new guide to

pregnancy
and babycare

from conception to age five

new guide to

pregnancy
and babycare

from conception to age five

general editor
Dr Penny Stanway

photography by
Sandra Lousada

conran
OCTOPUS

Project editor Cindy Richards, Alexandra Kent
Art editor Sue Storey, Isabel de Cordova
Photographic direction Nadine Bazar
Designer Sally Powell
Production Jill Macey, Alex Wiltshire
Photography Sandra Lousada
Illustrations Colin Salmon, Lucy Su
Picture Research Clare Limpus

The publishers would also like to thank
Liz Cowen, Caroline Davison, Felicity Jackson
and Donna Wood for editorial help, and Nicola
Collings for design assistance.

First published in 1994 by
Conran Octopus Limited
a part of Octopus Publishing Group
2–4 Heron Quays
London E14 4JP

This updated edition published in 2000

ISBN 1 84091 064 X

Typeset by Dorchester Typesetting Group Limited
Colour origination by Sang Choy International, Singapore
Printed and bound in China

CONTENTS

Foreword by Dr Penny Stanway

Chapter One
PREGNANCY AND BIRTH (0–40 weeks)

Chapter Two
THE YOUNG BABY (0–6 months)

Publisher's Note
We have used the pronouns 'he' and 'she' in alternate chapters throughout the book to reflect the fact that the text applies equally to male and female children. Where the text applies specifically to a male or female child, the appropriate pronoun has been used.

FOREWORD

This book, **New Guide to Pregnancy and Babycare**, is a team effort. Each of the seven writers brings her own professional expertise to her sections. More important, each writer has the common sense which comes from being an experienced mother. We hope that our combined contributions provide a useful and clear source of information for parents and others who care for young children.

Most young men and women today grew up in families which were smaller than those of their grandparents or great-grandparents. This means they had little chance of learning about childcare, let alone helping with younger brothers, sisters and cousins. Not surprisingly, most new mothers and fathers nowadays don't know that much about babies.

Our book can help fill the information gap and can offer new ideas and perspectives, though each of us learns most on the job itself. The experience of being a parent and coming to know, sometimes by trial and error, how best to meet your child's needs and your own, brings you wisdom and confidence. But never ignore your intuition, hunch or 'gut feeling'. This sixth sense can be very acute in parents and is frequently the most accurate barometer of what is going on with your child.

We have arranged the book in sections, starting with looking after yourselves immediately before and after conception. The rest of the pregnancy and birth section contains basic facts about your developing baby, how to look after yourself, including a section on antenatal exercise, and the choices you may need to make.

The next four sections are about the young baby (birth to six months), older baby (six months to a year), toddler (one to two-and-a-half years), and older child (two-and-a-half to five years). There is information about feeding, general care, equipment, play and toys, growth and development, health and common concerns. My family life section is followed by ones on looking after a sick child, common ailments, emergencies and first aid.

As I write this I am torn between wanting to say that having and caring for a child can be an incredible joy, gift and privilege, and knowing that being a parent can be tough and strains many a couple's relationship. However, love, humour and give-and-take give a child a secure base and help parents grow as individuals and, hopefully, as a couple too. Be prepared for ups and downs, laughter and tears, despair and delight. Children bring hope for the future and, as you welcome your child to the world, you begin the adventure of a lifetime.

DR PENNY STANWAY

GENERAL EDITOR

Dr Penny Stanway (MB, BS), as a doctor and mother of three children, is uniquely placed to give parents the information they need about all aspects of pregnancy and childcare. She worked in general practice and as a senior medical officer for London's largest health authority, looking after able-bodied and handicapped children in the community. She pursued her special interest in child health by studying developmental paediatrics and child neurology at the Institute of Child Health, London University.

After the birth of her first child, she gave up full-time practice. She now concentrates on writing about child health and development and has written many books including the classic bestseller *Breast is Best* and *The Complete Guide to Child Health*. She also writes a column on health for *Woman's Weekly*.

CONTRIBUTORS

Daphne Metland is a journalist and former editor of *Parents* magazine. She is an antenatal teacher for the National Childbirth Trust (NCT) and edits the Trust's journal *New Generation*. She has two children. (*Pregnancy and Birth*.)

Heather Welford has written several books including *The Mothercare Guide to Sleep and Wakefulness*. She is a columnist for *Parents* magazine and a NCT breastfeeding counsellor and tutor. She has three children. ('Feeding' and 'Sleep and Bedtime' sections; 'The Newborn Baby' in *The Young Baby*.)

Maggie Jones has written several books including *The Mothercare Guide to Safety and Your Child*. She is also a NCT breastfeeding counsellor. She has three children. ('Common Concerns' sections; 'Your Day Together' in *The Young Baby*; *Safety Around the House*.)

Carolyn Humphries is a journalist specializing in childcare issues and is a regular contributor to parenting magazines. She has two children. ('What Your Baby/Child May Need' and 'Play and Toys' sections.)

Jane Bidder is a journalist and writes regularly for the *Daily Telegraph* and *The Times*. She has three children. ('Growing and Learning' sections; 'Pre-School Play and Learning' in *The Older Child*.)

Gillian Fletcher is an obstetric physiotherapist. She is an antenatal teacher and is author of the NCT's *Get into Shape After Childbirth*. She has three children. ('Exercise During Pregnancy' in *Pregnancy and Birth*; 'Postnatal Exercises' in *The Young Baby*.)

PREGNANCY
AND BIRTH
0-40 weeks

The wonderful moment of conception happens when a man's sperm unites with a woman's egg deep within her body. The tiny embryo, nestling snugly into the lining of the womb, will be a separate human being within a few short months. But first the mother's body becomes  a safe haven, providing everything her developing baby needs to grow, until it's time for birth to part them.

Pregnancy brings enormous change and your baby will never be out of your mind for long, right from that very first day when you realize you are pregnant. Yet not until the hard work and excitement of labour and birth are over does the idea of your new baby become real and do your roles as mother and father begin.

PLANNING FOR A HEALTHY BABY

FOLIC ACID
- **Natural sources of this vitamin include: fresh fruit, beans and peas and green leafy vegetables.**
- **Beef and yeast extracts like Bovril and Marmite have folic acid added to them.**

Planning for a baby is exciting. Nowadays, with smaller families and readily available contraception, more people than ever before choose when to start trying.

We're all familiar with antenatal care but peri-conceptual care – looking after yourselves before and around the time of conception – is important too. Peri-conceptual care concerns everyday matters such as diet, weight, immunity, exercise, when to stop using contraception, alcohol, smoking and environmental influences.

Peri-conceptual care helps a woman enter pregnancy more capable of sailing through with no problems. And if both man and woman look after their health before they conceive, then in the early weeks after conception, before most women even know they are pregnant but when the human embryo is particularly vulnerable, they give their baby the best chance of developing safely.

DIET
- Eating a healthy, balanced diet with plenty of fresh fruit and vegetables will increase your chances of conceiving (see page 40).
- Try to avoid eating too many foods containing added sugar, refined grains (for example, white flour, bread, pasta and rice) and saturated or refined fats and oils (for example, animal fats, margarines and cheap cooking oils) too often.
- It's probably better to have fewer drinks containing caffeine.
- Make sure food is fresh – stale food generally has fewer vitamins and may contain moulds.
- If as a woman you need to lose weight, do it sensibly and slowly and aim to end your weight loss at least four months before trying to conceive.

IMMUNITY
Keeping fit and healthy helps your body to fight against disease, but two common infections are best avoided if at all possible in pregnancy as they can damage an unborn baby. These are rubella (German

measles) and chickenpox. If you haven't had a rubella immunization, arrange one, but ensure you don't get pregnant for three months afterwards.

EXERCISE
If you are fit you'll be able to cope more easily with your extra weight in pregnancy. Try to exercise at least three times a week for more than twenty minutes at a time.

ALCOHOL
Excess alcohol consumption within three months of conception can damage sperm and eggs as they mature and can also hurt the newly fertilized egg. Ideally, you and your partner should keep alcohol to a minimum for four months before you wish to conceive.

SMOKING
Women smokers are only half as fertile as non-smokers. Smoking makes men less fertile too: men who smoke between ten and twenty cigarettes a day are twice as likely to have a malformed baby as men who don't smoke. If you can't give up, cut down.

THE PILL
Stop taking the contraceptive pill at least three, and preferably six, months before trying to conceive. The Pill can alter body levels of certain vitamins and minerals. It can take several months off the Pill to right the balance and have the best chance of conceiving.

POLLUTANTS
A number of substances can interfere with conception and pregnancy and it's sensible to be on the alert as some of them are present in our everyday lives. For example, you and your partner should avoid extra exposure to any form of radiation including X-rays. It is also best to avoid excessive exposure to exhaust fumes from traffic, pesticides, household chemicals, paints and contact adhesives.

Finally, do not take any medicines without your doctor's approval.

10

See Looking After Yourself, pages 38–39; Healthy Eating, pages 40–43; Exercise During Pregnancy, pages 46-51

GET FIT FOR PREGNANCY
- Eat plenty of fresh fruit and vegetables.
- Take plenty of exercise.
- Give up smoking.
- Stop taking the Pill *at least* three months before trying for a baby.

11

Choose a form of exercise which you can look forward to because it's enjoyable and gives you a buzz, and then you're more likely to give it a regular time slot.

KNOWING YOU ARE PREGNANT

Some women seem to know they are pregnant almost immediately. Small changes in their body or how they feel, such as extreme tiredness or nausea from very early on, alert them to the fact that they have conceived. Other women experience no noticeable changes and may find it hard to believe they are pregnant.

Whether you just 'know' deep inside, or have to keep checking the results of a home pregnancy test to convince yourself, realizing you are pregnant can open the floodgates to a whole range of emotions. You may feel over the moon one day and quite low and worried the next. Even when the baby is much wanted, many ecstatic new parents-to-be find that concerns about the future momentarily cloud their happiness. Worries about how their relationship will be affected, how to manage financial changes and, of course, the health of the baby may crop up at some time. In the first few days and weeks of pregnancy they may seem overwhelming. However, most couples find a way to slow down and tackle these concerns one by one. Making time to talk things through now will stand you in good stead later.

HOPES AND FEARS
Try the following with your partner.
● **Each make a list of the things you are most looking forward to about having a baby and the things you are least looking forward to.**
● **Compare them and discuss the similarities and differences.**
● **This may help to avoid future misunderstandings.**

12

FIRST SIGNS
What you may notice
● Breasts may become tender and increase in size and the nipple area may become more pronounced.
● Some women suffer from morning sickness, others have feelings of nausea which last all day. This can begin very early on, but usually starts around six weeks and improves after about twelve to fourteen weeks of pregnancy.
● A missed period is the most obvious sign of pregnancy but occasionally a very light and scanty period may occur, which can be confusing. This happens because the normal female hormonal cycle continues despite being swamped by pregnancy hormones. If pregnancy hormones are on the low side, a small amount of bleeding can occur.
● The need to urinate frequently is caused by pressure from the developing baby, because the uterus sits just above the bladder. You may need to get up during the night to go to the lavatory, or find yourself going frequently during the day. This usually abates as the baby grows and the uterus moves off the bladder.

Pregnancy adds a new dimension to a relationship — it's a time when many couples recommit themselves to each other's wellbeing and happiness as well as their baby's future.

Many women find that their pleasure at being pregnant helps to compensate for the nuisance of any discomforts during the early weeks, such as tiredness and morning sickness.

How you may feel
- Many women say their sense of taste changes; foods may taste very strong, or favourite foods may develop 'off' flavours.
- Some women find they have a metallic taste in their mouth.
- You may go off specific foods completely: coffee, tea and alcohol are common aversions in pregnancy and this may be nature's way of making sure you avoid things which could be detrimental to you and your baby.
- You may feel very tired; to the point of needing to sleep during the day as well as in the evening and at night.
- You may crave certain foods; perhaps sharp fruity tastes or bland carbohydrates like potatoes and bread.

CONFIRMING THE PREGNANCY
The surest sign of pregnancy is missing a period, and many women are content to wait for this signal. It is not the only reason for periods to be absent, but if you are trying for a baby it is the most likely.

If, however, you want to find out as soon as possible, then home pregnancy testing kits are quick and easy to use. Many can give a result from the day you would have expected your next period. Most tests measure the level of pregnancy hormone in your urine, and are carried out first thing in the morning when urine is most concentrated. In ideal conditions they are very reliable but, because they have been known to give false results, some are supplied in sets of two, so that you can repeat the test later. Once the pregnancy test has confirmed the pregnancy or you have missed a period you can visit your doctor to discuss maternity care.

Knowing very early that you are pregnant enables you to eat and drink wisely and generally look after your health right from the word go.

CALCULATING YOUR DUE DATE
Pregnancy usually lasts 280 days or forty weeks; slightly longer than the nine months we usually refer to. For a rough calculation of the due date go forward nine months and one week from the first day of your last period.

To calculate your due date, find the first day of your last period by looking at the top line of figures in the chart below – your due date appears in bold type underneath.

JANUARY	1 2 3 4 5 6 7 8 9 10 11 12 13 14 15 16 17 18 19 20 21 22 23 24 25 26 27 28 29 30 31	JANUARY
OCTOBER	**8 9 10 11 12 13 14 15 16 17 18 19 20 21 22 23 24 25 26 27 28 29 30 31 1 2 3 4 5 6 7**	**NOVEMBER**
FEBRUARY	1 2 3 4 5 6 7 8 9 10 11 12 13 14 15 16 17 18 19 20 21 22 23 24 25 26 27 28	FEBRUARY
NOVEMBER	**8 9 10 11 12 13 14 15 16 17 18 19 20 21 22 23 24 25 26 27 28 29 30 1 2 3 4 5**	**DECEMBER**
MARCH	1 2 3 4 5 6 7 8 9 10 11 12 13 14 15 16 17 18 19 20 21 22 23 24 25 26 27 28 29 30 31	MARCH
DECEMBER	**6 7 8 9 10 11 12 13 14 15 16 17 18 19 20 21 22 23 24 25 26 27 28 29 30 31 1 2 3 4 5**	**JANUARY**
APRIL	1 2 3 4 5 6 7 8 9 10 11 12 13 14 15 16 17 18 19 20 21 22 23 24 25 26 27 28 29 30	APRIL
JANUARY	**6 7 8 9 10 11 12 13 14 15 16 17 18 19 20 21 22 23 24 25 26 27 28 29 30 31 1 2 3 4**	**FEBRUARY**
MAY	1 2 3 4 5 6 7 8 9 10 11 12 13 14 15 16 17 18 19 20 21 22 23 24 25 26 27 28 29 30 31	MAY
FEBRUARY	**5 6 7 8 9 10 11 12 13 14 15 16 17 18 19 20 21 22 23 24 25 26 27 28 1 2 3 4 5 6 7**	**MARCH**
JUNE	1 2 3 4 5 6 7 8 9 10 11 12 13 14 15 16 17 18 19 20 21 22 23 24 25 26 27 28 29 30	JUNE
MARCH	**8 9 10 11 12 13 14 15 16 17 18 19 20 21 22 23 24 25 26 27 28 29 30 31 1 2 3 4 5 6**	**APRIL**
JULY	1 2 3 4 5 6 7 8 9 10 11 12 13 14 15 16 17 18 19 20 21 22 23 24 25 26 27 28 29 30 31	JULY
APRIL	**7 8 9 10 11 12 13 14 15 16 17 18 19 20 21 22 23 24 25 26 27 28 29 30 1 2 3 4 5 6 7**	**MAY**
AUGUST	1 2 3 4 5 6 7 8 9 10 11 12 13 14 15 16 17 18 19 20 21 22 23 24 25 26 27 28 29 30 31	AUGUST
MAY	**8 9 10 11 12 13 14 15 16 17 18 19 20 21 22 23 24 25 26 27 28 29 30 31 1 2 3 4 5 6 7**	**JUNE**
SEPTEMBER	1 2 3 4 5 6 7 8 9 10 11 12 13 14 15 16 17 18 19 20 21 22 23 24 25 26 27 28 29 30	SEPTEMBER
JUNE	**8 9 10 11 12 13 14 15 16 17 18 19 20 21 22 23 24 25 26 27 28 29 30 1 2 3 4 5 6 7**	**JULY**
OCTOBER	1 2 3 4 5 6 7 8 9 10 11 12 13 14 15 16 17 18 19 20 21 22 23 24 25 26 27 28 29 30 31	OCTOBER
JULY	**8 9 10 11 12 13 14 15 16 17 18 19 20 21 22 23 24 25 26 27 28 29 30 31 1 2 3 4 5 6 7**	**AUGUST**
NOVEMBER	1 2 3 4 5 6 7 8 9 10 11 12 13 14 15 16 17 18 19 20 21 22 23 24 25 26 27 28 29 30	NOVEMBER
AUGUST	**8 9 10 11 12 13 14 15 16 17 18 19 20 21 22 23 24 25 26 27 28 29 30 31 1 2 3 4 5 6**	**SEPTEMBER**
DECEMBER	1 2 3 4 5 6 7 8 9 10 11 12 13 14 15 16 17 18 19 20 21 22 23 24 25 26 27 28 29 30 31	DECEMBER
SEPTEMBER	**7 8 9 10 11 12 13 14 15 16 17 18 19 20 21 22 23 24 25 26 27 28 29 30 1 2 3 4 5 6 7**	**OCTOBER**

13

FERTILITY CONCERNS

RIGHT Put a urine-moistened strip into this electronic ovulation-prediction monitor on 16 days per month for several months, and it will 'learn' enough about your hormone levels to predict your likely fertility on any one day.

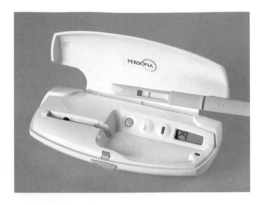

BELOW Above you see how one egg-follicle grows each month and releases an egg; afterwards its lining-cells swell as they produce progesterone, then the follicle shrinks. Below are the fluctuating levels of oestrogen (pink) and progesterone (orange), and the changes in the womb lining.

One couple in five having regular unprotected sex takes more than a year to conceive, and one in ten takes more than two years. The main thing affecting fertility is your age. You are most fertile when you are young. The average woman's chance of conceiving falls from her late twenties, and by thirty-five she takes twice as long to get pregnant as she would at twenty-five. By forty-four, only three to four per cent of women can conceive, partly because few eggs are left and partly because they are of poor quality. A year after the menopause any natural fertility ceases completely.

A man too is at his most fertile when young. As he grows older, his sperm count and sperm quality gradually decline.

A woman's fertility also varies with her menstrual cycle. However, ovulation nearly always occurs fourteen days before a period. If you have an average twenty-eight-day cycle, then taking the first day of your period as day 1, you'll probably ovulate on day 14, and be fertile on days 10–15.

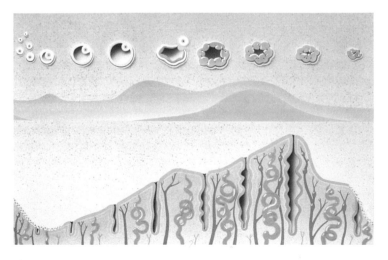

THE CAUSE

Of every ten couples who can't start a baby, the problem is the woman's in four, the man's in three, and is unexplained in the others. The most common problem of all is the man producing too few sperms, or too few good-quality sperms; this is the cause of one couple in four needing medical help.

One of the two most likely difficulties in women who cannot conceive is an ovulation disorder. Three times out of four this results from a hormone imbalance associated with the polycystic ovary syndrome. The other likely possibility is blocked Fallopian tubes.

Other causes include endometriosis (in which womb-lining cells stray outside the womb); cervical mucus that is hostile to sperms; a womb disorder; and exposure to pesticides or certain other poisons.

Very often a woman who thinks she is infertile is miscarrying repeatedly. In some women this is because they have antibodies that cause blood clots in their placenta.

IMPROVING YOUR FERTILITY

It's often possible to enhance your fertility, and it is worth following these guidelines.

Knowing when you're most fertile

For a baby to be conceived, an egg needs to be fertilized within twenty–four to thirty-six hours of leaving the ovary. Sperms generally survive for up to seventy-two hours (though some live for up to five days). So the most fruitful time for sex is from about seventy-two hours before to about thirty-six hours after ovulation. Research suggests that a couple trying to conceive should aim to have sex once a day in the week before ovulation.

There are many ways of working out when you'll be most fertile each month. One is to keep a period diary for several months. If you have regular cycles, you can then work out in advance the likely day of ovulation.

Another is by assessing your vaginal mucus each day. You'll notice the amount increases in the few days before ovulation. Once production is past its peak, you'll ovulate within twenty-four hours.

DO'S AND DON'TS

On the subject of hazardous chemicals, here is a list of 'don'ts', most of which it is best to follow at any time, but especially when you are trying to conceive.

- Wash, scrub or peel fruit and vegetables, or consider organic produce, as pesticide traces can lower the sperm count and might even trigger miscarriage.
- Don't touch or breathe vapour from pesticide-containing products.
- Don't ignore safety recommendations if working with industrial, agricultural or garden chemicals.
- Don't take illegal drugs such as cannabis, ecstasy and cocaine.
- Don't take medications without approval from your doctor or pharmacist.
- Don't strip lead-containing paint.
- Don't inhale smoke from burning PVC-containing plastic, or vapour from solvents, glues, marker pens and paints.

Advice for women:
- Taking a mineral and vitamin supplement formulated for preconception and pregnancy ensures you get all the nutrients you need.
- Health workers and airline crew exposed to ionizing radiation should ask for their official exposure limit to be lowered. Dental assistants and workers who are exposed to textile dust may benefit from changing their job.
- Weight loss may encourage conception in an overweight woman if tests reveal that she has polycystic ovaries and isn't ovulating. Losing weight gives overweight women who are having treatment with assisted-conception techniques 75% more chance of conceiving. Moreover weight loss in overweight women discourages miscarriage.
- Weight gain encourages fertility in underweight women, because being too thin makes you more likely to ovulate infrequently (or in some cases not at all) and to miscarry.

Advice for men:
- Taking a multimineral and vitamin supplement is a wise precaution.
- It's best to avoid too much beer, as its plant oestrogens and certain other ingredients can depress the sperm count.
- If you do long hours of driving or a job involving heat-exposure, such as welding, consider a change. Anything that heats the testes for a long time reduces sperm production, so avoid soaking in a hot bath, jacuzzi or hot tub.
- Weight loss may help an overweight man father a child because excess fat can interfere with sperm production.

15

One high-tech way of predicting fertility is to use an ovulation predictor kit to estimate your level of a hormone called LH (luteinizing hormone). Another is to use an electronic ovulation predictor monitor. A light comes on when you put a urine-moistened dipstick into it. A red light shows that you are fertile, a yellow one that you might be, and a green one that you're not.

Being health-aware
Looking after your health is an excellent way of boosting your fertility. This also reduces repeated unrecognized early miscarriages. Stop smoking and limit your alcohol intake as both decrease fertility. Some experts recommend giving up alcohol altogether. Researchers disagree about the effects of coffee, but some recommend no more than 320–360mg of caffeine daily. (One 6oz cup of ordinary ground coffee contains 80–90mg; a cup of instant coffee 60mg; and a cup of tea or can of cola, 40mg.)

Eat a healthy diet to provide you with nutrients such as vitamins C and E, folic acid, selenium, zinc and essential fatty acids that you need for optimum fertility. If you suspect sensitivity to wheat and other cereal grains, see your doctor for tests.

Try to manage stress effectively, as this can prevent ovulation and reduce the sperm count. It's good for you to take half an hour of exercise five days a week. This increases circulation to the ovaries, womb, pituitary gland, testes and penis.

A simple yet effective measure is to go outside in daylight for fifteen minutes each day, and to match your waking hours with daylight hours, as exposure to light boosts the levels of reproductive hormones.

FERTILITY TESTS
The time for a couple to consider getting medical help is when they have tried to conceive for two years if the woman is under thirty, or one year if over thirty.

SOME SEX TIPS: Having sex each day in the week before you ovulate will improve your fertility, particularly early in the morning. Lying with her hips raised on a pillow for half an hour after having sex may make the sperms' journey easier too.

YOU AND YOUR GROWING BABY

The first phase (weeks 0-12)

Pregnancy is divided into three phases, or trimesters. In the first, from conception until about twelve weeks, much of the hard work of growing a baby takes place.

WEEKS 0-4

The length of your pregnancy is calculated from the first day of your last period. The egg (ovum) is released from the ovary in the middle of the menstrual cycle (usually at around day fourteen). The sperm swim towards the egg, and surround it in the outer part of one of the Fallopian tubes. Once one sperm has penetrated the egg, the egg's surface changes to prevent other sperm getting through, and the fertilized egg journeys on down the tube. Six days after fertilization it has become a ball of cells that burrows into the lining of the uterus.

OPPOSITE In the first three months, before other people can even see that you are pregnant, your baby's organs are forming and he is already easily recognizable as a tiny human being.

You may begin to notice slight changes, perhaps in your sense of taste, some breast tenderness, or feelings of nausea.

WEEKS 5-8

Major changes now occur as the blueprint for your baby is laid down. His main organs begin to grow and the nervous system develops. The heart begins to beat at about week six and the limbs are developing. At first they look a bit like flippers, but gradually knee and elbow joints are formed. The face also begins to develop and the mouth and tongue are already visible.

Many women now notice they are pregnant. Your breasts may start to grow and you may feel tired and nauseous and go off certain foods like coffee and alcohol.

16

WEEKS 9-12

The embryo begins to look more like a baby now and is technically called a fetus. During this time all the major organs such as the lungs, kidneys and liver are formed. The skeleton begins to develop too. The ears and nose can be recognized, and the eyes are forming, but still closed. Fingers and toes are growing, and the baby even has the beginnings of external genital organs. He is floating about in amniotic fluid, which acts as a shock-absorber to protect him from bumps and falls.

You may find that any feelings of nausea begin to abate at this stage.

Your baby at week 12
Length: 8cm (3in)
Weight: 30g (1oz)

1. Stomach   **5.** Bladder
2. Intestine   **6.** Cervix (neck
3. Fetus   of the womb)
4. Uterus   **7.** Vagina

MISCARRIAGE
Miscarriages sometimes happen in early pregnancy, usually during the first twelve weeks. The first sign is often bleeding and you should call your doctor immediately and lie down if any bleeding occurs. However early the miscarriage, it is still very upsetting and you may feel a deep sense of loss, but try not to blame yourself.

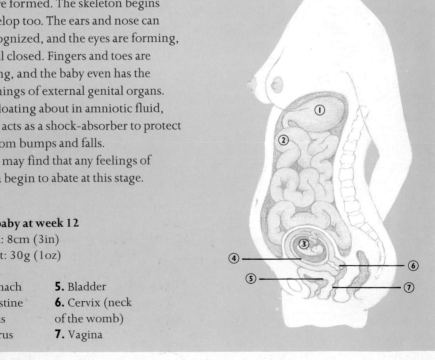

'I was really excited when I found out that I was pregnant and although I felt very tired at first, I found that exercise really helped. The more I did, the better I felt, so I continued swimming and playing tennis.'

The second phase (weeks 13–28)

The middle months of pregnancy are often the most comfortable. Sickness and tiredness usually improve, your body begins to grow and become quite rounded, and many couples feel they can make real plans for the baby, now that the pregnancy feels firmly established.

WEEKS 13–18
Your baby now looks like a baby, but in miniature. All the major organs begin to work, including the kidneys. Your baby makes breathing-like movements. These are not real breathing, as the lungs will not expand and work until after he is born.

His finger and toenails have formed, and eyebrows and eyelashes are beginning to grow. The baby's skin is covered with vernix, a white greasy substance that protects him in his watery environment. A fine downy hair also grows, called lanugo. He still has plenty of room to move around, and many mothers notice the first fetal movements at around eighteen weeks. Sometimes it is difficult to be sure that it really is the baby moving. The feeling can be so tiny, and so strange, almost like butterflies or bubbles in the stomach.

WEEKS 19–24
By now the baby is growing hair on his head, and may weigh around 450g (1lb) and be about 30cm (12in) long. There is still more fluid than baby, and he can easily turn around inside you. You may notice quite large movements and your partner or other children may be able to feel them if they place their hand on your bare skin. The baby can now react to outside influences and you may notice that he becomes much more active when you have a bath, or play loud music. You may find indigestion a problem and eating small, frequent meals may help.

OPPOSITE During the middle three months of pregnancy your baby's development shoots ahead – he can drink the fluid around him, he can move about in the womb and he can even suck his thumb.

WEEKS 25–28
By now the baby weighs almost as much as a bag of sugar, around 900g (2lb), and is about 40cm (16in) long. He is now laying down fat reserves under the skin, although, despite this, he still looks very red in comparison to a full-term baby. He may have definite periods of rest and activity. Some babies seem to kick and move around at the same time each day, and they then have set times when they keep still, and possibly are asleep.

His eyes are open, and he may respond to the small amounts of light filtering through the stretched abdominal muscles. He can suck his thumb, and may even get hiccups. This is a strange sensation for the mother, almost as if he were giving little regular kicks in the same place.

Your baby at week 28
Length: 40cm (16in)
Weight: 900g (2lb)

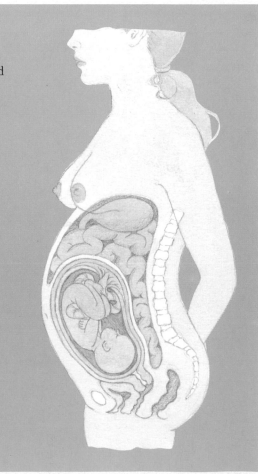

WHAT YOU MAY NOTICE
● You will feel the first fetal movements around week 18.
● By week 24 you will probably have developed a definite bump.
● You may notice 'practice' contractions, known as Braxton Hicks contractions, around week 28.

'The middle months were a really calm time and I felt amazingly good, both emotionally and physically. I felt properly pregnant: I looked pregnant, everyone knew and, best of all, I could feel my baby move.'

The third phase (weeks 29-40)

Reaching thirty weeks often feels like being on the home stretch; you can count the weeks until the baby arrives in single figures, and your plans become more definite. You may look forward to giving up work as you become bigger and need to rest more often. Listen to your body; some women are still full of energy, and quite happy working and keeping active. Others need to slow down, and begin to focus their attention on the baby.

WEEKS 29-32

Your baby is very well developed now. He can swallow, hear, suck his thumb, recognize your voice, and, if he were born now, would have a good chance of survival. However, the best place for him over the next few weeks is undoubtedly inside you, where he is safe, secure and continues to grow. He weighs around 1500g (over 3lb) now and may be about 45cm (18in) long.

You may notice that the baby's movements change as he gets bigger. He has less room to move around now, but you may be able to identify which is a foot kicking and which is an elbow poking. Ask your midwife to show you what position the baby is lying in. She can guide your hands to feel the head, and trace the smooth roundness of the back.

WEEKS 33-6

The baby continues to put on weight. He may weigh about 2400g (just over 5lb) and be about 50cm (20in) long. He will probably settle into the head-down position, and gradually move down or 'engage'. This happens as the lower third of the uterus softens ready for labour, and the baby fits into the brim of the pelvis.

WEEKS 37-40

Now your baby is plump, strong and ready to be born. He will be able to breathe and suck well from birth. He could arrive two weeks before or two weeks after your due date, so plan some things to do if you go overdue. You will probably find that you need to rest each day and conserve your energies for the hard work of labour. Gentle exercises and swimming will help keep you supple. Daily relaxation sessions will stand you in good stead for coping with contractions.

Your baby at week 40
Length: 51cm (20in)
Weight: 3400g (7½lb)

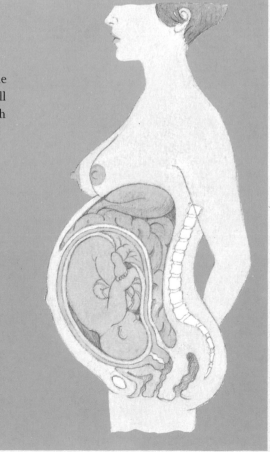

OPPOSITE *The last three months of pregnancy is a waiting time when your baby can continue growing and maturing in the warmth and safety of your womb, ready for the day you go into labour and birth.*

20

'I really enjoyed being pregnant, and felt much healthier than usual. I found it really exciting watching my body gradually growing and changing.'

ANTENATAL CARE

**BOOKING A
HOME BIRTH**
● If you want a
home birth, discuss
it with your doctor.
● If she is unwilling
or unable to care for
you at home, the
Director of
Midwifery will
arrange midwife
care.
● Write to her at
your local hospital,
stating that you plan
to have the baby at
home.

Antenatal care is designed to ensure that your pregnancy is as happy and problem-free as possible by keeping an eye on your general health and wellbeing. Any problems can be picked up at an early stage and quickly treated.

Taking measurements and doing tests early in pregnancy give a base line against which changes are measured as the pregnancy progresses. Regular trips to the clinic can be reassuring, and give you the opportunity to get to know your midwife or doctor. Antenatal care should start as soon as possible so, once your pregnancy has been confirmed, visit your doctor. He or she will be able to advise you on the antenatal and childbirth choices available in your area.

WHERE TO HAVE YOUR BABY

One of the first decisions you will need to make is where to have your baby. It is worth knowing what your options are and the advantages of each, so you can think everything through before you have to make up your mind. What matters most is having your baby where you will feel happiest and most secure.

Where you choose to have your baby will depend on your own personal needs and preferences. It is also important to remain flexible; if a medical problem crops up during pregnancy, it may well alter your views on where you want to have your baby.

Hospital birth

Almost all babies are born in hospital, and many parents are reassured by having access to specialist facilities and a wide range of pain relief options. If you need medical intervention such as a forceps delivery or a caesarean section, then there's readily available nursing care too. Many women like having a midwife on hand to help with feeding and looking after the baby, and enjoy the company of other new mothers. If you have other children, you may find a few days of resting and getting to know this newest baby invaluable before going home to resume the routine of family life.

Home birth

While some experts are against home births, others support it and some women feel sure home is the right place for them to

---

CHOOSING WHERE TO HAVE YOUR BABY

Asking yourself these questions may help you decide where to have your baby:

● Is being cared for by the same person or team throughout pregnancy and labour important to you?

● Do you feel more secure knowing that monitors, epidurals and the back-up of a hospital are there if you need them?

● How much responsibility do you want to take? Would you like to be consulted about decisions, or would you prefer others to decide for you?

● What type of pain relief would you like to have available? Remember, epidurals are only on offer in hospital, but you are less likely to need external forms of pain relief if you decide to have your baby in your own home.

● How confident do you feel about having your baby at home? If you are concerned and tense about the idea, then you are

unlikely to relax during the birth and that could slow down labour.

● How much support can you rely on after the birth? You will need to rest and have time to get to know your baby, and won't be ready to rush up and down stairs, do the washing or make the meals for a few days at least. Will your partner be able to take time off, or can a relative help?

● Do you like the idea of labour taking place in your own bed?

● If you already have children, will you feel able to rest with them around you?

● If you or your baby needed more help during labour than the doctor or midwife attending you at home could offer, is the journey to the maternity unit easy enough for you to be taken there quickly?

give birth. It avoids many of the interventions that are almost routine in some hospitals, like electronic fetal monitoring, and it is often easier to remain upright and mobile in your own home. Your choices for pain relief are more limited than in the hospital, but, in general, women labouring at home need less pain relief.

The statistics for planned home births are better overall than those for hospital births: women need less pain relief, have far fewer interventions, and their babies are more likely to do well.

Other schemes

Domino delivery is popular with mothers and it is unfortunate that this type of scheme is only available in some areas. The name is taken from Domiciliary, In Out, and reflects the fact that a domiciliary or community midwife will take you into

hospital, deliver your baby and then arrange for you to go home after a few hours. In the best schemes, a midwife you know will come to your home, assess how far into labour you are, take you into hospital and deliver your baby.

The main advantage of domino delivery is that the midwife visits you in your home when you go into labour. You can then stay at home as long as you are comfortable and you know that the same midwife will deliver your baby.

An alternative scheme that many areas are now introducing is the named midwife scheme, in which you have your own midwife appointed to you, who acts as co-ordinator of your care. That midwife may not be available to deliver your baby, but she will ensure that your other carers know what matters to you, and that they are aware of your needs.

Friends and neighbours enjoy sharing their experience of antenatal care but your doctor will explain exactly what's on offer.

INDEPENDENT MIDWIVES
● **Some midwives have set up as independent practitioners.**
● **A fee is charged which covers antenatal care, delivery and postnatal care.**
● **Some women choose independent midwives for the continuity of care they offer.**

OPPOSITE *A beautiful big belly like this changes the way you look and feel, walk and sleep — and is something to be really proud of as you near the end of your months of waiting.*

TYPES OF ANTENATAL CARE

Choosing the type of care you receive during pregnancy and for the birth of your child is very important to your health and wellbeing.

Discuss your options with your midwife, doctor and antenatal teacher. Talk it through with your partner too. But first consider your options locally: some types of care may be easier to obtain in your area than others.

Shared care

Most women are booked under shared care. This means that your doctor and midwife will look after you throughout pregnancy, and once you have had the baby. You will go into hospital for the labour and birth and, with a first baby, usually stay in hospital for a few days. You are likely to visit the hospital a couple of times during pregnancy, first to book in and have a scan, and later for a brief check-up towards the end of pregnancy. This system means that most of your care is given locally by people whom you can get to know.

Consultant care

A woman with an existing medical condition (such as diabetes) or someone who has had previous problems in pregnancy may be referred for consultant care. This involves going to the hospital antenatal clinic throughout pregnancy. Some women find this reassuring, especially if they are concerned about their own or their baby's health. It does mean that you are more likely to get to know some of the hospital staff, and the place will seem more familiar, but it can also involve extra travelling and long waits at the clinic.

Midwife care

Having a midwife with you whom you know and trust is a priority choice for many women. With team midwifery you are cared for during pregnancy by a small team of midwives. You know when you book in that one of these women will deliver your baby and the same team will also look after you and your baby postnatally (see also page 23).

THE ANTENATAL CLINIC

Most clinics are run by midwives and doctors together. You are more likely to see the same people at your local clinic and be able to get to know them than at the hospital, where staff move from department to department quite regularly.

The booking visit

The first visit is called the booking visit and is usually longer than later visits. A full medical history is taken, and you may also be asked for a family history to pick up the possibility of twins or illnesses that may be genetically linked. Routine tests such as checking your urine and recording your weight will be done at each visit. Other tests such as taking blood samples will be done occasionally.

The booking visit is the time to talk about your preferences for childbirth and to find out about antenatal classes.

Asking questions

Your midwife is a good source of information both medical and local, so it's worth thinking about what you want to discuss before you go to see her. You may feel that you definitely don't want any pain relief, but during labour you could change your mind so find out what's on offer. You may find the following list of questions helpful.

Labour and Birth

- Will my partner or friend be able to stay with me throughout labour?
- What pain relief will I be offered (see also Pain relief options, page 63)? Are epidurals available?
- Will I be able to move around freely during labour?
- Can I give birth in any position?
- What is your policy on caesareans and episiotomies?

After the Birth

- Can I breastfeed my baby immediately?
- How long will I stay in hospital?
- What are the visiting hours? Can my partner visit at any time?
- Is there a Special Care Baby Unit? If not, where is the nearest one?

JARGON BUSTING

On your first visit to the antenatal clinic you are likely to be given a card to carry with you, often referred to as the co-operation or co-op card. This has all the details of each antenatal visit written on it. In some areas you may carry your full notes. Either way, these notes give you a record of your pregnancy, although midwives and doctors tend to use a form of shorthand. If there are things you don't understand, ask your midwife to explain them. The following abbreviations are commonly used:

Ceph. short for cephalic, meaning head. It shows that the baby is in the head-down position. Some people also write V for Vertex or use an arrow pointing downwards for the same thing.

BP is short for blood pressure and will be shown by two figures with a line between. Most people have a normal blood pressure in the region of 120 over 70. Some women find their blood pressure drops in early pregnancy and rises later. An increase of more than about twenty to thirty points in the lower figure may indicate a condition known as pre-eclampsia, which is potentially dangerous for both mother and baby.

ROP, ROA, LOP, LOA describe the position of the baby. The O (occipito) is the back of the baby's head. R and L mean that the back of the baby's head is towards the right or left of the mother; P means the back of the head is posterior or towards her back, and A means that it's anterior or towards her front. So ROP would mean the baby is lying with the back of his head towards the mother's back, slightly to the right. Your midwife can show you how the baby is lying when she examines you. She will show you how to feel for the head and then follow the baby's curved back to work out which side she is lying. This can only be done late in pregnancy, when the baby is quite large.

FH stands for fetal heart, and an H will show that the heart-beat has been heard. This column is likely to be blank for the first few weeks, because the heartbeat cannot be picked up by a stethoscope until about week twenty-four.

Oedema means swelling and usually occurs in the hands and feet. A certain amount of swelling is normal, but if it is combined with high blood pressure it may be an early warning of pre-eclampsia.

HB is short for haemoglobin level. This constituent of the blood carries oxygen around the body. If the level is low you may be anaemic; a blood test is usually done at intervals in pregnancy to check the level.

Height of Fundus refers to the top of the uterus. As pregnancy progresses the uterus tends to move upwards. Feeling for the height of the fundus can give the doctor or midwife a rough estimate of the progress of the pregnancy.

Your womb rises as your baby grows and the fundal height increases (see right). Babies usually settle or 'engage' with the head or bottom against the cervix (see far right). A head-down baby faces forwards or backwards and to either side.

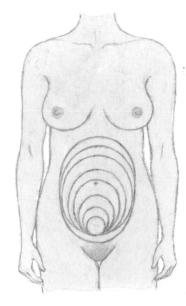

Height of fundus

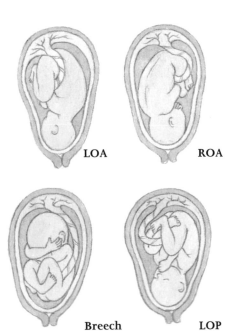

LOA   ROA

Breech   LOP

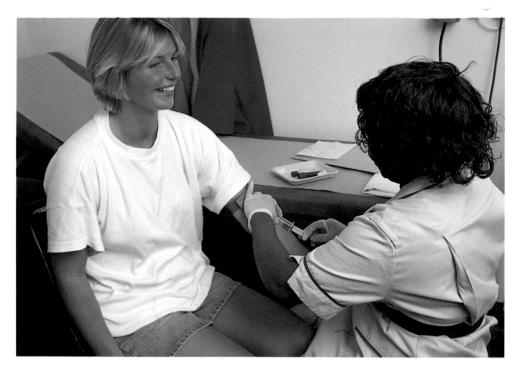

A variety of blood tests may be done during pregnancy. Early routine tests show your blood group, check that your blood contains enough iron, and discover whether you are protected from rubella.

BIRTH PLANS

Many couples find that writing a list of their ideas and preferences for the birth is very useful. This can then be added to your notes for those who care for you to read. Some hospitals encourage everyone to make a birth or care plan, others may be rather reluctant to use them, or feel threatened by them, so it is essential to word them carefully.

Bear in mind the fact that you may change your mind about things when you are in labour. If you simply issue a list of orders, your carers might feel awkward about offering advice. Birth plans can run to several pages, and a busy midwife may not have the time to read it all, or be able to remember what was in it. Ideally keep it to one page.

Writing your birth plan

● Begin by acknowledging the skills of the midwife and/or doctor. You will probably need their advice and help and they will have information, suggestions and ideas that they can offer you.

● Use a sentence or two to cover the general points such as, 'We would like to be kept informed about the progress of labour and the health of our baby, and be involved in making any decisions with our midwife and/or doctor.'

● Accept that you may change your mind and make a point of putting this in. Write things in an open-ended way such as, 'I realize I may feel differently when I am actually in labour, but . . .'.

● The decisions you make may vary according to what happens in labour. For instance, if there is cause for concern about the baby's health, you may want to change your views regarding monitoring, or where to have your baby. So you may want to say something like 'As long as the baby is well, we would prefer the midwife to monitor the baby using a hand-held stethoscope, or a portable monitor . . .'.

● Ask for your carer's help in achieving your wishes. For instance, you could state that you would like your midwife to help you remain mobile in labour, or try out different positions for the second stage.

● Write down any specific points that matter to you, such as 'I would really like my baby delivered on to my tummy . . .'.

● Try to expect the unexpected; half the women who have a caesarean section do so as an emergency, so think about what would matter to you if you did need one.

● If you have cultural or religious traditions that may be different from those which are routinely practised, it might be worth including them so that your carers know what matters to you.

SPECIAL TESTS

Tests of one sort or another are often carried out during pregnancy. A few are offered routinely to all women. Others are used where more information is needed in specific cases, or a particular problem has occurred.

ULTRASOUND

Almost all women are now offered an ultrasound scan. Your partner may be able to come with you for the scan, and many couples find it quite fascinating. A full bladder helps to give a clearer picture as it keeps the baby quite high in the abdomen. Your stomach will be lubricated, and the scanner passed over it. Sound waves are passed into the uterus to build up a picture of the baby and the placenta. The picture on the monitor may look rather indistinct, but usually the person doing the scan can point out where the head and limbs are. Often the baby's beating heart shows up quite clearly. In early pregnancy you can usually make out most of the baby, but later on, as the baby gets much larger, it is harder to see him all at once.

From a medical point of view the scan is useful to confirm the date of pregnancy. Measurements may be taken of the spine or head, or the long bones of the thigh. The scan date is a little more accurate than dating the pregnancy from the first day of your last period, if your periods are regular.

Ultrasound scanning is also used to check the development of the baby, to ensure that any problems are picked up early. Sometimes these can be dealt with during pregnancy, and in some hospitals procedures such as clearing a blocked urethra to relieve pressure on the kidneys can be done at once. Being forewarned of a problem may mean that the baby will have to be delivered in a specialist unit.

Scans can confirm a multiple or twin pregnancy, and they will also show where the placenta is lying (see also Low-lying placenta, page 30).

MATERNAL SERUM SCREENING

Many hospitals offer screening tests to women at between 15 and 20 weeks of pregnancy. First an ultrasound scan confirms the baby's age. Then a blood sample is taken and the laboratory staff do a double, triple or quadruple test to measure the levels of two, three or four substances (alpha-fetoprotein, chorionic gonadotrophin, oestriol, and inhibin A).

28

Most women who have a routine scan enjoy seeing an outline of their baby on the screen; and a few like to know whether the operator can tell if the baby is a girl or a boy.

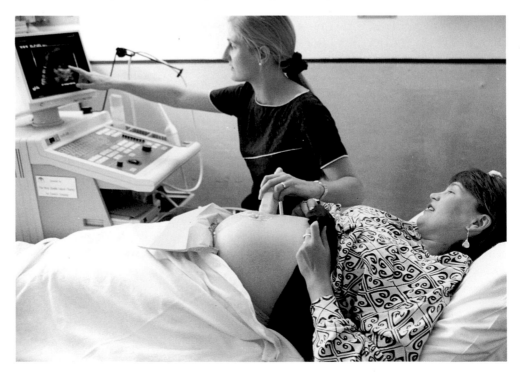

The results, combined with the woman's age, indicate up to seven or eight Down's babies out of 10, with the quadruple test being the most reliable. The results also indicate whether there is a high risk of the baby having a defect such as spina bifida. If the factor is high, you can then choose to have a more invasive test like amniocentesis.

At the moment these tests can throw up false positive readings and some of the women who are thought to have a high risk actually do not. For them, the test results cause unnecessary concern and worry. For others, a negative blood test rules out a more invasive test such as amniocentesis or chorionic villus sampling (see right). The term 'invasive' refers to the fact that these tests involve taking samples of amniotic fluid or cells from the placenta and carry the risk of miscarriage.

The extra information supplied by the serum screening, which carries no risk, can help parents decide whether or not to undergo further tests. Maternal serum screening is not available in all areas, and may not be offered to all pregnant women. The tests are currently being improved and refined and it is hoped that the false positive problem will decrease.

AMNIOCENTESIS

This involves taking a sample of the amniotic fluid that surrounds the baby. This test is used to check for chromosomal abnormalities such as Down's syndrome. As there is a risk of miscarriage after the test, it is only offered if the chances of Down's syndrome are considered to be higher than average.

The incidence of Down's syndrome increases with the mother's age, so in some areas women over thirty-eight or forty are offered the test. It may also be suggested if one of the diagnostic tests such as serum screening shows an increased risk. An ultrasound scan is used to show the position of the baby and the placenta, then a fine needle is passed through the abdominal wall to draw off some of the fluid. Most women find the process quite painless, although they are usually advised to rest for a day or two after the test.

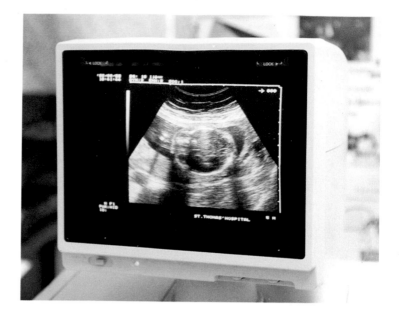

CHORIONIC VILLUS SAMPLING

In this test, a few of the cells of the placenta are taken, using a fine needle passed through the cervix. It can be done much earlier than amniocentesis, at eleven or twelve weeks of pregnancy. Unfortunately, the risk of miscarriage is higher than with amniocentesis, and there is also a risk of limb deformities. It tends to be used where the need for the information it can give outweighs the risks.

AFTER THE TEST

For many couples the greatest worry comes when deciding what to do if a test proves positive, which means that there may be an abnormality. Making a decision about continuing a pregnancy, or choosing a termination is never easy. Some couples feel strongly either for or against one option, while others feel unsure, confused and upset. Although you may wish to resolve the problem among yourselves, it is important not to feel isolated as there are people who can help. It may help to talk things through with your midwife or doctor. They will be able to give you more information and put you in touch with a local support group where you can contact couples who have gone through a similar experience.

You can also contact one of the support groups listed under the Useful Addresses section on pages 314–15 for further help or information.

The moving picture on the ultrasound screen may look fuzzy and indistinct, but to an experienced observer it can give clear information about the baby's age and wellbeing.

29

COMPLICATIONS IN PREGNANCY

Pregnancy is straightforward for the majority of women, but occasionally complications occur. The aim of antenatal care is to spot problems early on, and hopefully to resolve them before they result in miscarriage (see pages 32–33).

It helps to understand what is happening to your body and why, but if the problem cannot be resolved you may need extra support and help. Your doctor will be able to advise you of other organizations and support groups you can contact.

FALLS
As your bump grows you may find it harder to keep your balance.
● **Take care on stairs and don't go up a step ladder, or climb on chairs.**
● **If you need to reach something high up, ask somebody to help you.**
● **Your baby is very well protected inside the uterus and minor falls are unlikely to harm her.**
● **If you have a major fall, consult your doctor.**

ECTOPIC PREGNANCY
This is thankfully quite a rare condition in which the fertilized egg implants and begins to grow outside the uterus, usually in one of the Fallopian tubes. As the egg grows the tube begins to stretch, causing a sharp pain on one side of the abdomen. Other symptoms include vaginal bleeding and feeling faint or dizzy.

If you suffer from these symptoms, you should contact your doctor immediately. The pregnancy must be terminated, and usually the Fallopian tube has to be removed.

INCOMPETENT CERVIX
Usually the cervix (the neck of the womb) stays tightly closed throughout the pregnancy until labour commences holding the baby in place. However, in some women the cervix is weak and unable to support the growing baby and this can be the cause of a miscarriage later on in pregnancy, generally after the third month.

If an incompetent cervix is discovered before you miscarry, the cervix can then be held closed with a stitch, which is put in place during a minor operation. The stitch is removed late on in the pregnancy, usually about a couple of weeks before the baby is due to be born, so that labour may progress normally.

PRE-ECLAMPSIA
One in ten mothers suffers from symptoms of pre-eclampsia during late pregnancy. These include raised blood pressure, a swelling of the hands and feet, and protein being found in the urine. Regular and routine antenatal checks are vital to ensure that any of these symptoms are detected early on and preventive action taken. For example, if your blood pressure is very high, then bed rest may be suggested or you may be admitted to hospital for observation. In certain cases labour may have to be induced, and your baby may be delivered by caesarean section.

RHESUS FACTOR PROBLEMS
If a rhesus negative mother has a rhesus positive baby as her first child, it can then activate her defence mechanisms for dealing with foreign bodies. This means that in a subsequent pregnancy her antibodies may damage a rhesus positive baby's blood cells.

It is usual to check the blood group of a baby born to a rhesus negative mother and, if it is necessary, the mother can be given an injection to prevent problems arising with future pregnancies.

LOW-LYING PLACENTA
Usually the placenta embeds high up on the wall of the uterus. Occasionally it fixes low down and may cover the cervix. If this happens it is called placenta praevia. Often the first sign is bleeding, perhaps at about twenty-eight weeks. Sometimes a low-lying placenta is picked up by an ultrasound scan early on, but the condition may correct itself as the uterus grows. If it remains very low, or covers the cervix, a caesarean section will be necessary.

HEALTH PROBLEMS
An existing health problem, such as diabetes, epilepsy or asthma, can cause complications in pregnancy. If you are aware of any particular health problem, it is important to discuss your condition with your doctor before becoming pregnant as it is likely that you will need extra care and attention during pregnancy, and possibly in labour.

STILLBIRTH
It is rare now for a baby to die at or around the time of birth as routine antenatal

See Miscarriage and Premature Birth pages 32–33

care now picks up most problems which can then be treated, especially those related to developmental abnormalities or failure of the placenta. However, some babies do die before they are born, sometimes due to high blood pressure, haemorrhage from the placenta, or because of a pre-existing medical problem in the mother, which doctors have been unaware of, or unable to treat.

If, tragically, the baby has died in the womb, your midwife and doctor will explain to you what has happened and talk about the necessity of inducing labour. Once the baby is born, you may be asked if you want to see and hold her. Many parents find this extremely difficult at the time, but in fact it can help you come to terms with your grief in the future if you have a chance to say both hello and goodbye to your baby, to hold and look at her and perhaps also have photographs taken. It may help too if you choose a name for your baby.

GRIEVING

Losing a much longed for baby, whether through miscarriage or stillbirth, is a trauma for all members of the family and you need to allow yourselves time to grieve. This process may begin with anger, disbelief, despair and sometimes guilt, but eventually there comes a stage of acceptance and understanding. Some couples find it easier to talk alone, while others need a third person to help them work things through. (See Useful Addresses 314—15 for some organizations which can help.)

MISCARRIAGE

It isn't surprising that many of the things that encourage miscarriage also encourage a premature birth, because a miscarriage is simply an extremely early birth. One pregnancy in three ends in miscarriage, though most miscarriages happen so early that the woman didn't even know she was pregnant.

THE REASONS FOR MISCARRIAGE

Even today, doctors can find no cause in up to two in five miscarriages. The most common reason for the pregnancy ending in the other cases is that a genetic abnormality or some other damage means the embryo has not been properly formed. The woman's body then 'scans' and rejects this abnormal baby.

Your age affects your risk of miscarriage, because the older you are, the more likely you are to miscarry. Up to one in two pregnant women aged 40 or more loses her baby. Many of these lost babies have some sort of abnormality, and most are miscarried very early - perhaps even before their mothers know they are pregnant.

Pre-eclampsia (high blood pressure in the mother and possible growth problems in the baby) is another possible trigger for miscarriage (see pages 30–31). Some women have an immune reaction to their baby and produce antibodies which form blood clots in the placenta. Other causes include diabetes, a liver disorder, a poorly shaped womb, and a weak cervix.

There are also various other factors such as infections, too little folic acid in the diet, too much alcohol, smoking, fatigue, a shock, standing for long hours, a hormone imbalance (for example, from the polycystic ovary syndrome – see below) which may be to blame.

While many miscarriages and premature and 'small-for-dates' births are impossible to prevent, you can take steps to make some of their possible causes less likely. The best way to do this is by following the general advice of doctors and guidance which is provided in this book. It's especially important to:

- Eat a healthy diet.
- Take a supplement of folic acid.
- Avoid too much alcohol (or cut it out).
- Stop smoking (or at least cut right down).
- Avoid getting overtired.
- Go outside each day to get some daylight on your skin and in your eyes.
- Attend the antenatal clinic regularly.

PREVENTING REPEATED MISCARRIAGES

If you've had repeated miscarriages, it is important to investigate if there is a cause that is preventable for the future. Your doctor can arrange blood tests and an ultra-sound scan of your ovaries. There are two conditions in particular which can be treated.

HUGHES' SYNDROME
Blood tests in pregnancy can show whether you have any of the antibodies (called anti-phospholipid antibodies) that can cause blood clots in your placenta. This condition (Hughes' syndrome) is more likely in women who already have an auto-immune disorder called lupus (which also causes a variety of other problems). If this is your problem, your doctors will recommend a small daily dose of aspirin and also, perhaps, another drug called heparin. These will help to prevent the blood clotting in your placenta. This treatment will give you a high chance of having a successful pregnancy next time.

POLYCYSTIC OVARIES
A combination of an ovary scan and blood tests for hormone levels between pregnancies can show if your miscarriages result from a hormone disruption associated with multiple cysts on your ovaries. Such 'polycystic ovaries' are found in as many as four out of five women who keep miscarrying. Women with polycystic ovaries are particularly likely to be overweight, but researchers have found that the ovaries return to normal in many of those who manage to lose their excess weight and keep it off. So if you discover you have polycystic ovaries, and you are also overweight, it would be wise to lose weight well before you try to become pregnant again.

PREMATURE BIRTH

PRE-TERM OR 'SMALL-FOR-DATES' BABIES

Between five and seven in every hundred babies born each year in England and Wales are born early, before thirty-seven weeks. And one baby in ten is born 'small-for-dates' – weighing less than he or she should for the time spent in the womb.

There are many reasons for a baby being born exceptionally early or small. Perhaps the most important of these is a placenta that isn't working properly, which means that the baby doesn't get enough nourishment and oxygen. Sometimes doctors don't know why a placenta is unhealthy. However, it is known that many lifestyle factors and health problems can affect this.

Smoking is often responsible. Other possibilities include a poor diet, too much alcohol, and certain infections (such as flu and rubella, a urine infection, toxoplasmosis or listeria infection, or long-term gum infection). High blood pressure (perhaps from pre-eclampsia) is another culprit, as is Hughes' syndrome (see opposite). If the mother herself was a 'small-for-dates' baby, her babies are at a higher risk too.

Some women deliver prematurely because they have an underactive thyroid gland. Carrying twins, or more, encourages early birth, as does having a medical procedure such as amniocentesis (see page 29). Sometimes the waters break abnormally early because the cervix dilates too soon, the membranes around the baby are weak or a vaginal infection has spread into the womb; such an infection also encourages early contractions.

The list of possible reasons still isn't complete. If you previously had an early birth or small-for-dates baby, this is more likely to happen again. And if you've had two or more abortions, you are more likely to give birth prematurely. Being under sixteen when you have a baby also increases your chances of giving birth prematurely.

If you used the Pill or a copper coil right up until just before you conceived, you may have high levels of copper and low levels of zinc in your body, which can encourage

prematurity. If you had trouble conceiving, particularly if you had fertility treatment, your baby has a higher risk of a low birthweight. An unusually shaped womb, fibroids, or too much or too little amniotic fluid is occasionally to blame, as is untreated rhesus disease in the baby.

If you work long hours, you'll reduce your unborn baby's growth by an average of 80g (3oz). Feeling continually stressed makes both premature birth and a small-for-dates baby more likely too.

Illegal drugs can also cause problems. Taking cannabis regularly encourages a low birthweight; taking cocaine encourages prematurity; and amphetamines encourage both prematurity and being small-for-dates. All should be avoided at any time, but especially during pregnancy.

Exposure to lead reduces a pregnant woman's level of zinc and makes her baby more likely to have a low birthweight. This can result from stripping lead-containing paint, using lead-containing Indian cosmetics (such as surma), having prolonged exposure to traffic fumes, or drinking water with a high lead content.

Lastly, two upsetting factors can be responsible for premature birth. One is being subjected to physical violence. The other is the financial poverty that means a woman is more likely to have a tiring job and less likely to eat well and be healthy.

ABOVE: Let your body guide you over how much you need to rest. Aim to have at least half an hour each day lying with your feet up, and avoid being on your feet all the time.

33

ENJOYING YOUR PREGNANCY

Pregnancy is a natural changing point in your life; a chance to review your health and lifestyle and make changes that will stand you in good stead during the years to come. It's the perfect time to tune into your body and listen to what it is telling you. Women vary as to how they will feel. Some women bloom and their growing roundness suits them. Others find tiredness and sickness mar the first few months, and they feel large and cumbersome from the middle of pregnancy onwards. For most women, there arc ups and downs during pregnancy: times when you are glad that you are pregnant and enjoy the process, and times when you probably wish it could be over more quickly and you could feel like your old self again.

It's sensible in pregnancy, as in any period of major change, to let each other know how you are feeling and to listen to each other's hopes and doubts, excitement and concern.

Small changes to your lifestyle can help: a regular swim, sitting with your feet up in the evening, or perhaps switching your main meal to the middle of the day. The important thing is to experiment to find what suits you.

Your partner

Some men find pregnancy rather stressful. Finances tend to figure high on their list of worries, but they also have concerns about the health of both their partner and the baby, as well as the changes that the baby will bring to their relationship.

This is a good time to develop your communication skills so that you can begin to understand each other's worries and fears. Talk to your partner about the future and include him as much as possible, perhaps by inviting him to come with you to your antenatal classes or appointments. Let him know how you feel. Confiding in each other will help you both to feel confident in the strength of your relationship once the baby arrives.

SEX IN PREGNANCY

For some couples, pregnancy is a time when physical closeness matters a lot. The excitement both partners feel can be expressed physically, adding to the richness of the relationship. For others, physical discomforts can inhibit their sex life, and sometimes underlying tensions and worries mean that sex is not good. Some men find a partner's pregnancy enhances her attractiveness, and many women feel particularly good about their bodies at this time. Indeed, the pelvic congestion that occurs as the baby grows makes some women aroused more quickly.

Many couples are concerned about whether sex during pregnancy can harm the developing baby. For most pregnancies, most of the time, there is absolutely no need to worry, but there are some circumstances in which you may be advised not to have full sex. If you have a previous history of miscarriage, or had a threatened miscarriage this pregnancy,

some experts advise against having sex at the time your period would normally have been due. Also, any woman with a very low-lying placenta (placenta praevia) is usually advised to avoid sex. If you have any concerns at all about sex, do discuss them with your doctor or midwife. In a normal pregnancy, sexual intercourse is not a problem, though you may find as your bump grows that you need to use a little ingenuity, and avoid positions with the man on the top. Some couples prefer to avoid full intercourse later on in pregnancy, although you cannot harm the baby or break the waters by intercourse. For many couples, pregnancy provides a chance to develop and enhance their sex life to include more touching, stroking, cuddling and massage. Many of these skills can induce deep relaxation and are useful when you are in labour.

her into labour, and male semen contains substances called prostaglandins which can help start contractions. It will only do this, however, if you and the baby are ready for labour.

Even if you don't feel inclined to make love, simply stroking, massaging, touching and hugging can have the same effect, and if it doesn't work you can always console yourself with the fact that it was fun trying!

WORKING IN PREGNANCY

Most women choose to work through part of their pregnancy, and many women will be entitled to maternity leave. The length of leave and the value of benefits vary according to how long you have been with the company. You may plan to work until the last possible moment, but it is worth keeping your options open since in the early stages you cannot be sure how you

You can continue working for as long as you feel comfortable but listen to the messages from your mind and body. This way you can do what feels right to you and guard against overdoing things by taking extra rest if necessary.

35

In late pregnancy, sex may cause a few Braxton Hicks contractions to occur. These are 'practice' contractions, and some women experience them throughout the last few weeks of pregnancy. Others hardly feel them. Orgasm can set them off, but they usually fade away after a few minutes.

Sex can be a pleasant, natural way to start labour when the pregnancy is overdue. A woman's body produces hormones during lovemaking which can help nudge

will feel later. You may be able to adapt your job slightly to make things more comfortable, for instance by sitting instead of standing, or altering your hours. Jobs that involve handling or being near chemicals or radioactivity are unsuitable for a pregnant woman. Your midwife or doctor will be able to advise you on safety at work and your personnel department may be able to help you alter your working arrangements.

See Childcare Choices, page 262, for information on childcare and returning to work

ENJOYING YOUR PREGNANCY

36

Explain to your toddler that the only things new babies do are sleep, feed and need baths and nappy changes – then there'll be no disappointment when the baby isn't an immediate playmate.

RELAXATION ROUTINE

It's well worth getting into the habit of a daily relaxation session. This will not only help you to relax in labour but will also help you to recharge your batteries once the baby is born.
● **Sit comfortably on a sofa or lie on a bed, making sure you support your body with plenty of cushions or pillows.**
● **Begin by stretching out your right arm, making it long, tense and straight right down to the tips of your fingers. Then let it flop down.**
● **Now stretch and relax your left arm in the same way and then each leg.**
● **Push your bottom into the cushions or pillows and relax, then push back with your head and shoulders, and relax.**
● **Your whole body should feel heavy, warm and relaxed, and you can let your eyes close and concentrate on steady deep breathing. Listen to the sound of each out-breath, and let it become a gentle sigh.**
● **You may find you drift off to sleep. Avoid getting up too quickly after this routine.**

Women are entitled to take time off work for antenatal visits, and if you are unwell during pregnancy your doctor will give you a sickness certificate. Your doctor or midwife will supply you with the right certificate of pregnancy to use to claim maternity benefits and to notify your employer if you are taking maternity leave and plan to return to work.

OLDER CHILDREN

If you have older children you will need to think about when and how to tell them about the baby. Nine months seems a very long time to a small child and you may prefer to wait until the pregnancy is some way along before telling your toddler. However, there is a strong possibility that a child may overhear adults talking about the baby and, mentioned in a low-key way, early on, it gives her time to assimilate the news. She may find the whole idea of a baby growing inside you rather odd. Toddlers have been known to ask if you ate the baby, or they may expect the baby to share your cup of tea because it is 'in your tummy'.

ANTENATAL CLASSES

In some areas antenatal classes become very crowded, so it is worth finding out what is available early on. Most hospitals offer classes and some community midwives run them. These are usually free.

Classes run by independent teachers, for which a fee is usually paid, may also be available. Classes may be concerned with general preparation, active birth, pregnancy exercise, yoga in pregnancy, 'aquanatal' exercises (taught in a swimming pool) or discussion. Find out what is on offer locally, and consider what you would like from a class before booking.

Choosing a class

Some classes concentrate on relaxation techniques for labour, others focus on parentcraft skills, some only cover exercises, and others are more like discussion groups. Find out as much as you can about the classes before you begin. You may find it helpful to ask some of the following questions.

See Planning Another Baby, page 270, for more information on preparing your children for a new baby

- Are they women-only classes or for couples? You may prefer an all-female group or want to involve your partner.
- Are the classes nearby? Local classes mean that you are more likely to meet other local parents.
- Are they held during the day or in the evening? This may influence your choice, depending on whether you are working, how you can arrange transport and when your partner will be free to attend.
- What will they cover? If you feel strongly about wanting to concentrate on, for instance, active birth, you may be disappointed if labour skills are dealt with in a class or two and the rest of the time is spent on topics like baby bathing.
- Is a tour of the hospital included? It's useful to look around the labour ward before you have your baby.
- How large is the class? Discussion groups need to be small, but exercise classes can be larger. Hospital-based classes can be very large, and people may find it difficult to ask questions and discuss things in a big group.

Remember that you can choose to go to more than one type of class. You may, for example, want to go to an exercise class and a hospital course.

Women who have attended classes normally cope well with labour and tend to need less pain relief than women who have not attended any antenatal classes.

TRAVELLING

- Sitting in cramped conditions for long periods can be uncomfortable when you are pregnant, so you may need to break your journey more often.
- Wear your seatbelt, but wear it properly: between the breasts and under the bump is the guide, so the lower section of the seatbelt is over your hip bones.
- If you need to fly long distances late in pregnancy, discuss the flight with your doctor. Some airlines require a certificate of fitness to travel in late pregnancy.
- You may need to take out extra holiday insurance to cover pregnancy-related problems, or the baby, should you go into early labour.
- Make sure to check with your doctor about the safety of holiday immunizations during your pregnancy.
- Take your co-op card or hospital notes with you so that if you go into labour while you are away you will have any vital information for those caring for you.

Regular exercise, enough to make you warm, for twenty minutes three times a week – like this antenatal exercise class, or walking or swimming – will keep you fit while you're waiting.

37

See Exercise During Pregnancy, pages 46-51, for antenatal exercises

LOOKING *AFTER* YOURSELF

HEADACHES
- Headaches can be a sign of tension.
- If you suffer from these try to rest more.
- After the first three months of pregnancy, most doctors feel it is safe to take a small dose of paracetamol to ease a headache.
- If the pain is severe, or accompanied by vision disturbances, contact your doctor as this could indicate high blood pressure.

Pregnancy is a natural state, not an illness, and you can do a great deal to contribute towards your general health and well-being, and that of your baby. If you need to adjust your lifestyle, now is the right time to do it.

SMOKING
This is the time to give up smoking, both for your sake and for that of the baby. Some women find they go off cigarettes in the early stages, but even if you still have the urge to smoke, knowing that you are pregnant may provide the motivation you need to give up.

If you find it impossible to give up, do at least try to cut down. Babies born to women who smoke tend to be smaller, and may be less healthy than babies born to women who don't smoke, and they have a higher risk of cot death. Babies growing up in households where there is a smoker are more likely to suffer from chest infections.

Avoid using any smoking substitutes, like nicotine pills or patches. If your partner or others around you smoke, you may be subjected to passive smoking. Try to persuade others to limit their smoking to specific areas, so that you can avoid the smoky atmosphere.

DRINKING
The fetal alcohol syndrome can affect the babies of mothers who drink excessive amounts regularly. Some experts think that binge-drinking in early pregnancy may also lead to this condition. There is no evidence that the occasional glass of wine or beer does any harm, and very many women have one or two drinks in the early weeks before they even know they are pregnant, with no ill-effects whatsoever.

SLEEPING
Sometimes discomforts of pregnancy such as heartburn or cramp can keep you awake at night or you may need to go to the lavatory. A regular 'winding down' routine can help you sleep better. Perhaps a bath with a few drops of a calming aromatherapy oil (check that the oil is safe during pregnancy before doing this), a hot milky drink and a short spell reading would help you sleep. Experiment with sleeping positions, too.

TEETH
It is important to take extra care of your teeth during pregnancy as gums tend to become softer and more prone to disease. Regular cleaning, including flossing, helps to avoid this and prevent decay. A healthy

38

OPPOSITE *When playing the waiting game, look after your baby — and yourself — by stopping smoking and limiting your intake of alcohol.*

TEN WAYS TO GIVE UP SMOKING

1. Set a date to give up and stick to it.

2. Your partner can offer his support, if he smokes, by giving up at the same time.

3. Give yourself other rewards: have a snack, a fruit drink, rest with your feet up, or make a chatty phone call to a friend instead of having a cigarette.

4. Identify the worst times: perhaps you crave a cigarette most after a meal, or when you sit down in the evening. Plan your day to make sure you have someone around to help you resist the urge.

5. Change the pattern of your day to avoid crisis times; go for a walk, take a relaxing bath, or do something else that makes smoking difficult.

6. Remind yourself why it matters; pin a picture of a newborn baby on the wall, so that you can see it whenever you want to smoke a cigarette.

7. Add up the money you are saving; each day put the money you would have spent in a jar on the mantelpiece. At the end of the week buy something nice for the baby.

8. Take up knitting or sewing to keep your hands occupied.

9. Avoid smoky rooms and situations when everyone around you will be smoking, at least for the first week or two.

10. Ask for help if you need it; your midwife or doctor will be able to give advice, support and encouragement.

diet helps too; avoid sugary foods or drinks and eat plenty of calcium-rich foods such as milk, cheese, chickpeas, some fish and cereals. Regular visits to your dentist are important too.

VAGINAL DISCHARGE

An increased vaginal discharge during pregnancy is perfectly normal; however, if it becomes more profuse or discoloured, starts to smell, or you begin to itch, it may signal an infection such as thrush or bacterial vaginosis. Check this with your doctor.

WEIGHT GAIN

For many years a great emphasis was put on achieving the 'correct' weight gain during pregnancy. Now it is accepted that women vary, and so do babies, so it is less important to gain a set amount of weight than to eat a healthy diet, and feel well. You will probably find that you put on 7–18kg (15–40lb). Women who have a very poor diet in pregnancy and gain little weight tend to have very small babies. Women who overeat and put on a great deal of weight may be subjecting their bodies to great strain.

STRETCH MARKS

Some women find that as they grow larger their skin develops stretch marks. You may be prone to these or you may not: it seems to depend on skin type. Nothing can prevent them, but using a moisturizing cream at least helps keep the skin feeling smooth. Don't go out and buy special cream – use an old favourite or one that is not too expensive so you can use it generously rather than skimp on an expensive one.

BREASTS

Your breasts are likely to increase in size, and some women find they also develop stretch marks here. Use a moisturizing cream and always wear a good supportive bra. It's worth checking the fit at intervals during the pregnancy, since you may need to move up through the sizes as you grow. If you are not sure what size bra to buy, go to your nearest department store to be measured. Women with smaller breasts are no less likely to be able to breastfeed, but if you have very flat or inverted nipples it can make it difficult

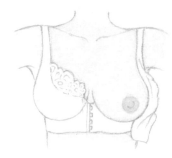

for a baby to fix on well. However, a baby's sucking is a very effective mechanism for pulling out an inverted nipple, so even if yours are flat or inverted at the start it certainly does not mean you will be unable to feed your baby.

As you expand, buy more comfortable bras. Measure under your breasts for the size and around the fullest part for the cup (above left). You could buy a front-opening nursing bra.

HEALTHY EATING

Eating well during pregnancy is not difficult so long as you have a varied diet, with as many fresh and wholesome foods as possible.

In early pregnancy you may suffer from nausea. For this short time it is best to eat whatever you fancy, whenever you can manage it. Small, light meals are generally easier to digest than heavy ones. Experiment with different mealtimes to find when is the best time for you to eat. Sometimes it helps to combat nausea by eating a plain biscuit and having a drink before you get up in the morning.

A healthy diet supplies you and your baby with all the vitamins, minerals, essential fatty acids and other nutrients you need, but a folic acid supplement is recommended too.

Easy steps to a healthy diet

A good diet has enough variety to ensure that both you and your baby receive everything you need. To begin with, try gradually introducing healthier versions of the food you usually eat (see Quick and easy ways to improve your diet, opposite). This way you can get used to new tastes and experiment with foods to see which you prefer.

Rather than thinking of foods as either 'healthy' or 'forbidden', simply make two lists, like the two below, one to eat more from, and one to eat less from.

You may find that you cannot eat if you are too tired or very hungry. Keeping meals small and frequent, and having a rest before eating may suit you best. Drink plenty of fluids (to prevent dehydration), and rest as much as possible. Even if you eat very little at the beginning, your baby is still tiny and your body will draw on its own reserves of vitamins and minerals to nourish him. Most women find nausea vanishes by fourteen weeks.

Eat more

Fresh fruits and vegetables; carbohydrate foods such as wholemeal bread, pasta, cereals, and brown rice; beans and pulses; chicken and fish; fresh and raw foods.

Eat less

Sugary food like cakes, sweets, biscuits, sweet drinks; high-fat food, like fried food; beef, pork and lamb; meat products like sausages; pastry-based food like pies; ice-creams, sauces and creams.

QUICK AND EASY WAYS TO IMPROVE YOUR DIET

1. Serve two fresh vegetables with your main meal.

2. Add a side salad to each main meal.

3. Replace sugary breakfast cereals with wholemeal, no-added-sugar varieties.

4. Add chopped fresh fruit to breakfast cereals.

5. Replace cream and ice-cream with yogurt or fromage frais.

6. Swop sugary drinks for low-calorie versions, or mix fresh fruit juices with fizzy water.

7. Trim all fat from meat and try grilling instead of frying.

8. Swop chips for baked potatoes.

9. Replace crisps with vegetable sticks, fruit, or unsalted nuts and raisins.

10. Make two or three puddings each week entirely from fresh fruit.

11. Eat three helpings a week of oily fish such as salmon, sardines or mackerel.

12. Serve a variety of breads and try new types and shapes.

13. Eat three pieces of fruit each day.

14. If you drink lots of tea or coffee match each cup with a glass of water or diluted fruit juice.

DRINKS

A high-fibre diet with plenty of fresh fruits and vegetables and wholegrain foods will help prevent constipation during pregnancy. It is also really important to keep your fluid intake up. This too will help with constipation, but many women find they have to make a special effort to remember to drink enough. If you have gone off tea and coffee, experiment with fresh juices diluted with still or fizzy water. You may particularly fancy milk-based drinks, and you can make an easy and filling milkshake using a ripe banana and about 100ml (5fl oz) of milk blended together. Add a strawberry yogurt for a complete meal in a glass.

CHOOSING CAREFULLY

Some foods are best avoided by pregnant women. A sensible attitude to your diet is vital here as the foods you can eat and those you ought to avoid will vary from time to time. For instance, liver was once recommended as a good food for pregnant woment to eat because it is rich in iron. It is now thought best to avoid it because many animal feeds are supplemented with vitamin A which builds up in the liver of the animal. Very high doses of vitamin A can cause fetal abnormalities. Eggs have always been seen as a good and cheap source of protein, but since the salmonella scare of 1989, pregnant women have been advised to avoid raw or lightly cooked eggs – you should cook eggs until the yolk is firm. Toxoplasmosis is an illness caused by organisms found in some raw or undercooked meats, and it can affect the development of the fetus if caught by the mother. It is wise, therefore, to avoid eating raw or undercooked meat, to avoid storing raw and cooked meats near to each other in the fridge, and make sure that you use different chopping boards for raw and cooked meats.

BASIC FOOD HYGIENE

● When using a microwave oven, stir food after cooking, allow it to stand for a minute or two and check that the food is hot.

● Don't eat raw or undercooked meat as this can be a source of toxoplasmosis.

● Avoid handling cat litter, as cats can very occasionally pass on toxoplasmosis.

● Store foods well; keep them clean, cool and covered.

● Reheat food only once, and then check that it is hot all the way through.

SUPPLEMENTS

Take a folic acid supplement from when you start trying for a baby until at least the twelfth week of pregnancy. A lack of this B-group vitamin has been linked to backbone and skull defects such as spina bifida. Some pregnant women add a multi-vitamin and mineral supplement formulated for pregnancy, and a supplement of the essential fatty acids (docosahexaenoic acid, arichidonic acid and gamma linolenic acids) that are important for a baby's developing brain and eyes.

FOODS TO AVOID

● Eggs unless well cooked until the yolk is firm.

● Liver and liver-based dishes such as pâté and liver sausage.

● Soft, unpasteurized cheeses.

TAKE EXTRA CARE WITH:

● Instant meals that are reheated in the microwave (reheat very thoroughly).

● Ready-washed salads.

CURRENT HEALTHY EATING GUIDELINES

As a pregnant woman the easiest way to boost your well-being and that of your baby is by eating a healthy diet. The guidelines for eating this way apply to everyone. They are remarkably straightforward and are summed up in the Food Pyramid. This shows the proportions of the various groups of foods you should aim to eat each day.

FOOD PYRAMID

● Complex carbohydrates form the base of the Food Pyramid. Experts recommend eating between six and eleven daily helpings of starchy foods. Examples include bread, breakfast cereal, rice, pasta, potatoes and yams. It's better to choose whole-grain bread, cereal and pasta, brown rice and potatoes in their skins. This is because these have higher levels of fibre than white bread, pasta and rice, refined cereal and peeled potatoes. Fibre is good at any time, but especially when you are pregnant, because it helps to counteract any tendency to constipation, and also helps guard against faintness, fatigue and pregnancy diabetes.

ABOVE Imagine the items in your shopping trolley in six piles – complex carbohydrates; vegetables; fruit; dairy foods; meat, poultry, fish, beans, peas and lentils; and fats, oils and sugar. Try to assess whether these piles match the proportions of the food pyramid.

● Vegetables and fruit come next in terms of bulk. The basic recommendation is to have five helpings a day of vegetables and fruit. Some experts recommend up to ten! Aim to have at least three and perhaps five daily helpings of a variety of different vegetables. Don't count potatoes, as these are included with complex carbohydrate foods.

Choose between two and four daily helpings of fruit. A banana is fine occasionally but it's wiser to choose other fruits more often than not. This is because bananas – especially ripe ones - contain rapidly absorbed sugars and so aren't as good as other fruits at helping maintain a normal blood sugar level.

● Next come dairy foods – milk, cheese, and yogurt and other cultured milk products. These are good sources of protein, and excellent sources of calcium. Aim to have two or three servings a day.

● Meat, poultry, fish, eggs, beans, peas and lentils provide you with protein and many other nutrients too. Opt for two or three helpings a day.

● Fats and oils are vital to good health but you don't need much of them. They are present in almost all foods, but especially meat, poultry, oily fish, eggs, dairy foods, nuts, seeds, whole grains and vegetable oils.

Fats allow you to absorb fat-soluble vitamins (A, D, E and K) from your intestine. Some fats, called essential fatty acids (linoleic acid and alpha-linolenic acid), are vital for good health and a healthy pregnancy. Nuts, seeds, whole-grain foods, and cold-pressed vegetable, nut and seed oils are the best sources.

It's a good idea to eat three helpings of oily fish (such as salmon, herrings and sardines) each week. This is because certain non-essential fatty acids, DHA (docosahexaenoic acid) and EPA (eicosapentaenoic acid) are particularly important for the development of an unborn baby's brain. Your body makes these from essential fatty acids but you can get them ready-made in oily fish. If you don't like oily fish, consider taking a supplement of fish oil (but not fish liver oil, such as cod liver oil, as its level of vitamin A is too high for a pregnant woman).

● At the top of the Food Pyramid comes sugar. This means 'non-milk extrinsic sugar', the sort – like table sugar, honey and golden syrup – you use to sweeten foods. Fruit juice is counted as one of these because its sugar is present in concentrated form and without the fibre of the whole fruit.

HOW BIG IS A HELPING?

● A helping of complex carbohydrates is a slice of bread, 25g (1oz) of breakfast cereal, or half a cup of cooked pasta, rice, potato or yam, or cooked cereal.
● A helping of vegetables is a cereal bowl of salad leaves, or half a cup of other salad or cooked vegetables.
● A helping of fruit is one piece of fruit, such as a small banana, apple, orange or similar-sized fruit, or half a cup of tinned or cooked fruit.
● A helping of dairy food is 300ml (½pint) of milk, 50g (2oz) of cheese, or a small tub of yogurt.

- A helping of meat, poultry or fish is 50–75g (2–3oz); a helping of cooked beans, peas or lentils is half a cup.
- You need only a little over 50g (2oz) of fats each day. This includes those fats naturally present in foods, as well as the fats (or oils) you add to food. Many people eat too much saturated fat in hard fats, meat and dairy foods.

FRUIT AND VEGETABLES

One way of ensuring you get a good balance of the nutrients available from vegetables and fruit is by choosing from different colour groups each day. Not only does this make meals attractive, but it also provides a variety of important plant pigments that help keep you and your baby healthy.

These pigments include carotenoids (such as the betacarotene that makes carrots orange), proanthocyanidins (that give a dark-blue hue to blueberries) and lycopene (that colours tomatoes red). Plant pigments often have powerful effects in the body. Betacarotene, for example, is a potent antioxidant which helps counteract inflammation.

OPPOSITE *Nature gives us several ways of selecting plant foods, and one is truly brilliant. Just ensure a variety of colours among the leaves, roots, stems, fruits and seeds on your plate.*

IMPORTANT NUTRIENTS

Some pregnant women don't get enough of certain important nutrients. The ones most likely to be lacking are iron, folic acid and calcium.

IRON You can boost your intake of iron by choosing iron-rich foods such as whole-grain foods, fortified breakfast cereals, dark-green leafy vegetables, beans and bean products (such as tofu), lentils, meat, fish and eggs (egg yolks, to be precise). Having citrus fruit or juice with iron-containing foods helps your body absorb their iron, whereas drinking tea or coffee with meals or within an hour of a meal reduces iron absorption.

FOLIC ACID Boost your intake of folic acid by taking a supplement (see page 41), and by eating more folic-acid-rich foods, including green leafy vegetables, citrus fruit and freshly squeezed juice, peas, beans and bean products such as tofu and beanburgers), whole grains, folic-acid-fortified breakfast cereal, nuts, dairy foods and yeast extract.

CALCIUM As for folic acid, you can boost your intake by opting for more dark-green leafy vegetables (broccoli is a particularly good source), swede, tinned sardines with their bones, soya-bean products that have been fortified with calcium, nuts, seeds and dairy foods. It's worth knowing that half-fat and skimmed milk, and low-fat yogurt and cheese contain as much calcium as their full-fat equivalents, yet much less saturated fat. Another tip for boosting your calcium intake is to make a chicken stock by boiling chicken bones for half an hour in water to which you have added two teaspoons of vinegar (which releases more calcium from the bones). Use this stock for making soup or gravy. Some people also like to eat the softened ends of cooked chicken thigh-bones.

LOOKING GOOD

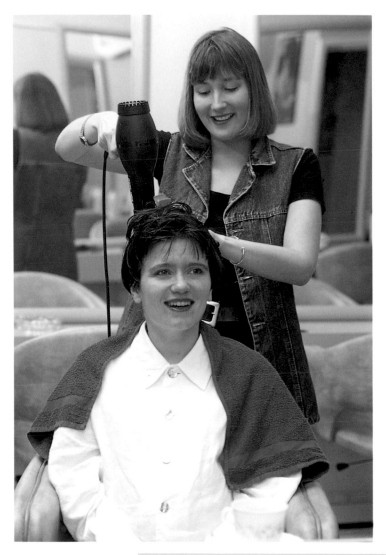

Looking good in pregnancy has never been easier. You will probably find that your baggiest existing clothes do for the first part of pregnancy, and the careful addition of a few new items should see you through the last half.

CHOOSING CLOTHES

What you wear will depend on what you are most comfortable in and the confines of your lifestyle. Many women opt for leggings plus a few loose tops, and they look stylish throughout pregnancy. You may not need maternity leggings, just your usual ones a size or two larger. If your figure or your job demand something a little more formal, you could opt for one or two well-cut outfits and vary them by wearing T-shirts underneath, or coloured tights, scarves and accessories. Often clothes can be adapted by wearing a shirt open with a T-shirt underneath, a waistcoat over a dress, or a loose jumper with leggings instead of a skirt.

Well-cut clothes may be expensive but they are usually flattering. If you need something for a special occasion like a wedding or dance, consider hiring an outfit. Accessories can be used to brighten things up, ring the changes or just detract from your growing bump. Scarves or

You've never looked so good! While you're pregnant your hair may be in peak condition, thanks perhaps to the pregnancy hormones, but it's probably best to avoid perms and colourings.

44

SPOIL YOURSELF

Make a point of spoiling yourself occasionally. Feeling good is important during pregnancy, and if you get into the habit of looking after yourself now, it will stand you in good stead once you are busy looking after a baby.

● **Treat yourself to some new underwear.** There's a wide range designed for pregnancy, including silky French knickers and pretty lacy bras.

● **Have a facial, or an aromatherapy massage. (Make sure you seek advice from a qualified aromatherapist who regularly works with pregnant women.)** Both are relaxing, and will leave you looking and feeling good.

● **Try some bath oils with aromatherapy extracts added to them (check with a qualified aromatherapist that they are safe to use), and put aside an evening to have a soak.**

● **Make time for a weekly swim; it's gentle and supportive and will help you keep fit.**

● **Book yourself in for a pedicure. It will keep your feet in tip-top condition, and a foot massage can be wonderfully relaxing.**

● **Make an appointment to have your hair cut and spend the time relaxing.**

● **Keep a 'post baby' basket. When shopping, buy extra moisturizer, make-up, bath oil, good tights, etc. and put them in the basket. This way you will have plenty of your favourite things for after the baby is born, when your time and money may be spent on the baby.**

bright jewellery at the neck help to draw attention to your face and away from your expanding figure.

TIGHTS AND SHOES

Hormone changes and the pressure of the uterus on veins make varicose veins in the legs more likely in pregnancy. They are one of the most unpleasant side effects of pregnancy, though they do not affect everybody. Good support tights can minimize them, and these are now available in sheer versions and in a range of colours. Try to avoid standing for long periods, sit with your feet raised when you can and avoid sitting with crossed legs. Well-shaped pregnancy tights are useful as you grow, as they have an extra section at the front. Comfortable shoes are essential. Avoid high heels, and choose stylish pumps and flatter shoes; you may find that you need a wider fitting in late pregnancy.

HAIR AND MAKE-UP

Many women find that their face shape changes during pregnancy. You may want to alter your style of make-up or have your hair cut into a new style, especially if fluid retention causes your face to seem rounder. Hair can be quite fragile in pregnancy, so avoid perms or colourings. Concentrate on a good cut and use gentle shampoos and rich conditioners to keep it in the best condition possible.

SKIN CARE

Your skin may change too; sometimes it becomes very dry in pregnancy and needs an extra-rich moisturizer, but often in the middle months skin and hair really do 'bloom'. Occasionally women develop a brownish marking on the face, or a brown line down the middle of the stomach from about the third month. These have no significance – they are caused by pregnancy hormones and usually fade after the baby is born. Similarly, freckles can become temporarily darker. If such changes in pigmentation bother you, particularly any blemishes on the face, try covering them up with a good foundation cream. It is also best to avoid strong sunlight as this can make the pigmentation worse.

EYES

Contact lenses, especially the hard variety, can become uncomfortable in pregnancy as fluid retention can change the shape of your eye. See your optician if this happens; you may need to cut down your wearing time, or change to glasses for a while.

MAKE YOURSELF FEEL GOOD

● Lie down and place some cucumber slices or cotton-wool pads soaked in witch-hazel over your eyelids. Not only will this feel wonderfully soothing but it will help to reduce any puffiness around your eyes caused by fluid retention.

● Give your skin a stimulating rub with a flannel or some special cleansing grains. This will help to remove any flaking skin. It will also unblock the pores and is good for the circulation.

Enjoy creating a 'new you' as your skin, face, hair and body adapt to the months of pregnancy. For example, your different shape and style of clothes may inspire you to experiment with your hair.

LOOKING GOOD

45

EXERCISE DURING PREGNANCY

Now that you are pregnant you may be wondering whether or not it is safe to continue with your regular exercise class or if you should take up exercise. Growing and carrying a baby around inside you for nine months is physically hard work and the labour itself, as the name suggests, may seem like a marathon. Physical fitness brings with it many advantages and you may find that now is the time you want to take a look at your lifestyle and see if there are some changes you could make so you feel fitter and healthier. Choose some form of physical activity that you enjoy as you are then much more likely to stick with it. Brisk walking is a very good form of physical activity and, provided it is brisk enough and done for long enough, can really help keep your heart and lungs healthy.

REGULAR EXERCISER

If you are a regular exerciser, taking part in some sport or attending aerobic, body conditioning or yoga classes, then there is no reason why you shouldn't continue with these throughout your pregnancy unless you have any specific problems such as an existing medical condition, bleeding in early pregnancy, a low-lying placenta or high blood pressure.

It is usually recommended that pregnant women avoid competitive sports and those sports which carry a risk of falling or hard contact with other players such as skiing, horse-riding, judo, squash or hockey.

NON-EXERCISER

If you have never been a regular exerciser then this may be a good opportunity to take up some form of physical activity or join an exercise class. Choose something that you think you will enjoy and is not too strenuous, and begin very gradually.

EXERCISING SAFELY

- Exercise regularly two or three times a week. This is much safer and more effective than doing it infrequently.
- Start slowly and build up gradually.

- Don't exercise in very hot or humid conditions.
- Make sure you take plenty of fluids as this will help prevent dehydration and overheating.
- Avoid high-impact activities such as jumping and jogging, jerky, bouncy movements and sudden, fast changes of direction, as these can put a strain on your ankles, knees and hips.
- Exercise should not raise your heart rate too high.
- If any adverse symptoms occur you should slow down gradually and stop, then talk to your midwife or doctor about what occurred before continuing with your exercise plan.

POSTURE AND BACK CARE

Poor posture can lead to constant fatigue and tension, which in turn can lead to aching shoulders and low backache. During everyday activities and before starting any exercise always check your posture.

Bending forwards to lift anything puts enormous pressure on the discs in your spine. When you are pregnant, it's even more important to take care to lift correctly as the ligaments become much more lax and stretchy and are more easily strained.

PELVIC FLOOR

The pelvic floor muscles make up an important sling of muscles which forms the floor of the bony pelvis and supports the internal organs. There are three openings in these muscles. During birth they get stretched and need exercise to make them strong again. Any weakness may cause leakage of urine when coughing or sneezing. Exercise helps to keep them strong and it's easier to exercise them after the birth if you have practised often in pregnancy.

Imagine you are desperate to empty your bladder when you get to the lavatory but it's occupied. Tighten up around the front passage as if to stop yourself leaking. Keep breathing, hold for a count of four and then release. Do it as often as you can during the day.

OPPOSITE *Movement and exercise are enjoyable and good for everyone in the family – not least for you and your new baby.*

47

The Pelvic Floor
1. Pelvic floor muscles
2. Urethra
3. Vagina
4. Anus
5. Coccyx
6. Buttock muscle

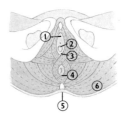

Good posture
Stand with your feet hip-width apart and your weight evenly distributed on both feet (far left). Tuck your bottom under and pull in your abdominal muscles. Think tall and try to lift your ribcage away from your hip bones. Relax your shoulders down, away from your ears, tuck your chin in and lengthen the back of your neck.

Poor posture
This is when your ankles are rolled in, knees locked back, pelvis tilted forward with the weight of the baby, resulting in an over-arched lower back (centre).

Lifting
Before attempting to lift anything: tighten your abdominal and pelvic-floor muscles, keep your back straight and bend your knees (left). Bring the object to be lifted as close to your body as possible and then straighten up from the knees. Breathe out as you lift.

48

WARM-UP
Before starting any exercises or heavy activities like gardening after a period of rest, it's vital that you gradually prepare your body first. During periods of inactivity the joints stiffen as the surfaces harden and dry up. Then, when the joints are used suddenly, they are more vulnerable to injury. These exercises will warm up and lubricate the joints to help prevent injury.

Start Position
Stand with feet hip-width apart, knees soft, bottom tucked under, tummy pulled in and ribcage lifted up (right). Think tall and breathe normally.

Shoulder shrugs
Shrug your shoulders up towards your ears and release (far right).

Arm circles
Bend your knees (far left)
and then straighten them
as you circle your arms up
and past your ears (left).

Heel to toe
Keeping your weight on one foot
with the knee slightly bent, touch
the other heel (right) and then
toe (far right) on to the ground
in front, then change feet.

Note: these exercises should be
done slowly and rhythmically,
about six to eight times each.

49

AEROBICS

Aerobic exercise is important for keeping your heart and lungs healthy. Many people think of jogging as the aerobic exercise, but it is not recommended during pregnancy. Any exercises that use the large arm and leg muscles in a repetitive way are effective.

Marching

Marching on the spot with your arms swinging rhythmically will work the heart and lungs well (far left). Don't bang your feet on the ground as this could jar the joints.

Knee lifts

Lift alternate knees and touch the raised knee with the opposite hand (left). Pull in your abdominal muscles, and keep your bottom tucked in and your hips level as you do this exercise.

50

Half stars

This is a low-impact alternative to star jumps and is a good aerobic exercise. Stand with feet together, tummy pulled in, bottom tucked under and knees slightly bent (right). Point your left toe out to the side and raise both arms out to the side (far right). Bring left foot back to the centre and arms down. Repeat on the right side.

ABDOMINAL EXERCISES

During pregnancy the abdominal muscles stretch to allow room for your baby to grow. To prevent them becoming too weak as they stretch it's important to keep them strong with exercise, but take care to work them safely. After sixteen to twenty weeks you should not exercise them while lying on your back.

Straight abdominals

Kneel on all fours with your knees hip-width apart and your hands underneath your shoulders (above). Keep your back flat and breathe in. As you breathe out, tighten your abdominal muscles and arch your back up towards the ceiling like an angry cat (left). Release and return to the start, trying not to let your back sag the other way.

Diagonal abdominals

Do the same as before, but as you arch up hitch your hips round to the side (left), making the distance between your ribs and your hips on that side smaller. Return to the centre and repeat on the other side.

51

STRETCHES

Stretching out the muscles at the end of an exercise session helps to avoid stiffness.

Inner thigh stretch

Sitting with the soles of both feet touching, gently ease your knees further towards the floor. You should be able to feel the stretch in the inner thighs.

COMMON DISCOMFORTS

Some of the minor problems of pregnancy like cramp or heartburn can be quite difficult to cope with at times. Although they don't pose any real risk to you or your baby, they can make you feel pretty miserable. Talk the problems through with your midwife, doctor, or antenatal teacher. She may be able to suggest ways that you can make yourself feel more comfortable, such as changing your diet, or experimenting with complementary treatments such as homeopathy.

AVOIDING BACKACHE
This pelvic tilt helps prevent backache and improves posture.
- **Stand with your back straight against a wall.**
- **Place your hand in the small of the back (you will feel a hollow).**
- **Tip hips slightly forward so that your stomach comes in and up (the hollow will get smaller).**
- **Repeat several times.**
- **Squat rather than bend when lifting things.**

BACKACHE
During pregnancy your body produces hormones which soften the ligaments joining the sections of the pelvis. This is to allow the pelvis to open slightly and make more space for the baby. Unfortunately, it can also cause backache. Standing and moving well will help (see left, Avoiding Backache). If backache is a major problem, you should discuss it with your doctor. You may choose to visit a qualified and experienced osteopath.

BREATHLESSNESS
The growing baby takes up quite a lot of space inside you, and many women find that at some stage they feel breathless. It usually occurs when the bump is fairly high up and improves once the baby settles down into the pelvis, often at around thirty-six weeks. It can help to ease breathlessness if you sleep propped up on several pillows.

If the breathlessness is prolonged, however, you should talk to your doctor.

CARPAL TUNNEL SYNDROME
The symptoms are tingling and sometimes pain and numbness in the thumb, index and middle fingers. They are caused by fluid retention, which puts pressure on the nerves in the wrist. Raising your hand can help, as can wrist exercises: circle your wrists several times in each direction, then bend and stretch your fingers. An ice pack can reduce swelling and if it is very uncomfortable a wrist splint can be worn at night. The condition usually goes once the baby is born.

CONSTIPATION
This is a common problem in pregnancy. It can be made worse by some types of iron

pill. If your doctor has prescribed iron tablets do discuss this with her. It may be possible to change the type of iron supplements. Diet, fluids and exercise all help relieve constipation. Make sure you eat high-fibre foods such as cereals, wholemeal bread and fresh fruits and vegetables every day. Drinking plenty of water or fruit juice diluted with water also helps. Exercise is important too: walking, swimming, cycling and yoga can all help with constipation as well as keep you fit, supple and generally feeling good.

CRAMP

This usually manifests itself as a sudden sharp pain in the muscles, often in the lower leg. It is not dangerous, and usually goes quite quickly, but you may find it occurs at night and wakes you. Firm massage can help, as can putting your foot on a cold floor. If you get cramp in your leg when you stretch, try turning your toes upwards rather than pointing them. There is some evidence that cramp

may be improved by taking calcium tablets, so discuss this with your doctor.

FEELING FAINT

Sometimes during early pregnancy women experience low blood pressure. This can make you feel faint or dizzy, especially when you stand up from a sitting or lying position. Don't get up too quickly; change position slowly, perhaps sitting up in bed for a few minutes before standing. You may also feel faint if you stand for long periods or in a stuffy atmosphere. Lying down or fresh air will help.

HEARTBURN

The same pregnancy hormones that cause backache may also contribute to heartburn. A ring of muscles around the entrance to the stomach usually help keep the acid contents in. However, the entrance can remain slightly open during pregnancy, allowing the stomach contents to seep back. Rich or spicy foods or alcohol may make the condition worse. Sometimes small, frequent meals help to prevent heartburn, as does sleeping propped up on several pillows.

ITCHING

This may be caused by the skin stretching over your stomach. Keeping your skin as cool as possible and wearing cotton next to you may make you feel better. A moisturizing cream rubbed in regularly may help as may homeopathic remedies. Consult your doctor if the itching becomes severe or widespread.

PILES

Constipation can occasionally lead to piles. These are swollen veins in the walls of the back passage. They can become very hot and itchy and may bleed occasionally. Avoiding constipation helps prevent them and resting in a warm bath is very soothing. Your doctor will be able to suggest a suitable cream.

VARICOSE VEINS

If there is a tendency towards varicose veins in your family, it might be worth wearing support tights from early pregnancy. Try to avoid standing for long periods and sit with your legs raised whenever you can.

STRESS INCONTINENCE

Some women find that when they cough, laugh or run they leak a little urine. This is caused by pressure on the pelvic floor, the sling of muscles under the baby. Regular pelvic floor exercises can help (see page 47).

PELVIC FLOOR EXERCISES
When you do pelvic floor exercises:
● Sit or lie down, with knees slightly apart and bent, and feet flat on the floor.
● If you aren't sure which muscles to tighten, then next time you pass urine, stop the flow in mid-stream. The muscles you use are the ones you need to tighten when exercising your pelvic floor.

COMMON DISCOMFORTS

53

PREPARING FOR THE BIRTH

It is worth getting organized for the birth in advance, as later you may need to slow down and take life more easily. Make a list of things you may need in labour, pack a small case for your stay in hospital and stock up on essential items for your return home, such as moisturizer, make-up, shampoo, bath oils and sanitary towels. Buy a few basics for the baby, like nappies and stretch suits (see What Your Baby Will Need, pages 56-7), but don't rush out and buy a complete wardrobe until after he is born and you know exactly what you need. Other people may buy clothes as presents, so you may have plenty of first-size outfits but little for when the baby is a few weeks older.

Remember also to keep practising your pelvic floor exercises (see page 47 and 53, and relaxation techniques (see page 36).

LABOUR BAG

In some hospitals your case may be taken up to the ward while you are still in labour. Keep separate a small bag of things you may need while in labour, and give it to your partner to look after. You may find some of the following items useful.
● Cotton nightdress or T-shirt to wear while in labour. Something old and soft will be more comfortable than a hospital gown, which can be stiff or starchy.
● Natural sponge. This can be really useful for moistening your lips as labour progresses and you need to take shallow breaths through your mouth.
● Toothbrush and toothpaste. If labour is long, cleaning your teeth can be refreshing.
● Hand cream for your partner to use when giving you a massage.
● Clean nightdress, sanitary towels and knickers to wear after the baby is born. Usually you can have a shower before being moved to the postnatal ward, so keep your washbag handy too.
● Books or magazines in case labour is slow.
● Tapes and a portable player.
● Hand-held mirror, so that you can see the baby's head in the second stage.
● Coins for the telephone box so that you can ring people.

Partner's labour bag

Your partner will also need a few supplies. Think about taking some of the following.
● Sandwiches and drinks, in case labour is long and there is nowhere to go for a snack.
● Camera to take some pictures of the new baby.
● Coins and a list of phone numbers so he or you can ring everyone straight away.
● Cotton T-shirt to wear if the hospital is hot.
● Spare T-shirt to change into once the baby is born.

HOSPITAL SUPPLIES

Once on the postnatal ward you may need supplies for both you and your baby. Check with the hospital whether they provide nappies, cotton wool and nappy cream. Some hospitals supply sanitary towels and others require you to take stocks in with you. When choosing sanitary towels, opt for really soft absorbent ones, as you may have to cope with bruising or stitching. Many maternity towels have a special covering to prevent the surface catching on stitches. Some women find using looped towels and a maternity belt comfortable, as the pad is held against the body as you walk. Others find stick-on pads better. It is not wise to use tampons at this stage.

As well as these disposable items you are likely to need the following.
● One or two nightdresses (hospitals are always hot, so choose cotton, and make sure they will be easy to unfasten when breastfeeding).
● Feeding bras.
● Washing kit.
● Slippers.
● Spare knickers. Buy cheap stretchy cotton ones that are easy to wash and dry quickly, and can be thrown away after the first few weeks if necessary. Stretch disposable briefs are particularly good if you've had stitches. Paper ones are not recommended as they tend to be quite scratchy and tear easily.
● Notepaper and envelopes so you can write to let everyone know the news.
● Coins for the phone.
● Books and magazines.

54

CONTACTING YOUR PARTNER

Think about how to contact your partner when you begin labour. You may need to arrange for him to phone you frequently, or hire a bleeper if you can't phone him. These are now available on short-term hire, so you can have one just for a month or so. It may also be worthwhile having a reserve labour companion on standby.

If you are planning to have your baby in hospital, think about how you will get there and tell the hospital if you will need an ambulance.

HOME-BIRTH PREPARATIONS

If you have arranged to have your baby at home, your midwife will drop off a home-birth pack at your house containing the medical necessities. Choose a room to have the baby in on the same floor as the bath and lavatory. You will need to warm the room quickly, and have a lamp or spotlight on hand. Spare sheets are useful, as is a plastic sheet to protect the bed. Somewhere for the baby to sleep, nappies and baby clothes are essential. Beanbags or a rocking chair could be useful during labour.

It helps to have home comforts at hand in hospital. How about packing something light and interesting to read, a bottle of mineral water to sip, and some fragrant relaxing massage oil for your back?

WHAT YOUR BABY WILL NEED

When your baby arrives, you will want to be ready for her. That doesn't mean buying every piece of high-tech equipment and adorable baby outfit under the sun before she's born, but you will need to make sure you have a few basic essentials from day one such as nappies and some clothes (see Baby Basics, opposite). Those first few weeks of parenthood will take some adjusting to, but if you are well organized beforehand you'll probably find that life is a lot easier.

SHOPPING FOR EQUIPMENT

When you are pregnant for the first time, you may feel like rushing out to buy up almost everything you can find in the baby shops, or you may feel that you don't want to tempt providence and would rather wait until the baby's born before buying anything. The best time to shop for basic equipment is in the middle stages of pregnancy when you are feeling on top of the world and the baby hasn't yet become too heavy or too uncomfortable. You may, however, prefer to wait until you are on maternity leave, if you are working, when you will have more time to look around.

MAKING YOUR CHOICE

It's easy to be overwhelmed by all the wonderful baby gear available – and to be lured into buying items you don't really need. Before parting with your money, wander around the baby shops and pick up some catalogues to browse through at home. Having got an idea of what you would like, work out what you can realistically afford and stick to that budget – it's easy to get carried away! Finally, remember that the most expensive isn't necessarily the best buy. You could be paying for an exclusive design, or extra gadgets which you may not need.

Ask yourself these questions before you buy any large items:
- Is it within your price range?
- Can it be stored away easily? If not, where will it go in the house?
- Does it suit your lifestyle? For instance, if you live in a first-floor flat, you don't want a heavy pram to drag up and down stairs.
- Is it durable? It's better to choose from the bottom of a good-quality range by a reputable manufacturer than the top of a poor-quality one.
- Is it simple and practical? Try it out before you buy. An uncomplicated design is easier to assemble, use and clean.

WELL DRESSED

Buy most of your baby's clothes after she's born. If she's bigger or smaller than expected you could have spent a lot of money for nothing, and remember she won't need different clothes for day and night. Also you will probably receive some gifts of clothes from friends and relatives.

When you prepare for your baby, hang a colourful, interesting mobile from the ceiling. You may be surprised how much your baby enjoys looking at its shapes and movement.

56

See What Your Baby May Need, pages 120–29

BABY BASICS

What you will need as soon as she arrives:

- Four wrapover vests or sleeveless bodysuits which fasten between the legs.
- Four stretchsuits (for tiny babies nighties are better, plus bootees or socks unless the nighties have drawstring hems).
- Four cardigans.
- A shawl.
- Woollen hat, mittens, socks or bootees (not necessary in summer).
- Sun hat.
- Disposable or terry towelling nappies (disposable nappies are more convenient if you are going into hospital to have your baby).
- Toiletries for nappy changing and bathing (see Nappy Changing and Bathing Your Baby, pages 108-15).

Tip: it is a good idea to wash new clothes before you use them in mild non-biological suds and rinse them thoroughly to remove all traces of soap.

If you are using terry-towelling nappies at home:
- Twenty-four nappies.
- Pins.
- Two nappy buckets.
- Sanitizing powder.
- Disposable day liners and more-absorbent night liners.
- Waterproof pants (tie-ons are good for tiny babies).

If you are not breastfeeding:
- Bottlefeeding equipment (see page 101).
- Sterilizing unit.

Other equipment:
- Changing mat.
- Baby bath (see page 128).
- Cot/crib/carrycot or pram (see page 124).
- Baby carrier (see page 127).
- Baby car seat if travelling by car (see page 126).

It pays to be prepared but don't worry if you haven't remembered everything. You can easily buy – or ask someone else to buy – whatever else you need after your baby arrives.

WHERE TO SLEEP

At first, some parents like to have their baby in their room. The advantages of this are that you know you'll hear her when she wakes and you don't have to stagger far to feed her (especially if you are breastfeeding). Also, your baby will be able to hear you, which will be comforting to her. There are disadvantages, however. You may find that her every grunt, wriggle and squeak can keep you awake. And sleeping in a room that is warm enough for a newborn baby can be somewhat claustrophobic.

- The room should be kept at a temperature of 18-20°C/65-8°F. Fit an individual thermostat to the radiator or buy a BEAB-approved convector heater, plus a nursery thermometer.
- Keep a changing mat, nappies and toiletries near where your baby sleeps.
- Don't put her 'bed' near a draughty window or door.
- Fit a dimmer switch to the main light or make sure your bedside light is fitted with a low-wattage bulb so you can feed and change her without disturbing either of you too much.
- If you are breastfeeding, keep a glass of water nearby in case you feel thirsty.

LABOUR AND BIRTH

Call the hospital if:
- **Your waters break.**
- **You have any bleeding.**
- **Contractions are coming every ten minutes.**
- **You think that the baby is not moving.**

Everyone worries about how they will know when they start labour. For many women, there is a longish phase when they simply are not sure; they may have odd aches and niggles, or feel 'different' somehow, but not really have proper contractions. This may be what is known as the pre-labour phase.

KNOWING YOU ARE IN LABOUR

If you notice the following, it is likely that you are in the early stages of labour:
- Low backache, caused by the baby settling down into the pelvis.
- A sudden desire to get everything finished and ready for the baby.
- Niggling contractions low down at the front. This may be the cervix becoming soft and ripe, ready for labour.
- Intermittent contractions that last a few hours then fade away. These could be practice contractions, or may result from the ripening of the cervix.
- Diarrhoea, or a frequent need to empty your bowels.
- A show. The cervix is sealed with a soft mucus plug that helps prevent infection. As the cervix begins to soften and thin this plug often comes away as a 'show'. It is a soft clear jelly, but may be streaked with blood from the fine blood vessels that are stretched by the thinning cervix.

When to call the hospital

You can stay at home during the first half of labour and spend a little time getting used to the feelings and dealing with contractions by relaxation, breathing, massage and so on. However, some situations require medical intervention or advice and you should phone the hospital or your midwife if: any of the following happens.
- Your waters break. If you notice a sudden gush of water or a constant steady trickle, the bag of waters surrounding the baby has probably broken. This does not usually happen until you are in established labour, but it can occur before labour starts. It is possible (though very rare) that the umbilical cord could become compressed once the waters have gone, and so most hospitals and midwives like to check the baby's heartbeat regularly afterwards. Some units also believe that the baby is more at risk from infection once the waters have gone and therefore prefer to induce labour.
- You have any bleeding. This could simply be the show coming away, but bleeding in pregnancy should always be checked.
- Contractions are coming every ten minutes, or less, or the pain is becoming too much to bear.
- You think the baby is not moving very much. In late pregnancy the baby often settles down and kicks less than in the middle months. But if you feel the baby is very much quieter than usual, it is worth consulting your midwife.

GOING INTO HOSPITAL

Most women are happy pottering about at home in early labour while the contractions are not too strong. As labour can take anything between twelve and twenty-four hours, it is worth keeping busy and distracted. In the first few hours at home you may want to have a shower or bath and wash your hair, finish packing your bags for hospital, go for a walk or have a light meal. Keep busy with gentle tasks and the time will go more quickly. You can always ring the maternity unit of your hospital for advice if you are not sure whether this is

58

Apart from when the midwife is checking you, there's usually no need to labour in bed. You may be more comfortable and your labour may be easier if you get up and move about.

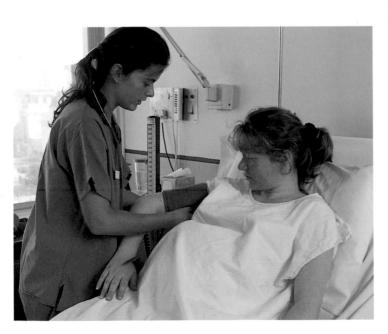

the real thing. Go by the length and strength of the contractions; lots of niggling ones will do less work than a few good strong ones. Powerful contractions take all your energy and attention. Stay at home for as long as you feel confident and comfortable. Once you feel you need a midwife go to the hospital, or ring for your midwife to come to you.

Meeting your midwife

Your midwife will carry out routine checks of your blood pressure, test a urine sample, and then do a physical examination to see how far into labour you are. She will use her fingers to feel the cervix, checking to see if it is soft and how dilated it is. The cervix has to open up into a circle about 10cm (4in) in diameter to let the baby through. Up until about 5cm (2in) the cervix opens quite slowly and gradually, then things usually start to speed up rapidly, so if your midwife examines you and you are about 4cm (1½in) dilated, you are already through the slowest part of labour.

IF BIRTH TAKES YOU BY SURPRISE

Considering how many babies are born each year, very few are delivered without the help of a midwife or doctor. If birth does take you by surprise however, try to stay calm; fast labours are usually straightforward ones. Often all you need do is make sure that you and the baby are warm and safe.

If birth seems imminent, call a midwife or doctor to you. Far better that the baby is born in your living room than in a cold car on the side of the road. If you are on your own, call in a neighbour or friend. If you are with a woman who is about to give birth, make sure help has been summoned, then get her on the bed or sit her on the floor. Put some towels or sheets under her, and help her remove her tights and pants if necessary. Talk to her, keep her calm, encourage her to listen to her body and do what seems right to her. If she is really thirsty offer her an ice cube to suck on, otherwise liquids should not be offered.

She may have an overwhelming urge to push, if so encourage her to push gently. Try to get her to blow out, or pant, so the baby's head is born as slowly and gently as

ARE YOU IN LABOUR?		
Have you had a show?	No.....	You may have missed it. Wait and see.
	Yes....	You may be in the pre-labour phase, wait and see.
Have the waters broken?	No.....	They often stay intact until late labour.
	Yes....	Contact your midwife or hospital.
Are you having contractions?	No.....	You may be in pre-labour phase, wait and see.
	Yes....	You may be in early labour, wait until they get stronger before going to hospital.
Are they long and strong?	No.....	Possibly in early labour, try to keep busy until they get stronger.
	Yes....	You may be in labour, so pack your bag.
Can you cope with the pain and intensity?	No.....	Contact your midwife or hospital.
	Yes....	Keep using your own skills, try a bath, change position, use massage, etc. Go to hospital or call your midwife when ready.

possible. Often the baby will be born quite quickly after this; encourage the mother to reach down and greet her baby, and be ready to catch him yourself. Check the cord is not around the baby's neck. Thankfully, umbilical cords are quite stretchy and can usually be lifted over the head if necessary. If you have to do this persuade the mother not to push for a few seconds. Lift the baby on to the mother's abdomen, keeping him quite low down. Do not cut or pull the cord. The midwife or doctor will deal with it, and there is no rush to deliver the placenta. The baby might be quite blue, but will pink up as he breathes.

Some babies have a lot of mucus in their mouths at birth, and as they try to take their first breath you can hear them making small gurgling noises. Lay the baby with his face downwards so that the mucus can drain out. If it seems to be a problem, gently clear the mucus away using a tissue or piece of clean cloth on your finger.

Keep both the mother and the baby warm. Wrap a towel or blanket around the two of them, letting them stay in skin-to-skin contact as this keeps the baby warm. Stay with them until the midwife or doctor arrives.

First stage

The first stage of labour is usually the longest, and can take anything between six and eighteen hours. During this time the neck of the womb (cervix) opens up to make space for the baby to pass through. The cervix begins as a firm muscular tube, quite tightly closed (see below). Gradually it softens, thins and then opens out. In a way, when the baby comes through it is rather like pulling a polo-neck jumper over your own head. Each contraction during the first stage helps to open up the cervix so that eventually it is fully dilated and the baby can be born. Therefore, each contraction brings you one step closer to the moment when at long last you will be able to hold your baby in your arms.

HOW THE CERVIX OPENS DURING LABOUR

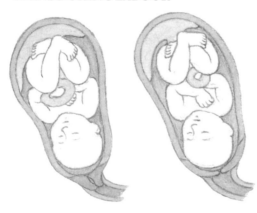

At the beginning the cervix is still thick and long.

Next the cervix is gradually 'taken up' — thinned but not dilated.

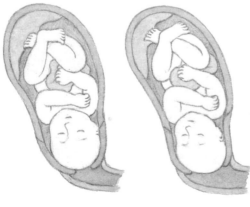

The first stage of labour is the longest, when contractions of the uterus slowly and gradually squeeze the baby onto the cervix and encourage it to dilate ready for birth.

Here the cervix is several centimetres dilated.

The cervix is fully dilated.

HOW CONTRACTIONS MAY FEEL

Contractions are most often described as muscular pulling sensations that come in waves. You can feel the beginning of each contraction, and experience it getting stronger and then reaching a peak before it fades away. There is then a rest, quite often a long one, before the next contraction. Contractions become longer, stronger and closer together as labour progresses. To begin with you may feel a contraction every ten or fifteen minutes that lasts perhaps thirty seconds. This may then step up to every five minutes, with contractions lasting perhaps fifty to sixty seconds. And in the last hour or so of labour you may have contractions that come every three minutes and last for around a minute or just over.

You may experience the contractions mostly as backache that gets stronger and more intense as labour progresses, or occasionally as 'referred pain' in the legs or thighs, but most often the strong pulling sensations are felt low down, just behind the pubic hair, which is where the cervix is. Many women say that in the first part of labour contractions feel much like very bad period pains.

SELF-HELP IN LABOUR

Self-help methods of pain relief are very effective during this stage of labour. Being frightened only makes you feel more tense, making you experience more pain which, naturally, causes more fear. Part of helping yourself in labour involves understanding what is going on in your body.

Relaxation

Learning to relax while you are in labour is important. Not only will this bring down the level of pain, it also means that you can save your energy for the hard work of pushing out the baby instead of wasting it fighting against your body.

It is well worth learning how to relax properly while you are pregnant. It is a topic that will be covered in antenatal classes and regular practice will help you develop the technique. Along with relaxation there are many other ways in which to help yourself. Think about the things you usually do when you are tired or in pain. Perhaps you take a leisurely bath, or curl up with a hot water bottle. Maybe you listen to music, or have a cuddle with your partner. Simple as they may seem, these things may help you to cope with labour too.

Positions

Being upright and mobile in labour can make the contractions less difficult to bear and at the same time make them more effective. It can shorten labour quite dramatically, and many women instinctively move around and experiment with positions. Try sitting cowboy-style on a chair, with a couple of pillows against the chair back, so you can rest your arms and head on them. Or lean on your partner with your arms around his shoulders. Leaning forward often helps, taking some of your weight on your arms. Lean on a worktop or table, over the ironing board or on to a hospital bed. Some women like to flop forward on to cushions or across a beanbag and, if you have backache, kneeling on all fours can help immensely. This may be because the baby's spine is lying alongside your spine, and lying in bed can feel very uncomfortable. Roll over on to all fours, so that the baby's weight drops off your spine, thereby reducing the feeling of pressure.

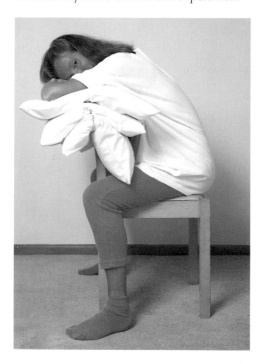

See if different positions help you through the contractions. Sit cowboy-style on a chair, leaning on cushions; bend over a work-surface; or kneel on all fours, rocking your bottom quickly up and down.

BREATHING

- **As a contraction starts, breathe in and out steadily through your mouth.**
- **Take lighter, shorter breaths as the contraction reaches its peak.**
- **Return to regular, deep breathing as the contraction fades.**
- **Remember to relax and breathe normally between contractions.**
- **At no stage should you breathe too deeply, and especially not deeply and fast, as this could make you light-headed.**

61

ABOVE Massage of the lower back muscles can be a great help — it's up to you to say where exactly is best and to choose whether you prefer a firm pressure or light, fast, 'butterfly' strokes.

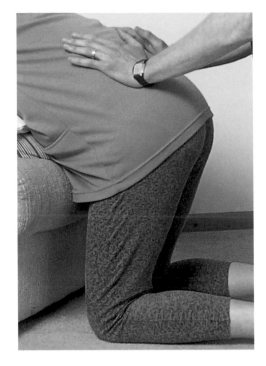

62

Massage

Good, strong massage can help a great deal on the lower back, where it will help to relax the muscles if you are tense, and distract you from the pain of contractions. Your partner can rub your back while you are on all fours, sitting on a chair or leaning over cushions. You may also find warmth helps in the form of a hot water bottle, although some women prefer cold, and like to hold an ice pack (carefully wrapped in cloth) over the affected area.

Your partner can also help you to relax with stroking massage. This can be done on the face shoulders and neck, or around your bump. Regular stroking of your forehead and face may also help you to relax and unwind.

Very fast, light stroking movements over the base of the spine can also bring great relief as your labour progresses.

Breathing

We alter our breathing patterns all the time without thinking about it. When we run for the bus or play a game of squash or take a quick swim, our breathing changes automatically. Part of learning to relax involves concentrating on deep, steady breathing with the emphasis on the 'out' breath. Our natural response to being in pain is either to hold our breath, or to take short sharp breaths. By breathing slowly and steadily, and as deeply as is comfortable, the pain is controlled and the body remains relaxed.

You may find a definite pattern develops. It is a good idea to take a deep, steadying breath at the beginning of each contraction, taking slightly lighter and shorter breaths at its peak. As the contraction fades away the breaths can become deep again, and you can take a good deep breath as it finishes. You do not have to use rigid breathing techniques, but can experiment

BELOW A head massage can be wonderful — but if your shoulders and neck feel tense, try some gentle head movements and shoulder hitches and rolls to stretch the muscles first.

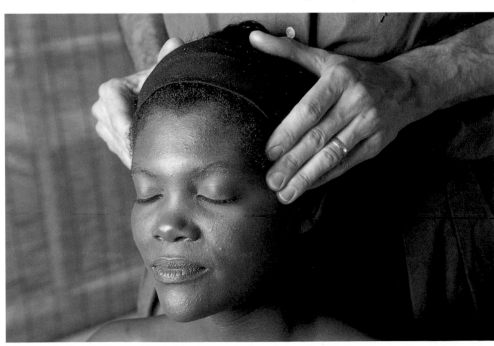

to find what suits you. Avoid breathing too quickly and/or too shallowly as this can cause hyperventilation, which means that there is too little carbon dioxide in the bloodstream. If you feel lightheaded or dizzy, or notice a tingling in your fingers, you are probably hyperventilating and should breath into your cupped hands for a couple of minutes.

WHAT YOUR LABOUR PARTNER CAN DO

A labour partner literally holds your hand through labour, and acts as a supporter, guide and interpreter. Many partners find that they spend most of their time giving massage, helping their partner to relax or assisting her to find a comfortable position. They may have to reassure, encourage and prompt her too. This enables the woman to cope better with the pain of labour, feel more positive about the experience, and need less pain relief.

For the partner, labour can be surprisingly tiring. It may be distressing to see the person you love in pain, it may take much longer than anticipated, and you may feel unable to leave for a rest or snack. Talk things through with your partner beforehand so that you know what matters to her. Practising massage and possible labour positions together will be useful. On the day wear light, cool clothing, and take along some snacks and drinks.

PAIN-RELIEF OPTIONS

You have several choices for pain relief in labour. You may not need any of them finding that you can cope purely with self-help methods. The pain of labour varies considerably from woman to woman and labour to labour.

Injectable drugs

A pethidine injection may help some women mind the pains of contractions less. However, pethidine is less popular nowadays because it has several disadvantages. It doesn't reduce the actual intensity of pain. It makes some women feel so sick that they need another drug to suppress the nausea. Some women feel disorientated and out of control, and most

feel very sleepy. This could be useful if you are finding labour long and tiring, but the downside is that some women wake at the peak of each contraction, which can be distressing. You are unlikely to be able to move around, and your speech may become slurred. Having pethidine late in labour could make your baby slow to breathe, and some babies need an antidote as soon as they are born. Babies may also be quite sleepy for the first few days and find it hard to feed effectively.

An **epidural** is undoubtedly the most effective form of pain relief. It usually removes all feelings of pain while leaving the woman clearheaded and able to cope. As it involves an injection into the spinal area, it is essential to keep still while the epidural is being set up, so it may not be possible to have one if it is left too late and contractions are coming thick and fast.

There are a few medical conditions that prevent an epidural being given, although very low blood pressure or a previous back injury may make it inadvisable. Most epidurals work by numbing the lower half of the body completely, but occasionally one may not 'take' correctly leaving you with one side of the abdomen that is not affected. There is an increased risk of forceps or Ventouse delivery with an epidural, and some women may suffer from long-term backache afterwards. There are no known side-effects on the baby.

When your epidural is in place, try to remember to move your back and legs every so often and to avoid an awkward posture. This may prevent backache afterwards.

63

RIGHT If you need something to help you through the contractions, take several big breaths of gas and air from the mouthpiece or mask as soon as you feel a contraction coming on.

FAR RIGHT Borrow, hire or buy a TENS machine if you wish to try this pain-relieving electrotherapy. It has a similar effect to continued quick, light strokes of lower back massage.

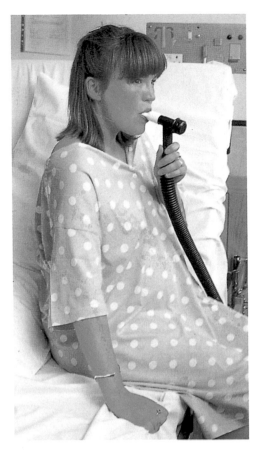

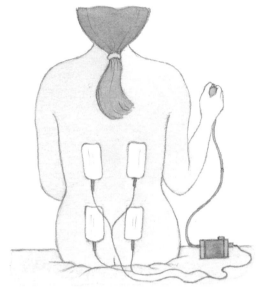

64

'Gas and air' (nitrous oxide and oxygen) or **Entonox)** is breathed in through a mouthpiece or mask. You may find it makes you feel rather lightheaded, but it can be very effective at taking the peak intensity of the contraction away. It is usually only offered towards the end of the first stage of labour, often at around 8cm (3¼in) dilation, and is designed to be self-limiting; if you take too much it will make you feel floppy and inclined to drop the mask. Nobody else should hold the mask on you. Since it takes a few seconds to build up in your bloodstream it is important to begin taking it as the contraction begins. A few women dislike the mask and some find the gas makes them feel sick, but it is quite effective and does not seem to have any harmful side-effects on the mother or baby.

TENS
A TENS (which stands for transcutaneous electrical nerve stimulation) machine comes with two battery-operated pads. These are stuck on to a woman's back. When the machine is turned on, electrical stimulation by these pads may block some of the pain

coming from the contractions. It can also increase the level of the body's own natural painkillers (endorphins). A woman attached to a TENS machine can move around and control the stimulation level herself. But, using the machine interferes with electronic fetal heart monitoring. TENS may be useful in early uncomplicated labour, especially if you have backache. If your hospital doesn't have a machine, you may be able to hire one. Your local antenatal teacher or community midwife should be able to give you details.

RELAXING IN WATER
Relaxing in warm water can be very comfortable and some women choose to spend part of their labour in a special pool. Most ordinary baths are not deep enough or wide enough to give a labouring woman enough room, which is why some hospitals have installed special pools. It is also possible to hire a portable pool to use either at home or in a hospital that does not have a pool.

Your midwife or doctor will advise you about the water temperature and how long to spend in the pool.

MONITORING
In most hospitals your midwife will monitor the baby using a belt monitor. This has two straps that fit around the abdomen: one to pick up the baby's heartbeat and one to measure the contractions. Often this is

used intermittently and you are free to get up and move around between times, but some hospitals prefer you to keep the monitor on all the time. Some women find this reassuring, but if you should find it uncomfortable and restricting, discuss your feelings with the midwife. Even if the hospital has a set policy, your opinion and preferences matter. You may prefer the midwife to use her small stethoscope, or a hand-held 'sonic aid' type of monitor. If there is concern for the baby, a scalp electrode may be inserted through the vagina and fixed on to the baby's scalp to monitor his heartbeat. Routine electronic fetal monitoring is a controversial issue in low-risk labour. Some critics say it leads to more intervention, and it does limit mobility.

STARTING OFF LABOUR

Sometimes medical problems such as a malfunctioning placenta or the mother's high blood pressure mean that a baby is better born early. If this is the case, labour is then artificially started off (induced) by hormones administered via an intravenous drip. Pessaries or tablets may also be given to make the cervix ready and labour easier.

Induction may also be suggested if you go past your due date as sometimes the placenta becomes less efficient after about forty weeks. However, some women naturally have longer pregnancies and a healthy baby and placenta. Unfortunately, it is difficult to assess how well the placenta is functioning, and many consultants suggest induction once you are one or two weeks overdue. Some women are very keen to begin labour while others are reluctant to interfere with the natural process. Discuss the situation with your midwife, antenatal teacher and consultant before making a decision.

SPEEDING UP LABOUR

Occasionally progress in labour is very slow and it may even stop and start. In this case labour can be accelerated in one of two ways. The midwife may suggest breaking the waters surrounding the baby in order to speed things up. This is bound to make the contractions feel more

painful, and seems only to shorten labour slightly. However, experienced midwives often find this technique useful, as some women seem to reach a plateau; they dilate steadily but then stop for a couple of hours. Rupturing the waters may provide the nudge that labour needs to get going again.

If the contractions are not very effective, yet prevent you from resting, it can feel as if labour is going on for ever. If you have lost a night's sleep and still have most of the work of labour to come, you may prefer to have a hormone drip run directly into a vein in your arm to get things going properly. Again, discuss the situation with your midwife.

Alternatively, taking a good walk around the hospital corridors, eating a light meal or relaxing in a warm, deep bath may help to establish labour properly and it could be worth trying the less-invasive techniques first, then moving on to medical help only if they do not work.

You may like to lean forward like this. Or, standing, lean forward with your elbows on a table or high bed; or kneeling on the floor, lean with your elbows on a chair.

65

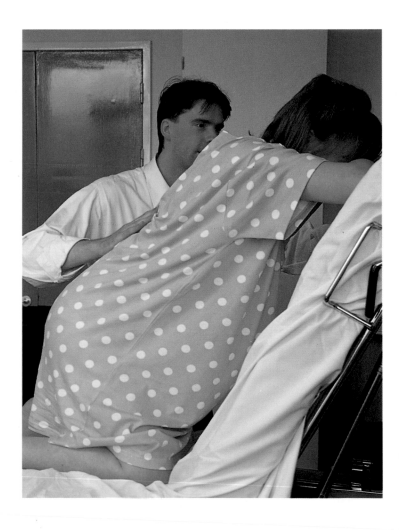

Transition

The very end of the first stage of labour can often be quite difficult to deal with. Contractions may be long and strong, come thick and fast and feel irregular. Often this is because one part of the cervix is not as fully dilated as the rest. Usually it is the front part of the cervix that is slower to dilate and this is known as an anterior lip. If you feel the urge to push, tell the midwife straight away, and she will do an internal examination to check that the cervix is fully dilated. If there is a lip she will ask you to wait a while. Changing position can make this easier; try sitting up or turning on to all fours for a few contractions. Blowing out will help prevent you holding your breath and pushing. Use gas and air at this stage if it helps.

Your partner can give a great deal of support during this hectic part of labour. He may be able to lift you up and help you change position, or encourage you to blow out by gently blowing on your cheek. He may be able to offer you a cool drink, or wash your face, or best of all remind you that you are nearly there. Transition is a bridge that you need to cross to reach the calmer second stage, when you can begin to push your baby out into the world.

Little, shallow blowing breaths may help you manage during the transition between first and second stages; and kneeling on all fours takes some pressure off the cervix and lets it dilate evenly.

Second stage

The second stage of labour is the active phase of pushing the baby out. Now each contraction helps to push the baby down the birth canal. It's a very short journey but can take one or two hours. The vagina is made up of lots of muscular folds which stretch and give way to accommodate the baby. With each contraction the baby moves further down, but slips back a little after the contraction has finished. The birth canal is not a straight line; the baby has to turn as he moves along, and he needs to be in just the right position to fit through. It's rather like fitting a key into a lock.

POSITIONS

You can use gravity to help you during the second stage. The more upright you are, the easier it is to push the baby out. Many women find that sitting propped up is comfortable, while others prefer to semi-squat, lie on their side or kneel with their arms and shoulders raised. Experiment until you find a position that is comfortable to push in and which seems to be effective.

Sometimes working out how to push is really difficult at first. You may need to wait for a couple of contractions to sort out what the feelings are like and think about how you will help this baby out. Try sitting on the lavatory at the beginning of the second stage. Often the firm support allows you to sit upright and push really effectively.

You may want to try several positions during the second stage, or you may find that everything happens so quickly that you simply stay where you are and push. Your partner can help to make sure you are as upright as possible. Hospital pillows often slip and leave you almost lying on your back, which is not the easiest position to push in. Some hospitals have special beds or chairs to help you stay upright, or some can supply beanbags or large foam cushions for you to lean against.

Even if you have an epidural in place you can usually still sit propped up to push. You are unlikely to know when a contraction is coming, so your midwife may have to tell you when to push and when to rest.

Pushing

It has been traditional for mothers to be told to hold their breath and push as long and as hard as possible with each contraction. This can be effective but it can also make the mother's blood pressure rise very high and then fall, which is not very good for the baby. Some women feel happier giving little breaths and little pushes, usually making a noise, sometimes almost grunting, with each push.

Try to listen to your body and go along with what it is telling you to do. If you feel unsure, try giving little pushes and little breaths with each contraction. If this does not seem to be effective, you can then move on to holding your breath and pushing as hard as you can.

HOW YOUR PARTNER CAN HELP

Most women need a great deal of encouragement during the second stage. It seems such hard work to move the baby

'Labour began with backache, and that continued right the way through. I couldn't lie down, so I spent most of the night either running to the loo, or sitting on a chair in the dining room, leaning on the table and dozing. I woke Richard at about dawn, and felt much better once he was with me. I could deal with contractions as long as I was upright and could lean over a piece of high furniture, or on Richard's shoulders. I managed to eat in early labour, but later felt sick and was sick, so I stopped. At 7 o'clock we left for the hospital. Oddly I had no contractions in the car. I was examined and the midwife told me that I was 5-6cm (2-2½ in) dilated. We were really pleased. Things began to hot up a bit and I had to deal with contractions by kneeling over a beanbag. Richard massaged my back very firmly which helped a lot. By around 9 o'clock I began to get lots of little contractions between the big ones and they really hurt. I got very hot and sticky and needed my face washed in between contractions, and felt quite shaky. The midwife checked a urine sample and said my blood-sugar level was low, so she gave me hot sweet milk to drink. It helped a bit, but I remember wishing it was all over. The gas and oxygen was quite effective and I used that for the last hour or so.'

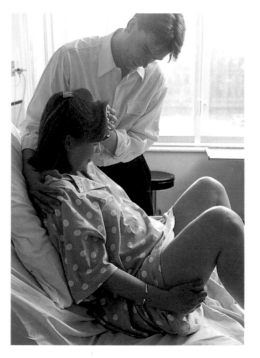

FAR LEFT When you labour in a kneeling position, try resting on all fours between contractions. Then you can straighten into an upright kneeling position like this to ease the discomfort of the next contraction. LEFT It helps enormously to have someone to encourage you, someone to lean on, and someone just to be there with you when you're in the thick of things and there's no going back.

such a short way, and a long second stage can be quite demoralizing. Many women find it helps to feel the baby's head once it is nearly out, or to put a mirror on the bed, and look down as they push.

Strangely enough, many women say that the second stage of labour is not painful. Some actually enjoy the pushing, feeling that at last they can do something active to help

the baby out. Other women describe the stretching of the tissues of the vagina as a hot or burning sensation. It is often quite hard to stop pushing when the midwife asks you to, and to pant the baby out slowly, but try as this increases the chance of your tissues stretching, so avoiding a tear or cut. You may find that it helps if your partner pants with you, or reminds you what to do.

The birth

The second stage is hard work, but when you realize that the baby is about to be born, you may find new reserves of energy. In fact some women describe this stage as positively enjoyable especially once the head can be seen. Until then you will have been pushing quite hard, but as the head appears the midwife will ask you to pant and push gently so that the head is born slowly. When the head is through, the baby turns inside you and the shoulders are born one at a time. Often this happens very quickly, and the next thing you know the baby is being delivered, perhaps up on to your tummy, for you to greet each other.

Your baby is well on the way to being born – with each contraction her head gradually widens the opening of the birth canal and is a little more visible to the outside world.

68

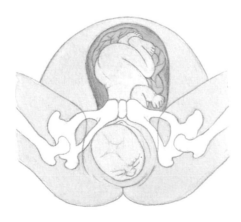

As the baby emerges beneath the archway formed by your pelvic bones, her head turns, then the rest of her body quickly slithers out, still attached by the cord to the placenta inside.

ABOVE RIGHT It's over and you've done it! As you gaze at your newborn baby it may be hard to imagine that those waving arms and legs could ever have fitted inside you.

A HELPING HAND

Some babies need to be born quickly; some get stuck during the second stage and need a little help. Babies who are in distress may be delivered using forceps or a Ventouse vacuum extraction to speed things up. Sometimes a baby does not achieve the right position, and forceps are needed to turn him round and help him out.

EPISIOTOMY

Sometimes the midwife makes a cut at the opening of the vagina to increase the space for the baby to get through. This is called an episiotomy. It may also be made if the baby is very small, very early, or if forceps or a Ventouse (vacuum extraction) is used. With a normal delivery, the midwife watches the area called the perineum at the base of the vagina. This small triangle of muscle thins and stretches to allow the baby to get through. Ideally, the midwife will help you to give birth slowly, so that it has enough time to stretch

properly, but sometimes it tears as the baby is born. If she feels it will need to tear quite a lot she may cut it instead, to direct the lesion away from the anal sphincter. An upright position, and controlled breathing as the baby is born, can help avoid a cut. Either a cut or a tear will need stitching.

FORCEPS

If forceps or Ventouse vacuum extraction are needed, the midwife will call a doctor. Your legs are put in lithotomy straps (stirrups), leaving you in the rather inelegant position of lying on your back with your legs in the air. A local anaesthetic is given to numb the area, then a cut is made into the muscles of the vagina. The forceps are put in one at a time to cup the baby's head and guide him out. A Ventouse vacuum extraction uses a suction cap fixed to the top of the baby's head. The doctor then pulls steadily as you push with each contraction, until the baby is born.

A baby born using either of these methods may have marks on his head, and sometimes the head looks rather pointed. All babies' heads tend to mould to the shape of the birth canal as they are born, even with a normal delivery, and some look quite pointed for the first few days. Forceps marks will fade and the head will soon resume its rounded shape.

CAESAREAN SECTION

You may know before you go into labour that you will need a caesarean section. This may be because the placenta has embedded low down in the uterus (see Complications in Pregnancy, page 30) or because your pelvis is an awkward shape or too small.

Caesareans are also performed as an emergency if the baby is in distress, or if there are other complications and the baby needs to be born quickly.

With a caesarean birth, the baby is delivered abdominally and many are now carried out under an epidural. This means you are awake all the time, your partner can be with you, and you can both greet your baby as soon as he is born. Sometimes this is not possible, however, and the

'I had planned to move around in labour and just have gas and oxygen, but it didn't work out like that. We stayed at home for ages, and I was really disappointed when I got to hospital and found I was only 2.5cm (1in) dilated. The baby had his spine against mine, and the midwife felt it would be quite a while before he was born. I tried some pethidine, which helped a bit but made me feel quite sick and woozy. When that wore off Steve and I talked things through and decided on an epidural. The doctor was great and explained exactly what he was doing. It felt icy cold at first but then wonderfully numb. I could sit up in bed and talk quite calmly. I did need forceps, but then Angus was over 4.3kg (9lb) so I might have needed them anyway.'

caesarean has to be done under a general anaesthetic. If this is the case you may feel disappointed that you missed the moment of birth, although some hospitals take a picture as soon as the baby is born, which is especially comforting if your baby cannot be beside you when you wake up.

STITCHES

If you have had a tear or a cut, the midwife or doctor will stitch the area soon after the baby is born. If you just need one or two stitches, this can be done while you sit on the bed. If more major stitching is needed, you will be asked to lie in the lithotomy position: on your back with your feet in stirrups or straps. A local anaesthetic will be given to numb the area.

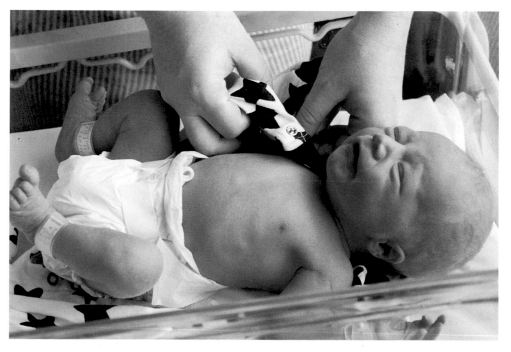

Newborn babies sometimes have a surprisingly wise and knowing expression on their faces and, once comfortable and warmly dressed, they may like to have a good look around.

After your baby is born

Soon after the baby is born, the midwife will clamp and cut the cord and wait until the placenta (afterbirth) has been delivered. This has supported the baby throughout most of the pregnancy, but now comes away from the wall of the uterus, where it has been embedded. After it is delivered, the uterus contracts quickly, closing off the blood vessels and minimizing bleeding. This usually happens naturally and with little effort.

NATURAL THIRD STAGE
In most hospitals the mother is given an injection into her thigh as the baby is born. This is to speed up the delivery of the placenta and to prevent sudden bleeding after childbirth: if the large blood vessels

My baby – you've been so close to me. Now here you are – I wonder what you'll be like as you grow up. Getting to know your baby is a process which starts now and continues throughout the rest of your life.

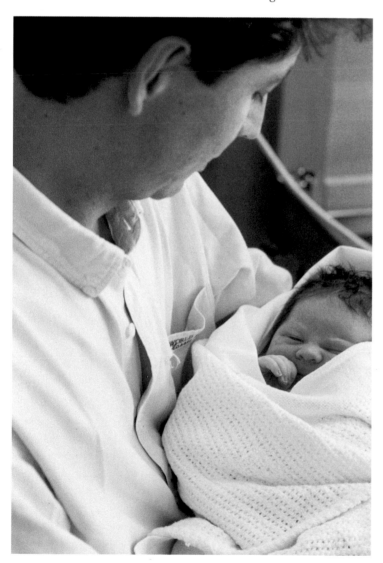

inside the uterus do not close down, the mother can bleed very quickly and suddenly. Using the injection seems to have cut down the likelihood of post-delivery bleeding, but brought about an increase in the risk of retained placenta, when the uterus clamps down before the placenta is delivered. If this should occur, the placenta has to be manually removed, usually under a general anaesthetic.

Some couples prefer a natural third stage in which the cord is left to stop pulsing before it is clamped and cut, thus allowing extra blood through to the baby. There is no injection to hasten the third stage, but the mother holds the baby, perhaps putting him to her breast to stimulate hormones that make the placenta break away and the uterus clamp down. It is important to be as upright as possible for a natural third stage, and to have plenty of skin-to-skin contact with the baby. This process usually takes longer than a managed third stage.

THE PLACENTA
After the placenta has been delivered the midwife examines it to ensure it is complete. She also checks that it has the right number of veins and arteries, and that there are no lumps or pale spots in it. Most new parents are so busy with the baby that they hardly notice this happening.

FATHERS
During the third stage of labour you will probably hold your baby for the very first time, especially if your partner has to have stitches. Like her, you may feel nervous about handling him. This is only natural and you will soon gain confidence if you cuddle and hold your baby as often as you can right from the start. It will help if you can get used to changing nappies, bathing your baby or settling him down to sleep. Not only will this ensure that you get used to helping with your baby, but it will give your partner a rest as well. Shared parenting is much easier, especially if you both learn together from the earliest days.

YOUR NEW BABY

Almost as soon as she is born, your baby will be thoroughly checked by the midwife or doctor. They will ensure that she is breathing well, her skin is 'pinking up', and her muscle tone is good. These basic checks are done when the baby is one minute old, then again at five minutes. They are often done so quickly that sometimes the new parents hardly notice them. The results of these tests are recorded on your notes as an Apgar score, which shows how vigorous the baby was at these times. Many babies score seven or eight out of ten. Babies with a score under about five or six may be seen by a paediatrician just to check all is well.

HOW YOUR BABY MAY LOOK

● To the new parents the baby is, or soon will be, quite beautiful. At first babies are often quite blue or grey, and then pink up slowly as they breathe and cry. Hands and feet often stay rather grey and sometimes feel quite cold for several hours.

● Many babies have vernix on their skin. This is a greasy, creamy substance that coats the skin while they are inside the womb. Often it can be seen in the folds of the skin of a newborn baby.

● Some babies, particularly if they are born a little early, have a fine down-like hair on their backs and shoulders. This disappears quite quickly.

● In order to fit through the birth canal the baby's head has to mould to the shape of the vagina, and at birth it can look quite pointed and misshapen. Don't worry – this will resolve itself eventually. Babies born by caesarean section often have very round heads, as they have not passed through the birth canal.

● New parents often remember special things about this first meeting with their child. Some notice how silky the baby's skin is; others feel that newborns have a really special smell; and some always remember the sound of the first cry. Most parents find themselves counting fingers and toes, marvelling at how tiny the fingernails are, and looking into eyes that

seem large and deep. It is a special time, and under most circumstances you are left alone with your baby to get to know each other. Others, however, may simply be too exhausted to remember much at all.

THE FIRST FEED

Most newborn babies go through a wakeful period some time during the first hours. Some are very alert right from the start, while others need a little while to recover from the birth. During this wakeful time your baby may begin to 'root' for the nipple. Babies are born with an instinct to look for the breast and feed, although she will probably need help to latch on properly. You may hear your baby making sucking sounds and notice her turning her

Newborns not only look fascinating but often smell distinctive and attractive too, probably because of the subtly scented chemicals called pheromones secreted by their skin.

71

head from side to side. This is a good time to help her go to the breast and try feeding. Some babies get the hang of it straight away and suck strongly, while others simply smell or lick the nipple. It is not vital that she feeds properly at once – she may be more interested in a rest.

'He seemed quite interested in going to the breast, but I couldn't quite work out what to do. The midwife showed me how to hold him turned towards me, and how to stroke his cheek with my nipple so he turned and latched on. I was surprised at how much of the breast had to go into his mouth. He only had a few good sucks, and then gave up but was quite happy. By the next feed, we had both had a sleep and he fed for much longer.'

YOUR BABY'S FIRST DAYS

Your baby needs lots of loving attention — but remember that you've been through a tumultuous experience giving birth, so you need plenty of rest, care and cosseting too.

The first few days after your baby is born will be both exciting and demanding. You are recovering from the hard work of labour, your body is adapting and changing, and you have a new baby to care for and get to know. Many women feel euphoric and quite energetic but they can feel sore, tired, battered and bruised, too.

Your stomach will seem about the size it was when you were four or five months pregnant, but will feel quite soft and flabby. You will bleed quite heavily at first and you may need to use two sanitary towels at a time for the first day or so. Many women find that their bruising or stitching is uncomfortable and need to sit on a

cushion for the first few days. You may find some of the following helpful.

● Fresh air speeds healing; try to sit on an old towel for some time each day with nothing on.

● Some women also find salt baths very soothing; place a handful of salt in the water and then sit in it. The salt will slowly dissolve and soothe the affected area.

● You may find that taking the homeopathic remedy arnica (in tablet form) helps prevent bruising and discomfort.

● If bruising is a problem, an ice pack can help. Your midwife can make one up, or at home you can use a small packet of frozen peas, wrapped in a cloth.

SELF-HELP

● Take it easy at first and do things gradually. As each day passes you will manage a little more and gradually feel more energetic.

● Deal with any problems as they occur; if stitches and bruising are very sore, try doing some pelvic floor exercises, having a salt bath or using an ice pack.

● Afterpains are a good sign that the uterus is contracting back down in size, but they can be uncomfortable. Second-time mothers will probably notice them much more than first timers, and you may

feel them especially while feeding. Take a paracetamol tablet if they are very bad, and use the breathing and relaxation techniques which you learned for use in labour. The pains usually fade away over the first day or two.

● Ease bruising with arnica cream, and soothe stitched skin by sprinkling a few drops of witch hazel on your sanitary towel.

● Talk to your midwife if you are worried or in pain. She will be able to check things out, and reassure you.

Lie down with the ice pack between your legs for twenty minutes or so each morning and afternoon.

CARING FOR YOUR BABY

All new parents find bathing, changing and handling a baby difficult at first, but by the end of the first week you begin to look, and feel, like an old hand. After all, you will have changed forty or fifty nappies by then! No one is expecting you to be an instant expert. It is much more important to tune in to your baby and learn to respond to his needs than to be able to tie the perfect nappy, or wash his hair properly.

Your relationship

Your relationship with your baby is unique, just as your feelings for your partner are unique. Many new parents feel they must instantly love their child, and that bonding should be instant, like glue, but it can take time to get to know a baby and for love to grow. After a long hard labour, you may want nothing more than a good sleep. Many men too need time to come to terms with becoming a father.

First feeds

You and your baby will learn to breastfeed together. It may take you both a while to get the hang of it, and you may need quite a lot of help with positioning and latching on at first. Sometimes things are not right; perhaps the baby is not in the right mood or you feel uncomfortable. If this is the case, try again a while later and things may just click. Sitting or lying in a different position may help, or holding the baby differently. Experiment to find what suits you and your baby. Whatever position you use, the important thing is to make sure that the baby has a good mouthful of breast and does not fix on the nipple only (see Breastfeeding, pages 92-99).

POST-BABY BLUES

Feeling over-emotional in the first few days after the baby is born is very common. This is often at its height on day three or four, when the excitement of the birth is wearing off. You may have odd aches and pains and your milk may be coming in, making your breasts feel hot and full. It's not surprising then that some women feel tearful and easily upset for a while. Tell yourself that these feelings will not last forever. Probably you will feel calmer and stronger within a few hours, or the next day.

One woman in ten suffers from postnatal depression. For them the feelings of not being able to cope may build up from the early days, and gradually become a real illness. Often it is just exhaustion brought on by the hard work of labour, and subsequent broken nights. The loss of your pre-baby lifestyle and friends at work may be upsetting too. A good sleep and a helping hand with the baby can make you feel much better. If you think it is possible that you might be suffering from postnatal depression do talk to your midwife or doctor about it without delay.

Joy, admiration, pride, relief, amusement, curiosity, concern or tiredness? A welter of feelings may abound for both mother and father as they watch their baby feed.

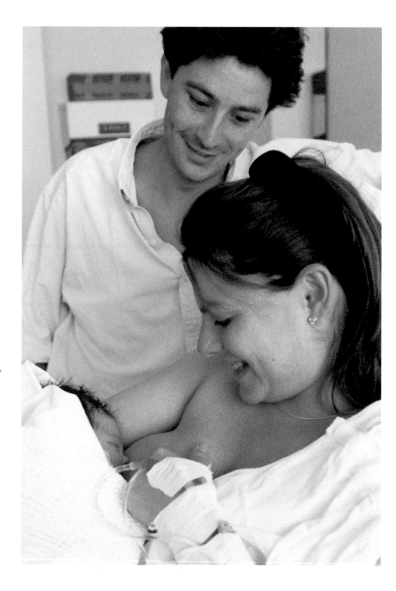

73

BABIES NEEDING SPECIAL CARE

While most babies are born fit and well, some need extra care. If your baby is born very early, has a medical problem, an infection or a very low Apgar score, she may be taken to the special care baby unit. Here, babies can be monitored constantly by trained staff. Some babies only need special care for a short period, while others may need nursing for days or even weeks.

LOOKING AFTER A BABY IN SPECIAL CARE

Monitors, drips and incubators can all look rather frightening, but the staff will explain what they are all for, and help you to hold your baby, or reach inside the incubator to touch her. If she is too small or weak to breastfeed you can express your milk, so that she can be given it by tube or cup. Many mothers find that expressing milk makes them feel that they are doing something to help their baby. It also means that once she can feed from the breast there will be ample supplies of milk for her. Most units have an electric breast pump that you can use regularly, several times a day, but hand expression works easily as well.

PREMATURE (PRE-TERM) BABIES

Some babies decide to arrive early, and some babies have to be delivered early because of problems arising during the pregnancy, such as the mother having very high blood pressure. Either way, a baby born too early is likely to be small. She will need to be kept warm in an incubator, she may need help with her breathing, and she may need tube-feeding. The expression pre-term is usually applied to babies born before about thirty-seven weeks of pregnancy, but the earlier in pregnancy they are born the smaller they are and the more nursing they need.

Survival rates are increasing all the time. Babies born as young as twenty-seven weeks' gestation now have a good chance of survival, although they may need to remain in hospital for many weeks. Generally, the longer into the pregnancy the baby can stay in the womb the better her chances of survival, but some babies born at the expected time are still quite tiny. These babies are usually called 'small-for-dates' and have a birth weight below 2500g (5½lb).

74

Welcoming two small babies who need an incubator is an emotional business, but you can do a great deal for them, including providing your milk, stroking, speaking and simply being nearby.

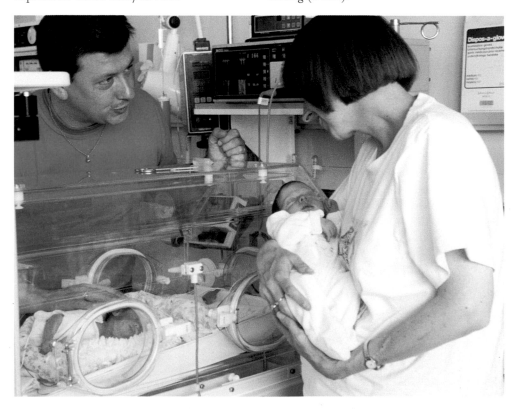

See Feeding Your Baby, page 96, for expressing

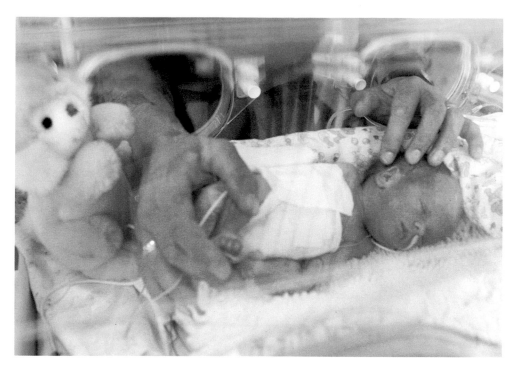

How large the father's hands look! Remember that stroking, handling, talking and singing are vitally important for babies, so don't stop because you feel silly or the incubator puts you off.

TWINS

Twins are often born early. One of the factors which influences the beginning of labour appears to be the total weight in the uterus so, because two babies usually weigh more than one, women carrying twins generally go into labour early. Sometimes one twin grows at the expense of the other, and a delay in the delivery of the second twin can mean that she has breathing difficulties. Nevertheless, many twins are born a reasonable size and both quite healthy, and they should be able to go straight to the ward, alongside the mother's bed. Feeding twins can be hard work, and you may need a hand with the everyday care, but most parents soon work out various ways of coping. If you feel you need help, ask your midwife or health visitor for advice or contact a local support group (see Useful Addresses, page 314).

JAUNDICE

Some babies develop jaundice. The commonest cause is a slight immaturity of the liver which means that bile pigments cannot be broken down and excreted. The baby begins to store one of these pigments called bilirubin under the skin, making her look yellowish. If left untreated the condition may progress and cause brain damage. Blood samples are taken to measure the bilirubin level in the blood. If this is high or rising, it is usual to treat the baby with ultra-violet light. In some hospitals the baby has to go to the special care baby unit for this, while in others it is done on the ward. Jaundiced babies are quite often sleepy and reluctant to feed. You may have to wake your baby up frequently to give her little breastfeeds so she has plenty to drink.

BABIES WITH SPECIAL NEEDS

Nowadays we expect pregnancy and birth to go well, and our babies to be fit and healthy. But some babies are born with medical problems, and it can be a great shock to find your baby is one of them. Some problems, like a club foot or hare lip, can be treated. Others, like cerebral palsy or Down's syndrome, have long-term implications both for the baby and the family. It often takes a while for the extent of the problem to be discovered, and for all the implications to be realized. It may help to talk through your fears, feelings and worries with a relative, friend or professional counsellor. Many people find contact with parents who have been through a similar experience useful. There are support groups for a whole range of conditions and situations. Your health visitor will also be able to advise you.

75

See Useful Addresses, page 314, for list of support groups

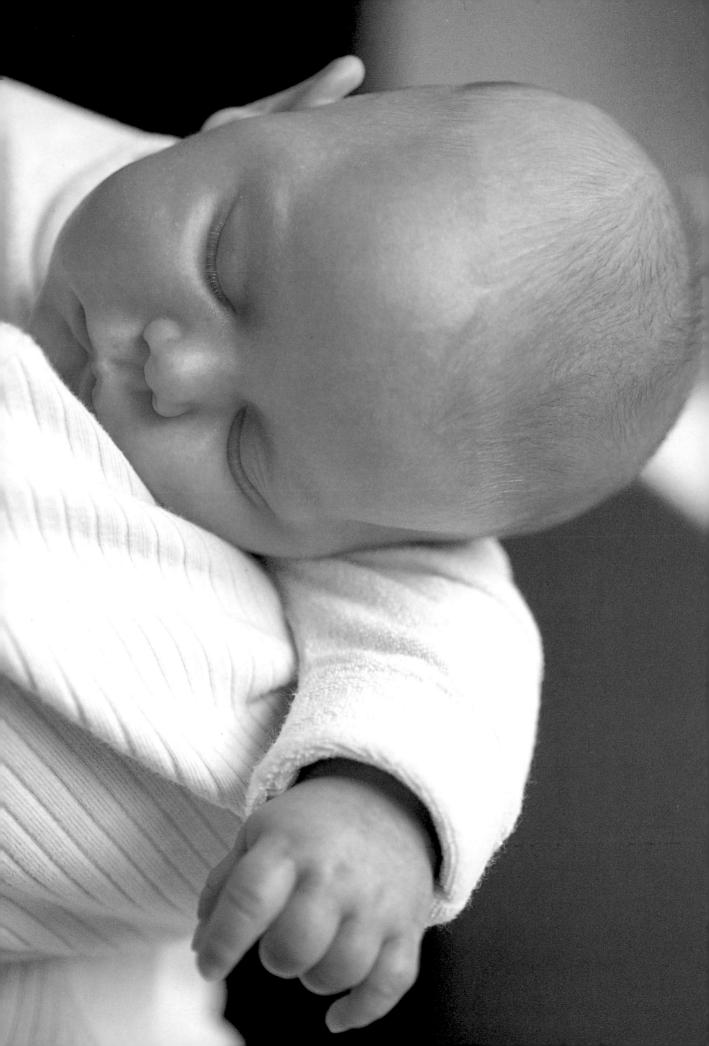

THE
YOUNG BABY

0-6 months

Once your baby is born you can greet her face to face and welcome her to the big wide world. Looking after a young baby may seem daunting but all you really need are common sense and love. The rest you can easily learn from other people. The fragile helplessness of a newborn baby is very

appealing and you'll want to do all you can to make her comfortable and happy. Yet sometimes you may feel vulnerable and needy too and it's then that you'll welcome help, encouragement and tender loving care yourself.

As the days pass, your baby will grace you with enchanting smiles, coos and gurgles and a gaze firmly fixed on your eyes. And you'll know you are hooked for ever.

YOU AND YOUR YOUNG BABY

BELOW You and your baby have been close for months, intimately sharing your lives day and night during your pregnancy, yet now perhaps you feel as excited — or even apprehensive — as if this were your first meeting.

OPPOSITE **There's** something intensely appealing about a baby's big eyes, and captivating smiles.

Labour and birth follow months of anticipation and preparation. When the baby finally arrives, everything changes abruptly as you see each other for the first time. Greeting your baby you forget any tiredness or pain. The miracle of new life rarely fails to give a thrill of amazement, delight and even awe, and many parents want to stare at their baby for ages. New born babies may look squashed, red and sometimes a little ugly but to their mothers, fathers and grandparents they are quite fascinating.

The excitement and euphoria of the first day or two tend to calm down as you begin to adjust to your baby. You may feel low and weepy but these baby blues usually go quickly. Most women find that their emotions see-saw up and down for months with the enormous change in lifestyle on becoming a mother or adding to the family, and with the work of caring for a baby. Tiredness, joy, pride, delight, frustration, satisfaction, helplessness and relief become close companions.

It isn't surprising that a couple's relationship changes and may grow or falter at different times. Parents give a great deal to a baby and may not always have enough energy to maintain good communications. Looking after yourselves and each other is particularly important while you are responsible for your lovable yet demanding and totally dependent baby.

Settling down to life with your baby and getting used to your new role with all the breast- or bottlefeeding, cuddling, calming, nappy changing, playing, disturbed nights, washing and bathing takes time. But you'll soon become more confident in balancing your life and looking after and learning about your baby.

One of the biggest changes of the early months comes when your baby discovers other foods. When you give him his first try of solids, watch while he sucks and experiences the surprise of the new taste. A look of interest, pleasure or downright dismay soon conveys whether he thinks it's a good idea. Be prepared for the food to come dribbling out, because eating is difficult at first and he'll spit it out if he doesn't like it, but before long he'll be leaning forward with his lips pursed to have more, or even helping himself to a fistful of food from the plate.

Babies vary as to how much sleep they need but during periods of wakefulness you can enjoy each other and take it in turns to talk. Your baby will move his head and sometimes his whole body as he coos, gurgles and concentrates on your face and voice with all his being. You'll find yourself moving your head when it's your turn too. By six months your baby may be saying 'da-da', 'ma-ma' or 'ba-ba'.

This 'babbling', along with other sounds, paves the way to matching words to things or people. Your baby loves you to spend time conversing and it's by listening to you, making noises and having you respond that he learns to understand, communicate and eventually speak.

There's amazing developmental progress in the early months. Sucking fingers or thumb, lifting the head, rolling over, holding a rattle, and putting pieces of food in the mouth are wonderful achievements. And as your baby practises sitting, the nerves and muscles supporting his back and head become stronger.

Babies smile earlier than most books say and it's a red letter day when you see the first crooked little heavenly grin. Smiles become larger until the really big ones almost split the face with delight. Many parents say that their biggest rewards are their baby's smiles. Babies thoroughly enjoy games if you catch them in the right mood, when they're ready to laugh, sing or play peep-bo. When it's time for a nap their attention flags rapidly and many a baby falls asleep there and then in the parent's arms or in a baby-sling.

If I could sum up what your young baby needs most on top of basic creature comforts, I'd say you can't go wrong with your company, cuddles, laughter and love.

Dr PENNY STANWAY

OUR CHILDREN

Penny Stanway: 'I'd never imagined how I'd feel about our first baby – all I'd thought about was the pregnancy and labour. But when Susie arrived I was stunned with delight and couldn't take my eyes off her for ages.'

Daphne Metland: 'One of my best-ever moments was discovering one-week old Caity fast asleep on her dad's chest, and he was fast asleep too.'

Gillian Fletcher: 'I remember taking my two-year-old son Andrew swimming and introducing his three-month-old brother Robert to the water for the first time. There were so many comments from other swimmers at seeing this little baby bobbing around in the pool with his water wings on, trying to copy his older brother and the two of them giggling with obvious delight.'

Heather Welford: 'Some of my best memories are to do with breastfeeding my babies. It was so relaxing and rewarding to sit down at the end of a hard day, with a little one getting love, comfort, food and security direct from me . . .'

Carolyn Humphries: 'When she was only a few weeks old, Katie was given a tiny musical box which hung from the bars of her cot. It seemed to calm her as if by magic. She played it every night until she was about three, then a tape recorder took over. And even today she still loves to go to sleep listening to music.'

Maggie Jones: 'My second child was a crying baby – as a newborn he slept little more than ten hours out of twenty-four and then only for short periods, and while he was awake he was either feeding or crying. The only thing which worked was carrying him round in a sling all day but this was exhausting to do and drove my toddler mad! Now he needs more sleep than anyone in the family and has the sunniest temperament!'

Jane Bidder: 'When my third child (Giles) was born, he had a rather chubby little face with only a smattering of very fine hair on his head. He looked like this until he was about six months and then his face fined down and he grew lots of blond hair. Now he has very fine features. And it's only when I look back at old photographs that I remember how chubby his face seemed in those early months.'

THE NEWBORN BABY

The first days and weeks at home with your new baby can be terribly exciting – and a bit frightening too. Even if other family members offer help and support, the responsibility of caring for your baby and getting to know her can feel hard to cope with. Taking each day as it comes and accepting you'll learn about each other as you go will help.

Everything will feel different for you and your baby once you're at home. Your baby may seem to realize she's somewhere new, even after only a few days in hospital. Smells and sounds are quite different, for example, and she may respond by appearing more unsettled than she was in hospital. She may need the reassurance of being held close to you, so she can sense some things haven't changed. It's also normal for babies who were sleepy at first to perk up a bit. It's likely too that your baby will need feeding more often than before, and she may stay longer at the breast.

HOLDING YOUR BABY

Cradling a newborn baby in your arms is a lovely feeling but, at the same time, you may be a little unsure as she seems so fragile and dependent. However, plenty of practice will soon put you at your ease. Each day, you will hold her for feeds, sit comfortably with her on your lap and talk to her, cuddle and enjoy her. You will dress and undress her, change her nappies and wash her. It will not be long before you feel relaxed and confident and know what's right for your baby.

Your baby can enjoy the warmth and closeness of your body if she's carried in a sling while you move about. This sometimes helps soothe a fractious, unsettled baby. Make sure any sling you use is comfortable to wear, and gives her good support (see What Your Baby May Need, page 120). You may find your baby falls asleep and you can remove her from the sling, still asleep, and place her in her cot.

HOW TO PICK UP YOUR BABY

80

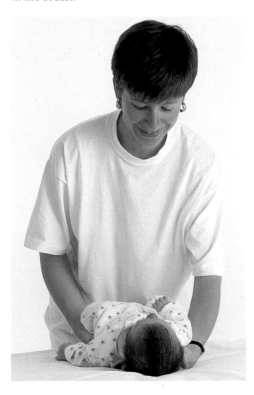

1. *A newborn baby has very little head control so you need to make sure her head is well supported when you pick her up. Slide one hand under her neck and head and the other under her lower back.*

2. *Gently lift your baby up, continuing to support her head and back. Try to make your movements as smooth and reassuring as possible. Talking softly to your baby as you pick her up will also help.*

See Sleep and Bedtime page 116: What Your Baby May Need, page 127, for slings

PICKING UP YOUR BABY

At first, you may feel rather nervous about picking up and cuddling your newborn baby: she may seem so little and fragile. But so long as you remember to support her head properly, she will be fine (see How to pick up your baby, below). Young babies don't have much control over their heads, and they need a gentle hand, arm or shoulder to lean or lie on. Most babies enjoy being rocked, and having a nice, soft, soothing voice murmuring or singing near their ear. Again, with time, you'll learn what your baby likes best.

TIREDNESS

You're bound to feel tired in the first few weeks – and possibly for longer. Practise feeding lying down, or in bed. Try sleeping when your baby sleeps, and aim to get to bed by mid-evening if you can. It's helpful to spend at least some of the day with your feet up, at least, even if you don't go to bed. Accept any offers of help gladly and use the time you save to rest, not to catch up on other chores.

Carrying your baby in a sling leaves your hands and arms free as you go about your day, and the warmth, sounds and movements of your body help your baby relax into peaceful contentment.

REGISTERING YOUR BABY'S BIRTH
- You must register your baby's birth by six weeks after his birth.
- One parent needs to go to the register office in the town, district or borough in which the baby was born.
- The registrar will give you a birth certificate, and a form with your baby's National Health Service number on it. You will need this to register your baby with a doctor.

3. *Cradling your newborn so that her head is supported in the crook of your arm is a secure and comfortable position for her and also means that she can see your face.*

4. *Your baby may also like being held against your shoulder. Use one hand to support her bottom and the other to cradle her head gently so that it doesn't flop backwards or to one side.*

See Becoming a Parent, page 244, Tiredness

81

YOUR DAY TOGETHER

Coming home from hospital with your baby is an exciting moment. You can now relax and enjoy your baby in your own home; he can sleep in his own Moses basket or cot, close by you, and you can do everything when you and your baby want to rather than fitting in with the hospital routine. Don't worry if you feel slightly nervous too: there is a lot to do. Your baby may wake frequently, want to be fed, need his nappy changed, and need to be soothed, clothed, bathed and cared for. In addition, there are all the normal baby, but ask other people to help entertain them as well. Grandparents often welcome the chance to spend more time with their grandchildren.

MANAGING VISITORS

It will obviously give you great pleasure to show off your new baby to family and friends but make sure you are in control of the situation. Most people will be willing to help and, if they have had children themselves, will be only too well aware of how you are feeling.

Sometimes you'll want to enjoy a cuddle while your baby rests, but make sure he can't fall off the sofa or bed just in case you fall asleep as you relax.

HELPING TO ESTABLISH A ROUTINE
● Always bath your baby at the same time each day.
● Differentiate between quiet play times and more boisterous play.
● When you start to give solids you can gradually try to co-ordinate your baby's feeding times with those of the rest of the family.

household tasks to be done, which is why it is a good idea to ask for some help during the first week or so at least.

ASKING FOR HELP

It helps a great deal if you can have someone at home with you to lend a hand. If your partner can take time off work, he may be the ideal person, as he can also get to know the baby; otherwise your mother, or a close friend or other relative might take over some of the household tasks while you rest and concentrate on being with your baby. In the first weeks, it's best to dedicate yourself entirely to the baby and not try to achieve anything else. If you have other children you'll need to spend time with them so they don't get too jealous of the new

They will understand if you say that you don't want visitors in the first two weeks. If people do come, make use of them. Ask them to get some shopping on the way over, to make their own tea or coffee, empty the rubbish, hang out the nappies or hold the baby. If you are exhausted, get them to rock the baby in the pram while you have a quick sleep.

HOW SOON CAN I GO OUT WITH MY BABY?

Going out with your new baby for the first time is a big step and you will feel justifiably proud as you wheel your baby along in his pram. Don't worry, however, if you feel uneasy about going out and keep putting it off, just go when you feel ready.

After two or three weeks people will assume that you are 'back to normal' and you will probably be left on your own more. Your nights may be broken; you may not be getting enough sleep; and it may still seem to take hours to feed, change and dress the baby. By the time you are ready to go out yourself, it's time for another feed again. If you feel frustrated by this, try to relax because soon things will take less time as you and your baby become more used to each other.

FORGETFULNESS

Some mothers are shocked by the way in which they can no longer concentrate on anything and find they are forgetting little things all the time, such as where they put their purse five minutes ago and whether they remembered to lock the back door. It's a good idea to leave a spare door key with a neighbour in case you lock yourself out, leaving the baby inside. Saucepans get burned because you forgot you were cooking some pasta and you come back from shopping to realize you forgot to buy the main thing you went out for. Writing a letter to a friend becomes impossible and it seems difficult sometimes to finish a single sentence. Don't worry, you are not going mad and you are not alone; this happens to almost every mother.

ROUTINES

In the early weeks most babies' behaviour is fairly chaotic; it is impossible to predict how long the baby will sleep, how often he will feed, or when she will settle again. It is therefore difficult to plan ahead.

Some babies get into a routine sooner, but somewhere between six weeks and three months many babies will have sorted out day from night, will have predictable times when they are awake and other times when you can usually be sure they will have a long sleep. If you have other children, the new baby tends to get into a routine sooner because he has to fit into an already busy and predictable day. If you want to encourage your baby into a routine see our box of suggestions (left) but don't worry if your baby does not co-operate – not every baby has to have, or wants, a fixed routine.

See Becoming a Parent, page 244

83

GETTING THINGS DONE?

Having a small baby in the house frequently means that the usual household tasks just don't get done. It's important to work out the things that do matter and the things that don't. People often say, 'Don't worry about the housework.' This is fine if you really don't mind a certain amount of mess, but some mothers find this irritating. If the house gets really untidy it can make more work for you because there's so much to sort out in order to find anything. Try to set limits to what you can do and don't expect too much of yourself (see Becoming a Parent, page 244). Remember, if you feel you need help, ask your midwife or health visitor for support, they will understand how you feel.

Even if you think you can predict when feeds, sleeps and wakeful times for play will be, remember to be flexible because babies' needs can change quickly as they grow.

POSTNATAL EXERCISES

In the first few days after your baby's birth, exercise may be the last thing on your mind, but doing these few simple exercises will speed up the process of healing and returning to normal. If you are in hospital you will probably have a visit from a physiotherapist, who will show you exactly what to do.

SIX WEEKS PLUS

You may be wondering how soon you can return to regular exercise classes. It is wise to wait until you have had your postnatal check-up, which usually takes place six weeks after a normal delivery and eight to ten weeks following a caesarean section. If possible, choose a class whose teacher is trained in the specialist field of postnatal exercise. It is very important before progressing to strong abdominal exercises to check that the gap in your muscles has closed, otherwise you could make it worse. Start gradually and progress slowly with any return to sport. Your joints and ligaments will still be lax for about three to five months, so you need to pay attention to safety. Some exercises may cause your breasts to feel tender. Avoid those and always try to breastfeed before exercising or playing sport.

PELVIC FLOOR

If you have stitches or feel swollen and bruised, tightening and relaxing these muscles as you learned to do antenatally improves the circulation and helps to avoid problems such as incontinence. The muscles tire quickly so a few contractions repeated many times throughout the day are most helpful.

MOTHERS WITH A DISABILITY

There is no doubt that becoming a mother is a very exciting time. You will be amazed at the wide range of emotions you can experience in a day – the highs and the lows, the many physical changes and the tiredness. As a mother with a disability there may be extra factors which you have to consider as you try to work out ways of coping with a young baby. You may have problems with balance or co-ordination and if you have a visual or hearing impairment you may be particularly concerned about safety. The difficulties vary according to the disability and it is therefore only possible to give some general guidelines here.

Many mothers feel extremely tired much of the time during the early weeks, whether they have a disability or not. Your lack of mobility and the extra physical demands this makes on you may mean that tiredness is even more of a problem. Try to make allowances and ask for and accept all offers of help. It is important to discuss with the people offering help what will be of most practical use to you. Health visitors and midwives are very experienced in childcare matters but may not have the special knowledge and experience of your disability that you have. Together you should be able to work out the best ways for you to manage. It is really important to make time to continue with any special exercises you normally do as well as to find time for regular rests.

If your disability affects your ability to contract your muscles then some of the exercises shown on pages 86-8 will not be appropriate for you. If not, then many of the exercises can be adapted to different starting positions, such as sitting down. They will be just as effective but this will remove the instability of having to stand while trying to concentrate on the exercises.

If you are in contact with a physiotherapist, ask her to help devise a specific programme of exercises to suit you while you are pregnant or recovering from the birth. The warm-up exercises on pages 48-9 will help relieve tension in the upper body caused by holding and carrying your baby. Pelvic tilting (page 86) can be done sitting as well as lying down.

Pelvic-floor exercises are very important and can be done anywhere. The golden rule for pelvic-floor exercises is to do them little and often to avoid overtiring the muscles and, in general, this is a useful rule to exercise by.

OPPOSITE *A wakeful and contented baby can join in the fun of an exercise session. Make the time to say 'hello' and her rapt interest and warm smiles will encourage you to get fit.*

84

POSTNATAL EXERCISES

STRESS INCONTINENCE

This is a distressing condition in which you cannot control your bladder properly if you cough, laugh or sneeze. Doing your pelvic-floor exercises many times each day can help improve the strength of these muscles and avoid or improve this condition. If you are suffering from stress incontinence do talk about it with your doctor or health visitor and ask if you can see an obstetric physiotherapist. Many women feel they just have to put up with these problems because it's all part of having a baby, but this is not true – help is available.

Pelvic tilting

Lie on your back on the bed with your knees bent and a pillow under your head. Tighten your abdominal muscles and press the small of your back flat against the bed as you breathe out. Hold for a count of four then relax. Repeat the exercise six to eight times.

Leg sliding

Lie on the bed with your knees bent (right). Tilt your pelvis flat as before, and slide both legs away from you slowly, using your abdominal muscles to keep your back flat on the bed (below). When you reach a point when your back is starting to arch then, keeping your tummy tight, carefully bring your legs back to the start position and repeat the whole process six to eight times. It is most important to keep breathing rhythmically throughout the exercise and to make sure that each time before you start sliding your legs away you have your abdominal muscles tightened and your back flat. At first you will find you cannot go far as the muscles are still weak.

86

Rec check

Lie flat on your back with your knees bent. Place the fingers of one hand, palm facing you, just above your tummy button (right). Breathe in and as you breathe out lift your head and shoulders off the bed and slide the other hand up your thigh towards the knee. This will make your abdominal muscles tighten and you should be able to feel between the two edges of the muscles if there is a gap. A gap of one- or two-finger widths apart is quite usual and means you can move on to stronger exercises, but if you have a wider gap then you need to do lots of pelvic tilting and leg sliding to help narrow it. When you do curl-ups, use your hands to help keep your tummy really flat as you tighten your muscles and lift your head and shoulders. When you can easily manage sixteen head-and-shoulder raises you can progress to the curl-ups.

Curl-ups

Lie on your back with your knees bent and your hands resting on your abdomen (centre). Breathe in and, as you breathe out, tighten your abdominal muscles, flatten the small of your back against the bed and raise your head and shoulders off the bed (below). Slowly lower and repeat the whole process six to eight times.

Note: it's important that you don't do all these abdominal exercises at once or the muscles will get very tired. A good idea would be to do pelvic tilting, pelvic floor, leg sliding, and more pelvic floor exercises, then have a rest and later do some curl-ups.

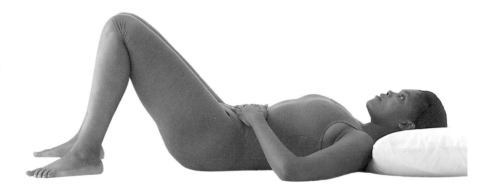

87

POSTNATAL EXERCISES

Curl-ups: diagonal

If you have a wide abdominal gap (see Rec check) *do not attempt this exercise*. Lie on your back, feet flat on the floor (top). Breathe in and, as you breathe out, lift your head and shoulders off the floor, sliding your right hand up and across your thigh towards the outside of your left knee (below). Return to the start position and repeat six to eight times, then repeat six to eight times on the other side. Whenever doing curl-ups make sure you maintain the normal angle between your chin and your chest. Avoid forcing your chin on to your chest or letting your head sag behind as you lift it off the floor or bed as this can strain the little neck joints and cause pain.

88

Curl ups

Curl ups are a good way to strengthen the upper body muscles needed for carrying your baby around.

Start on all fours with your knees directly below your hips, and hands slightly more than shoulder-width apart (top). Keeping your back flat and tummy pulled in, gently bend your elbows (below) and then straighten again. Repeat six to eight times and then rest. Keep breathing normally throughout and don't lock your elbows when you straighten them.

Exercise, relaxation and massage

Sit comfortably supported and place your left hand over the muscular part of your right shoulder and then slowly shrug and circle your left shoulder so that as it moves up and down, your left hand massages the tense muscles. Repeat on the other side.

Making little circles with your fingertips over your temples or the area at the back of your head where the neck muscles join the head helps to relieve tension headaches. It might be useful to mark in your 'diary' a set time each day for you to practise relaxation and to exercise.

POSTNATAL EXERCISES

89

MANAGING STRESS

Whenever we feel anxious, frightened or stressed by too many demands upon us our bodies switch on the 'fight or flight' response. This is a normal protective mechanism to keep us out of danger. When we have fought or run away from the cause of stress the body returns to normal. Unfortunately, in most everyday stressful situations it is not appropriate to fight or flee, so we can be left feeling all wound up by the stress hormones. In the long term this can be harmful to health.

One way of getting rid of pent-up feelings is to use regular exercise to help disperse the harmful stress hormones. Brisk walking or swimming are both very good stress-relievers, and relaxation is another very important skill that will help you to unwind and return the body to normal when under stress. One of the most common signs of stress is tension in the shoulders and back of the neck and jaw, often causing headaches. The shoulder exercises are useful for releasing this tension, as is massage (see above).

Good health is a matter of balancing the physical, emotional and mental aspects of your life and being a mother places so many new demands upon you that it's easy to feel that you have no time left for yourself, or to feel guilty about snatching a few minutes when there is so much to be done. It helps to remember that by looking after yourself you will be more able to give your baby the best start in life.

FEEDING YOUR BABY

However you decide to feed your baby, you'll discover that when it goes well you'll feel close to him and you'll enjoy being together. Babies get a lot of satisfaction and comfort from feeding, and you'll find your baby's responses and obvious pleasure are rewarding to you, too.

Feeding can bring its own problems, even so. It can be distressing when things don't go smoothly. And though you may not be facing major difficulties, you may still feel confused about what to offer your baby when, and what sort of foods ensure the best and healthiest start in life.

MAKING CHOICES

Most women plan to breastfeed, mainly because they know breast milk is the best food for a newborn baby and because the idea of feeding their baby nature's way just feels 'right'. Even if you know nothing about it, you can be confident your milk is ideal for your baby, and that with the right information and support, you should feed happily and successfully.

A smaller number of mothers decide to bottlefeed instead, using one of the formula milks available (see Bottlefeeding, page 100). If you feel you'd prefer to bottlefeed, it may be because you're embarrassed or uncomfortable with the idea of breastfeeding, or perhaps you feel rather put off by the prospect of having the total responsibility for feeding your baby.

It can be helpful to leave your options open, and decide when the baby actually arrives what you'd like to do, as your feelings could change. If you're not sure what you want, you can talk over the pros and cons with a midwife or breastfeeding counsellor. They won't try to persuade you to do something you're not happy with, but they may be able to suggest ways of coping with your feelings. For example, if you think you'll feel shy breastfeeding in front of others, you could decide to feed only at home until you feel more comfortable and relaxed.

The antibodies in your milk mean breastfeeding helps protect your baby from a wide range of illnesses, including diarrhoea, chest infections and, if you or your partner have a history of allergy, possibly also from asthma and eczema.

Cuddling your baby at the breast and letting your warm, nourishing milk flow can feel intensely intimate and loving; it also helps you both adjust to your new life together.

90

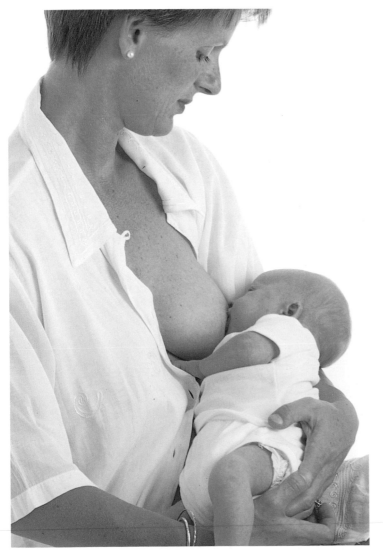

'The best thing about breastfeeding for me has been the convenience of it all. I can't imagine how I'd have coped if I'd had to sterilize bottles and take feeds with me. I just know that wherever we are, Lily can have a feed without a fuss.'

See The Child Health Clinic, page 130

HOW LONG TO FEED?

Breast milk or a suitable formula milk are all your baby needs for the first three to six months. Bottle-fed babies may need extra drinks of cooled, boiled water, especially in warm weather.

You'll carry on with milk (breast or formula) after you have introduced other foods, of course. Milk should be a major part of your baby's diet for the first year. Breastfeeding can continue for as long as you and your baby want it to; some mothers carry on well into toddlerhood and early childhood.

If you're bottlefeeding, you may want to think about phasing out bottles of formula milk round about the first birthday. This is because it's easy for a baby to 'fill up' on bottles of milk, leaving less room for a varied diet of other foods (in contrast to older, breastfed babies, who typically take comparatively small amounts of breast milk, even if they're feeding several times a day). A bedtime bottle is fine, however, as long as your baby doesn't remain asleep or dozing with the bottle in his mouth, which could affect his teeth. This is because a bottle teat in your baby's mouth while he's asleep and not swallowing means his teeth may be bathed in milk for a long time. You should never leave your baby alone with a bottle as he may choke.

HOW FEEDING CHANGES

As your baby gets older, his feeding pattern will change. Breastfed babies often become very efficient at feeding, and feeds may take less time (although some feeds may be longer, if your baby enjoys snuggling or falling asleep at the breast). Bottlefed babies, too, finish more quickly. Older babies become more predictable, and are happy to have most of their feeds at set times if that's what you prefer. This is worth knowing if you're planning on going back to work, or if you have older children and you know you'll need to establish some sort of a routine to make life easier.

Don't think that the length of time your baby spends feeding (or sleeping) one week is necessarily going to set the pattern that will follow for the rest of his babyhood. While many babies do work towards some sort of feeding routine, there are bound to be times when things are different. A baby who usually feeds a predictable number of times a day may go through periods when he wants extra feeds. This is likely to pass and the previous pattern may return after a few days.

As your baby feeds, she drinks in your attention and love along with the protection and nourishment from the milk.

'For me, bottlefeeding was the right choice. I just wouldn't have enjoyed breastfeeding, and I didn't really relish the thought of having to struggle with my feelings as well as getting used to another little person in my life, and all the changes that would bring.'

FEEDING YOUR BABY

Breastfeeding

Breastfeeding is the best and healthiest way to feed your baby, and helps you to get back into shape. You can get off to a good start by knowing something about how it works, and how to get it going well.

FIRST FEED

If you feel like it, put your baby to the breast straight after the birth. But don't worry if you need to be separated from your baby at this time or just feel too exhausted to try feeding, it doesn't mean you won't be able to breastfeed. When you do give your first feed it's as well to ask your midwife for help in getting your baby well positioned (see below).

BEGINNER'S CHECKLIST

It's important you and your baby learn to feed in a comfortable, effective way. Why? Because if your baby isn't correctly positioned (it's called being 'well latched on' or 'fixed') you are more likely to develop sore nipples. Also, your baby is less likely to get a satisfying feed, and your breasts may not get the stimulation they need to make enough milk.
● Hold your baby so he is chest-to-chest with you, and his mouth is in front of your nipple. He shouldn't have to turn or try and flex his head to feed.

● When your baby's mouth is wide open (as wide as a yawn) bring him on to your breast. Keep your fingers and thumbs out of the way.
● It will help if you're comfortable and relaxed. You may need to raise your breast from underneath and put a pillow on your lap so that your baby is at the right level.

HOW YOUR BODY PRODUCES MILK.

Your body makes milk under the influence of the hormone prolactin. When your baby feeds and takes milk from the breast, this stimulates the production of prolactin, which in turn causes your breasts to make more milk. The more your baby feeds, the more you'll make (that's why the mothers of twins can successfully feed their babies as they make twice as much milk).

Your baby takes the 'foremilk' first. That's the milk in the reservoirs behind the nipple. When the baby sucks, this milk runs down the short ducts from the reservoirs to the nipple, and is available to your baby as soon as he comes to the breast. This thinner milk quenches your baby's thirst. His continued sucking also stimulates the hormone oxytocin, which causes the let-down reflex. This makes the tiny muscles around the milk glands in your breast contract, squeezing the milk

HOW TO BREASTFEED

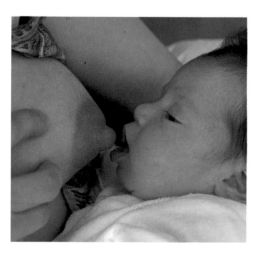

1. *Ready to go. Your baby's mouth should be wide open, and his tongue well forward. If you touch your baby's cheek with your breast he should automatically open his mouth, ready to feed.*

2. *Position your baby so that he is chest-to-chest with you. Now bring your baby on to your breast. His mouth should cover most of the areola (the dark area around the nipple).*

out into the ducts, through the reservoirs, and then out through the short ducts to the small 'exit' holes in your nipple. This milk –

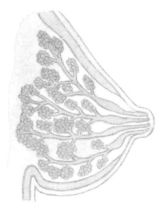

Milk from the tree-shaped milk glands and ducts supplies just what your baby needs to grow.

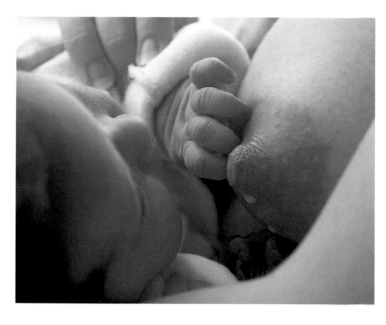

called 'hindmilk' – is creamier and higher in calories than the foremilk and satisfies your baby's hunger. It is important to allow your baby to feed from one breast for as long as he wants. If you swap from one breast to the other your baby may only be getting the 'foremilk' from each breast which will not satisfy him.

KEEPING UP THE SUPPLY

Every mother makes colostrum, the nutritious first milk some women notice even in pregnancy. Then, after a couple of days or so, the milk comes in (see page 94).

The best way to keep up your supply is to make sure your baby is correctly positioned and feeds as often as he wants to. This tells your body that more milk is needed, so it is best to feed your baby as often as he asks. He'll tell you he's hungry in lots of different ways.

Don't try to time your baby at the breast. Let him feed as long as he wants to on the first side, and then offer the second side. It doesn't matter if he takes it or not but, if he does and still wants more, wait until he has finished the second side and then offer the first again. In any case, aim to offer the second side first at the next feed, to equalize the supply and demand on each side. You may find that you change your baby from one breast to the other several times during a feed.

Seeing your baby, thinking about her, hearing her, smelling her and having her suck your areola or touch your breast with her tiny hand all help encourage the milk to flow.

93

3. *As your baby sucks and swallows, he becomes more contented and relaxed as the feed progresses. He may enjoy touching you, or prefer feeding with his arms tucked away.*

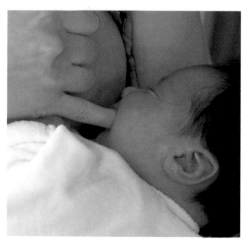

4. *If you need to take your baby off the breast before he comes away by himself, don't pull the nipple away as this will hurt. Gently break the suction by inserting a finger between his lips and your breast.*

FEEDING YOUR BABY

94

Help to avoid sore nipples by feeding your baby in different positions from one feed to another. This 'rugby hold', with your baby's feet tucked under your arm, is a good one.

CHANGES TO YOUR BREASTS

Your breasts will feel different when your milk comes in and the colostrum in your breasts gives way to larger quantities of milk. There's also an increase of blood and fluid in your breasts, and this means you might feel full and a little uncomfortable for a day or so. You may need to express a little milk to soften the breasts which will help you to position your baby correctly. Some mothers find their breasts become swollen and hard, and quite painful. This is called 'engorgement' and you can help prevent it by feeding the baby frequently and by expressing some milk, if necessary, to keep the breasts soft. Severe engorgement can sometimes be helped by one or two sessions expressing as much milk as possible (see Expressing your milk, page 96). Ask a midwife or breastfeeding counsellor for advice.

You may feel rather fuller and larger – though not uncomfortably so – for a few weeks. Then, when breastfeeding is well established, your breasts may change again, and feel softer. This is normal, and not a sign you have less milk – in fact, at this stage you are producing milk very efficiently and quickly, and in just the quantity your baby needs.

FREQUENCY OF FEEDS

Babies differ from one another in the number of times they want the breast. Some babies feed a lot from the very beginning; others take a little while to get into their stride. However, a baby who regularly feeds fewer than half a dozen times or so in twenty-four hours may need some encouraging or even waking up in order to feed more often. He could be sleepy, or jaundiced, or lacking the energy to ask for feeds.

Most babies feed very frequently in the first weeks of life, and then space their feeds out as time goes on. Feeds tend to take less time, too, after the first couple of months or so, though there may always be the occasional longer, more restful feed, especially at bedtime. It's normal for many babies to be on and off the breast in the evenings. Sometimes, you won't be at all clear when one feed ends and the next one begins. This pattern will tend to change after the first few months, and it's then you can start having a bedtime routine, if that's what suits you and the baby (see page 116).

Your baby is likely to have several different feeding patterns as he grows. There may also be times when he feeds very frequently for some days, before going back to whatever he was doing before.

'At first I was sore because she wouldn't latch on and people around me kept telling me to give her a bottle. But the midwife was really helpful. Eventually Sarah took my breast beautifully. It felt just great, knowing it was going to work after all.'

See Sleep and Bedtime, page 116, for How much will your baby sleep?

BREASTFEEDING TIPS

● Feeding is thirsty work at first! You'll find it handy to have a drink already at your side when you start to feed (for safety, make sure it's a cold one).

● Leaking is not uncommon in the early weeks. You can buy special breast pads which you tuck into your bra, or use old cotton hankies, folded to fit. Remember to change them regularly so that your nipples stay dry, as this will help prevent soreness.

● You don't always have to wait for your baby to ask for a feed. If it suits you to feed him earlier (because you're going out, for instance) then wake him and feed.

● Similarly, if your baby regularly wakes at midnight for a feed, and you go to bed at eleven, try waking him an hour earlier to give you a longer period of uninterrupted sleep.

● Experiment with feeding lying down. It makes night feeds simple if you can doze while your baby feeds.

MAKING YOURSELF COMFORTABLE

It's very important that you should feel happy about feeding, as well. Make sure you always feed in a comfortable chair, with extra cushions to support your back and arms if you need them.

It will help to wear a well-fitting bra – probably a special nursing bra. You'll find it easier than a normal one, as you can open it one side at a time. Check that whatever sort you choose has no tight or restrictive elastic or seaming. You may also find it easier, when breastfeeding, to wear loose clothing that you can lift up at the waist rather than dresses that fasten down the back, or front opening blouses which can be more revealing. With practice, you'll find that very little, if anything, is on view.

Lying down to feed your baby in the middle of the night or the first thing in the morning can be much more comfortable and restful than sitting up in a chair.

Experiment as much as you like to find the best way of feeling relaxed while you feed your baby. Feeds can be precious times and the last thing you want or need is aching shoulders.

See Nappy Changing, page 111, for bowel movements

The World Health Organization recommends exclusive breastfeeding for six months. The Department of Health in the UK says three to six months. Both organizations recognize that breastfeeding ideally continues for much longer, and the American Academy of Pediatrics recommends breastfeeding babies for at least one year.

EXPRESSING YOUR MILK

Expressing your milk is a useful skill to learn, especially if you anticipate being away from your baby for more than a few hours in the first few months. It can mean some forward planning and extra organization on your part, but it does mean your baby can continue to have the benefits of breast milk. You can express milk from your breasts by hand or with a pump (make sure all parts are sterilized before use, see page 101). Store it in the fridge in a sterilized plastic container or in the freezer if you're not using it within twenty-four hours. It can then be given to your baby in a cup, off a spoon or in a bottle. Make sure that whatever you use has been sterilized.

You might want to express your milk if you're planning to go out for the evening, or if your breasts have become engorged. You may also wish to express breast milk on a more regular basis if you are planning to return to work while your baby is still young. If you want to do this, you'll find it easier if you have a way of expressing milk at work. You will also need a fridge to store it in and a cool bag in which to take the expressed milk home.

When?

You can express milk at any time that's convenient for you. Some mothers express from the 'unused' breast while the baby is feeding on the other side (possible with 'one-handed' pumps). You may find straight after a feed is a good time, or, if you're at work, halfway through the day may be the easiest. You may find that once is enough, and you can express again at home if you need to leave an extra feed.

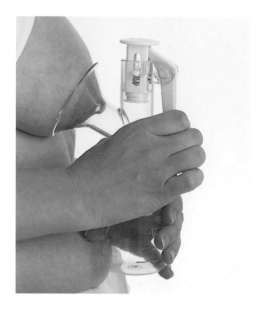

You can use a breast pump as an alternative to hand expressing.

How much?

This varies from one individual to another and you can't equate a breastfed baby's needs with those of a formula-fed baby.

This is because breast milk is digested more completely than formula, which means that breastfed babies need smaller volumes of milk. If you want to collect milk for someone else to give your baby, express what's left after each feed for a day or two. You'll probably collect only a little each

HOW TO EXPRESS

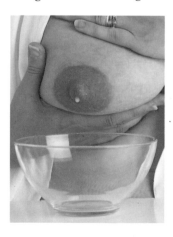

1. *Supporting your breast with both hands, exert a gentle massaging action with your thumbs.*

2. *Continue the pressure with the flat of your hand, moving your fingers towards the areola.*

3. *Squeeze your thumbs and forefingers together and push backwards as you squeeze.*

Your body makes twice as much milk for twins as for one baby, because two babies stimulate the breasts and the pituitary gland's milk-producing hormones twice as much as one does.

time, but a small amounts soon add up. You'll learn how much to collect for your baby by experience. Always leave more than you think your baby will need. A young baby should take your milk from a cup. An older one can have it from a bottle; avoid waste by using two bottles and putting half your milk in each.

Store frozen expressed breast milk (EBM) in small containers such as sterilized ice cube trays or special breast milk freezer bags, so you only defrost what you need. Defrost in the fridge, or by standing in a jug of hot water if you're in a hurry. Don't use the microwave; it destroys some of the nutrients, may heat unevenly, and you could scald your baby's mouth.

FEEDING A BABY IN SPECIAL CARE
If your baby is born prematurely, or has to spend any time in a special care unit, you may find that breastfeeding is more of a challenge at first. Small, sick, or very pre-term babies may not be able to suck at the breast. They may need feeding through a tube that goes through their nose and into their stomach. To keep up your milk supply, you'll need to express more than six times every twenty-four hours – an electric pump is easiest for this though hand expression is more efficient.

Your baby can be given your EBM through a tube. Some special care units then suggest bottlefeeding with EBM but the evidence shows this is more tiring for the baby than coming on to a breast with a good milk supply. There is also a possibility that the teat could confuse the baby's sucking reflex and make it harder to establish breastfeeding. Many hospitals have good results by offering EBM in a tiny medicine cup. The baby then laps at the milk with his tongue.

Research has shown that breast milk can help protect vulnerable premature babies from serious, sometimes life-threatening infections. Mothers often say that expressing breast milk is a way of feeling close to their pre-term or ill babies.

The amount you express might seem very small, but pre-term babies only need a little. Some mothers find it helps to look at a picture of their baby as they express, if they can't actually be next to their baby at the time.

If you are discharged from hospital before your baby, you may be able to borrow or hire an electric breast pump. If this isn't possible, the hospital staff may be able to put you in touch with an organization which hires them out (see Useful Addresses, page 314).

The health visitor can be a godsend when you need someone expert to answer all your queries and listen carefully to your concerns about feeding and caring for your baby.

98

COMBINING BREAST MILK AND FORMULA

Some mothers consider breastfeeding *and* giving bottles of formula milk. This gets over the business of expressing in advance, which needs a lot of organization, particularly on a long-term basis.

However, it's not usually a good idea to mix breast and formula in the early days and weeks. This is because the regular use of a bottle will reduce your milk supply and confuse your baby's sucking technique. In fact, it's been shown that the more bottles are used, the sooner breastfeeding ceases. A very occasional 'convenience' bottle probably won't make much difference to your supply.

Once a mother and baby have had three months or so of successful breastfeeding, the milk supply is far more flexible. Some working mothers breastfeed when they are with their babies, while formula is given by the carer the rest of the time. You will, of course, have to make sure that your baby is happy taking formula from a bottle or a lidded beaker before leaving him. Express (and discard) your milk at work to keep your breasts comfortable and to maintain your milk supply.

FOR HOW LONG SHOULD I BREASTFEED?

It's up to you and your baby. Breast milk remains a first-class, nutritious food and drink for as long as you give it, so there are no health reasons for stopping. In our society, however, it's uncommon to feed babies into toddler- or childhood, although in the past and in other parts of the world, there would be nothing unusual about it at all. If you are happy to carry on breastfeeding, don't feel pressured into giving it up.

HOW DO I KNOW IF I HAVE ENOUGH MILK?

When you are breastfeeding you can't actually see how much milk your baby is taking, but if he is growing and seems content after most feeds, then you can be assured that he's getting enough milk. If you have any reason to think you haven't enough, then checking your baby's position (to make sure he's stimulating your supply and getting a good feed), encouraging your baby to feed more often, without any restrictions on time or frequency, and trying to avoid large gaps between feeds, both during the day and at night, will help to build up your milk supply.

INCREASE YOUR MILK SUPPLY BY:
- Encouraging your baby to take extra feeds.
- Giving two-hourly feeds.
- Expressing milk between feeds.
- Letting feeds continue for as long as your baby wants.

YOUR QUESTIONS ANSWERED

My sister had several problems with breastfeeding, and gave up after three weeks. I'm expecting a baby shortly – but what if I have problems?

Always ask for help if you need it! Midwives – in hospital and outside – will help you at first. Later on, you're more likely to be in close touch with your health visitor at the baby clinic.

Breastfeeding counsellors are trained volunteers who belong to one of the organizations concerned with breastfeeding (National Childbirth Trust, La Leche League, or The Association of Breastfeeding Mothers). They're trained to give you information and support, and to help you make the right choice for you. (See Useful Addresses, page 314.)

With my first baby my nipples became so sore I couldn't bear to feed. How can I stop this happening again?

Sore nipples can make breastfeeding a misery. They can be caused by poor positioning, which means the baby clamps his gums on the end of your nipple and tries to suck the milk out as if it were coming through a straw. Good positioning allows his jaw and tongue to 'milk' your breast – and it doesn't hurt. So try to change the way your baby comes on to the breast (you may need help to do this) – and take him off if you find it hurts. Also, experiment by feeding your baby in various different positions. But try not to cut down on how often you feed your baby as this would make your breasts over-full and engorged and reduce your milk supply.

Sometimes, sore nipples are caused by thrush, which may also be present in the baby's mouth too. (If it is, you'll be able to see whitish deposits in it.) Your doctor can help by giving you both an anti-fungal preparation.

Do any of the creams and sprays available help if you have sore nipples?

All the available research shows that nothing can actually help or prevent sore nipples other than getting the baby correctly positioned. However, some mothers find such products are soothing and pleasant to use, and there's no evidence they do any harm except to the few mothers and babies who may be allergic to them. However, some experts are wary of creams and sprays because their taste and smell may mask the mother's own taste and smell – and that could be important to a baby who is just learning to feed. If you are sore, avoid using soap on your nipples, and make sure you keep them dry between feeds.

I'm expecting my first baby in about two weeks and I'm worried that I won't be able to breastfeed him properly because I'm very fair-skinned and have been told that I will develop sore nipples. Does hair and skin colour really make a difference?

No it doesn't. Research has shown that a mother's colouring makes no difference. It's poor positioning that causes sore nipples; if your baby's not well positioned, he'll make you sore whether you are fair or dark-skinned.

My baby seems to cry the whole time. Do you think my milk is satisfying him: it looks very thin and watery compared to cow's milk?

Breast milk often does look thin compared to cow's milk, but it's meant to be that way. In fact, breast milk is not always the same. When your baby starts feeding, the milk he takes is thinner than the fattier milk – called hindmilk – which he gets after he has been sucking for a while (see How your body produces milk, page 92).

I've been told that I need to pay special attention to what I eat and drink when I'm breastfeeding, or I won't produce good enough milk. Is this true?

Many mothers find that they're rather hungrier and thirstier while feeding, especially when their baby is very young. That's normal. Simply respond to these 'messages' from your body by eating and drinking what you feel you need, just as you would at any other time. Generally speaking, you don't need to make any special effort to eat or avoid certain items as long as you eat a healthy diet.

With my first baby, I developed mastitis after three weeks. I felt dreadful – as if I had flu. The doctor explained it was a blocked milk duct and gave me some antibiotics which seemed to clear it up quickly but how can I prevent it happening with my next baby?

Inflammation can occur if the milk ducts are not emptied properly, for example, if you aren't feeding often enough, or you have an ill-fitting bra. If part of your breast becomes sore, feed your baby more frequently, and don't let more than two hours pass between feeds during the day, or three by night. Feed your baby in different positions. Massage the sore area gently towards the nipple after each feed and also while lying in a warm bath. Do arm-swinging exercises before each feed. If the lump doesn't go away, see your doctor in case a blocked duct has caused some infection.

Bottlefeeding

If you decide to bottlefeed your baby, either from the start, or after any time spent breastfeeding, you'll need to make sure that the milk you choose is suitable for your baby. A midwife or health visitor will help you decide. Most babies thrive on ordinary formula milk. A few need a special formula instead. Don't change your baby's milk without checking first with your health visitor or doctor.

BABY MILKS

In the UK, all milk sold for babies under the age of six months has to follow Department of Health rules about the ingredients used,

and their quantities. Manufacturers offer two main sorts of baby milk: whey-dominant, and casein-dominant. They're both based on cow's milk, which is modified to make it more suitable for babies, and then dried and packaged in granule or powder form.

What's the difference?

Whey-dominant milks take most of their protein from the whey of the milk. Case in-dominant milks take most of their protein from the curd. Casein is supposed to take longer to digest, and this is why casein-dominant milks are sometimes recommended for hungrier or older bottlefed babies. Some casein-dominant milks contain different sugars; again with the claim that this is more likely to satisfy a hungrier baby.

Whey-dominant milks are promoted as being more similar to breast milk, because their protein pattern is closer than that of casein-dominant milks. This is why they are recommended for babies from birth, or for babies who are making the change from breast to bottle, or who are having both breast and bottle milk for a time. Some milks are available to buy in cartons, in a ready-to-feed formulation. You don't have to add any water to the milk, you simply pour it direct from the carton into a sterilized bottle. This is a very convenient, but expensive option.

Other milks

There are also milks for pre-term (premature) babies, and for babies with a diagnosed intolerance to cow's milk formula. Your doctor may prescribe a formula from which the allergenic proteins have been removed. 'Follow-on' milks for babies over six months are promoted as a healthier alternative to cow's milk because they have a higher iron content. Don't give cow's milk to babies under six months of age; ideally you should wait until they are twelve months old, although small amounts can be used in cooking (see Feeding Your Child, page 218).

Most bottlefed babies drink diluted dried infant formula. Manufacturers make this formula by modifying cow's milk so it is more like breast milk, then drying it into a powder or granules.

100

HOW TO STERILIZE BOTTLEFEEDING EQUIPMENT

Note: You can sterilize all the equipment by boiling the items in a pan for ten minutes, draining and keeping them covered until used. Or, by using a steam or microwave sterilizer according to the manufacturer's instructions. There is a microwave sterilizer made especially for the purpose, so don't use your microwave oven as a substitute.

1. *Wash all the equipment in hot water and detergent. Use a bottle brush to clean inside the bottles and round the necks thoroughly. Turn the teats inside out, and make sure all deposits of milk are removed: you may find a teat cleaner helpful. Rinse everything carefully under running water to get rid of any soap suds.*

EQUIPMENT
You will need:
- At least six bottles plus teats and caps.
- Bottle brush for cleaning.
- Sterilizing tank or steam sterilizer.
- If not using steam sterilizer, sterilizing liquid or tablets.
- Knife.

101

2. *Fill the tank with clean cold water and add the correct number of sterilizing tablets or amount of fluid. Allow the tablets to dissolve.*

3. *Put all the equipment into the tank filled with the sterilizing solution and leave for the recommended time.*

4. *Make sure you use the float and ensure that all the items are properly submerged. Rinse in cooled boiled water before use.*

CLEANING THE EQUIPMENT

Bottlefed babies don't have the same protection against infection as breastfed babies, and stale milk is a good breeding ground for germs. For both these reasons, it's important to keep everything that's involved with your baby's feeding as clean as possible. Dummies should be sterilized daily and never put back into a baby's mouth if they have fallen on to the floor.

Leave the equipment in the sterilizing solution until you need it. You can, if you want, take the teats out after the minimum time as they tend to wear out more quickly if stored in the solution. Keep them in a sterilized container.

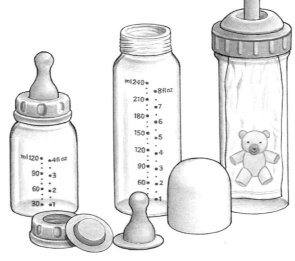

Bottles come in all shapes and sizes, including ones with disposable liners (right).

HOW TO MAKE UP A FEED

Note: you can make up more than one bottle of feed at a time and store the bottles in the fridge for up to twenty-four hours. If you're storing the bottles, invert the teats inside the bottles and put the bottle caps over the tops.

1. *Fill the sterilized bottles up to the required level with freshly boiled cooled water. Check that the volume of water is correct at eye level.*

2. *Using the scoop provided, measure out the correct amount of powder. Don't pack the measure full. Level off any excess.*

3. *Add the correct number of scoops of powder to the water in the bottle.*

4. *Screw the disc and ring on to the bottle and shake well to dissolve the formula.*

5. *Remove the disc and ring, replacing the disc with the teat and placing the cap over the top.*

MAKING UP A FEED

You'll soon develop a routine for making up feeds. The main points to remember are to keep everything clean, to follow the instructions on the packet or tin, and to measure out the water first and then add the measures of milk. If you do it the other way round, there won't be enough water in the feed, which could be dangerous for a young baby.

GIVING A FEED

Shake a few drops of milk on to the back of your hand or the inside of your wrist. It should feel slightly warm. Some babies are happy to take their milk straight from the fridge, but if you need to heat the milk, stand the bottle in a jug of hot water for a few minutes. The microwave should never

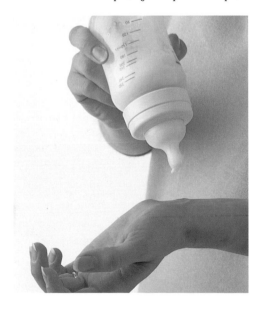

1. *Test that the milk is slightly warm by shaking a few drops on to the inside of your wrist.*

be used because it may heat the milk unevenly, creating hot spots which could scald your baby's mouth.

Hold your baby close, and settle down to feed him. Rotate the bottle or take the teat out of his mouth occasionally, as the sides of the teat may stick together, preventing a free flow of milk. Keep the bottle tilted so the teat is always full of milk.

Different teats

The teat you buy is a matter of preference. There is no good evidence that 'orthodontic' or shaped teats promote dental health or mimic breastfeeding.

Generally speaking, smaller, younger babies cope better starting with a smaller-holed teat and graduating to larger holes later. Silicone rubber teats are more expensive than latex ones, but they last quite a bit longer. You should always change a teat if it looks cracked or worn or feels sticky.

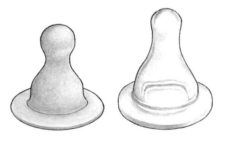

Silicone Teat   Latex Teat

BOTTLES WHEN YOU'RE BREASTFEEDING

You may feel sad if you have to give bottles – for whatever reason – if you'd planned on fully breastfeeding for longer. Feeding, whether by breast or bottle, is much more than just a way of getting milk into your baby. It's a close and loving part of his care.

Firstly, remember it may well be possible to go back to full breastfeeding if that's what you want. Seek the support of someone you have confidence in during this time, increase the number and length of breastfeeds, express your breasts after each feed to stimulate your milk supply, and then you should be able to phase out the bottles after a few days. Secondly, always offer the breast before the bottle, to keep up your breast milk supply longer.

If you do end up bottlefeeding, your feelings may be tinged with relief that whatever the problem was with breastfeeding, it may now go. Babies who have been difficult to feed because of problems with breastfeeding sometimes settle better on the bottle – and you're bound to have mixed feelings about this. Share your thoughts, if you can, with someone who will be sympathetic. Don't give up breastfeeding suddenly. You need to stop gradually, because any quick build-up of milk could cause blocked ducts and mastitis (breast inflammation).

GIVING YOUR BABY A BOTTLE

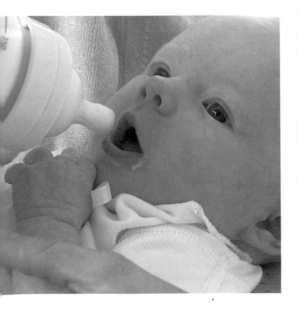

2. *Hold your baby close to you when you offer the bottle. His mouth will probably open in anticipation.*

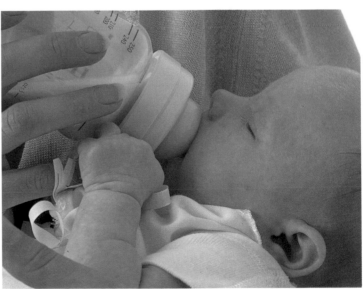

3. *Keep the bottle tilted so the teat is always full of milk. This prevents your baby swallowing too much air.*

Introducing solids

Most babies in the UK start solids at between three and four months on average, though there is no precise 'right' time. Official Department of Health advice is to start no earlier than three months, and no later than six. Your health visitor will help you decide when it's time for you to start thinking about solids.

Open wide and in it goes. Once your baby tastes the food she'll soon show you whether she likes it and wants more. Whatever she thinks of the food, the mess is half the fun.

Starting solids – and that means any food other than milk – can be enjoyable and even exciting for you and your baby. Think about it as a big social step forward, rather than a physical stage of development. After all, the very first foods your baby has are more of a learning (and playing) experience for you both than a major addition to his intake. Your baby clinic will have lots of information on the foods you can offer your baby and how to prepare them. Whenever you decide your baby is ready for solids, remember to take things slowly and do what your baby wants. If he seems totally uninterested then leave it for a few weeks before trying again. And don't expect solids to make your baby suddenly sleep through the night or wake less often.

WHEN TO START

The majority of babies do very well on milk – breast or formula – alone for the first few months of life. Breast milk actually changes its composition to cope with the changing nutritional needs of a growing baby.

There's usually no need to start offering your baby anything other than milk for the first three to six months, especially if you're breastfeeding and still feeding as and when your baby wants. Offering solids too early runs the risk that non-milk foods will replace milk sooner than necessary in his diet, and for a few babies early solids carry the risk of triggering an allergic reaction. Milk is the ideal food for a young baby; why

replace or add to it sooner than you need to? If your baby is happy on milk alone and is continuing to thrive, don't feel pressured into offering other foods.

FIRST FOODS

Whenever you start, keep your baby's first foods simple, and only introduce one taste at a time. If he's very young (three or four months) he may prefer lump-free textures such as purées which he can suck or lap off the spoon. Don't bother making everything super-smooth for an older baby; mashing is usually quite sufficient.

Good first foods include apple, pear, gluten-free cereal such as ground rice or rice flakes, mashed potato, mashed carrot, mashed turnip and swede.

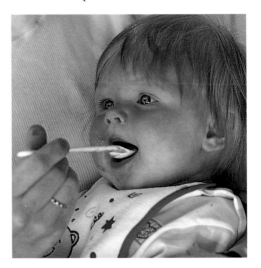

Apple: choose a ripe, dessert apple. Peel and chop it finely. Place in a small saucepan with a little water and heat until boiling. Simmer until soft and then mash or purée by passing it through a sieve.
Rice: buy baby rice, rice flakes, or ground rice. Mix, according to the instructions on the packet, with water, expressed breast milk or formula milk.
Potato: choose a medium potato and peel and remove the eyes. Boil with water (no salt) until cooked. Mash with water, expressed breast milk or formula milk.
Carrot: choose a fresh, clean carrot. Scrape off the skin. Chop and boil with water (no salt) until cooked. Mash or chop finely.

FIRST TRIES

Don't feel your baby has to be spoonfed, or fed from your fingers, all the time. Give him a chance to pick food up from his plate or directly from the table or tray. When you use a spoon, give him one to play with too. In time, he'll try to put it in the bowl himself – unsuccessfully at first, but he'll get there. Vary the lumpiness of the food you give your baby. It can be a mistake to rely on smooth, bland mixtures for too long. Even babies without teeth can chew or use their tongues and saliva to make lumps easy to swallow.

Tips

● If you're spoonfeeding your baby, offer tiny tastes at first.
● Be guided by his appetite and remember that more solids may make him thirstier, so he'll need more to drink.

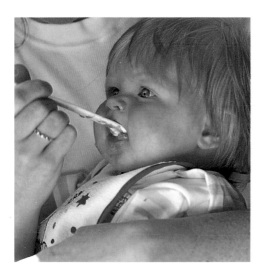

● Try to offer solids at a time your family would normally eat as this will make things easier for you.
● Don't add extra salt or sugar to your baby's food.
● If your baby rejects or dislikes a certain food, don't offer it to him again for a couple of weeks.
● For even young babies holding and manipulating food is fun and helps them to learn about new tastes and textures. (It is easier with banana or a very soft pear than a purée, of course.)
● Remember that the contents of your baby's nappies will change even after small amounts of solids.

COMMERCIAL BABY FOODS

Commercially made baby foods offer a good variety of meals for growing babies. However, they're more expensive than your own home-cooked food, and may contain additives like thickeners and stabilizers to improve the product's shelf-life and appearance in the shop. Food bulked out with starch, cornflour and other thickeners may also have a lower nutritional value than you imagine. A diet containing bought, pre-packaged foods is not harmful, though, and babies on the whole enjoy the tastes and textures of baby foods (the manufacturers test all their products before they sell them, to make sure of this). Socially, however, it's good for your baby to have whatever the rest of the family is eating (without added sugar or salt, and mashed or sieved to the appropriate texture). Yet there will be times when

you're eating food that's highly seasoned, for example, or which your baby doesn't like, so it's always useful to have a jar or packet of something as a standby.

In the end, it's up to you. Feeling guilty because you don't give your baby home cooking all the time is not worth it. Read the labels on commercially made foods and avoid those containing added sugars, such as sucrose or dextrose, and salt. Remember, the first item listed is the main ingredient. Buy a variety, and use them when it fits in with you and your lifestyle. Give your baby what you're having at other times, as this will get him used to the textures of home-made food.

WHAT YOU CAN GIVE YOUR BABY

STAGE 1 At first (at about three to four months).	STAGE 2 Later (after a few weeks).	STAGE 3 Still later (when your baby's around six months).
WHICH FOODS Fruit or vegetable purées such as pear, potato or carrot. Rice.	**WHICH FOODS** Everything he's had so far, plus pulses; meat (avoiding fatty varieties such as pork and lamb); a wider variety of fruit and vegetables.	**WHICH FOODS** Everything he's had so far plus food made from wheat or other grains; yogurt; cottage cheese; fromage frais; citrus fruits; well-cooked egg yolk.
HOW Hold your baby on your lap, securely and comfortably, and offer the food on a teaspoon, one small taste at a time. Don't overload the spoon with food. Be guided by your baby. If he doesn't seem to want it, don't insist.	**HOW** Larger tastes, and less-smooth textures. Keep your baby on your lap, as he will probably be too small to sit comfortably in a highchair.	**HOW** Try your baby in a highchair, well-strapped in, and with a cloth or mat underneath to collect the mess. Try some finger foods.
WHEN You can offer the solid food after one of your baby's milk feeds, or halfway through it – whatever works best for you and your baby. You could try starting solids at his lunchtime feed.	**WHEN** Try giving solids twice, and then three times a day, with a milk feed.	**WHEN** To fit in with your normal mealtimes. Offer a milk feed before, after, or during the solid feed. You can start substituting a drink of cooled boiled water or diluted fruit juice for a milk feed if you like.

WHAT YOU WILL NEED

None of these is essential – after all, you can feed your baby on your lap from an ordinary plate – but most parents find them useful.

- Bibs, wipes and cloths.
- Highchair (from about five to six months).
- Small-bowled plastic spoons.
- Shallow plastic bowl.
- Cloth or plastic mat to place under the highchair for easy wiping.
- Blender, food mouli or sieve.
- Safety harness.
- A plastic beaker with a spout for first drinks.

OPPOSITE It's a great day when your baby can hold a beaker in both hands, close her lips around the spout and give herself a drink. Having an extra beaker saves a fuss if one goes missing.

STARTING DRINKS

Breastfed babies need only breast milk to meet all their food and fluid needs. Bottlefed babies may need extra fluids, especially in hot weather and babies on solids generally get thirstier. If you feel your baby needs extra fluids then offer cooled, boiled water. If you use bottled water you should check that it's suitable for babies. It also needs to be boiled and cooled.

There is actually no need to offer your baby anything other than milk or plain water to drink. If your baby refuses to drink water, then from the age of three months you can offer your baby diluted fresh unsweetened fruit juices. Mix up any baby juice according to the instructions on the packet and dilute fresh juices using one part juice to three parts water.

Check the labels on all commercially made drinks for their sugar content, as some of the 'baby' juices contain added sugar. Remember that ingredients such as 'glucose' or 'dextrose' are types of sugar and should be avoided as sweet drinks are harmful to your baby's teeth.

Which cup?

You can help your baby use a normal cup, but he won't be able to lift, balance or tip it by himself for some time. Instead, you can try him with a lidded, spouted beaker at any age from about four months.

Is my baby getting enough to drink?

If you're worried your baby isn't taking enough fluid, make his solid food more watery. If you offer a cup at every meal, and a cup, breastfeed or bottle is on offer at other times, and your baby has plenty of wet nappies, he is probably getting enough to drink.

NAPPY CHANGING

You will be doing a lot of nappy changing over the next couple of years or so. Don't look upon it as a chore but as an important way of caring for and getting to know your baby. She will enjoy the close, physical contact it offers and it'll give you the opportunity to talk to and play with her.

TERRIES AND DISPOSABLES

Most parents these days use disposable paper nappies, but a sizable minority choose reusables, like the traditional terry-towelling squares which almost everybody used until the 1980s.

Disposable nappies are very absorbent, and they fit well. Reusables are available in the old-style square which you fold to shape, and also ready-shaped secured with velcro fastenings. With the latter, you buy a bigger size of reusable as your baby grows, just as you do with a disposable. Normally, you would also use a pair of waterproof pants over the nappy.

In some areas, you can pay a nappy service to do the washing and drying for you. These firms collect your dirty terry nappies and replace them with freshly laundered ones. Cost-for-cost, reusables work out cheaper if you wash and dry them yourself – and you can use them again with your next baby. However, the difference is not as great as you might imagine when the laundering costs are included. Nappy services tend to aim to match, rather than beat, the cost of using disposables.

The green issue

Disposable nappy manufacturers are keen to demonstrate that they use environmentally-friendly materials and methods, but their arguments may not take into account hidden factors such as the cost of transporting the nappies from factory to shop and from shop to home.

Despite their name, disposable nappies are not easy to dispose of either, and there may be hazards in putting them out with the household rubbish. They go to landfill sites

It doesn't seem to matter to babies whether they wear disposable or reusable nappies as long as they have a change before a cold, wet or soiled nappy makes them uncomfortable.

where, wrapped in plastic bags or folded up, they take a long time to bio-degrade (some estimates say hundreds of years). Campaigners also express concern about the risks of nappy contents (like bacteria, or polio vaccine) seeping out into the earth and affecting the land and the water supply.

Many parents decide that the disadvantages of disposables are worth it overall for the sake of convenience.

THE NAPPY-WASHING ROUTINE

1. Take off the dirty or wet nappy and place in nappy bucket 1, already filled with sanitizing solution.

2. When you have about a day's worth of nappies, remove from the bucket and place in bucket 2, which doesn't contain any sanitizing solution.

3. Renew the solution in bucket 1.

4. Place all the next day's nappies in bucket 1, and then put them in bucket 2.

5. When bucket 2 is full, put the nappies in the washing machine. Wash on a hot cycle if badly stained, otherwise just rinse them through.

6. Hang the nappies out to dry on a washing line, if possible, as sunlight has a natural bleaching effect. Do not dry close to direct heat as they will go hard.

Variations

● Some people don't use sanitizing solution because a 90°C hot wash destroys most bacteria. They soak the nappies in cold water only.

Oblong Fold

2. *Fold the nappy into three. Put it long-side down. Place your baby on the top, and bring it up between*

● You can use just one extra-large bin (such as a plastic swing bin) for your nappies. It holds two-to-three days' worth. You may need a hose to fill it with water.

FOLDING A NAPPY

It is not hard to fold a terry-towelling square. Here are a couple of methods:

Kite Fold

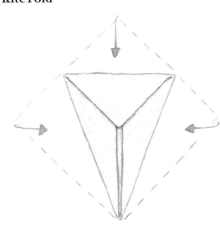

1. *Place the nappy flat in front of you and imagine the corners are the points of a compass. Bring 'west' and 'east' to the centre, under 'north'. Bring 'north' down, to form a straight top edge and fold 'south' up to meet 'north'.*

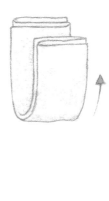

her legs. Fold over the top edges if necessary, and fold in the legs. Pin at each side.

WHAT YOU WILL NEED
If you choose reusable nappies, you will need twenty-four to begin with: buy the best quality ones you can afford.
● **Two large plastic buckets with lids.**
● **Sanitizing powder or liquid (you can buy 'green' varieties).**
● **Three or four pairs of waterproof pants.**
● **Nappy pins.**
● **Disposable nappy liners – useful if your baby dirties a lot of nappies instead of just wetting them.**

KEEPING YOUR BABY CLEAN AND DRY

Although many babies don't seem to mind if their nappy is wet or dirty – except if they're sore – it's obviously important for hygiene reasons to change your baby regularly and to clean her at every change. Good-quality disposables leave very little wetness on the skin, but even the best of them stop working when they're very full. The nappy will then leak out at the edges. A terry nappy stops absorbing beyond a certain point as well.

You will find your baby goes through between five and eight nappies every twenty-four hours and will probably need changing at every feed (apart from little feeds). Change her when it suits you – before, during or after the feed. New babies often dirty a nappy during a feed anyway, so you might find it easiest at first to change your baby halfway through a feed, so you don't need to disturb her if she then falls asleep.

Plain, warm water is fine for cleaning your baby's bottom, but baby wipes are convenient. If you're using terry nappies, you may find you need to use a barrier cream such as zinc and castor oil cream to keep your baby's skin dry and prevent any soreness from nappy rash.

NAPPY RASH

Don't feel guilty if your baby occasionally gets a red or sore bottom which develops into a nappy rash. This can be caused by bacteria reacting with the baby's urine or motions. You can go some way to prevent it by changing your baby's nappy whenever it is wet or dirty. If you feel your baby is particularly susceptible to nappy rash, you can use a protective barrier cream. Your midwife or health visitor may recommend a brand.

HOW TO CHANGE A BABY'S NAPPY

1. Lie your baby on a changing mat. Unpeel the tapes, or undo the pins if using a terry nappy, and remove the soiled or wet nappy (use any spare clean corners to give your baby a quick wipe down).

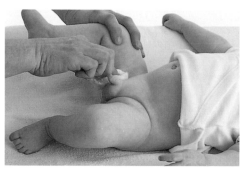

2. Clean your baby's nappy area with warm water and cotton wool, baby wipes or a clean cloth. *Always wipe girls from front to back. Dry gently – especially in the creases around the thighs – if you need to.*

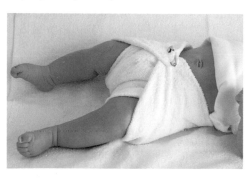

5. If using a terry nappy, lift up your baby's legs and slide the nappy underneath. Bring the nappy up between her legs and bring both side pieces into the middle. Fasten the three pieces together with a pin.

6. For a larger baby, repeat as before but instead of using one safety pin, use one at each side to give extra room around the waist. The nappy shown here was folded using the kite method (see page 109).

Other forms of rash are caused by thrush, eczema or a reaction to traces of sanitizing powder, soap or detergent in the nappy. So, if you are using terry nappies, make sure you rinse them thoroughly. Ask your health visitor or doctor for advice if your baby's rash doesn't go in a few days.

BOWEL MOVEMENTS

The first bowel motions your newborn baby passes are black, tarry and very sticky – they are called meconium. After a few days your baby's motions will change to a greenish-brown colour and, after a week or so, they'll change again. If your baby is fully breastfed her motions will be bright yellow and very loose, whereas the motions of bottlefed babies are light brown and more formed. Some formula milks make the motions greenish in colour.

The occasional green motion in a breastfed baby, or in a bottlefed baby, may look alarming but is nothing to worry about. However, if it happens several times, it is worth seeing your doctor.

Bottlefed babies usually pass a motion once a day. Breastfed babies are more variable. Some pass one at every feed. Others go for a week or more without one.

WHAT'S IN A NAPPY?

Black, tarry and sticky	Meconium, the first motions of a newborn baby.
Greenish-brown	Known as 'changing stools', these are passed in the first couple of days after birth.
Bright yellow, very loose	The motions of a fully breastfed baby, passed from round about the fifth day after birth.
Light brown, more formed	The motions of a bottlefed baby, passed from round about the fifth day after birth.

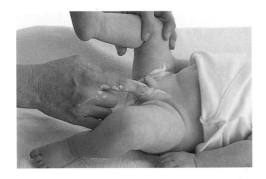

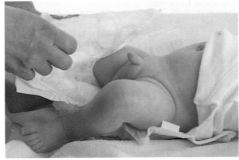

3. *Apply any baby creams or lotions. You don't need to use anything unless your baby has a tendency to a sore bottom. Lift your baby's legs up and slide the clean nappy underneath, soft-side up, with the tapes at the top.*

4. *Bring the front of the nappy up between your baby's legs and unpeel the fastening tapes. Pull the nappy as closely as you can around your baby's middle and then fasten the tapes round the front.*

TIP
● **Don't bother changing your baby's nappy when she wakes in the night unless her bottom is sore, or she is wet.**

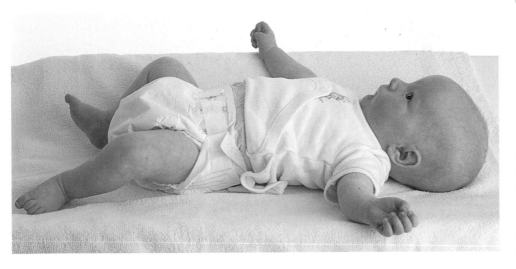

Practice makes perfect. A warm, dry, comfortably fitted nappy leaves a baby free to breathe, feed, have a cuddle, play, kick his legs and sleep without restriction.

See A-Z of Healthcare, page 288, for constipation and page 291, for diarrhoea

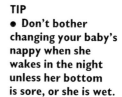

BATHING YOUR BABY

The idea of bathing your tiny, new baby can be quite daunting. But you'll soon gain confidence, and start to enjoy it. Don't feel you have to follow any rules about timing. In fact you can bath your baby at any time that suits you. Use a baby bath (or even a large washing-up bowl for a new baby) if you like, or the family bath.

A baby bath uses less water, and is portable, so you can bath your baby in a warm room. If you use it with a stand or on a table there is less bending and lifting for you. However, a baby bath is awkward and cumbersome to fill and empty (though the ones with a plug hole are slightly easier to manage). Some parents use the baby bath in the big bath or the shower tray, which avoids having to fetch and carry water, or having to lift a baby bath full of water. There are also foam rubber baths available which fit neatly around your baby's body and can be used in the big bath, and plastic baby baths that fit over the top of the big bath, so they can be filled from the taps and emptied from their own plug holes. Most

parents find they use the big bath after the first few months, especially if they have other children.

PREPARATIONS
Gather all the items you will need together – towels, clean clothing, nappy, flannel, toiletries and changing mat. This avoids the nuisance of forgetting something, and having to take your baby out of the bath while you fetch it.

TOILETRIES
A very young baby has sensitive skin, so avoid using toiletries with strong colours or perfumes that could cause irritation. In fact, although there's a wide variety of baby toiletries available, if you stick to mild, unperfumed products you don't need to buy anything special for your baby unless you want to, or unless your baby has a skin condition (such as eczema) which makes special products necessary. Shampoo is only necessary if your baby has a lot of hair; otherwise water will do.

HOW TO BATH YOUR BABY

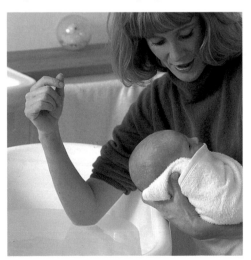

1. Fill the baby bath with water to a depth of about 10cm (4in). You should avoid making the bath too hot by adding the cold water first, and then the hot. Check the temperature by dipping your elbow into the water (do not use your hand because it can withstand much higher temperatures) or by using a bath thermometer. The water should feel just warm. Add any baby bath liquid.

2. Undress your baby down to her nappy and wrap her in a towel. Wash her face with cotton-wool dipped in cooled boiled water. Bath water will be fine once the baby is older (about four months old) unless you have added any bath preparations. Supporting your baby's back along your forearm, and her head in your hand, gently pour some water over her scalp with your free hand. Then pat her head dry with the towel.

See What your Baby May Need, page 128, for information on bathing equipment

Talcum powder smells delicious but is not essential. Shake it into your hands and then smooth it over your baby's skin, avoiding his bottom as it could set up an irritation. You should *never* use it near the face or in a newborn's navel, and must avoid shaking it near your baby as it could get into his nose, throat and lungs.

If your baby has dry or flaky skin you may want to use baby oil. Massage it in (see What Children Need, page 249), remembering it will make him slippery. A barrier cream for your baby's nappy area is useful if your baby is already sore, or if you find he has a tendency to get a sore bottom.

CUTTING NAILS

The simplest way to trim your newborn baby's nails is to bite them off gently yourself. If you find this difficult, try using a round-ended pair of baby nail scissors. You can even use an emery board to smooth down your baby's sharp nails.

A funny nose rub, a big cuddle in a warm fluffy towel and then, perhaps, a long, relaxing feed are just what you need when you've splashed and played in the bath to your heart's content.

3. *Remove her nappy and, cradling her in your arms, lower her gently into the water. Make sure her shoulders and head are supported on your forearm and your hand is firmly holding her shoulder and upper arm. Put your other hand under her bottom.*

4. *Keeping hold of her arm and continuing to support her head and shoulders, gently swish the water over her body. Lift her out of the bath and wrap her snugly in a towel straight away. Lie her on the mat and, with another towel, pat her dry all over. Pay special attention to the folds and creases of her skin. Put her nappy on and dress her. Sing or talk to her if she seems distressed.*

TOPPING AND TAILING YOUR BABY

Your baby doesn't need to be bathed every day when he's small. As well as a bath, or instead of it, keep him clean and fresh with a daily topping and tailing. Lots of babies seem to enjoy being topped and tailed. Just keep it gentle and relaxed.

Gather together everything you will need – some cooled boiled water in a bowl, cotton wool or a clean flannel, and a towel. Lie your baby on the changing mat. Make sure there are no draughts to make him uncomfortable. A towel on the changing mat makes it a little cosier for him.

HOW TO TOP AND TAIL YOUR BABY

1. *Dip a piece of cotton-wool into the water and wipe it across the eyes from the inside corner to the outer corner. Remember to use a fresh piece of cotton-wool for each eye.*

2. *Wipe over the face, neck and ears, hands and fingers with some moistened cotton-wool or a damp flannel. Use a fresh piece of cotton-wool for each ear.*

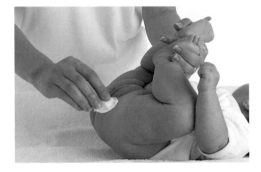

3. *Remove the nappy and clean the bottom with some more moistened cotton-wool or a damp flannel. Remember to wipe a girl from front to back.*

4. *Pat gently dry with a towel. Your midwife or health visitor will tell you if the umbilical cord stump needs special attention.*

WHAT YOU WILL NEED
● **Changing mat.**
● **Bag or bowl for the used nappy and cotton-wool or baby wipes.**
● **Cotton-wool and bowl of water, or baby wipes.**
● **Barrier cream or lotion, if necessary.**

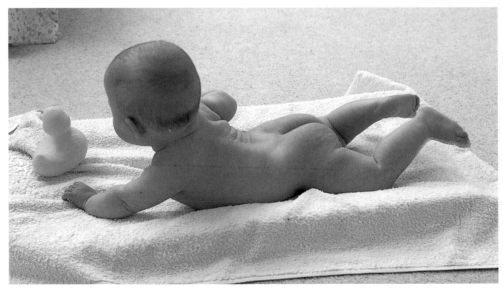

Babies enjoy being free to kick and play with no clothes in a warm place. What's more, exposure to light and air encourages healthy skin and helps prevent nappy rash.

HAIR WASHING

Brushing and rinsing keep soft baby hair clean. Once your baby's hair grows a bit, however, you will need to use shampoo – especially when he starts to get pieces of food stuck in it.

Using a mild shampoo, wash your baby's hair when he's in the bath. Hold him so you can rinse the water over his head but away from his face (see Nappy Changing and Bathing, page 154). Use a small amount of shampoo.

Cradle cap is a condition brought on by excess oil in the scalp and causes scaly crusts to form on the baby's head. It's harmless but can be unsightly. If you want to get rid of it, you can loosen it by rubbing in baby oil, or a special cradle-cap shampoo available from the chemist. It should then come off when washed, although you may need to treat it several times before you get rid of it all.

TO THE BIG BATH

If you've used a baby bath in the early weeks, you'll find you need to transfer to the big one at some stage. Try taking the baby in with you, or putting the baby bath inside the big one at first. Bathing a baby and a toddler together makes bathtime fun and cuts down on time, too. Be sure never to leave them alone. Take your baby out after a short time, as he may get cold.

Always hold your baby securely, just as you do in the baby bath. Even when he can sit up, stay with him at all times. A non-slip mat in the bath will make things less nerve-racking.

DRESSING YOUR BABY

Some babies really don't like being dressed and undressed, but they tend to get used to it as they get older. It helps if you make sure you're quick and fairly smooth in your movements and the room is warm.

HOW TO DRESS YOUR BABY

115

1. Put your baby's nappy on first, then the vest. Stretch open the neck as wide as possible so that you can slide it over his head.

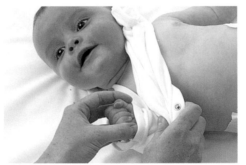

2. Holding the armhole open, gently ease your baby's hand through the sleeve. Do the same with the other sleeve. Do up the fastenings between his legs.

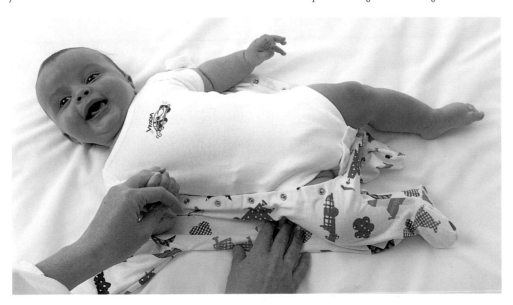

3. Lay out a stretchsuit and place your baby on top. Take one leg of the stretchsuit and gently ease your baby's leg into it. Do the same with the other leg. Then gather up one sleeve and hold it open while you guide your baby's hand through. Repeat with the other side. Finally do up the fastenings.

SLEEP AND BEDTIME

There is nothing as peaceful-looking as a contentedly sleeping baby – and nothing feels nicer than having a drowsy little face snuggled up against your cheek or resting on your shoulder. It feels good, too, when you see your baby fall asleep at the breast.

Life with a young baby may not have enough of these peaceful, rewarding moments, and one problem with a wakeful baby is that the parents tend to lose out on much-needed sleep. The good news is that even very wakeful babies usually become more predictable and sleepy as time goes on, and that there are ways of coping with babies who seem to need very little sleep.

HOW MUCH WILL YOUR BABY SLEEP?

Newborn and young babies vary a great deal in the amount of sleep they need. For the first few days after birth, many babies remain quite sleepy. This is especially likely to happen if you had a long labour, or needed pethidine to relieve the pain, or if your baby has jaundice (see Babies Needing Special Care, page 74).

After this time, your baby will probably sleep several times in twenty-four hours during the first few weeks. By the age of six months, she may be having one major sleep through the night (though she may wake for shortish periods once or twice in that time), plus a couple of daytime naps. It is very common for all babies – breast- or bottlefed – to have a wakeful time from early to late evening (see page 118).

WHERE SHOULD YOUR BABY SLEEP?

Your baby can sleep anywhere that is clean, warm, free from draughts and safe from any household pets. In practice, most families have a cot, a Moses basket or a carrycot for their baby to sleep in. Keep your baby in the same room as you to begin with so that you can check she's alright and hear when she wakes. Night-time feeds are also easier to give and cause less disruption if your baby is near you. Some parents, however, put their babies in a separate room right from the start. There is no

evidence to show that this helps babies sleep through the night any sooner, and night-time wakings are more inconvenient if you have to go to another room to settle your baby. In fact, you may find an unsettled baby sleeps better if she's in the same room as you are.

Can she sleep in your bed?

Babies all over the world sleep next to their mothers at night, and in this sense it's a normal way to behave. It gives babies (and their mothers) a lot of comfort and the freedom to breastfeed easily when they want to. However, some experts worry that being in the parents' bed may dangerously overheat a young baby. Also, one study found that babies who slept with mothers who were smokers had a higher risk of the sudden infant death syndrome (cot death). If you feel anxious, feed your baby in bed and then put her back in her cot or Moses basket afterwards to sleep.

Positions for sleeping

Lie your baby on her back to go to sleep. A baby sleeping on her side can easily roll on to her tummy, and recent research indicates that babies lying on their tummies have a higher risk of cot death (see Cot death, page 118).

NIGHT CRYING AND WAKING

Babies cry for many different reasons. You can find more information on why your baby might be crying on page 132. Some babies cry for a short while before they go off to sleep. If your baby is distressed, the crying will last longer than a minute or so.

A few whimpers in the middle of a deep sleep aren't usually anything to be concerned about. If your baby is unhappy, hungry or uncomfortable her crying will get louder and more insistent. Sometimes, however, you may feel your baby is crying because she's tired and needs to go back to sleep. If this is the case, it can help to find a quiet corner where you can calm her without any distractions, or alternatively rock her to sleep.

Sleeping gives your baby time to recharge those batteries and offers you the chance of having a lovely quiet cuddle or time on your own to work, exercise, relax or sleep.

Lie your baby on her back to sleep as research shows that babies who lie on their tummies have a higher risk of dying from a 'cot death' (sudden infant death syndrome).

A very new baby may have no sense of night or day, and you may not see any difference in your newborn's sleeping and waking patterns throughout the twenty-four hours. Within a few days, however, you may notice that her longest sleeping time is at night.

Expect to be woken two or three times at first (it can depend on the time your baby had her last feed of the day); most babies then settle to wake once or twice at night. There may be occasions when you have very disturbed nights, when your baby is very difficult to settle, and when you feel you can't console her. She may seem to want an endless feed, when all you want is to get off to sleep yourself. You'll need extra support through this time, and a chance to catch up on some lost sleep during the day.

EVENING WAKING

Most babies start to have a wakeful period after the first couple of weeks or so – and it's often in the evenings. It doesn't last, and it can be easier just to accept it while it's happening.

Some babies are more fractious in the evenings; others are fine as long as they get attention and plenty of cuddles. Breastfed babies may sometimes want to be on and off the breast all evening, so you're unsure when one feed ends and the other one starts.

COT DEATH

Cot death is the everyday term for the sudden infant death syndrome, which kills many babies every year. Experts now know enough to identify certain risk factors, and give the following advice to parents.

● Always lay your baby on her back to sleep (remember: 'back to sleep').

● Don't smoke with your baby in the room; discourage others from smoking in the same room as your baby; keep your baby out of smoky atmospheres.

● With a comfortable room temperature of 18°C (65°F), most lightly-clothed, healthy babies only need a sheet and 1–3 blankets, depending on their type.

● Make sure your baby isn't too warm when sleeping, even in winter, and especially if she is feverish. You may need to reduce the amount of bedding on your baby's cot, or the amount of clothing she has on.

● Seek medical advice if your baby seems ill, listless, uninterested in feeding, feverish or has difficulty with breathing.

● Breastfeed your baby. (Scientific evidence does not consistently show that breastfeeding protects against cot deaths, but it never shows that bottlefeeding does.)

For further information and advice on the subject of cot death, contact the Foundation for the Study of Infant Deaths (see Useful Addresses, page 314).

**CHECKING
YOUR BABY'S
TEMPERATURE**
● **Place your hand
on her chest.**
● **If it feels warm,
she's fine.**
● **Hands and feet
are not good guides
as they often feel
misleadingly cold.**

HOW MUCH WILL MY BABY SLEEP?

Three mothers were asked to record their babies' sleeping patterns over a single day. Both said no day was exactly the same as the one before.

Karen is the mother of James, aged two weeks. He is totally breastfed.
6.30am: Feed, in bed with mummy and daddy. Light snooze.
7.30am: Wakes again and is fed, changed, washed and dressed. Wakeful.
8.30am: Falls asleep in pram.
10.30am: Wakes and needs a feed.
11.30am: Awake, but happy to look around.
12pm: Feed – he usually feeds rather sooner than this!
2pm: Goes to sleep in crib.
5pm: Wakes, feeds, cries, needs a lot of cuddling.
6.30pm: Has a bath, followed by another feed.
7.30pm: Settles down to sleep in his crib.
10.30pm: Wakes, feeds, cries, takes a while to settle down again.
3.30am: Wakes for a feed.

Karen says: 'James is far more placid and contented than his older brothers. They needed more frequent feeds and more attention.'

Chris is mother of Caitlin, aged four months. She is breastfed, and Chris has just started introducing solid foods.
4.15am: Wakes for a feed, and then goes straight back to sleep.
8.30am: Wakes again, is washed and dressed and has a short feed.
10.30am: Goes to sleep in buggy.
11.30am: Wakes, has a quick feed and is happy to look around.
12pm: Lunch – a spoonful or two of packet baby food, followed by a breastfeed.
2.30pm: Falls asleep in buggy.
3.15pm: Wakes and grizzles a bit. Needs a feed.
4.30pm: Asleep in cot.
5.30pm: Awake, and needs cuddles and attention.
6.15pm: Has a bath, more cuddles and a feed.
7pm: Very sleepy, but only happy if she's on my lap feeding.
8.30pm: Asleep in her cot.

Chris says: 'Caitlin always takes a little time to settle down for the night, but once there, she usually sleeps through.'

Jill is the mother of Matthew, aged five weeks. He is breastfed.
6.30am: Wakes for a feed.
7am: Matthew cries and whimpers, needs comforting.
8am: Falls asleep in his carrycot.
10am: Wakes and has a feed.
11am: Awake, needs cuddling and rocking.
11.30am: Asleep in his pram.
12.30pm: Wakes for a feed.
1pm: Settling, but grizzly.
1.30pm: Asleep.
2.30pm: Awake, needs lots of attention.
3.00pm: Asleep.
4.30pm: Feeds.
5.30pm: Asleep.
6.30pm: Has a bath, needs rocking and cuddling.
7.30pm: Short feed, then falls asleep.
8.30pm: Wakes crying and needs rocking.
9.30pm: Has a short feed.
10.00pm: Falls asleep.
11.30pm: Awake again for another feed.
12am: Put down to settle in his carrycot.
12.30am: Falls asleep.
4.00am: Wakes for a feed.
5.00 am: Settles down to sleep.

Jill says: 'Matthew's routine is far from settled. He takes a lot of cuddling in order to calm him down before he'll sleep. Alternatively, I take him out in the pram.'

Some babies are content to lie in their cots for a while before going off to sleep, or after waking up, but others become very upset and prefer not to be left on their own.

WHAT YOUR BABY MAY NEED

Always take the time to ensure that your baby is safe, wherever she sleeps, and secure her with a safety harness if there is the remotest chance of her falling or climbing out.

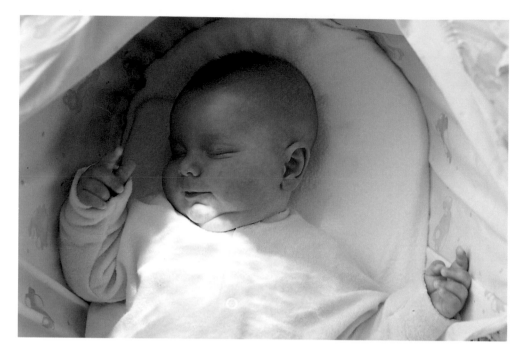

You may have already bought some items of equipment before your baby was born but there will undoubtedly be items that you hadn't considered or you were perhaps cautious about buying before your baby's birth. Once you are at home with the new arrival things can be hectic and you may not have much time to go browsing round shops looking for equipment. The following pages have been designed to help you, with tips on decorating and advice on buying pushchairs, prams, car seats, baby carriers and clothes.

A ROOM OF HIS OWN
It's best for your baby to sleep in your bedroom at first, but at some stage you'll want to move him into another room. It can be fun to plan and decorate it before the baby arrives, but don't worry if you haven't time. All that matters is that it's clean, warm, practical and draught-free.

The decor
For DIY enthusiasts there are whole ranges of colour co-ordinated wallpapers, curtains and furnishings to choose from for children's bedrooms. Or you could try some of these less expensive alternatives:
● Paint the walls in a pastel shade or white

then add a frieze, transfers, a few posters or framed prints. Or paint one wall in a toning primary colour.
● Paint the walls in one of the many whites available that contain just a hint of colour. You can then pick up that colour as a stronger gloss shade for the woodwork.

Tips:
● Avoid a dark, plain carpet as spillages of milk, creams, lotions and cotton-wool fluff will all show up horribly.
● Go for a washable floor-covering instead of carpet. Cork tiles or cushioned vinyl feel warm and are easy to clean.
● Use unleaded paint on all surfaces.
● Paint is generally easier to keep clean than wallpaper.

FULLY FURNISHED
You don't need to fill your baby's room with loads of cupboards and shelves – but you'll probably find the following items make things easier:
● A low chest of drawers or cupboard to keep nappies and clothes in.
● An upright, comfortable chair for you to sit in while feeding your baby.
● Table for a night light and feeding bottle.
● A baby monitor.

120

SAFETY
● **Don't give your baby a duvet or a pillow until he is a year old.**
● **Lay him on his back to sleep, never on his tummy.**
● **Check the drop-side mechanism (if your cot has one) cannot be operated by a child.**
● **Make sure there are no horizontal bars that could help him climb out.**

See Safety Around the House, page 306, for information on safety

Sleeping soundly

One of the first and most important items
of equipment you'll have to make a decision
about is what your baby is going to sleep
in. For the first few months a carrycot or
pram is fine and cosier for a tiny baby than
a large cot.

CHOOSING A COT

As a general rule, the more intricate the
design, the more expensive it will be, but if
it's a reputable make, the quality will be the
same. If you choose one with an adjustable
base height, have it raised at first, so you
don't have to bend over so far to put your
baby down to sleep, then lower it as he
becomes more active so he can't climb out.
Sheets: You'll need about four pairs for the
cot and three pairs for the pram/carrycot.
Invest in fitted bottom sheets and you'll find
cot-making easier.
Blankets: Lightweight cellular ones are best
and be sure to choose machine-washable
ones. You'll need at least two blankets in the
winter plus spare ones if it gets cold or you
need to wash them. A shawl can double as
a blanket in cold weather.

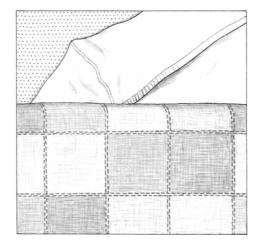

CHOOSING A MATTRESS

Most cots and mattresses are a standard size,
but check before you buy that the mattress
will fit the base. There should be no gaps
between it and the frame where your baby
could trap an arm or a leg.

Some foam-filled mattresses have
ventilation holes and a removable mesh
cover at the head end; others have a sprung
interior or are made of natural fibre.
A plastic covering means a wet or soiled
bed can be wiped clean.

SAFETY
Don't buy a
secondhand cot if:
● It has any
horizontal bars.
● The bars are too
wide – your baby's
head could get stuck.
● The bars are too
narrow – his arms
and legs could get
caught.
● Always buy a
new mattress even
if you buy a
secondhand cot.

121

Moses basket

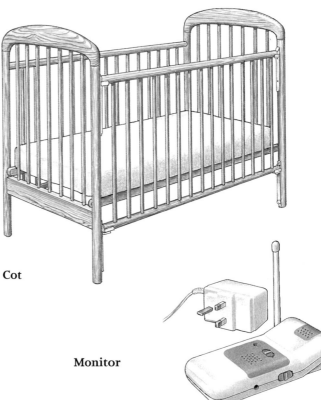

Cot

Monitor

Daytime needs

Your newborn baby will most likely spend a lot of time asleep unless he needs feeding or changing. But in a very short time he will become more alert and won't want to lie around in his cot all day. He needs to be with you, to watch you and hear your voice. His eyes will follow you and you move around the room, he will start to smile and gurgle and the two of you will begin to communicate. But you won't want to carry him around constantly so you need somewhere to put him that's comfortable, convenient and transportable.

Sitting pretty

It wasn't so long ago that being on the floor, propped up and surrounded with cushions was the only safe place to put a baby unless he was strapped in a pram. But now there is a whole range of equipment to choose from.

BABY GYM
(From about six weeks until around six months)

Your baby may enjoy lying under a baby gym trying to reach the toys suspended from the bar. Some come with a washable floor mat.

+ The activity toys will fascinate your baby and probably keep him amused for far longer than if he were just allowed to lie and kick on a mat.

– Some types of baby gym are tricky to take apart for cleaning. They also take up quite a lot of room.

BOUNCING CRADLE
(From about three weeks to six months)

The cradle supports your baby's back, head and legs and gently rocks as he starts to wriggle and kick. Make sure you always place it on the floor.

SAFETY FIRST

● Don't leave your baby – even for a second – on a chair, table or any other raised surface. He could roll off.

● Never put your baby in a bouncing cradle or baby chair on a table or worktop – it could slip off.

● Don't leave your baby unattended in a baby bouncer.

● Always use the safety straps provided or fit a harness in a seat.

● Don't leave your baby alone with a bottle or any food.

● Don't leave objects lying around – especially on or near the stairs – you could trip and fall while carrying your baby.

● Check there are no flexes or leads which you could trip over while carrying him.

● Always hold the banister when coming downstairs carrying the baby. Make sure others do the same.

● Avoid having rugs or mats on slippery floors and don't wear loose slippers.

Bouncing Cradle
+ Light and easy to move from one room to another.
– Some babies don't like such a reclining position once they're alert. If this is the case, try supporting the back with a soft cushion so the baby is in a more upright position.

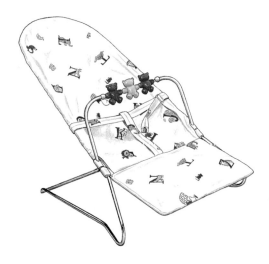

See Feeding Your Baby, page 101 for bottles and sterilizing equipment

BABY ROCKER
(From birth to around nine months)

This is a padded seat which rocks gently. It can be fully reclined for your newborn baby or adjusted to a more upright position for an older baby. It also converts to a rigid low chair, so is ideal for mealtimes once he's moved on to solids.

Note: A baby rocker is not a car seat and should never be used as one.

+ Good for babies who prefer to be more upright once they're alert.

– You'll still need a car seat, which could double as an indoor seat.

MULTI-PURPOSE CHAIR
(From birth until toddlerhood)

Some start as a baby gym with toys suspended from a bar (see below), and can convert to a swing, rocker, low and highchair. You will need a separate safety harness to strap your baby in, especially when using it as a highchair (see What Your Baby May Need, page 166).

Babies like something to do or watch — but never give your baby a better view of what you're doing by putting her bouncing cradle on a table, because it might bounce off.

WHAT YOUR BABY MAY NEED

123

Baby Gym

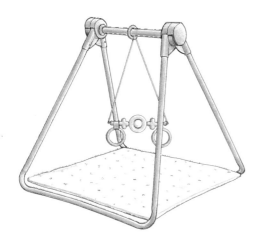

Low chair

Multi-purpose chair

+ Even if you don't use one function much, it is still a very useful piece of equipment which saves you the expense of buying all the items separately.

– The initial outlay makes it seem like an expensive option although it will save you money in the long run.

Baby rocker

Out and about

It may be a few weeks before you venture any distance with your baby. But when the time comes you'll need some sort of transport for him. The choice is really between a pram (or carrycot with chassis) and a fully reclining lie-back stroller plus a car seat if you have a car.

PRAM OR CARRYCOT WITH CHASSIS (From birth)
A pram or carrycot is warm and snug – especially for a winter baby – because the high sides protect him from the wind and draughts. It can also double as a first bed. But it's difficult to store when not in use.

COMBINATION PRAM/PUSHCHAIR (From birth)
This has a fully reclining pushchair with a carrycot that clips on to the same chassis.

TWO-IN-ONE (From birth)
The two-in-one has four different reclining positions, and a fabric hood and base, which allow you to convert it from a pram to a pushchair without removing it from the chassis.

THREE-IN-ONE (From birth)
This has one chassis which takes a carrycot, a reclining pushchair and a car baby seat. You can wheel your baby round the shops in the car seat without having to disturb him, but need room to store the parts not in use.

RECLINING STROLLER (From two months)
The reclining stroller is an expensive pushchair, but it can be used even with quite a young baby in the fully reclined position. It is compact and folds easily.

SAFE AND SNUG
● Even tiny babies must be properly strapped into a lie-back stroller.
● Put your baby in a harness in a pram or fully reclined pushchair from about two months. Even before he can sit up, he could pull himself up by the sides and fall out.
● Always make sure the brake is on correctly before you leave any pram or pushchair.
● Don't hang shopping from the handles of a pushchair as it could tip over – buy a proper shopping tray if it does not have one.

24

Combination pram/pushchair
+ The carrycot is snug for a new baby and he can sleep in it day and night.
+ The chassis folds flat.
– Need room to store the part not being used.
– Awkward to take on public transport.

ACCESSORIES
Essentials
● Most pushchairs have integral harnesses. If yours doesn't, buy one and fit it – it's essential for your baby's safety.
● Rain canopy – a transparent hood and apron which clips on to the chassis of the pushchair to protect against wet weather.
● Cat net – vital to put over a pram if your baby is sleeping in the garden. A fine mesh one is best as it will also stop insects settling on him.
● Parasol or sun canopy – to protect against strong sunlight.

Other accessories
● Head-support cushion (for a newborn).
● Cosytoes – this fits around your baby's lower body and is useful in winter to keep him warm and snug.
● Coverall – this is a zip-up waterproof cover which fits neatly round the pushchair and your baby to keep him warm and dry.

Reclining stroller
+ The rigid seat-back is suitable for young babies (from about three months).
+ Folds easily, so can be used on public transport.
– You will need to buy a rain canopy for protection from bad weather which means extra expense.

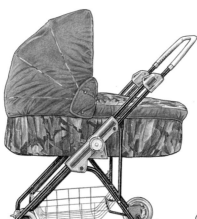

Have wheels, will travel! When you have a carrycot and chassis, you and your baby can see each other, there's a safely positioned tray for your shopping and outings are convenient and easy.

125

Two-in-One
+ No extra parts to store.
– Pushchair is rather bulky and heavy – especially for an older toddler.

Car seats

Even travelling back from hospital in the car for the first time, your baby should be in an approved car seat. Holding him tenderly in your arms is not a safe method and would not stop him being crushed by your body or the seat in front, or being thrown through the windscreen in a collision. Travelling with your baby in a carrycot strapped on to the back seat with carrycot restraints is not recommended either, but as a last resort it is safer than nothing (see below for advice).

If you do not want to buy a car seat then some hospitals run a seat hire service. All the equipment is thoroughly and regularly checked so you can be sure your baby will be safe.

CARRYCOT WITH RESTRAINT
(From birth to about six months)

If you have a carrycot, you can buy restraining straps which are attached to anchorage points in the back of the car. These may have to be fitted to your car. Make sure the straps are properly fastened or the carrycot could slip in an accident. Your baby should also be wearing a five-point safety harness and for further protection the storm cover should be fitted to the carrycot.
– This method is not recommended and should only be used as a last resort.

REAR-FACING BABY SEAT
(From birth to about nine months or 10kg/22lb in weight)

This is the safest option. The seat can be fitted to the front or rear passenger seat using the adult safety belt. The advantage of having the baby in the front seat is that it enables the driver to see the baby and vice versa. It has an integral harness to keep the baby secure, and is light and easy to carry if the baby is asleep.

COMBINED BABY/CHILD CAR SEAT
(From birth to four years or 18kg/40lb in weight)

This seat can be rear-facing at first and forward-facing later. It is fixed with the adult belt. You can buy an extra head-support cushion for a tiny baby. It is heavy to carry in and out of the car with ease if your baby is sleeping.

26

CAR SAFETY

● **Your baby must be properly strapped in to a car seat. Any car seat should conform to British or European safety standards.**
● **Always read and follow the product's fitting instructions.**
● **Don't buy a secondhand car seat as it may have been damaged in a previous accident.**
● **Only use a carrycot with restraints If you have to and make sure the restraint is easy to use, with a quick-release buckle.**
● **Don't travel with your baby in your arms, or try to strap him in with you with an adult seat belt.**

Rear-facing baby seat
+ Comfortable for your baby to sit in both in the car and indoors.
– Can be used only until he is about nine months old.

Combined baby/child car seat
+ Will last from birth to around four years.
– It may not be the ideal choice if you are planning to have more children.

See What Your Baby May Need, page 164

Baby carriers

There may be times when you want to carry your baby around but need to keep your hands free whether you're indoors or out. A sling or backpack can be the best solution. A sling is ideal from birth while a backpack is only suitable once your baby can fully support his head. Before buying make sure it's easy to get on and off and comfortable to wear.

BABY SLING
(From birth to around six months)

If your baby cries a lot he probably needs to be rocked and cuddled more than most. Pop him in a sling and your body movement, warmth, soothing words and heartbeat will help to settle him while you are free to get on with a variety of tasks. You can even breastfeed at the same time. It's often easier, too, in the supermarket for instance, to have both hands free.

BACKPACKS
(From around four months)

These are suitable only when your baby can hold his head up. An older baby loves to see what's going on but still needs to

Slings and backpacks rightly deserve their popularity — babies like being held securely and parents enjoy being close to their babies and being independent of prams and pushchairs.

be close to you, which makes a backpack a good choice. It also leaves your hands free for shopping.

Made of strong, weatherproof material with steel supports, a backpack can hold even quite a heavy toddler.

127

Baby sling
+ Ideal for use on public transport.
− Some are easier than others to get on and off and if your baby is sleeping it can be difficult to remove him from the sling without disturbing him.

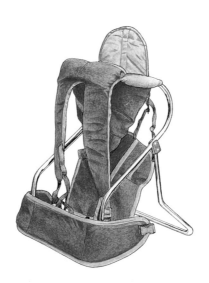

Backpack
+ Ideal for getting out and about as a family.
− Offers your baby little protection from bad weather.

Bathing and changing

Bathing your baby can be great fun but is not always as easy as it sounds. Babies don't all lie gurgling in your arms while you splash water lovingly over them. Some wriggle and scream and thoroughly protest at the whole business.

It makes life easier if you get everything ready to bath and change him before you get him undressed. The easiest place to bath your baby is in the bathroom, but if the only warm rooms in the house are the bedroom or the kitchen, use one of these.

BABY BATH

Most parents choose to buy a baby bath to use until their baby can sit up comfortably on his own but it is not essential – a washing-up bowl will do at first. You can use a basin or sink but make sure he doesn't bump or burn himself on the taps. Wrap flannels around them for safety.

Most baby baths are made of rigid plastic and some have a removable back and headrest and a slip-resistant inner surface. You can buy a folding stand but any low, flat surface is fine. Some baby baths fit over the adult bath. These can be filled directly from the taps and mean you don't have to bend over too far or carry a heavy bath full of water.

BATH SUPPORT

Made of foam rubber, it fits neatly around your baby, leaving your arms free for washing and playing.

CHANGING MAT

A waterproof wipe-clean changing mat is ideal for changing your baby on the floor or on a low flat surface. It's also comfortable for him to lie on and kick about without a nappy after his bath (provided the room is warm enough).

Bathtime accessories and toiletries

- Two-compartment bowl for 'topping and tailing', or two small plastic bowls.
- Soft sponge.
- Baby nail scissors or clippers.
- Soft hair brush and comb.
- For terry nappies – two buckets.
- Soft bath towel or towelling wrap with or without hood.
- Baby lotion.
- Baby wipes (for a quick clean-up).
- Zinc and castor oil cream (or a brand name baby cream to protect against nappy rash).
- Baby bath liquid (you don't need separate shampoo for a young baby).
- Cotton-wool.

BATHTIME SAFETY
- **Always check the water is the right temperature with your elbow before you put your baby in. It should feel pleasantly warm.**
- **Never leave your baby alone in the bath even for one second.**
- **When changing your baby on a raised surface, have everything to hand so you don't have to turn away even for a moment.**

128

Baby bath

Bath support

See Nappy Changing, pages 108-9 and Bathing Your Baby, pages 112-15

The well-dressed baby

Clothes can be practical and pretty but most of all they should be comfortable. As a rule of thumb, your newborn baby will need at least four changes of clothes every day at this stage. You don't have to have different clothes for day and night – but it's a good idea to get into the routine of giving your baby a bath or top and tail, then putting on a stretchsuit or nightie at bedtime.

CHOOSING CLOTHES

● Avoid tight necklines – most babies hate having clothes pulled over their heads. Envelope necks or clothes which do up down the front or back are best.
● Zips or front fastenings should be generous enough so you don't have to bend your baby's legs double to get them into the suit.
● Avoid frills around the neck – they get damp with dribbles and will make your baby's chin sore.
● Make sure the feet of all-in-one suits, socks and tights have enough room. If they're tight, you could damage your baby's feet.
● Avoid buckles and sharp fastenings.
● Soft, stretchy fabrics are comfortable to wear and easier to dry than denim, cord or other tough fabrics.

● Avoid open lacy-patterned cardigans and jumpers – little fingers can easily get caught in such patterns.
● Choose play and stretchsuits with fastenings down both legs, then you don't have to take the whole thing off every time you need to change a nappy.
● Choose clothes suitable for the time of year – warm, long-sleeved playsuits plus one or two outdoor pramsuits or snowsuits for winter; shortsleeved or sleeveless romper suits or dresses and a sunhat in summer.

Wash day wisdom

Every day is a wash day when you have a young baby!
● Whenever possible choose machine-washable clothes.
● If he has hand-knitted garments ask the maker to save a ball-band from the yarn because it will have the washing instructions on it.
● Put small machine-washable items, like socks, in a pillowcase so they don't get lost.
● Use a mild non-biological powder or liquid as baby's skin is very sensitive.
● To hand-wash delicates, use warm, soapy water. Rinse clothes thoroughly to remove all traces of soap then blot on a towel. Dry flat.

129

Imagine the time, effort and 'tlc' (tender loving care) that go into getting this lovely pair of five-month-old twins fed, washed, dressed and ready to go for an outing in their double pushchair.

THE CHILD HEALTH CLINIC

Whether you had your baby at home or in hospital, the community midwife will visit you for the first ten days after delivery. After that, responsibility for your baby is handed over to the health visitor based at your doctor's surgery or at the local child health clinic.

At the child health clinic, a number of health visitors will be available to check

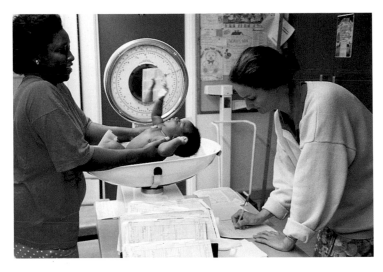

Child health clinic staff use their experience and skill to see how your baby is doing. They also provide a listening ear and give you any information you request.

your baby's progress, offer information and advice about any worries or problems you may have, and talk to you about how you are feeling. If there are any medical problems, a doctor there will look at the baby. It is also an important social centre where you may meet other mums and find out about local baby groups.

BABY'S SIX-WEEK CHECK

At around six to eight weeks, a doctor will examine your baby to check for any developmental problems. She will repeat some of the tests which were done in hospital, looking for major problems such as congenital dislocation of the hips, heart defects, breathing problems and undescended testes. She will also check the baby's reflexes and may ask you about any worries you may have.

Further developmental tests are done at around six to nine months when sight and hearing are usually tested, at eighteen to twenty-four months, at three to three-and-a-half years, and at school entry.

WEIGHT GAIN

Most health visitors encourage you to have your baby weighed regularly in the first few weeks and months, and to discuss any feeding problems. Don't worry too much about each week's weight gain; babies sometimes show a poor weight gain one week but compensate with a larger one the next. The health visitor will check that your baby's weight gain isn't straying too far above or below the average weight gain curve on the weight chart.

Your health visitor is well trained in different aspects of baby- and childcare and can advise you on breast- and bottlefeeding, weaning, sleep problems, colic and crying, and vitamin and fluoride supplements.

IMMUNIZATION

One of the most important things you can do for your baby is to ensure that you have her immunized against serious diseases. Not only are you protecting your own child, but also your next baby and other people's children who have not been or cannot be immunized.

Your baby should be immunized against serious diseases according to the timetable opposite. It is important that your baby has all the immunizations at the right time, otherwise she will not be properly protected. Just before your child starts school at between four and five years old she may need a booster.

The vaccines given are for polio (given as drops), diphtheria, whooping cough (pertussis) and tetanus, given in single injections as the 'triple vaccine', HiB (Haemophilus influenzae group B – which causes some strains of meningitis, croup and pneumonia), given as injections, and the combined mumps, measles and rubella vaccine (MMR), also given as an injection. BCG vaccination against tuberculosis (TB) is recommended for babies living in inner city areas where TB rates are rising. This is normally given when the baby is six weeks old. It is important to keep a record of the immunizations your baby has received.

YOUR SIX-WEEK CHECK

At six weeks after delivery you will also have a check-up, either back at the hospital or at your doctor's surgery. This is an opportunity to ask questions about anything that is worrying you. You will be weighed; by six weeks, you may be nearly back to your usual weight. Your urine will be tested to check that your kidneys are working properly and your blood pressure checked. If you had stitches they will be examined to make sure you have healed, and the doctor will feel your womb to see if it has returned to its normal size. A routine cervical smear will be taken, and if you have not been vaccinated for rubella (German measles) before, the injection can be given now to protect future babies, though it is essential that you don't get pregnant for three months after the injection.

CONTRACEPTION

Your doctor will ask about your plans for contraception. Many doctors believe it's safer not to have full sexual intercourse during the first six weeks after childbirth. After that, you will need to decide about contraception before you begin having full sex again.

Remember, you can get pregnant very soon after the baby is born, even if you have not yet had a period, and especially if you are not breastfeeding. Full breastfeeding – which means feeding frequently during the day, and at least every four hours at night, and giving the baby no other nourishment at all – *may* protect you from pregnancy. Some mothers do not have periods at all as long as they are breastfeeding and assume that they are unlikely to get pregnant, but this is not necessarily the case as they may ovulate before their first period. If you are anxious about getting pregnant again so soon, don't rely on breastfeeding and use another form of contraception as well.

The Pill

If you are bottlefeeding, you can take your usual contraceptive pill. If you are breastfeeding this may tend to reduce your milk supply, so the progestogen-only pill, which does not contain oestrogen, may be recommended instead.

IMMUNIZATION TIMETABLE		
Age	*Immunization*	*Method*
2 months	**Diphtheria** **Whooping cough** **Tetanus**	injection
	HiB	injection
	Polio	drops by mouth
3 months	**Diphtheria** **Whooping cough** **Tetanus**	injection
	HiB	injection
	Polio	drops by mouth
4 months	**Diphtheria** **Whooping cough** **Tetanus**	injection
	HiB	injection
	Polio	drops by mouth
12-18 months	**Measles** **Mumps** **Rubella**	injection
About 5 years	**Diphtheria** **Tetanus**	injection
	Polio	drops by mouth

The cap or diaphragm

This can be fitted six weeks after the baby is born, usually at your six-week check. The size you need may have changed after having a baby so don't use your old one.

The IUD, coil or loop

This plastic or copper device is placed inside the womb by a doctor and can be fitted six weeks after the baby is born.

The sheath or condom

This is a very good method after childbirth as it does not affect the mother's body.

Natural family planning

This can be used effectively after the birth of a baby, but as the menstrual cycle may not be back to normal you should seek advice and follow the instructions to the letter.

Sterilization

If you wish this to be your last baby, you or your partner might consider sterilization (tying the tubes or vasectomy).

WHY IS MY BABY CRYING?

All babies cry, but some cry more than others. Most mothers find that the sound of their baby crying arouses very powerful emotions such as protectiveness, pity, a desire to help – and it can be distressing if all their attempts to console him fail. It can also be very exhausting while it lasts but remember that it is his only means of communication and that from about three months the periods of crying will lessen as he becomes more aware and used to the world around him.

If your baby is crying the first thing that is likely to occur to you is that he is hungry, especially if it is some time since he has been fed. Feeding a baby will usually leave him contented or asleep, but not always. If he still doesn't settle, you may assume that he has wind and hold the baby upright over your shoulder, perhaps stroking or gently patting his back. If he brings up wind and still doesn't settle, and starts crying again, you may wonder what to try next.

HUNGER ISN'T THE ONLY REASON FOR CRYING

Many mothers, especially if they are breastfeeding and can't see how much milk the baby has taken, assume that their crying baby is still hungry. This isn't always the case. If your breastfed baby is gaining weight steadily, has plenty of wet nappies and is alert, hunger is unlikely to be a reason for constant or inconsolable crying.

If you are bottlefeeding, you may assume that the baby needs more feeds, but again, if his weight gain has been good, this may not be the reason. Remember that a bottlefed baby may just be thirsty and offer some cooled boiled water.

Your baby may also cry if he is too hot or too cold. Check his temperature by feeling his chest or the back of his neck. If it feels cold, take him into a warm room and put on some extra clothes. If the chest or back of his neck feel warm and slightly clammy then remove some items of clothing. Remember your baby's hands and feet are not a good guide to his temperature as they often feel quite cold.

Illness can also be a reason for crying especially if it is a different cry from normal, although often an ill baby is unusually sleepy, especially if he has a high temperature. A cold can stop your baby from feeding properly if his nose gets blocked. If you think this is a problem you should consult your doctor.

If you have gone through all the above possibilities and none seem to be the cause of your baby's crying then you must try and soothe him the best way you can. Most crying babies respond to being held, rocked, pushed in a pram or driven in a car. Babies

If your baby won't settle, try putting him in a sling – he may find being so close to you very soothing – and you may do too.

usually like sound and movement more than lying still in a motionless crib in a silent room.

You can try the following:

Massaging: this is a relaxing way to soothe and comfort your baby.

Rocking: a rocking cradle is a time-honoured way of soothing a baby to sleep. If you don't have a cradle, you can try rocking the baby in a pram.

Walking: if you carry the baby and walk up and down, the rhythm will usually soothe the baby. Holding the baby close to you, for example in a sling, also helps.

Noise: babies often settle better in an environment where there is background noise rather than in a quiet room. The sound of human conversation, a vacuum cleaner

CRYING OR COLIC?

Colic is a much-misunderstood word. Some babies may suffer from pains in the gut after a feed and this may cause some crying. But persistent crying after a feed, especially in the evenings, has never been proved after medical investigation to be caused by wind trapped in the gut or by digestive problems.

In cultures where a baby is permanently carried round by the mother, grandmother and other carers and is fed on demand, colic does not seem to exist. Unfortunately many mothers in our society are alone with their babies for most of the time so this is difficult. Some babies need very much less sleep than others, and these babies cry if put down when not sleepy.

Life may feel brighter for a 'colicky' baby when you hold her upright, or you could try massaging her tummy in wide, gentle, smooth, slow, rhythmical clockwise circles to help her relax.

or washing machine, or a special soothing baby tape or singing a lullaby can work wonders.

Sucking: it may help to soothe your baby to sleep if he is allowed to suck at the breast at the end of a feed or to suck a dummy.

Sometimes trying one thing after another can keep the baby awake. If all else fails, and you're hot and bothered, and at the end of your tether, ask someone else to try to soothe the baby. Letting him cry for ten or fifteen minutes will not harm him and he may cry himself to sleep.

If you have a baby who cries a lot, don't think it's because you're doing something wrong; it's more likely that you've just got one of those babies. Take heart from the fact that many crying or colicky babies are over the worst by three months. In the meantime, take up any offers of help and try to ensure that you get as much rest as possible, especially if you are woken a lot in the night. If your baby's excessive crying is making you desperate, then seek help from a doctor, health visitor, breastfeeding counsellor or mother's support group.

GROWING AND LEARNING

After all those months of waiting, your baby is finally here. She may not be quite what you expected. The damp little yelling bundle lying on your tummy can seem far removed from the rosy-cheeked baby which you fondly pictured during pregnancy. And what a funny little wrinkled old man's face . . . But don't be fooled. Inside that strange little wrinkly head which flops against your shoulder, she's already an individual. Just look at her eyes, which might already be focusing on you if you hold her close enough. She's probably wondering what on earth is going on after being safely cocooned for nine months. Imagine how you would feel if someone suddenly plonked you down on an alien planet.

Trying to understand how your baby feels can help if you're feeling frustrated because she won't stop crying. It's soothing to remember that each baby has her own character and personality, just as you are different from your next-door neighbour or the mother in the hospital bed next to you. And because she has her own personality, your baby will grow and learn in a different way from other new babies. In fact, right from birth, your baby will develop and change in appearance dramatically fast. You may not notice it, from day to day. But when you look back at early photographs, you'll be amazed by the difference even after only a few months.

SIZE, WEIGHT AND SHAPE

One of the first questions people ask new parents is 'How much did your baby weigh?' It's amazing how worrying this can seem, especially if your baby is smaller (or larger) than other babies you know of a similar age. But average full-term, healthy babies weigh anything between 2250-4050g (5-9lb). Your midwife (and later, the health visitor) will weigh your baby regularly and monitor her growth (see The Child Health Clinic, page 130).

Many new mothers are surprised by the shape of their baby's head. If it seems rather squashed and oval-shaped at birth, don't panic. Think how squashed you would look if you'd had to squeeze through a small tight tunnel.

YOUR CHILD'S PHYSICAL PROGRESS

You may be surprised by how quickly your newborn baby develops and grows — it won't be many months before she'll be able to twist sideways on her back to reach out for something, or sit up supported by cushions.

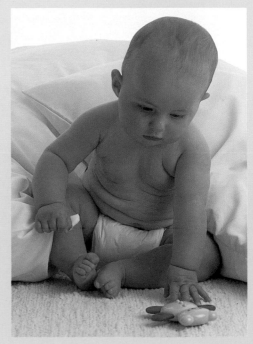

USING HER BODY

Even a tiny baby can be surprisingly strong. Put your finger in her hand and feel how tightly she can grip you. This is called a reflex action. At this age, babies can't decide for themselves whether to stretch out their left or right leg or arm. Instead, nature gives babies reflex actions over which they have little control. Indeed, you might find your baby has trouble letting go once she has something in her grip so you have to gently ease off her fingers.

Other reflex actions include 'stepping' automatically. If you trail a baby's feet over a flat surface, she will probably start to put one foot in front of the other as though she's walking. And if a loud noise startles your baby (like the doorbell or someone shouting suddenly), she may throw back her arms as though she's falling. This is known as the 'Moro' reflex.

During the first few weeks, a baby's head seems strangely floppy. She can't yet hold it up on her own so she relies on you to support it when you're carrying her around or holding her. By three weeks you'll notice her head getting stronger. You will find that when she's 'playing' on her stomach, she can automatically turn her head to the side. By about three months, your baby may be lifting her head and looking around, doing what look like mini press-ups. Encourage this by squatting in front of her and dangling or squeaking an interesting toy.

Your baby's body will gradually 'straighten out'. After birth, it's natural for her to look rather curled up, in something resembling the fetal position (the position she lay in while inside you). Then, over the first few weeks, she will gradually begin to straighten out.

Around four or five months, your baby will probably surprise you by rolling over – from her back to her front. You can encourage this through play. Smile and clap when she rolls as the action might amaze her and she may need reassurance.

This is a really exciting time for your baby. Every day she is learning to do more. At around four months you can try propping her up in a sitting position against a big cushion (on the floor in case she falls) or the bottom of a sofa. She may look rather hunched up and uncomfortable at first, but slowly, between about six and ten months, she will be strong enough to sit more independently.

When this baby holds his head steady while he pushes up with his arms, he not only strengthens his muscles but also has a better view of what's going on.

GROWING AND LEARNING

Your baby loves looking at your face and listening to you talking sweet nothings. Before long he'll start making conversation by cooing and gurgling when it's his turn to talk, then quietly listening when it's yours.

SEEING, TOUCHING AND HOLDING

Imagine you have just woken up and have something in your eye. Everything seems blurred and out of focus. That's how your baby sees things at the other end of the room in the first few weeks after birth. Close-up objects are a different matter. Hold your face close to hers from birth onwards and talk to her. She will soon focus on your face and get to know your facial features, as well as learn to recognize that your voice goes with your face.

By about six weeks, your baby's eyes may follow a brightly coloured moving toy. Lights and patterns are equally enticing to her.

Amuse your baby by:
● Pointing out birds/traffic/planes during pushchair walks.
● Putting a coloured low wattage light bulb in your baby's room for her to focus on.
● Propping up a baby mirror next to her.

Just as your baby wants to look around her, so she naturally wants to touch what she sees. Babies follow a distinctive pattern of hand development. In the early weeks, her hand is often tightly closed like a fist.

Gradually, she will open her fingers and bring her hands together in front of her.

You can encourage this hand development by:
● Holding out a toy to her and seeing if she'll try to grasp it.
● Playing finger-games by holding out your own finger and pulling it away.

Before long your baby will try to pick up a toy from the floor and bring it towards her mouth. At first, it will be easier for her to pick it up rather than let go. And she'll use her left hand as much as her right (until around the age of three).

GURGLES, COOS AND SQUEALS

By around three months, your baby will turn towards you when she hears your voice. She will also start to make all sorts of different noises.

Encourage your baby to talk by:
● Repeating the same coos or noises back. It soon becomes a game.
● Play music. Even little babies like this and learn to recognize favourite tunes.

Smiles are another breakthrough. You can expect your first real smile at around about six to eight weeks, although many babies smile earlier than this. Encourage your baby to smile by frequently smiling at her. It's a good habit to get into and makes you both feel better on a bad day.

Treat crying as one of your baby's methods of communication. You'll find it less annoying if you imagine yourself going around with a gag on. You simply *have* to tell someone that you're thirsty or hungry and crying might be the only way of attracting attention. Listen to those cries carefully. You may be able to pick up the message behind them. Some babies have different cries for different needs and only you may be able to distinguish one sort of crying from another. There will be tired cries that say, 'I want to be rocked to sleep,' or angry cries that say, 'I'm starving.' It can be like deciphering a code and you will soon become adept at understanding it. Interestingly, real tears don't usually trickle out until a baby is four months or so.

YOU – THE CENTRE OF HER WORLD

This is both wonderful and – let's not be afraid of saying it – a huge responsibility which can be daunting. You are her entire world. You pick up your baby when she cries, change her when she's wet and feed her when she's hungry. And as your baby grows older, she needs you as much as ever.

By around three months – probably earlier – she'll be recognizing your face and may cry when a stranger suddenly looms over her in admiration.

Not all babies will be doing this . . .

If your baby was born prematurely, you'll probably find that it takes time before she can do the same things as other children of her age. Your year-old baby, for example, might not be crawling if she was born early. Don't worry. Most health visitors assess a pre-term child's development from the time she *should* have been born.

Some babies are born handicapped. This can be a difficult time for you but there are organizations that can help (see Useful Addresses, page 314).

WHAT YOUR BABY MAY DO BY SIX MONTHS:
- Support her own head.
- Roll from front to back.
- Sit up with support.
- Reach out for interesting objects. Clutch a toy and pass it from one hand to another.
- Smile and make different noises.
- Recognize different faces.

GROWING AND LEARNING

You know you're in control but for your baby lively play has an exciting whiff of danger which can be great fun. She will soon let you know whether she's happy and wants more or whether enough's enough.

PLAY AND TOYS

SAFE TOYS
- **Soft toys should *be* soft. Tug eyes and limbs to check they are secured properly. Avoid glued-on features that may come off in your baby's mouth.**
- **Avoid toys with small parts which may get stuck in your baby's nose, ears or mouth.**
- **Check that any moving parts could not trap tiny fingers.**
- **Paint or other materials should be non-toxic.**
- **All edges should be smooth and rounded. Run your fingers over them to check for any sharp bits.**
- **Check any fabric is colour-fast and non-flammable.**

Every day of your baby's life is a voyage of discovery, adventure and play. As he grows, he'll explore everything using his five senses – touch, taste, smell, sound and sight. The right toys can perform an important role in his development but remember you are the one that can make his playing – and his learning – fun. You are your newborn baby's best toy. He'll love being carried around by you and hearing your voice.

YOUR ROLE

All your communication with your baby at this stage is, in a way, play. You'll talk to him, tickle his tummy, cuddle him and smile at him. Most of the time he will respond with smiles, chuckles, wriggles and gurgles, and both of you will love it.

Bathing and changing your baby, provide ideal opportunities for you to play with your baby and for him to experience new sensations. After the first few baths, which can be rather frightening for a newborn baby and for new parents, most babies enjoy the feel of the warm water against their bodies and will begin to kick around with their legs. Let your baby lie on the changing mat, too, without any clothes or a nappy on: he will appreciate the freedom to move his arms and legs around without any

restrictions. Try holding your hands against his feet and see if he pushes against them. It may surprise you to feel just how strong your baby is getting.

TOYS AND YOU

Bright colours – especially reds and greens – will attract your baby's attention. He won't be able to select or hold his toys at first but that doesn't mean he's not interested in them. This is where you come in. Show him what his toys can do. Shake the rattle, squeeze the squeaker or pat the plastic toys strung across his bouncing cradle or pram so he can see what happens. He will endeavour to copy you and it won't be long before he can bash the toys within his reach and gurgle with delight if they make a noise or move about.

Hold a toy mirror in front of his face or let him see himself in a mirror on the wall. He'll be fascinated by his reflection.

CHOOSING SAFE TOYS

You can tell an older child how to avoid dangers – like not putting beads in his mouth because he might swallow them. But your baby's safety is in your hands entirely. He hasn't the faintest idea what is dangerous or potentially harmful.

A play gym with plenty of interesting things to look at, touch, move and hear, means your baby can practise his arm, hand and finger co-ordination skills and lying down isn't boring.

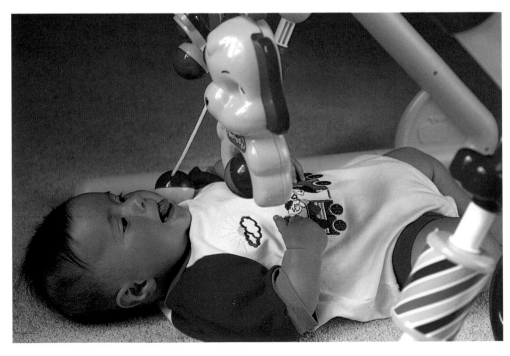

It won't be long before whatever your baby is examining goes into her mouth so she can explore its taste, texture and shape with her tongue as well as with her fingers.

TIME TO PLAY

It's hard to believe a tiny baby can make so much work. But don't be a slave to the chores. You don't have to prove you're a good mother by keeping everything ship-shape all the time. Your baby is an important person who needs you as his playmate as well as teacher.

Organize your day

The best plan is to decide when you get up what are the essential jobs and get them done while your baby is sleeping (but make sure you get enough rest too). Then, when he's awake and contented, you can have some fun together. Show him how his rattle works or pat his soft ball to and fro.

SMILE AND CHAT

You've probably thought other people look really daft when they coo and talk to a baby in a silly voice with their face right up close to him. But you'll find yourself doing it as soon as your baby is born and it's the most natural thing in the world. Your baby can focus on your face much more easily if it's close up. And as you smile and chat he'll soon begin to respond with delighted squeals and gestures of his own. Your first 'conversation' is the beginning of learning through play and is an immensely rewarding experience.

Obviously you can't spend every minute of his waking time actually playing with him, but while you're pottering around, talk to him. He won't care what you say – he'll just love hearing your voice and you'll enjoy his company too.

SONGS AND GAMES

The first parts of his body your baby will discover are his hands and feet. You can sing the nursery rhymes you remember from your childhood like 'This Little Piggy', tickling each toe one after the other, or 'Round and Round the Garden', stroking his hand, but there's nothing to stop you being more original. Make up your own songs to your favourite tunes while kissing his hands or gently pretending to nibble his toes. For example, 'ten tiny fingers, ten tiny toes. I can kiss those fingers and gobble up those toes!' Singing lullabies is still one of the best ways of calming a baby down and soothing him to sleep. Good old favourites like 'Bye Baby Bunting' or 'Rock-a-Bye Baby' should do the trick. But, again, singing softly to him your own song, which includes his name and how much you love him, will give you as well as him infinite pleasure. A nightlight with a built-in musical box can help to lull your baby to sleep once you've put him down – but it shouldn't be used instead of cuddling and singing to him.

FIRST TOYS
First toys should have some – or all – of the following qualities:
● **Be colourful.**
● **Feel soft or smooth to the touch.**
● **Be easy for a baby to hold.**
● **Make a noise.**
● **Move when he touches them.**

DANCE AND RHYTHM

Babies instinctively respond to sound and rhythm but it's a response that needs developing. From the word go you'll sway or bounce gently when you're cuddling him and this can be turned into a pleasurable game for you both. Start singing or put on the radio, a CD or tape and dance to the rhythm with him held securely in your arms.

MUSIC AND MOVEMENT EXERCISES

Try the following exercises and see if your baby likes them. You can lay your baby on the floor to do them rather than on your lap, if you prefer.

1. Lay your baby on your lap. While singing, counting or listening to music, let him grip your thumbs while you gently stretch his arms out to the sides, then down on his chest, then up above his head. Smile and look at him all the time.

2. Lay your baby on your lap. Hold his feet and gently rotate his legs in a cycling movement first one way a few times, then the other. Sing an appropriate song like 'The Pushbike Song' or 'Daisy, Daisy'.

Old wives' tales

Some people will tell you that you'll spoil your baby if you keep picking him up and cuddling him. This is rubbish.

Dancing raises the levels of endorphins or 'feel-good' chemicals in the bloodstream, and the pleasure you get from moving to music adds to your baby's own natural enjoyment of sound and rhythm.

PLAY SAFE

A young baby can often be overwhelmed by the generous attentions of an older brother or sister. He is likely to be hauled out of his pram the minute he squeaks or have the family pet dumped on top of him for a 'cuddle'. He's also likely to be showered with toys that are perfectly safe for an older child, but potentially lethal to him so you will need to be on your guard at all times.

Explain to your older child that the baby can't play with big children's toys yet so he must not be given:

● Anything small he can put in his mouth like a hard sweet or bead. Even quite large objects like pen tops or small building bricks can get stuck in a baby's throat if he's lying down.

● Anything sharp or pointed that he could cut himself on or jab in his eye.

● Heavy objects that he could hit himself on the head with.

● Anything with long strings or ribbons – he could get tangled up in them and strangle himself.

● The family pet – even the smallest fluffy kitten – could suffocate him if it lay on his face, and all pets carry germs.

If your older child is playing in a paddling pool make sure he doesn't try and drag the baby in with him.

TOYS FOR YOUR YOUNG BABY

WHEN your baby: can focus and follow movement and respond to sounds.	**WHEN your baby:** can grip your finger so he can hold on to an object.	**WHEN your baby:** starts to gnaw or suck his fists.	**WHEN your baby:** is happy to lie on a mat or sit supported; can wave his arms about.
WHAT he will enjoy: mobiles, musical boxes, moving lights, chiming balls etc.	**WHAT he will enjoy:** rattles with easy-to-hold handles, little soft toys, blocks or balls – especially if they make a sound when shaken.	**WHAT he will enjoy:** soft rubber squeaky toys, teething rings, smooth, hard plastic baby toys which are easy to hold.	**WHAT he will enjoy:** baby gym, a string of toys that spin or rattle within his reach. Soft toys or small ones which make a noise.
WHY he needs them: to stimulate and/or soothe him, to attract and hold his attention, to encourage him to use his eyes and ears.	**WHY he needs them:** to encourage him to use his eyes and hands at the same time to study his toys and feel their texture. To develop his co-ordination – the ability to turn the toys in his hands and to drop and (later) pick them up again.	**WHY he needs them:** to help him discover his toys by their taste and texture. To develop holding and chewing skills which he will need later when he starts to feed himself. To ease his gums while he's teething.	**WHY he needs them:** to encourage him to stretch out his arms and hands and grasp objects within his reach. To help him discover that when he touches something it moves and/or makes a noise (and the harder he hits it the more it responds). To learn how to pull and push.

THE
OLDER BABY

6-12 months

Never again will your
baby make so many
changes so quickly as she
grows and develops at
a record rate. This is the
time when she learns to
sit up and perhaps stand
as well. A few babies take
their first hesitant steps.
She wants to try new tastes
– and she'll want to feed
herself too.

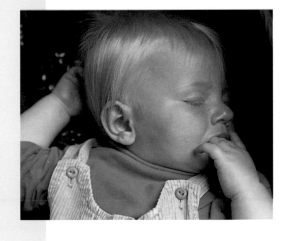

A very important member of the family, she notices everything
and knows how to make her presence felt. Her early practice sounds
of ma-ma, ba-ba and da-da become increasingly noisy until one day
when she begins to realize that her sounds have meaning, and da-da
becomes Da-da, and ma-ma, Ma-ma. She loves to play and chuckles
with delight over hide-and-seek games, wanting them again and
again until she's had her fill.

YOU *AND* YOUR OLDER BABY

Your baby has come a long way in the last few months. Just remember how she was in the earliest days and consider the progress. Your little one is longer, twice as heavy and may even be able to sit up. She probably makes lots of experimental sounds and is fascinated by everything you do and say. Her sleep-wake pattern is changing and the dietary revolution from milk to milk-plus-other-foods may already have begun.

Now think of what's happened for you since you gave birth. You've had to trust your instincts and you've cared for your baby through the early months of extraordinarily rapid growth. Never again will it be so fast – and never again will you put so much time and effort into providing feeds twenty-four hours round the clock.

There will be many more momentous developments for you both before the first birthday. Your baby has to learn to sit steadily without tipping and wobbling every which way. The next stage is the colossal one of becoming mobile. Slowly and with many

setbacks your baby discovers the exhilarating independence of moving from one place to another, whether by crawling, bottom-shuffling forwards or sideways like a crab, or walking like a bear on hands and feet. Some babies pull themselves up into a standing position and a few even start walking before they are a year old.

Nothing is safe from being handled, inspected, mouthed, chewed and tasted. Older babies are pioneers and investigators, fascinated by everything and wanting to find out what things are, how they feel, taste and smell, what they sound like and what they do. They have no preconceived ideas but great interest and magnificent powers of concentration. Your baby probably takes great delight in doing the same thing over and over again. Watch what happens when she pushes a brick or a spoon from the highchair tray to the floor. After her initial surprise as it vanishes, she does it again as soon as you've picked it up. You can keep her amused for a long time with hide-and-seek

The first summer brings a feast of pleasure – like the freedom to sit and play on the grass and enjoy the warmth of the sun and the delight of bare feet.

games involving losing and finding. This is all part of her coming to realize that things and people are still there even when she can't see them.

Indeed, knowing you'll come back may remove some of her anxiety when you leave her, but won't prevent many babies being upset to see their mothers disappear, even if they are left with someone well-known. You can't explain when you'll be back to your baby and the only way she can let you know that you're the one she wants is to cry.

Emotions often run high when you have a baby. There are those heart-stopping moments of pleasure as you look into your baby's adoring eyes, watch those huge smiles, or simply give thanks for the privilege of being able to care for her. There are also feelings of huge relief when you get away from parenting for a while and have a chance to be unencumbered by a baby who needs so much attention. Then there are more difficult emotions. There may be painful feelings of guilt and anguish over leaving your baby with someone else, especially if she makes a fuss when you leave. Being a parent has great rewards but isn't always comfortable.

Thinking about your baby's eating habits brings you down to earth. Babies are as individual in their likes, dislikes and the amount of food they want as older children and adults. You'll soon be expert at knowing what to offer your baby, or she may beat you to it by taking food directly from your plate or hands. Don't worry how much she eats because breast milk (or milk formula) continues to provide much nourishment. What's important is to let her become used to tasting and enjoying other foods so they gradually become an increasingly important source of nutrients. Carry on adapting to your baby's pace as she grows and learns at her own individual rate, ready for the hurly-burly and excitement of being a toddler.

DR PENNY STANWAY

OUR CHILDREN

Penny Stanway: 'It was a strange feeling to have a baby old enough to crawl away and then climb back on my lap for a breastfeed, but two of mine did that and it was a wonderful way of calming them if they were upset.'

Daphne Metland: 'You have to learn to trust your instincts. Sam did everything early, crawled, walked, talked and hardly ever slept. Caity was much more self-contained and took her time about things. I came to realize it would have been just as wrong to hold Sam back as it would have been to push Caity.'

Gillian Fletcher: 'I played tennis regularly with a friend who had a baby the same age as Richard, until one very cold morning both boys sat in their pushchairs and grizzled and complained all through our game. We decided we would have to find other ways of exercising until they were older. Now, twelve years on, both boys are keen tennis players and we can enjoy a good game together. I am very relieved to know that those early memories did not in any way put them off the game.'

Heather Welford: 'I found it easiest to abandon spoonfeeding as soon as I could, and just offer finger foods. I reckon babies prefer feeding themselves, given the chance – it's all so interesting for them.'

Maggie Jones: 'My first child had absolutely no sense of self-preservation at all at this age so the house had to be made completely toddler-proof. He crawled before he sat so missed out on the wonderful stage when you can sit the baby amid a heap of toys and know he will be quite safe.'

Carolyn Humphries: 'Katie and James both loved a wobble globe with a rubber-suction base. They would unscrew it and gnaw the rubber (it tasted horrid), use it as a bath toy filled with water, and bash it mercilessly on the highchair as a distraction when lunch was getting boring.'

Jane Bidder: 'My first child William did everything by the book: including crawling very early. But my daughter Lucy couldn't seem to master the knack. Instead, she preferred to sit on her bottom and push herself along with both hands. My mother was enchanted: she'd been a "bottom shuffler" herself.'

145

FEEDING YOUR BABY

Babies of six months old vary greatly from baby to baby in what they eat. Some are still on milk (breast or formula) only, with little or no experience of other foods. Others may be taking smooth fruit purées while some will have been on three hearty meals a day, plus milk, plus snacks, for several weeks.

It's now, though, that the majority of babies progress to a mixed diet, that is a diet based on a mixture of solid foods plus milk. Your baby's reliance on milk decreases over the second half of the first year. This is simply because a widening variety of other foods leaves less room for it, in terms of calories, but it is still an important part of his diet and a source of great comfort.

You'll share many peaceful, precious times of intimacy and delight when your baby relaxes and snuggles into your breast, then reaches up to explore your face and give you an adoring smile.

A VARIETY OF TASTES

Now that your baby is over six months, you can offer him a growing range of solid foods including protein foods such as eggs, pasteurized hard cheeses, chicken, fish, beans and peas. It's sensible to continue introducing lumps and soft, chewy vegetables and fruit. Beans and peas, possibly difficult for a very young baby to digest, should be well tolerated now. Go cautiously with very fatty foods (such as bacon, or the fat on meat) until your baby is a little older.

SPECIAL NEEDS

A few babies are intolerant of or allergic to certain foods and may need to avoid some items. For instance, babies with coeliac disease must avoid cereals containing gluten, including wheat, which is found in bread, breakfast cereals and rusks. Don't make this sort of diagnosis yourself. You need the support of an expert before you start altering your baby's food intake. This is to make sure your baby doesn't miss out on the calories and nutrients he needs to grow, especially when he reaches toddlerhood and will be taking fewer calories from milk.

If you suspect that your baby reacts to a food, or a group of foods, ask your doctor to refer your baby to a paediatrician. From there, if necessary, you'll be referred to a community dietitian once a diagnosis has been made.

If you are vegetarian, you may wish your baby to be so, too. This shouldn't cause any problems, because the nutrients present in meat are also available in other foods. As he grows older, your baby will need grains, pulses, eggs, cheese, milk and green vegetables, to obtain the protein and the iron which he would otherwise get from meat and fish.

A vegan diet omits all animal products. This means that babies, toddlers and children on vegan diets could miss out on certain vitamins, as well as the protein they need to grow, though careful combination of grains, pulses and vegetables can supply everything that's needed. If you want your child to follow a vegan diet, it's sensible to continue breastfeeding for as long as possible and to take expert advice on any necessary supplements, for example of vitamin B12.

EATING PATTERNS

Most parents find it easiest to adjust their baby's eating times to fit in with the rest of the family when they can, though this isn't always possible, or you may prefer to do things differently.

It may suit you best, for instance, to give a breast- or bottlefeed or cup of milk when your baby wakes, and a 'good breakfast' when the workers or scholars of the house have left you in some peace. However, that early morning milk feed may have taken place at 6am and, if he doesn't go back to sleep again, he won't be able to wait until around 9am for breakfast. You'll therefore have to feed him earlier at around 7.30 or 8am with the other members of the family.

Lunch can be at whatever time suits you and your baby – and that could change through these six months. A baby who drops off to sleep at midday may need his lunch at 11.30am in order to avoid having it at 2.30 or even 3pm when he wakes – which may not fit in with your afternoon plans. Similarly, teatime will change. Tea is likely to be easier before the bathtime/bedtime events. But a baby who's had lunch at 11.30am will be ravenous by 4pm . . . maybe three hours before you'd expect to start getting him ready for bed.

For a while you will find you have to fit in with these needs, but you can gradually adjust the times of meals by offering healthy snacks and drinks (see page 148) to keep your baby going until a time you find convenient.

FAMILY MEALS

Try to have at least the occasional meal, even during these transitional days, when all your household (even if there are only two or three of you) actually eat together. Making mealtimes sociable, friendly occasions is good for both you and your baby. He will enjoy watching other people eat and will probably eat more as a result.

147

COMFORT FEEDS

Babies of a year and older may still enjoy sucking on a bottle for comfort. This has several disadvantages. It's possible that a baby who has several bottles of milk a day at a year old may be filling up with milk at the expense of a wider variety of nutrients. Just as importantly, dentists are concerned that the 'all-day' bottle can affect the teeth (see page 148). Try to offer your baby a cup at every mealtime. Keep bottles to waking and going to sleep, and don't let your sleeping baby keep a bottle tilted into his mouth.

Breastfeeds can be comfort feeds, too, at this age. If you want to decrease your baby's dependency on you for comfort, you can try offering a cup before you think your baby may ask for a breastfeed. Eventually, so long as you are consistent, your baby will know only to expect a breastfeed at certain times.

Your baby will relish a lovely long drink of warm milk in your arms when she's worn herself out and simply wants to drift off slowly to sleep.

See Sleep and Bedtime, page 159, for night feeds

FEEDING YOUR BABY

HEALTHY EATING

Like everyone else, babies thrive on good food. This means the best food for your baby is fresh and wholesome, with few artificial additives and little added sugar. This is a good time to help your baby learn to enjoy a wide range of foods and a variety of different tastes – although you shouldn't worry if he seems cautious and uninterested at first.

As he grows, your baby will need protein (found in beans, peas, fish, meat, cheese, milk, eggs, cereals), carbohydrates (in rice, pasta, cereals, bread, potatoes), fats, vitamins and minerals. It's actually quite difficult for a baby of this age who's drinking milk and being given even a small variety of food to suffer from any real deprivation.

TOOTH DECAY

Protect your baby's teeth by avoiding giving too much added sugar, which is present in many foods. If your baby does have sugary foods, keep them to mealtimes only. That way the mouth's own defences against decay can take effect. You can offer between-meal snacks, of course, but make sure they are low in sugar or without any added sugar at all. Babies enjoy small pieces of fruit or peeled, washed vegetable sticks to chew.

Dilute fruit juice with water. Offer juice in a cup, not a bottle, unless you only ever offer the bottle at a mealtime. There is a risk of tooth decay when a baby sits or lies for a long time with a bottle of juice (or even milk), as this allows the teeth to be bathed in a sugary, sticky fluid.

148

Your baby will thoroughly enjoy the independence of using a trainer cup with handles and spout, but choose the drink carefully so those perfect new teeth aren't constantly bathed in sugar.

The risk of severe dietary deficiency in older babies comes from under-eating. Healthy, happy babies don't under-eat, even if they're a bit fussy and appear to eat less than the baby next door. However, a baby can become short of nutrients if he relies on one or two foods only (although this is more likely to occur in toddlerhood), as this can mean he isn't getting a balanced diet.

Your health visitor can help you decide if your baby is eating well, and eating enough. Looking at your baby, weighing him to check he's growing and developing as he should, and talking with you will probably be enough for your health visitor to reassure you.

PROTECTING YOUR BABY'S TEETH

- Keep sugary foods to a minimum, especially between meals.
- Encourage a liking for fresh fruit and vegetables and other sugar-free items as between-meal snacks.
- Offer fruit juice in a cup rather than in a bottle.
- Don't get into an 'all-day bottle' habit.
- Offer your baby sticks of vegetables to chew.
- Clean your baby's teeth at the beginning and end of each day with only a tiny blob of toothpaste.
- Ask your dentist about fluoride drops.
- Read the labels of bought foods to check if they contain added sugar.

See Nappy Changing and Bathing, page 155, for more information on teeth

PREPARING YOUR OWN BABY FOOD

It's not hard to make your own food for your baby – and it's a lot cheaper than relying on dried or canned food. Don't imagine you have to do anything particularly fiddly or time-consuming. It's true that young babies eat small quantities at a time, especially at first. But even if you're making something for your baby alone, it makes sense to prepare a larger amount in one go, and put the remainder in the fridge or the freezer.

Don't:

- Think you have to reduce everything to a purée. You can sieve or blend some foods if you want to, but total smoothness isn't necessary, even for young babies. Mashing or chopping is often enough.
- Add any salt or sugar. Babies often prefer bland flavours at this stage.
- Mix more than one flavour together at first. Build up blends of taste gradually.
- Forget that babies able to hold objects and direct them to their mouths can start to feed themselves with 'finger foods'. It's a good idea to encourage.

HYGIENE

The usual kitchen hygiene rules apply when you're preparing food for your baby – young babies' immune systems are not fully developed for some time, and they are more likely to succumb to infections. The

'Mirror, mirror, on the wall . . .'. But who cares what you look like when you're a budding gourmet savouring the smells, tastes, textures and mouth appeal of new foods?

rules are even more important if your baby is bottlefed. He won't get the antibodies and resistance to infection he would from breast milk, so you need to be even more meticulous.

Wash your hands before handling food, and make sure any utensil you use or surface you work on is clean. Sterilization is not necessary, although you should still sterilize your baby's bottles (see How to sterilize bottlefeeding equipment, page 101). Use a chopping board you can wash thoroughly (wooden chopping boards are not suitable for preparing baby food) and keep leftovers covered and in the fridge.

QUICK AND EASY FOODS YOU CAN GIVE YOUR BABY

- Mashed potato, sprinkled with grated cheese.
- Soft dessert pear, peeled and mashed.
- Banana, mixed with unsweetened desiccated coconut.
- Grated apple, peeled, with whole-milk yogurt.
- Grated carrot mixed with mashed potato.
- Home-made rusk (wholemeal bread fingers, hardened in a slow oven).
- Squares of thinly sliced soft bread, with soft cheese spread.
- Pasta shapes with cheese sauce.

- Mashed turnip or swede, with cheese on the top (melt the cheese under a medium-hot grill).
- Chopped satsuma pieces with whole-milk yogurt.
- Finely chopped pieces of cooked chicken mixed with a little cooked tomato, chopped.
- Soft dessert pear mixed with oatmeal and softened with milk (expressed breast milk, baby's usual formula, or cow's milk for babies over six months).
- Finely chopped white fish – make sure there are no bones.

See Healthy Eating, page 40, for more information on food hygiene

PREPARING FOOD FOR THE FREEZER

1. Wash and peel a couple of medium potatoes and a large carrot. Cook together until soft. Drain, then chop and mash with a little knob of butter and/or some milk (see page 153).

2. Alternatively, if you prefer, you can purée the vegetables once they are cooked and soft enough, using a food mouli, blender or sieve. Add a little butter and/or milk as before.

3. Spoon out the mixture into three well-washed containers. Yogurt pots, margarine tubs or any other freezable containers are fine.

Note: Put lids on the containers or cover with cling film. Label with the use-by date, which is three months on. Although safe, the food will start to lose nutrients and be lower in quality after this time. Put in the freezer.

The quantities given here will make approximately three meals for a six-month-old baby. To make larger quantities you could add another vegetable such as parsnip or swede.

When you serve the meal, heat it through, and vary the topping, or combine with other foods. Grated cheese, hard-boiled egg yolk or breadcrumbs can be added for variations.

Tips
● Freeze food in small amounts (use empty yogurt pots or ice-cube trays for even smaller quantities). This avoids defrosting more than you need and takes less time to defrost.
● When warming a previously cooked meal from the fridge or freezer, make sure you heat it thoroughly. Take it up to boiling point, let it cool and serve as soon as it is cool enough for your baby.
● You can use a microwave for heating up your baby's food (not recommended for bottles, however, see page 102). Make sure you give the food a good stir to even out the temperature, or you may risk 'hot spots' scalding your baby's mouth.

● Baby rice is very handy as a thickener for other foods, though you can serve it on its own, too, mixed with water or some appropriate milk (see page 104).
● An alternative cereal for young babies is oatmeal. Make your own finely ground oatmeal by putting some cooked rolled oats through a food processor.

'I know you're supposed to expect a lot of mess, but I've found it quite difficult to cope with and I've had to develop ways of making it easier for myself. I put James in a bib with sleeves and I put a big sheet of plastic under his highchair.'

OPPOSITE *Grated cheese tastes very moreish and your baby will have wonderful fun picking up those curly yellow shavings and stuffing them in. You also know they contain calcium-rich goodness.*

Give your baby a piece of bread to hold and gnaw as a quick and easy way of allaying hunger pangs when it's time for a snack. Chewing may help to soothe sore, itchy teething gums too.

52

WHEN YOUR BABY CAN FEED HIMSELF

Throughout these second six months, your baby will become more and more adept at feeding himself. He won't be proficient with a spoon yet, but his co-ordination, curiosity and dexterity will develop rapidly. This means that by the age of eleven to twelve months, he'll be able to pick up even tiny pieces of food – like a single pea – and pop them in his mouth. Such achievements will probably delight your baby as much as they will you.

It may seem at times that your baby is 'just playing' with his food – but that play is very important. He's learning to relate the texture of the food in his hands to the texture of it in his mouth. He's learning that the way things look and feel is sometimes reflected in the way they taste – and sometimes not. Of course you won't want him to throw his food around, or tip his bowl of pasta and tomato sauce up over his head, or sprinkle his juice around like salt and pepper. But he's bound to do these things sometimes as it will be great fun as far as he is concerned. Firmly, but gently, discourage him and let him play with food that's not quite so messy instead, such as toast or a finger of carrot.

COMMERCIAL FOODS

As we have seen (see page 105), there are many proprietary baby foods available, and you may find them useful for your older baby, especially as a standby when you're out and about, in other people's houses or if you're eating in a restaurant.

Keep aiming to offer your baby home-cooked or freshly prepared food when you can, however. Commercially prepared puddings may be high in added sugar, for example. A piece of fruit makes a far healthier, cheaper and easier dessert than a 'chocolate delight' – and as your baby becomes more expert at feeding himself, you'll find chopping up fruit for him to hold and eat without help is easier than opening a jar and spooning it into a bowl for you to spoonfeed him.

A few bought baby foods are well worth considering as an alternative to their 'adult' equivalents, however. Baby yogurt, for example, is based on whole milk, whereas many 'adult' yogurts are based on skimmed milk, which has fewer vitamins and little fat. If you offer puddings, then baby varieties may have fewer artificial additives compared with an instant, packet dessert aimed at adults (though it is always worth checking the labels).

See Feeding Your Baby, page 105, for more information on commercial foods

YOUR QUESTIONS ANSWERED

Is it safe to give a baby eggs?
Current advice is to avoid eggs until the age of six months, when well-cooked eggs are considered to be safe and acceptable. Start with the yolk; move on to the white.

When can my baby drink ordinary milk?
Current guidelines on milk for babies of weaning age and up to a year say that the best milk drink is either breast milk, or an appropriate baby formula. However, the guidelines add that once a baby reaches six months old, small amounts of whole, pasteurized cow's milk can be used in cooking. You can of course carry on using formula or expressed breast milk in your cooking, if you want to, and if your baby prefers this (for more on milks, see page 218).

What sort of cheeses can my baby eat?
Hard, fatty cheese, such as Cheddar, is best given in small quantities at first, simply because it is harder to chew and digest. But as your baby grows, you don't need to be quite so cautious.

Soft pasteurized cheeses and cheese spreads can be given from about four or five months.

Does my baby need vitamin drops?
Most babies don't, but ask your clinic for advice. Routine vitamin drops are a sort of 'insurance policy' for babies and toddlers to make sure they don't miss out on vitamins because of illness or food fads. Standard recommendations are to give drops every day between the age of six months and at least two years, but if you are in any doubt ask your health visitor for advice.

My baby only likes sweet foods – and I can't get him to take many savoury dishes at all. How can I change his likes and dislikes? He's nine months old.
It's not at all uncommon to find babies exercising this sort of preference, but at nine months old your baby has plenty of time to change.

You don't have to insist on savoury foods – in fact, making mealtimes into battles can make the situation worse. Don't offer artificially sweetened foods, or foods with extra sugar in, however.

You'll probably find he likes naturally sweet foods like banana or sweet-tasting apples and pears. And some vegetables have a naturally sweet taste, including fresh, young carrots, peas, parsnips and courgettes. Stick to this type of food for a while, and don't offer sweetened juices to drink. Give him sugar-free rusks (or your own rusks made from wholemeal bread, see page 149) instead of biscuits or commercially made rusks which contain sugar. Avoid the food you know he'll refuse for a few weeks, and then re-introduce it gradually.

My baby is eight months old, and still breastfeeds four or five times a day. She doesn't seem interested in solid food, though she'll occasionally take a piece of fruit or bread, if I eat it with her. Do you think I should worry?
If your daughter is healthy and continuing to gain weight, and she has the opportunity to have solid food, then her reluctance to take to solid food is probably not a problem.

Ask your health visitor for hints on how to increase her intake, however, and see if she feels your daughter needs vitamin drops. It's very likely that your daughter is taking all that she needs at the moment, and in a short time she'll start to enjoy these shared 'meals' with you even more – and start to let you know she wants extra. Let her sit in a highchair at the table whenever you eat, and put a selection of easy-to-hold foods on her tray, including the bread and fruit you know she likes.

Some foods seem to make my six-month-old son constipated. He goes several days without opening his bowels, and then when he does, it takes a lot of effort and makes him very uncomfortable. What can I do to help?
Sometimes, the change from a milk-only diet to mixed feeding has this effect on a baby's digestive system. Have a word with your family doctor to reassure yourself it's just a temporary problem, and do what you can to increase the amount of fluid and fruit in your baby's diet. This will keep the system working well, and make sure the stools are soft and easy to pass. If you think there's one food that always causes a problem, then leave it out of your son's diet for a couple of weeks before introducing it again, in small quantities at first.

153

See Feeding Your Child, page 218, and Food Sensitivity, page 293, for more information on milk

NAPPY CHANGING AND BATHING

You will probably find by this stage that you have developed your own dressing/washing/changing and bathtime routines for your baby. Bathtime, in particular, is a good chance to play, and your baby will probably have overcome any bathtime fears and thoroughly enjoy the chance to get wet and splash around.

NAPPY CHANGING

Most older babies go through fewer nappies per day than younger ones. That's because their feeding and drinking patterns are more regular, and also because their digestive systems have matured a little. By now, for example, you may find your baby has only one dirty nappy every twenty-four hours – though don't worry if it's more frequent than this, or less, as long as your baby isn't constipated (see page 288).

During this time, your baby becomes mobile, one way or another. This means she may not be keen on staying still for more than a few seconds. Life is too interesting, and full of too many challenges, to want to co-operate with nappy changing. Your baby may start to object to lying patiently on her back while you fiddle with her nappy, and wriggle and roll out of

your way. If she's crawling or walking, you may end up scrabbling across the floor trying to catch her as she gets away. It can be irritating when this happens, and you may have to think of ways you can keep your baby still while you do the necessary.

Try these:
- Change your baby while she's standing up, leaning against something.
- Change your baby on your lap.
- Have a special box of interesting objects she can hold and examine while you're changing her (keep their novelty value by putting them out of sight between each nappy change).
- Sing loudly and raucously to keep her attention.
- Make peculiar faces and noises and have a giggle together.
- Enlist the help of an older brother or sister to keep the baby occupied.

BATHING

Keep bathtime safe by following the safety rules on page 112. Now your baby is mobile, avoid scalds by wrapping a cloth around the hot tap.

154

HOW TO WASHYOUR BABY'S HAIR

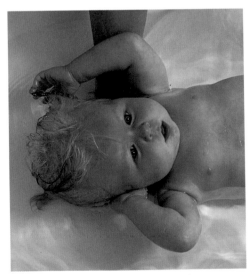

TIP
A flannel held in front of your baby's face – if she'll let you – absorbs stray trickles before they sting her eyes.

I. *Lay your baby back in the water, supporting her head and shoulders on your arm. Gently wet h er hair with your free hand. Apply the shampoo, lather and rinse off.*

2. *If your baby can sit up sturdily, you may find a shampoo shield is easier to use. This keeps the soap and water off her face and prevents drips from running into her eyes.*

See Nappy Changing and Bathing, page 188 for bath toys; Nappy Changing, page 110, for nappy rash

What is it about water that makes it such a constant source of fascination, wonder and amusement? A shared bathtime can be the high spot of the day and the washing purely incidental!

155

TEETH

Right from the start, you'll need to look after your baby's teeth. Use a clean cloth, a cotton bud or a piece of cotton-wool, to clean the very first teeth. When a few more come, use a soft baby toothbrush, and the tiniest pea-sized blob of child-strength fluoride toothpaste, once or twice a day. Let your baby play with the toothbrush.

Sit her on your lap, facing away from you, or to the side. This makes it easier for you to brush her teeth. However, if she doesn't like that, she can face you or you could try cleaning her teeth while she's in the bath. Remember to clean all the surfaces of the teeth – front, sides and back. You should aim to clean your baby's teeth at least twice a day; first thing in the morning after her breakfast and last thing in the evening before she goes to bed.

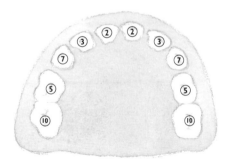
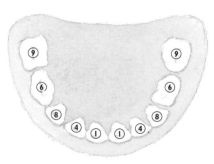

In an 'average' child, the lower incisor teeth come first (6-10 months), followed by the upper central incisors (8-12 months), and the upper, then lower lateral incisors (9-16 months). Next come the first upper, then lower molars (13-19 months), then the canines or eye teeth (16-23 months). Last are the second molars (23-33 months).

SLEEP AND BEDTIME

By the age of six months your baby will be spending more time awake and you can encourage him to sleep at times that suit you and fit in with your routine. Some parents find they can do this from the time their baby is just a few months old, but don't worry if your baby still doesn't seem to have an established pattern of sleeping, feeding and play times. Do what suits you and him. If your baby still sleeps at different times, and both you and he are happy with this, then carry on. It suits some couples, for example, to allow their baby to continue with a late afternoon nap so that if one or both of them are working they can see their baby in the evening.

You'll soon recognize the signs that show your baby is ready for a sleep — there may be a certain heaviness of the lids, a wish to be held, or a slightly distant look.

DAYTIME NAPS

Between the ages of six and twelve months, your baby may change his sleep needs. Many babies at the younger end of the age group are still having two or even three daytime naps a day of varying lengths. You may find your baby drops off to sleep in the car or the pushchair, and snatches sleep here and there when he needs it. Or you may be putting him to sleep after breakfast, after lunch, and then again in the later afternoon. The chances are that sometimes you put him in his cot and at other times he'll sleep where he happens to be at the time. It could help you plan your day better to combine these naps into one longer sleep. Some parents find this makes evening settling easier and quicker.

Decide when you'd find it easiest for your baby to have a nap. Most parents find some time between late morning and early afternoon is the ideal time, as any earlier and your baby will need another sleep; any later and he will be super-refreshed and lively at bedtime. For a few days, you may have to work towards that time. If your baby normally goes to sleep shortly after breakfast, wake him after a very short time, and put him down again later. You may also need to keep your baby awake if he looks like falling asleep too soon. So don't put him in the car or the pushchair if he's likely to drop off, and serve him an early lunch if necessary, so he can go to sleep afterwards. It's important to be consistent, however, until you have established a routine. Eventually, you'll be able to break the pattern, once your baby has grown accustomed to having a nap, and have the occasional different day. If you have other children who are at school or nursery, you may find that a routine

'I always knew when Jamie was tired. He'd be crabby and whinge the whole time, and want a lot of cuddling and stroking. But he seemed to fight sleep. It was better if I lay down with him on our bed, talking gently to him. He'd drift off, and then I could lift him into his cot without waking him.'

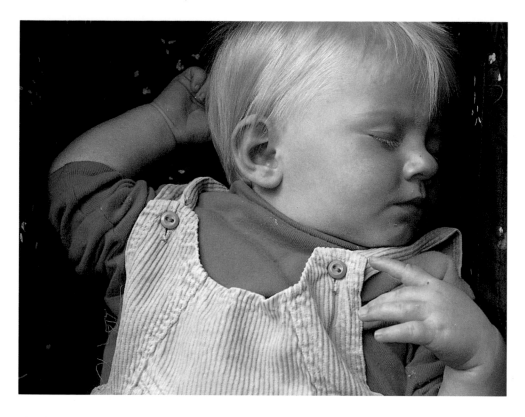

A good sound sleep during the day leaves your baby refreshed and happy, ready for the next few hours of playing, feeding and learning about the world around him.

157

develops naturally whereby your baby has a nap in the pushchair or car seat when you drop off or collect the other children.

Breaks in routines, such as holidays, or weekends away, will upset the pattern temporarily, but once you are at home be consistent and you will soon be back on course again.

BEDTIME ROUTINE

Here's a suggested bedtime routine you can consider for your baby. It'll help you both wind down at the end of the day. The timing is flexible.

Tea – early evening, between 4.30 and 6.30pm, followed by . . .

Quiet play – twenty minutes or so, some time between 5 and 7pm, looking at a book, cuddling and singing together, followed by . . .

Bathtime – as lively as you like. But try to quieten things down as you dry and dress your baby in his night clothes. At some time between 6 and 8pm, he'll probably be ready for a . . .

Milk feed – breast, bottle or cup, followed by . . .

Bed – at some time between 6.30 and 8.30pm.

You may prefer to have the quiet time (or another quiet time) between the bath and the feed. Babies in busy, noisy households may settle better if they don't go downstairs where all the action is, after their bathtime.

Changing patterns

Be prepared to adapt your routines as your baby grows, and to expect changes when his surroundings are different. However, most parents do find that a regular routine is a help when away from home.

AVOIDING SLEEP PROBLEMS

● **Don't expect too much of your baby. Some babies simply dislike sleeping on their own. They may be happier settling down where they can see you or hear you nearby.**

● **Don't insist on darkness. A soft light, enough to see quite clearly by, can be soothing.**

● **Leave the door to your baby's room open (unless he really does settle better with it closed).**

● **If you've decided on a routine, then try to stick to it as far as you can. Chopping and changing is confusing and upsetting for your baby.**

RELUCTANCE TO SLEEP

If your baby seems reluctant to sleep
ask yourself:
Is he too hot?
Is he too cold?
Is he too excited and stimulated, needing
a quiet time to wind down?
Is he hungry or thirsty?
Is he worried or frightened by shapes
or noises?
Is he just not tired?
Is he in pain or distress?
Is he uncomfortable?
Is he lonely?

Early wakers

It's not uncommon for older babies to go
through a stage of waking up early and
wanting to start the day's activities as early
as 4 or 5am! The baby who does this may
not want to go back to sleep again,
demanding your attention and a play
session . . . Take heart from the fact that,
usually, this stage passes.

Here are some ideas to try to hasten the
end of the stage, and/or to cope with it
while it lasts:
● Snuggle up together in bed so you can
at least try to doze.
● Offer a feed (he may go back to sleep after
this).
● Put some safe toys in his cot for him
to play with in the morning.
● Make his bedtime a little later.
● Let him play on your bedroom floor with
some safe toys, so you can watch him from
your bed.
● Get up early and have breakfast together
(in summer you can go for a walk).
● Take it in turns with your partner to play
with your baby in the mornings. Sharing
the responsibility makes it much easier
to deal with.

Night waking

Many babies still wake up once or more in
the night at this age. If your baby is difficult
to settle when he wakes up, it can be
especially tiring for you. You can:
● Make sure night-time wakings are as low-
key as possible. Don't switch the light on
and don't play with your baby. Offer quiet
reassurance, and whatever he needs to get

back to sleep again such as a breastfeed,
a bottlefeed, a drink or a cuddle.
● Consider taking him into your bed until
he settles and then putting him back in his
cot once he is asleep.
● Leave a nightlight on in his room all night
as he may not like the dark.
● Check he's not too hot or cold at night
by feeling his chest or the back of his neck.
A baby's hands and feet are often cool
so they can be a misleading guide to his
temperature.
Towards the end of the first year you can
consider following some of the suggestions
on page 194.

Night feeds

Babies over six months who are eating as
much as they want in the day may not be
really hungry at night (though on warm
nights they could wake up feeling thirsty).
However, giving a bottle- or breastfeed is
often a good way to get a wakeful baby
back to sleep.

Babies still have a strong need to suck
at this age. Bottles and breasts offer that
important comfort and help a baby calm
down enough to settle and go back to sleep.
A breastfed baby is unlikely to take a large
volume of milk in the night, so it won't
interfere with his appetite the next day.
That may not be the case with a bottle;
to get enough sucking time, a baby ends
up taking several ounces.

You may need to consider substituting
a dummy, watering down the formula milk,
or offering it in smaller amounts and
soothing your baby by cuddling or rocking
him back to sleep. Yet there's no real rush
to do anything at this stage. Your baby may
simply grow out of waking for a feed
without you taking any special steps.

'When Ellen was eleven months old, she started
wanting to begin the day at 5.30am every
morning. We'd take her into bed with us,
and she'd actually try to prise our eyelids open.
As she got older, though, she gradually grew
to understand that it was still night-time,
and lay awake singing and chatting to herself,
without disturbing us.'

OPPOSITE *Sometimes
you may be pleasantly
surprised to find that
the baby you thought
was having an extra long
sleep has in fact woken
up to amuse herself by
playing contentedly
with the toys in the cot.*

159

See Sleep and Bedtime, page 194, for night waking and difficulties in settling

WHAT YOUR BABY MAY NEED

Once your baby starts to become more active, you'll need to find ways of keeping her safely occupied. Although none of the following equipment is essential, she may well enjoy it.

BABY BOUNCER
(From about six months)
Your baby is held firmly in a padded support which is suspended from a doorway by steel clamps. She can then bounce and stretch her legs in preparation for walking later.

BABY WALKER
(From about six months)
Before your baby can walk, she may like cruising around for short periods in a baby walker. Walkers can be square or round and some fold up for ease of storage. She should always be supervised. Don't buy one if you have steps, uneven floors or narrow passageways.
+ Your baby can follow you around under her own steam.
− You will need a large area for your baby to be able to use it safely.

PLAYPEN
(From about six months to two years)
There are two main types of playpen: the traditional, square, wooden-style one with a built-in floor and the light, easily assembled, mesh-sided one with a raised floor and padded rim. There are folding styles in both designs. Make sure before you buy a playpen that your child can't climb out of it.
+ Gives you peace of mind if you have to leave the room.
− Make sure you don't leave your baby in it for long as she may need your attention and get distressed.

TRAVEL COT
(From about three months)
Some travel cots are specifically designed to double as a playpen. And any travel cot that's large enough, has mesh sides and is deep enough to prevent your child from climbing out can be used in this way. When buying, you should make sure that the cot is easy to assemble and fold, and feels rigid when standing. Most come complete with mattress and carrycase.

Travel cot
+ Once your baby has outgrown her carrycot or Moses basket, a travel cot is ideal if you go away often.
− Make sure it fits into the boot of your car as some are quite large.

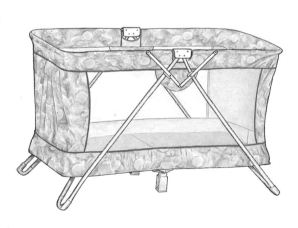

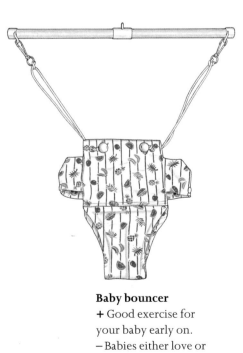

Baby bouncer
+ Good exercise for your baby early on.
− Babies either love or hate them so, if possible, try before you buy.

See What Your Toddler May Need, page 199, for choosing a cot

Dressed, ready and looking good enough to eat, today's well-turned-out babies wear comfortable clothes which are easy to remove and wash.

WELL DRESSED

Your baby's needs won't change that much over the next six months, although obviously you'll have to buy the next-size vests and so on. But as she'll soon be on the move, some clothes are more practical than others. Most of all they need to be machine-washable as she'll get very grubby from crawling around on the floor.

● Stretchsuits are still ideal – they will keep your baby warm and allow her plenty of freedom to move around. Make sure there is enough room for her toes.

● Avoid dresses or skirts if she's crawling as they give no protection to her knees.

● Avoid elasticated waisted trousers, tights or skirts – they'll soon come off as she crawls across the floor.

● Choose dungarees or stretchy trousers with bibs or straps and T-shirts or jumpers. Those with poppers down the legs make changing easier.

● For outdoors in winter, a snowsuit is ideal. Make sure it has generous fastenings so you can get your baby in and out easily.

● In summer a sunhat is essential to protect your baby's head and neck. Buy one which ties on if she's likely to try to pull it off.

● For bedtime, stick to a stretchsuit with a sleepsuit over the top in winter.

Safe and sound

Your baby will soon be rolling, crawling and pulling herself up. You won't be able to leave her kicking happily on a mat while you pop into another room to answer the phone or tidy up. She'll be up and away. Her safety is all important at this stage so you'll need to think of everything – before she does.

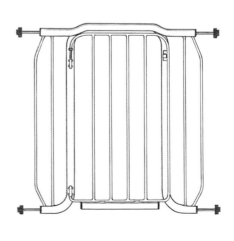

PROTECTING YOUR BABY
You can't put your baby in a playpen all day to keep her out of danger. What you can do, however, is to make your home safe for her to play in.

FIRE GUARD
A guard that fixes to the wall is safer than a free-standing one and should be fitted to every gas, electric and open fire. Never put anything on top of the guard and don't let your baby post things through the bars.

STAIR GATE
A steel one which opens and can be moved from one place to another is the most practical and means you only have to have one. You can put it at the bottom of the stairs during the day, and move it to the top at night or when she's upstairs playing. It's also useful for keeping your child in or out of a room. Before buying, make sure you can open it one-handed (you may have

What is this contraption that's stopping me from exploring? Your baby's expression says it all, but your constant vigilance over using the stair gate gives you peace of mind and may prevent a terrible accident.

162

your baby in your arms) but that a child can't. You also need to check a child won't be able to climb over it.

WINDOW LOCKS
To prevent hinged windows being opened too far, fit window locks. If you have sash windows, a small bracket screwed to the frame at a suitably low height on either side will prevent them from being pushed up any further.

Fire guard

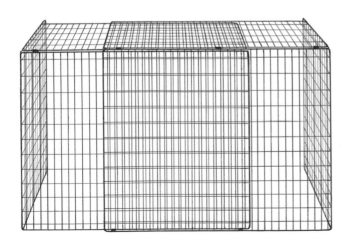

Stair gate

See Safety Around the House, page 306

COOKER GUARD

A hob guard could help prevent a nasty accident. Make sure you always turn the pan handles towards the back of the cooker. Ideally, keep young children out of the kitchen when you're cooking.
Note: If your oven has a glass door, you could buy a door guard which prevents the front becoming dangerously hot.

SAFETY CATCHES

Even if you think your child isn't of an inquisitive nature, you should fix safety catches to all doors, cupboards and drawers containing potentially dangerous items – cleaning materials, cutlery and cooking utensils, medicines, even make-up.
Tip: Have a special cupboard for your baby in the kitchen where she can keep an old saucepan, wooden spoon, and plastic boxes to pull out and play with when she likes.

SOCKET COVERS

All electric sockets should have special safety covers plugged in when not in use. Little fingers love little holes – but they can be fatal.

OUT OF HARM'S WAY

● Keep all cleaning materials and medicines out of your baby's reach in a locked cupboard and NEVER leave pills on a bedside table.
● Don't leave alcohol where your baby can reach it – it's highly poisonous to children.

Your baby will naturally want to open cupboards and drawers like you so often do. But they may contain hidden dangers, so fix safety catches to cupboard doors and drawers to guard against any harm.

● Keep all sharp knives and utensils, scissors and gardening equipment high up and out of reach.
● Don't leave matches or smoking equipment lying around.
● Be careful when drinking hot drinks close to your baby – a cup of coffee or tea can cause a nasty scald.
● Put all electrical appliances out of reach and keep leads short so they don't hang over work tops.

163

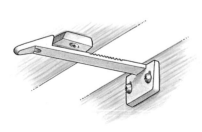
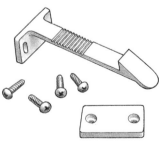

Safety catches

Socket cover

Travelling safely

BELT UP!
● Put your child
in a suitable car
restraint even for
short journeys.
● Make sure any
integral harness is
properly adjusted.
● Make sure the
seat is properly
fitted following
the manufacturer's
instructions.
If in doubt, get it
checked by your
garage or local dealer.
● Choose the right
seat for your child's
weight, NOT age.
● Replace the seat
after an accident
as it may no longer
be safe.
● Check the seat
regularly for wear
and tear.

WHAT YOUR BABY MAY NEED

164

Always make sure that your child is
protected properly when travelling in a car.
The law says that every child under eleven
must wear a suitable child restraint if
available. (A child under three must NEVER
be in the front seat without one.) The adult
belt alone is not safe for a young child. It will
not fit across her in the correct places and
could cause severe internal and neck injuries
in an accident.

Once your baby has outgrown her first
rear-facing seat, at about six to nine months,
you'll need a forward-facing car seat suitable
for the next years of her growth.

FORWARD-FACING SEAT
(From around six months to four years
or from 9kg/20lb to 20kg/40lb.)

Once your baby has outgrown her first baby
seat, she will need a forward-facing seat.
This is fitted into the car using the adult
seatbelt and has an integral harness to hold
the baby in for maximum safety. If your car
does not have rear seatbelts, you can buy a
special anchorage kit which bolts on to the
car's structure.

The seat is padded for comfort and can easily
be removed for washing. Choose one with
'wings' so your child can rest her head when
she falls asleep. Some have a reclining
position for added comfort.

LIGHTWEIGHT SEAT
(From around six months to six years
or from 9kg/20lb to 25kg/55lb.)

This forward-facing seat is light and easily
transferable from one car to another. The
child is strapped in by the adult belt, which
is held in place and kept in the correct
position by special locks. Some have an
adjustable headrest which makes them
suitable for a baby as young as six months.
Others have a detachable back, leaving a
booster seat for an older child (see What
Your Child May Need, page 225).

A basic model is an inexpensive buy.
But others, with extras like headrests,
pockets to put toys in or padded detachable
play trays are as dear as steel-framed seats.

One drawback is that as they are only
as high as a booster seat, so small children
can't see out of the windows very well.

Lightweight seat
+ Ideal if you want a forward-
  facing car seat that will last
  a long time and are not
  planning on having another
  child for at least four or
  five years.
− Ones without an adjustable
  headrest are not suitable for
  children much under three
  years of age.

Forward-facing seat
+ The most sensible option
if you are planning to have
more than one child is to
buy separate rear-facing
and forward-facing seats
(see page 120) rather than
the combined seat.
− Heavy to transfer from one
car to another, or to carry
your baby in if she is sleeping.

See What Your Baby May Need, page 126, for more information on seats and backpacks

Out and about

If your baby enjoyed being in a sling when she was tiny, she'll most likely take to a backpack like a duck to water! It's a good way for an older baby or toddler to travel. She'll be high up near your shoulders so she can see where she's going, instead of being thrust into a crowd of legs in her buggy. She can hear what you're saying to her and can talk back to you. She can touch you and feel your warmth too. But best of all, provided she is strapped in with a harness (which is a MUST), she's safely with you at all times. However, a backpack offers little protection from bad weather.

Umbrella-fold pushchair
(From six months)

The simplest pushchair of all; lightweight and easy to fold even one-handed. Some have a partial reclining facility but are not suitable for young babies.

It's also the ideal buggy when your child begins to want to walk, but inevitably gets tired before you get her home. Being so light, you can trail it or push it along folded without too much effort, until it's needed.

165

Footloose and fancy-free? Perhaps not quite, but you clearly have all sorts of delightful options open to you when your baby is happily ensconced on your back and a brisk walk beckons.

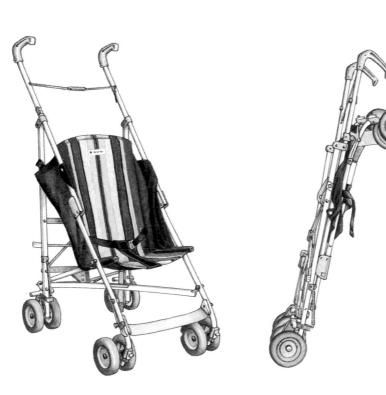

Umbrella-fold pushchair

+ Good – and inexpensive – for a toddler when you had a pram or pushchair with a chassis for her from birth.

+ Lightweight and easy to manoeuvre. Ideal for taking on holiday.

+ Good for use on public transport because it is so easy to fold.

– Not suitable for young babies.

Dining in style

Up until now you may have had your baby on your lap to give her little tasters of solids, or perhaps you may have fed her in her bouncing cradle or first baby seat. But once meals become established, a highchair makes life a lot easier. Your baby will be at a more comfortable height for spoon-feeding and she'll enjoy sitting up in her own chair at the table for family meals.

CHOOSING A HIGHCHAIR

It must be safe, sturdy, easy to clean, tough enough to last and easy to store when not in use. There are three main types to choose from: folding, convertible and rigid. Whichever one you choose, make sure it has:

- Attachment points for a separate safety harness.
- A removable cover for washing or a wipe-clean seat.

- A detachable tray, so it can be pushed right up to the table when your child joins in family mealtimes.
- An integral crutch strap so your baby can't slip out.
- No crevices where food will get trapped.

Tip: To keep mess to the minimum, stand the highchair on a plastic sheet.

FOLDING

If space is limited or if you travel a lot, a folding highchair is ideal. Choose one with braced legs for extra rigidity.

CONVERTIBLE

A convertible high/low chair means your child can sit up to the table with you or can sit in the low chair for less formal meals. It also converts into a child's table and chair, which makes an ideal first desk. But check

HIGHCHAIR CHOICES
Folding: takes up little space when not in use, ideal if space is limited.
Convertible: once your child is older it can be used as a desk and chair but is not so practical if you are planning on having more than one child.
Rigid: very sturdy but is a permanent fixture.

166

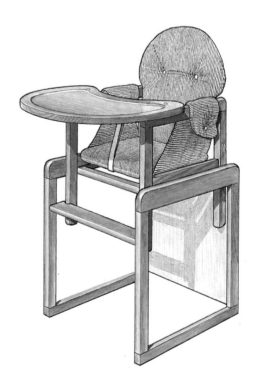

Convertible highchair
+ Many uses (see right) and is very sturdy.
− Takes up a lot of space as it cannot be folded away.
− Some are not very easy to convert.

Folding highchair
+ Ideal if space is limited.
− Not as sturdy as some rigid highchairs.

how it works, as with some makes it's more trouble than it's worth to convert once erected as a highchair.

RIGID

The beauty of a rigid chair is that it has fewer nooks and crannies for food to lodge in. And a wooden, cottage-style one can also be an attractive piece of furniture. Its main drawback is that it can't be folded and put away when not in use.

SAFETY AT MEALS

• Always use a safety harness to strap your child in a highchair.
• Don't leave her unattended while eating or drinking because she could choke.
• Wipe off spills at the end of every meal or germs could breed.
• Some highchairs have wheels or castors on the legs so the chair can be moved easily; check there is a brake fitted so the baby won't be able to move the chair herself.
• Check the highchair feels sturdy and stable.

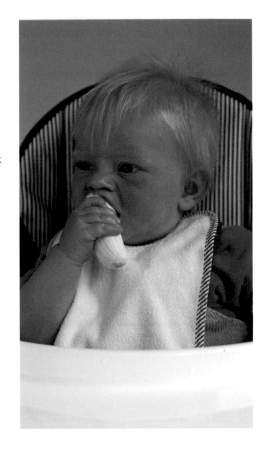

However expert your baby is at feeding himself, never leave him unattended while eating. A bit of food can all too easily go down the wrong way and he may need urgent first aid.

167

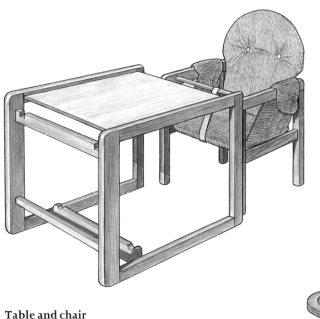

Low chair
+ Ideal if you don't want to feed your baby at a table.
– Not always easy to convert from the highchair.

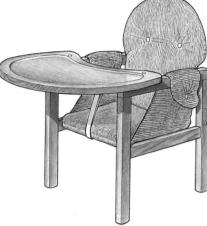

Table and chair
+ Ideal first table and chair for a toddler.
– Converts from the highchair (left) and may not get used if you are planning on having more than one child.

COMMON CONCERNS

Some babies suck their thumb, others one, two or sometimes even three or four fingers, and the good thing is that they're always there and can't get lost like a dummy or comforter.

168

My baby puts everything in his mouth. Should I sterilize toys? How can I stop him eating bits off the carpet and what should I let him touch?
You don't need to sterilize rattles or other playthings because your baby will be developing resistance to ordinary household germs, though it helps to give them a wash when they get grubby. At this stage, when your baby is crawling, you do need to keep the floor clean.

A baby of this age learns a great deal about objects by putting them in his mouth. Anything, from rattles to paper, a cup to a pebble, will go straight there. Because of this, it's very important that any tiny objects on which he could choke, or anything sharp that might cut him, are safely stored away. Then you can give him a whole range of safe toys and household objects to explore.

My baby is now ten months old and still uses a dummy – will this harm his teeth? Is it all right to give him a bottle in bed at night?
Some babies who have had a dummy in the early months become very attached to it at this stage. Your baby may have come to rely on sucking on his dummy as the only way to get to sleep. If you don't mind about him using a dummy, find it convenient to get him to sleep without tears, and don't use it all the time, let him carry on; there is no reason why it should affect his teeth. Never dip a dummy in

sweet juice or honey, and don't use it all the time as this can prevent the baby practising his pre-speech babble.

Sometimes the dummy becomes a nuisance if it falls out at night and the baby repeatedly wakes and cries for you to go and put it back. If this happens it may help to get your baby used to falling asleep without his dummy. Never tape a dummy to the bars of the cot or round your baby's neck as the string could strangle him.

Some babies suck their thumb or fingers as a comfort habit and parents may worry that they will damage their teeth. There is no danger of this while the baby is young and most children give it up of their own accord, or they can be helped to with a little encouragement later on.

It's best to give your baby a bedtime feed on your lap and then put him to bed without a bottle. If the baby feeds from a bottle while lying down this can lead to ear infections and, at worst, may cause him to choke. Once your baby is a year old, you may prefer to give a bedtime drink in a cup as this may be better for the teeth than a bottle (see Feeding Your Baby, page 148).

My baby still wakes several times a night and I'm exhausted – what can I do?
If when your baby wakes he is missing his comfort object, whether it be breast, bottle, dummy, or simply being held, it is likely that he will continue to cry until he gets it back again.

You can help your baby sleep through the night by trying to ensure that he doesn't fall asleep at the breast, over his bottle, or while he is sucking a dummy. Allow him to learn to fall asleep by himself by putting him into his bed just before he falls asleep. When he wakes in the night, check briefly that he is all right, perhaps give him a drink rather than a feed if you think he might be thirsty, and leave him to go back to sleep again. Sometimes this leads to more crying at first, but if you are determined and persist your baby will probably learn to sleep through after a few nights.

See Sleep and Bedtime, page 159, for night feeds

I can't get my seven-month-old baby into a routine. Sometimes he sleeps all morning and is up all evening, sometimes he is in bed by six.
Some babies are very flexible and will adapt their sleep needs to fit in with a varied and chaotic schedule. Others, however, really need to have their sleep at fixed times and become crabby and irritable if their routine is broken.

Many babies of this age thrive best if there is a definite structure to the day. Probably your baby needs two naps, one in the morning and one in the afternoon, though one of these may be very short. If you are not at home your baby can always nap in the car or in his pushchair. He will get hungry at fairly frequent intervals and will not be able to wait for a meal, so if you are out and about you need to remember to take provisions with you.

My baby clings to me and cries every time I go out of the room and won't let me hand him over to anyone else. How can I encourage him to be more independent?
This is a normal phase in every baby's life. To begin with he thinks that you are part of him, then when he realizes you are someone else and can come and go, he is afraid he might lose you. The best thing you can do is gradually to instil the basic security of knowing you are there or, if you have to leave him, of learning you always come back. At six to nine months your baby may show strong anxiety if you give him to a stranger. It helps to have other adults around with whom the baby is familiar and whom he will go to – fathers, grandparents, older brothers and sisters of course, but also friends or perhaps a childminder. If you get your baby used to being left sometimes he will adapt, though crying when you leave is usual and may persist till your baby is much older.

My baby dribbles a lot, and sometimes has red cheeks and frets all day. Do you think he is teething? Is there anything I can do to help him?
Teething usually begins around five to six months and goes on until a child is two or more. The teeth move slowly through the gum before they appear and this takes some time. Some babies may experience

discomfort or irritation when the teeth are actually breaking through the gums. Giving your baby a dose of paracetamol syrup or using a teething gel may provide short-term relief and some mothers find that homeopathic teething granules are helpful although they do contain milk sugar (lactose). However, the old-fashioned remedies such as chewing on a teething ring or a raw carrot, may be best. And others find that rubbing their baby's gums helps to soothe them. It also helps to give your baby lots of hugs and cuddles to distract his attention.

Dribbling and red cheeks are symptoms of teething, as is the desire to chew on something hard, sleepless nights and a loss of appetite. Teething, however, should not be blamed for a fever, vomiting or other signs of illness.

Welcome your baby with open arms whenever she needs them and you'll find she develops a deep inner sense of security and trust. She'll become independent soon enough in the months and years ahead.

169

See Sleep and Bedtime, page 156, for daytime naps; Becoming a Parent, page 244

GROWING AND LEARNING

Look how your baby has grown! It scarcely seems possible, does it? Suddenly, that tiny scrap who simply lay passively in her carrycot is now an inquisitive little person, looking around her and making her presence known. She's growing up in leaps and bounds. In fact, did you know that the brain develops more in the first five years than at any other time of your life? Now you can already spot your child's emerging personality and the difference between her and her contemporaries. Your baby may be shy compared with your friend's, who is always reaching out to other people. Your baby might be crawling while your friend's child is merely sitting up. They all grow at different rates.

FIRST MOVES

Already you can see your baby reaching out for toys, her comfort blanket or car-seat straps. It's the first step to mobility. She may be able to roll from her back on to her front. She then begins to twist her body and reach out for something just beyond her grasp. It is incredible the determination with which she attempts these first moves.

By about six months, you can help her sit up, propped against the foot of the sofa. At first, she'll wobble and probably fall down, so place lots of cushions or padding around her. Her shoulders will look all hunched up and she won't seem very comfortable, but keep going. Think of it as her exercise class – you probably have one too. Within weeks, your baby's body will become stronger. At first she'll need to bend forward and will use her hands to keep her balance. Gradually she will gain confidence and sit with a straighter back. She will no longer need to use her hands for support and will be able to use them for exploring. You can help your baby to sit independently by doing the following:

• Putting toys in the space between her knees to divert her attention from this difficult balancing act. She can also use them for support.

• Dressing her in loose, comfortable clothes and not something tight which will restrict her mobility.

Now your baby is sitting, she's halfway there. Place a toy just out of her reach and watch her reach forward, grab it and perhaps topple over. After a few practice runs, she'll be strong enough to lean forward for the toy and then sit back up again. Clap her – she's a clever girl.

Leaning forward will give her ideas – when she turns her feet and moves those legs, she'll be off. And so will you, in hot pursuit! But don't despair if she's not ready. Some children never crawl but simply bottom-shuffle by sitting on their bottom and skilfully propelling themselves forward, using hands and legs. Some bottom-shufflers progress to crawling and others don't. After all, if they can get where they want without crawling, why bother? Non

bottom-shufflers might look as though they're about to crawl for months before they finally learn how.

By ten to twelve months, you can watch your sitter-upper pulling herself up on the furniture (make sure it's stable). Soon she'll walk round it, holding on tightly. It's both a thrilling and a daunting development. You'll have to child-proof your home (see What Your Baby May Need, page 162 and Safety Around the House, page 306), but praise her too. Remember what it was like when you learned to swim.

Now your baby's on the last lap and learning to walk. Give her a pushstart by:

• Buying a toddle truck.

• Standing in front of her and holding out your arms encouragingly.

• Reaching out your arms, holding both her hands and walking her towards you. Don't worry if she's not quite there. Like crawling, your baby may look as though she's nearly cracked it but can't quite make the final effort. She'll get there in the end, even if it takes a few months.

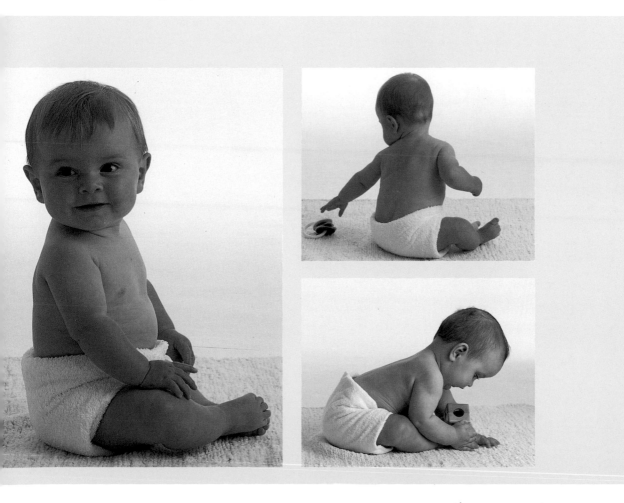

USING HER HANDS

Toys are becoming more and more important. Look how she can sit or lie on her tummy to finger toys inquisitively. 'What on earth is this?' she seems to say, as she passes an interesting-looking brick from one hand to another. These hand movements are becoming increasingly deliberate and accurate. If she likes the look of that rag book lying in front of her she'll pick it up – and throw it down when she's had enough. She'll also 'feel' it with her mouth. This is an important way of exploring for a young baby even if it does become rather unhygienic. Toe-sucking is equally popular at this age. Watch her lie on her back and try to 'pick up' her toes or push them towards her mouth. It makes a lovely photograph to embarrass her with when she's a teenager.

As the months progress, your baby will be able to pick up increasingly small objects. At first, she'll cup her whole hand round a toy in a clumsy attempt to pin it down. Soon she'll learn to be more skilful and accurate by using her thumb and first finger (known by health professionals as the 'pincer grip'). She'll become

Picking up and playing can be fun for both of you. Try setting aside a special ten minutes in each day to help your child explore this new skill.

Games could include:
- Banging objects together to make interesting noises (for example, let her bang a wooden spoon against a saucepan – if you can bear the noise).
- Playing the dropping game (letting toys or a spoon fall from the highchair). She'll love it but it will soon become monotonous and tiring for you.
- Waving goodbye. Practise through the window with your baby in your arms when your partner leaves in the morning. Or wave goodbye to each other when standing in front of a full-length mirror.
- Encourage independent playing too. Place a basket of interesting-looking toys and safe household objects in front of her for her to investigate while she's sitting.

CAN I PLAY TOO?

She may only be tiny but already your baby will want to join in with what's going on around her.

Soft squashy toys are just the job for learning manual dexterity skills such as gripping and squeezing, while other toys help a baby become ever more capable with fingers and thumb.

astonishingly adept at this – even that minute piece of thread on the carpet will be picked up carefully and examined. She'll become logical too – or attempt to be – when trying to fit pieces of a toy together. It's still early days for success but she's going to have a jolly good try! Don't be surprised if your baby is still using her left hand as much as her right. You won't know if she is going to be right- or left-handed until she is about three or four.

Give her the go-ahead by:
- Letting her hold a spoon while you're feeding her.
- Encouraging older children to join in brick-building. Watch the delight on her face – babies love company.
- Playing peek-a-boo games. They never seem to lose their appeal, and they are easy to teach older children to play, provided they don't smother the baby with the peek-a-boo cloth.

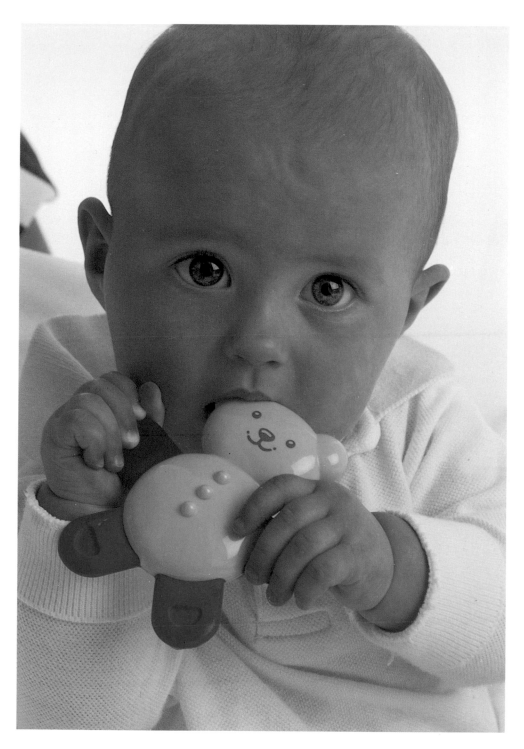

At this age using hands is fascinating, but there comes a time when the toy simply has to go into the mouth to be tasted, sucked and generally explored with lips, cheeks and tongue.

LISTENING AND CHATTERING

Suddenly, your baby is starting to make all sorts of different noises ranging from surprised 'ooohs!' to 'daaas'. As her first birthday approaches, you might well spot a 'dah' for Daddy or 'Mum' for Mummy amongst all those sounds. It doesn't mean she prefers her father if 'dah' comes out first. It's simply that some sounds are easier than others for her to master, and she probably hears them more than others. You can almost recognize different noises which indicate whether she's feeling frustrated or simply entranced by the wonders of the world around her. Don't be surprised when your baby wants to tell you something. It just goes to show that the chatty talk, shouting and babbling which you'll now start to notice are very important to that small person who hasn't yet even reached her first birthday. In fact, it's so important that she wants you to talk back.

GROWING AND LEARNING

WHAT YOUR OLDER BABY MIGHT DO:
● **Sit with a straight back without using her hands for support.**
● **Crawl or bottom-shuffle.**
● **Haul herself up on furniture.**
● **Stand unaided – even for a few seconds.**
● **Pick up objects.**
● **Shout and babble.**
● **Clap her hands together and wave.**
● **Play games (peek-a-boo, etc).**

With your baby on your lap and a book in your hands, you kindle an interest in words, open up a whole new imaginary world and pave the way for hours of future amusement and interest.

Sometimes we feel rather silly about this, especially if other people are around. But don't take any notice of them. Let yourself relax and repeat your baby's noises back to her like a game. Continue talking (in ordinary adult language) as you tackle the daily tasks ('That's right, in you go to your car seat'). The more you talk, the more she'll pick up. It's rather like learning a foreign language; you're more likely to acquire the genuine accent if you live there and are surrounded by native speakers.

Your baby will listen carefully to the words you use and the way you say them. She'll soon know if you're in a bad mood from the tone of your voice, so don't be too unkind, even if you're having a bad day. Life is still very new. Even accidental noises (like a sudden sneeze) can be frightening unless you make them fun by smiling broadly and saying, 'What was that?' A big smile will soon take away those fears and you can make a game out of it with Mickey Mouse sneeze impersonations (AAAAAChooooooo!). She may try and mimic the sound you have just made, which will delight both you and her. Keep repeating the noise if she likes it.

Give your chatter-box a headstart by:
● Sitting her on your knee (facing you) and singing nursery rhymes. Even small babies can learn to recognize tunes. The words will follow later.
● Putting together actions with words, such as waving exaggeratedly and saying, 'Bye bye'. Even if she doesn't make any sounds she will probably try and copy your actions.
● Playing clapping games like Pat-a-cake or Round and Round the Garden so she learns to identify key words and phrases (like 'tickly under there').

WATCHING AND WONDERING
Oh, what a wonderful world it is out there. At least, that's what your baby seems to say as she looks around her. She's noticing so much now: her own special plastic bowl in front of her on the highchair, the noise of the traffic going past or the aeroplane overhead. She'll start to watch now, rather than just feel. She'll really look at that toy car which moves along rather than simply putting it straight in her mouth. And she'll notice things that you do and even try to copy you.

Encourage her by:
- Pointing your finger at something and saying 'Oh, look' in an interested tone.
- Pushing a car or some other mobile toy towards her and helping her push it back.
- Letting her look at herself in a full-length mirror. She will love trying to touch her reflection and yours.

Occasionally you might wish your child *weren't* so observant. You'll have to hide things which she wants but which aren't safe (like that fascinating corkscrew, someone has left within reach). And then you'll need to prevent angry tears by providing something which is equally interesting but less dangerous, although this is not always easy.

Don't underestimate your child's comprehension skills. She'll understand more than she can say. She's beginning to understand situations like elevenses time, when you ask if she wants a drink and she may be able to hold out her cup to you or put it down when she's finished. Equally, she may decide she wants the cup back again. Maddening as this is, try to be sympathetic. You never know, maybe she just doesn't know what she wants, just like all of us at some stage.

There will also be times when your child is scared by what she can't understand – like that noisy dog which has just walked past you in the street. She might be frustrated that you haven't understood her cries which mean so clearly (to her) that she's tired and bad-tempered. That's when a comforter can come in handy. It might be a muslin cloth, a much-loved toy, a thumb or even a dummy. Don't deprive her of this. We adults have our comforters in life, be it the occasional drink or a bedside lamp.

ASSERTING HERSELF

You may be told, 'She's got you where she wants you.' And why not – up to a point? After all, you've been encouraging her to grow and learn and, like any human being, she likes to have her own way whenever possible. It is also important for her to know that you will respond to her needs.

It's natural, now that your child is nearly a year, that she should want to do more for herself. She hasn't quite reached the stage

where she physically refuses to let you dress her. (That tricky stage comes a little later.) But she'll try to tell you what she wants with other bodily movements like sitting at your feet with her hands outstretched, as if to say, 'Why haven't you picked me up?' She will also let you know how frustrated she feels when you prevent her from doing something she wants but which is dangerous, for example, crawling up the stairs.

Her personality will really be coming through now. Perhaps she'll bestow broad grins on everyone she meets. Or perhaps she's more withdrawn and hides her face when well-wishers try to tickle her cheek. Maybe she can crawl faster than you can run. Or she may be quite content to sit still with some toys at her feet watching the world go by. Group gatherings such as mother and toddlers can make you feel quite worried about these differences. But remember, none of us is the same, whether we're children or adults.

You'll feel like the best entertainer in the world when you take the time to play games and sing songs with your hugely appreciative, enthusiastic and participatory audience of one.

PLAY AND TOYS

This is when the fun really begins! Your baby will be growing and developing fast. He'll be able to sit up now and it won't be long before he's on the move. He can reach out for a toy and as he becomes more dexterous, he'll grasp it, turn it carefully in his hands and scrutinize it with deep concentration. Then it'll go into the mouth for a quick chew, taste and texture test before it is waved around in glee or discarded for another one. He'll also scream and cry with frustration if he can't reach

cubes or balls will give endless pleasure and it won't be long before he'll pick one up and throw it across the room.

PLAYING WITH YOU

A pleasurable game for you and equally enjoyable for your baby is to encourage him to hand you a toy. You say 'Thank you' then pass it back. Play this first with one hand then the other.

You can also play hide and seek games with your baby but be warned: you need

what he wants or can't make it work. This is all part of learning – and playing.

Your baby will concentrate on one new skill at a time. But once he's mastered it, he'll soon move on to another. So multi-function toys which can 'grow' with him are good buys.

An activity centre is a good choice. At first your baby will only be able to manage one or two of the functions, but with your help he'll gradually learn the others.

SIGHT, SOUND AND MOVEMENT

Your baby will love to sit and play with paper. It crackles, it scrunches up, it flaps, it tears and it tastes interesting. (See Play safe, page 179). He'll also enjoy shaking a musical rattle or chewing and squeezing a squeaky toy. Patting (and sucking) soft

patience when you decide to play such games with him because he'll want you to repeat them again and again. However, they do help him to get used to the idea of things – and people – going but coming back. Hide behind a door, pop your head round and say 'boo'. Or hide a toy behind your back, and ask him where it's gone.

Play 'Peter and Paul': draw a bird face on one finger of each hand, or attach a feather to them with sticky tape. As you say the following rhyme, make one, then the other 'bird' disappear then reappear.

'Two little dicky-birds sitting on a wall,
One named Peter, one named Paul.
Fly away Peter, fly away Paul,
Come back Peter, come back Paul.'

REACHING AND CRAWLING

Your baby will soon be getting around the room one way or another. He may or may not crawl, but you can encourage him to move towards you by holding out a favourite toy and asking him to come and get it.

He'll get very frustrated when fast-rolling toys move out of reach, so go for soft rather than hard balls and avoid toys with wheels until he's fully mobile or you'll be constantly fetching and carrying. He will enjoy any toys that can be moved easily, especially if they make an interesting sound as they go along.

Blow-up peek 'n roll-type toys can be great fun. They, too, are soft to fall on and feel nice to bash and chew. But they aren't that durable and invariably spring a leak after a while. Make sure you dispose of them once they do in case your baby chews the deflated plastic and chokes on it.

Once he is standing holding on, encourage walking with a toddle truck, push-along toy or baby's buggy. Your baby will love this new-found mobility, although you will have to be on hand to rescue your little walker when the toddle truck gets stuck in a corner. Make sure it is weighted so it won't tip up easily.

First approach the pan on hands and knees, then stir gently with a wooden spoon; examine the pan carefully, then sample your recipe. Have you had enough? Then upturn the whole thing over your head and see what happens.

177

MAKE YOUR OWN

You don't have to spend a fortune on toys. Many ordinary household goods will give as much, if not more, fun.

● Make a simple post box by cutting a round hole in the lid of a shoe box. Give your baby a few safe objects to 'post' through the hole, like a wooden egg cup, cotton reel and clean fromage frais pot.

● Use different-sized plastic yogurt cartons for stacking beakers.

● Different-sized plastic or cardboard boxes are great for putting inside each other.

● Use a large cardboard box and open up the top and bottom to make a tunnel for him to crawl through.

● A biscuit tin or old saucepan makes a good drum when bashed with a wooden spoon!

● Make a shaker out of a tin or cottage cheese-type carton with a plastic lid. Add a few grains of rice or some dried beans or lentils then secure the lid on firmly with sticky tape.

● A plastic bowl full of water placed on the floor or outdoors will provide great entertainment – especially if you can find an assortment of empty yogurt pots and plastic bottles for your baby to play with.

● Find an old handbag and put a few objects in it. Your baby will love emptying out the contents.

BUILDING FUN

He's not yet ready for intricate designs, but stacking beakers or simply piling up building blocks, first on your own, then with his help, will give hours of fun. He is bound to prefer knocking them down to the construction, so be prepared to do a l ot of rebuilding. Stacking rings help his colour recognition and hand-eye co-ordination. He'll soon remember which one goes on next. He may also be able to manage simple push-and-lock shapes, but some babies don't achieve that degree of co-ordination until later.

WATER PLAY

Bathtime isn't just for getting clean. It's a time full of fun and discovery, and once your baby can sit on a non-slip mat in the big bath he'll love to play with the water. A water activity centre which attaches by suction to the side of the bath will give hours of fun. There are lots of inexpensive water toys too: a whale which pours water out of its spout, a plastic doll, boats and ducks all float or can be sunk. But, as with just about all types of play, everyday objects are often more fun, for example, clean yogurt pots or plastic bottles.

A set of colourful stacking plastic beakers is an excellent investment because there are so many ways of playing with them, including making a nest or stacking them up and filling them with water or sand.

FIRST BOOKS

It's never too soon to start introducing your baby to the world of books. He will start to recognize shape and colour from a very early age. Washable cloth or thick, wipe-clean board books with simple, bright pictures of everyday objects and very few words will give him lots of pleasure. If you sit together with you telling him what the objects are as you turn the pages, he'll begin to point, gesticulate and 'talk' as he sees something he recognizes, like a ball or a cat. Reading a book is also a very restful way of entertaining your child.

PLAY SAFE

- Keep plastic bags and cling film away from your baby – he could suffocate.
- Never let him play with expanded polystyrene packaging. It clings in position if swallowed or stuffed into ears or noses. It cannot be broken down by the body and does not show up on X-rays.
- If using cardboard boxes as playthings, make sure you remove any metal staples. If necessary re-seal the sides with sticky tape.
- Keep tiny items like coins, small marbles, lego and buttons away from him as he could choke if he swallowed them.

TOYS FOR YOUR OLDER BABY

WHEN your baby: is showing pleasure in his toys and in your company.	**WHEN** your baby: can reach out and pick up things using both hands and fingers.	**WHEN** your baby: can sit on the floor before becoming mobile.	**WHEN** your baby: can pull himself up and is trying to walk.
WHAT he will enjoy: simple cloth and board picture books, music, songs and rhymes, simple musical instruments like shakers, drums and bells.	**WHAT** he will enjoy: activity centres, building or stacking toys, suction toys (like a wobble globe) and shape sorters.	**WHAT** he will enjoy: toys he can throw, like soft balls or blocks. Ones that move easily like peek 'n roll blow-up toys that he can grasp and roll backwards and forwards (when out of reach, encourage him to retrieve them).	**WHAT** he will enjoy: toddle trucks, push-along toys.
WHY he needs them: to help him learn to communicate. To begin to recognize colours, shapes and sounds and to derive pleasure from them.	**WHY** he needs them: to help him become more dexterous – that is, to use his hands and fingers to grasp, push, pull. To discover what happens when he does these actions. To teach him to think for himself and to develop early construction skills.	**WHY** he needs them: to encourage him to move by himself. To learn that once out of reach, a toy cannot come back by itself, but needs to be fetched (a game he will love to play with you, getting YOU to do all the work at first). To begin to learn how to throw and (later) catch.	**WHY** he needs them: to help him to balance. To develop his confidence and stability. To strengthen his leg muscles ready for walking unaided and to help him get around the room without holding on to the furniture.

179

THE TODDLER

1-2½ years

Some babies walk much earlier than others but once your baby's appetite is whetted, there'll be no stopping her. Walking brings increasing independence but she'll still need you nearby to catch her when she falls and wants a cuddle.

Endlessly inquisitive, your toddler will be 'into everything' and you'll have your work cut out to keep her safe as she explores the world around her. Bowls and boxes, spoons and paper, all are toys for building, banging, tearing and posting as she tirelessly learns about shapes and sizes, how things work and how things fit together. Then suddenly your toddler will flag, exhausted, ready to recharge her batteries for another day.

YOU AND YOUR TODDLER

Most older babies love crawling, bottom-shuffling or walking like a bear but when they walk their joy knows no bounds. It's a momentous day when you watch those first few steps. Full of concentration and determination, your toddler stumbles towards your open arms for congratulations and a warm hug. This progress is wonderful and your heart will burst with pride, but it's nerve-racking as well because toddlers take many a tumble.

Now is the time to toddler-proof your home. More accidents happen here than anywhere else, so time spent on thinking how to protect your child is an excellent insurance policy. Toddlers like to be 'into everything' and see no danger from stairs, steps, knives, hot drinks near the edge of a table, the projecting handles of pans on the hob, loose drawers, trailing flexes, fragile ornaments or expensive electronic equipment. You need eyes like a hawk with a mobile child around.

Young children like to experiment with independence by toddling off alone but your child will almost certainly want to be able to get back to you quickly. It's best to let her be as dependent on you as necessary, and always to make her feel welcome. Young children who are allowed to be as dependent as they want usually become very independent when they are older. Your toddler's developing personality becomes increasingly obvious as she delights in her new-found independence. She'll watch you doing things and want to do the same, often trying again and again until her determination and curiosity reap the rewards of success or end in helpless tears of woe and frustration. You need plenty of time and patience, because any attempts you make to take over will be met by insistent cries of 'no' or 'me do it' and you should try to respect these wishes even though it is difficult at times.

Absolutely everything commands attention now, including 'poos' and 'wee-wees'. When the first wee lands in the potty your child will want a good look at what she's done. A poo there is an even bigger feat. Your pleasure when she uses the potty instead of a nappy and your calm practicality if she can't get there in time or has a wet bed help make potty training easy for both of you.

Your toddler will probably like to eat little and often, which means planning the day around mealtimes. Once full, food all too easily becomes a plaything. She may find she can draw lovely lines on the table with egg yolk, throw buttery pieces of bread-and-butter soldiers at the cat, or make bright red

Though increasingly independent and eager to explore, your toddler will give you frequent updates about what she's doing. She also likes to know you're nearby in case she needs you.

patches of tomato ketchup on her denim dungarees. This is not so much fun for you if you have to clean the floor, wipe the table and wash the clothes. But remember, young children aren't being deliberately naughty when they make a mess. They're learning about the possibilities of everything they touch.

Being two can be difficult and sometimes this year is called 'the terrible twos', partly because of temper tantrums. When some toddlers can't have or can't do something they want, the enormous frustration bursts out in a fit of screaming and kicking. Tiredness makes tantrums more likely and they often happen in the most embarrassing situations like a supermarket check-out queue when your attention is distracted. They are frightening for a child and can be bewildering for parents, but if toddlers can trust their parents to handle their behaviour calmly, without exploding or collapsing, they learn eventually to cope in more acceptable ways and things become easier.

Understanding and speech development now progress in leaps and bounds. Single words join into twos then, gradually, little sentences emerge. Sometimes completely new words come out and you'll probably find they enter your family's vocabulary quickly. Accept whatever comes with warm interest and try to make plenty of time to be with your child so you can talk and listen to each other.

All this enthusiasm and concentration can be exhausting, leaving a parent craving adult company and someone to listen to *them*. At other times a toddler's fascination and zest for life are infectious. Life with a toddler is never dull and being with her can give life a special sparkle as you share a delight in things you previously took for granted – the bubbles in the bath water, for example, or the rustling sound of crisp autumn leaves as you shuffle through them or the wonder at flickering candles on a birthday cake. Showing things to a receptive toddler, enjoying them together and helping her to widen her horizons are some of the great rewards of parenting at this stage.

Dr Penny Stanway

OUR CHILDREN

Penny Stanway: 'Susie and Amy were close in age and liked to copy each other as well as me. They had blue-and-white striped toy buggies and occasionally we would go out in a cavalcade with me pushing Ben in his buggy and the girls pushing their dolls in theirs.'

Daphne Metland: 'One day Sam just took his nappy off and refused to have it back on, so I rushed out and bought a potty.'

Gillian Fletcher: 'Richard learnt to walk just before his first birthday by pulling himself up on the camp chairs when we were on a camping holiday. One day we heard him screaming because he'd pulled himself up on an empty chair which had fallen over with him.'

Heather Welford: 'The one thing I can always remember carrying with me when my children were toddlers was a banana. They all liked bananas and you can't get a more instant, healthy food.'

Carolyn Humphries: 'Neither Katie nor James learned to crawl and by nine months were wanting to walk everywhere, holding on to me. My back couldn't stand it so the sturdy toddle truck with bricks (so it wouldn't tip too easily) really came into its own.'

Maggie Jones: 'Tantrums were undoubtedly the feature of this period with all three children – tantrums because a biscuit was broken, because he couldn't get his own shoes on, because he didn't want to get out of the car. Tantrums and tiredness seemed to go hand-in-hand and the best policy seemed to be to ignore it while it was happening and distract the child as soon as it was over.'

Jane Bidder: 'All three of my children have hated lumpy food and "gagged" in the most alarming manner. I persevered with my first and second but gave up by the time the third came along. Even at sixteen months I'd blend Giles' food or even buy a tin meant for small babies. It took the pressure off eating for us both. By the time he was twenty months, he'd "relaxed" enough at mealtimes to learn to chew.'

FEEDING YOUR TODDLER

Toddlers can be very different from each other in the amount of food they eat, and in their likes and dislikes. During this next year or so, your toddler will grow to let you know much more clearly what he likes at mealtimes. But these are the years when arguments and battles over food can start – and where small concerns can develop into huge problems.

Parents with a toddler who is still keen on the breast or the bottle may start to wonder about the 'right' thing to do. It's certainly very natural and normal for toddlers and small children to get a lot of comfort from sucking. Toddlers who don't

good. Breast milk retains its quality, no matter how long it's made. You only need to be concerned if your toddler is still very slow to take to solid food, and this is affecting his health and development.

Nevertheless, if you want to retain the initiative in weaning, start thinking about reducing your toddler's time or frequency at the breast. Mothers of older breastfed toddlers report that it can be more difficult as their toddlers become more adept at insisting on what they want. Younger ones can be distracted more easily.

Bottlefeeding into the toddler years does carry a risk to dental health. This is because

have bottles or breastfeeds often suck fingers, thumbs, dummies or blanket corners – anything in fact that's fairly portable! So your child's not doing anything abnormal in continuing to show this need.

CARRYING ON WITH
BREAST OR BOTTLE

Different issues apply, according to whether your toddler is continuing with the breast, or the bottle.

Some people don't approve of a toddler at the breast. The reasons are complex. However, if you and your toddler are both happy to carry on, you can rest assured that it's nobody's business but your own, and you are not doing your toddler anything but

toddlers tend to carry their bottles with them, taking swigs over a longish period of time. They may also fall asleep or relax sleepily with them. This bathes the teeth in the bottle's contents, which are only harmless if the contents are plain water, which many toddlers reject. If your toddler still uses bottles, restrict them to mealtimes. Offer a cup for thirst at other times. If the bedtime bottle is still important, remove it when your child is almost asleep.

All toddlers benefit greatly from milk as a drink and mixed with other things. But if your toddler is having a lot of milk to drink – say more than a pint a day – then he could be restricting his appetite for other foods. Have a word with your health visitor if you think this could be the case.

HELPING OUT

Your child can 'help' in the kitchen as soon as he can hold a spoon. There will be many occasions when for safety reasons, or lack of time, you can't really involve your toddler in preparing a meal – but when you can, give him a chance to join in.

Depending on age and dexterity, he can:
- Set the table.
- Stir the mixture in a bowl.
- Sprinkle some salt or other flavourings into a dish.
- Roll out some pastry.
- Spread a filling on a sandwich.
- Wash up the things you've used.

A poor eater may try new things when he's been helping to make them.

GETTING EMOTIONAL ABOUT FOOD

Don't fall into the trap of making a fuss over what your toddler eats. Accept his likes and dislikes, and encourage him to widen his repertoire by serving food in imaginative ways that you think might appeal to him (see recipes, page 187). But if he doesn't want it, then fine. There is no point in trying to persuade your child to eat food he just doesn't want. Simply take the plate of unfinished food away without making a fuss. It may be hard to do, but you can be assured that he won't starve himself. As long as he's well and growing, and you don't feel he's regularly filling up on just sugary foods, or milk, you don't need to worry.

Food is such fascinating stuff that it's tempting to stare at it and suck it from your fingers as well as to practise using your spoon and to have a drink every so often.

185

QUICK AND EASY MEALS FOR YOUR TODDLER

Here are some quick-and-easy meals you can share with your toddler:

- **Pasta with peas, mushrooms and a cheese sauce.**

- **Pasta with ham strips or pieces of sausage in a tomato sauce.**

- **Jacket potato with salad and baked beans or sweetcorn.**

- **Poached egg and tinned spaghetti hoops on toast.**

- **Tinned or home-made vegetable soup with grated cheese sprinkled on top, served with fingers of wholemeal buttered toast.**

- **Toasted cheese made with wholemeal bread.**

- **Home-made burgers (minced steak with breadcrumbs and beaten egg, shaped and fried until cooked through) in a wholemeal bun, with ketchup, oven chips and carrot sticks.**

- **Sandwiches made with wholemeal bread and filled with flaked tuna, ham, chicken or sliced avocado.**

For a quick dessert, you can offer fresh fruit on its own, or ice-cream, yogurt or fromage frais with the fresh fruit mixed in with it.

- **Don't offer your toddler whole or chopped nuts because there is a risk that they may cause your child to choke. You should also avoid adding salt to your toddler's food.**

FEEDING YOUR TODDLER

Children have strong likes and dislikes and use meals for learning to say no as well as eating and playing.

186

Let your toddler join in as many family meals, including celebration ones, as you can. This helps him learn about acceptable 'table manners', and encourages him to think of mealtimes as enjoyable, sociable events. If there are other children present who eat absolutely everything then you may be surprised to see your toddler tucking into something he would normally reject. However, small children can't be expected to sit still without eating for long, either before the meal is served, between courses, or afterwards while waiting for others to finish – at least not without making rather a fuss! If you expect and accept this, you can be firmer about other basics of good table behaviour, like not getting down from the table in the middle of a course and then returning.

WEIGHT

Routine developmental assessments for your toddler (see page 130) include a height and weight check. You may in any case still be making occasional visits to the baby clinic, where your child will be weighed. Ask the health visitor or the doctor to show you the chart where your toddler's weight is plotted. If there's any concern about his growth, they may ask about his feeding patterns.

If you are concerned that your toddler is overweight, bear in mind that most children of this age have little pot bellies and it may just be a chubby stage he is going through. If your child is getting most of his nourishment from high-fat, sugary foods such as cakes, biscuits and pastries he may have a weight problem. If you think your toddler is underweight, this too may just be a temporary phenomenon, perhaps as a result of a bout of illness, or a period of fussiness over food. However, either extreme of weight, whether under or over, is potentially more serious than this. If you or the clinic are concerned, then ask for a referral to a paediatrician.

A HEALTHY DIET FOR YOUR TODDLER

Your toddler needs a varied diet, though you may find yours goes through stages when he has strong likes and dislikes. Try to avoid letting him snack between meals on sugary foods, such as sweets, biscuits or cake. Instead, offer a snack of fruit, or a vegetable stick, or a slice of wholemeal bread topped with a savoury spread.

You may find that the various recipe ideas for toddlers opposite are useful. Most are fairly quick and simple to prepare – and they're healthy too!

See The Child Health Clinic, page 130

Quick Pizza Faces
Serves 1
Slice of wholemeal bread
1 tsp tomato purée
28g (1oz) grated cheese (mild Cheddar)
2 slices of fresh tomato and 1 slice of red pepper
for the face (optional)

Lightly toast the bread under the grill.
Spread with the tomato purée and top
with grated cheese. Make the face with
the tomato slices and pepper, if wanted.
Place under a medium-hot grill until the
cheese is melted and bubbling.

Tuna Baked Potato
Serves 1
1 baked potato, halved
½ 200g (7oz) can tuna, drained and flaked
15g (½oz) margarine
60ml (2fl oz) whole milk

Scoop out potato flesh and mash with the
tuna, margarine and milk until combined.
Spoon the mixture back into the potato
skins and bake in a pre-heated oven
at 180°C (350°F) Gas 4 for about
10 minutes or in a microwave until
well heated through.

Baked-bean Shepherd's Pie
Serves 4
400g (14oz) can baked beans
2 large potatoes with skins left
on, chopped
60ml (2fl oz) whole milk
Knob of butter or margarine
25g (1oz) grated cheese

Cook the potatoes in boiling water until
soft. Drain and mash the potato together
with the milk and butter. Pour the baked
beans into a suitably sized serving dish
and top with the mashed potato. Sprinkle
over the grated cheese and bake in a
pre-heated oven at 180°C (350°F) Gas 4
for 15 minutes.

If wished, you could divide the
baked beans and potato mixture into
four individual portions and freeze.

Banana Whip
Serves 1
1 ripe banana
120ml (4fl oz) whole milk

Place the banana and milk in a blender
and process until smooth. Pour into
a cup and serve with a straw.

187

*Choosing fruit for a
snack or dessert provides a
good helping of nutrients
such as vitamins,
minerals and fibre, and
also a chance to admire
the varied colours, shapes
and flavours.*

NAPPY CHANGING AND BATHING

At some point during the toddler months, you'll start to think about teaching your child to use the potty and the lavatory – and by the age of two-and-a-half, she's likely to be either fully toilet-trained, or well on the way. During this time, she'll also learn to wash her hands and clean her teeth (with help from you) and she'll make good progress in learning to dress and undress herself. It's important to allow your toddler to try and do all these things for herself, even though it sometimes means extra work for you if, for example, she ends up soaking wet after an enthusiastic hand-washing session.

NAPPY CHANGING

Your toddler will use fewer nappies – maybe three or four a day – as she won't urinate as often as she did. She may start to be aware of having a wet or dirty nappy, and actually ask you to change it. This might be the first sign of being ready to use the potty. She may still resist nappy changes, or start to resist them, by wriggling and writhing, but if you persist and stay calm (see page 154), she will learn to accept that a nappy change is a bore, but one she just has to put up with. It sometimes helps to enlist an older brother or sister to amuse her.

Give your toddler the chance to run round without a nappy on now and then, perhaps after her bath would be a good time. It's worth the occasional accident to let her enjoy the feeling of freedom.

BATHING AND DAILY CARE

Toddlers get pretty dirty, and most need a good soak and scrub every night. Topping and tailing is still probably the handiest way to give a younger toddler a good wash. If she has a bath in the evening, she'll need a morning top and tail. If she wriggles try some of the ideas suggested on page 154 for changing her nappy. You may find it's easiest to top and tail and put on a fresh nappy while she's still in her cot and can't crawl or walk too far away. Encourage handwashing before meals, especially after any outside play, or if you have animals. As your child grows, she can wash and dry her own hands. Put a step by your washbasin so she can stand on it (you may have to turn the taps on) and have a towel she can manage to reach, too.

Hair washing

Try a shampoo shield (see page 154) if your child hates having her hair washed. Or she might tolerate it if she can slosh the water over her own head, or use a hairdresser-style hose by herself, although she is likely to get shampoo in her eyes unless you can hold a small towel or dry flannel over her eyes.

Fun in the bath

Bathtime is a great chance for chatting and playing with a toddler whose skill in language is growing day by day. You don't need lots of special bath toys – though there are some extremely imaginative ones

Surely not this again . . . I wish it were over . . . Let's be off now, please . . . It's good to be in a clean, dry nappy but wouldn't it be lovely not to wear one at all?

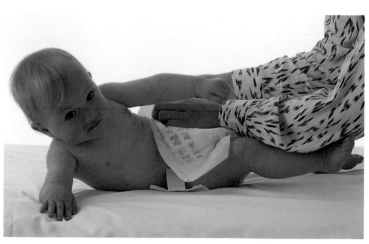

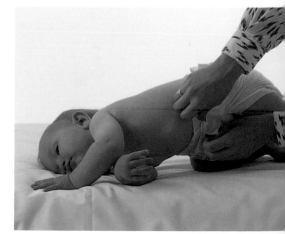

See Nappy Changing and Bathing, page 154, for more information on nappy changing

Use child-strength toothpaste (with less fluoride than other types) so there's little risk of your toddler getting an excessive fluoride intake from swallowing too much.

available. Plastic cups and crockery, and old plastic bottles and tops equip a toddler with many different ways to pour, sprinkle and slosh about and to have impromptu tea parties with a range of pretend delicious drinks. It's handy to have a special bag strung between the taps in which to store all the toys.

Bathtime fears

Although most toddlers enjoy bathtime, some refuse to go in the bath and seem genuinely frightened at the thought of it. If this is the case then it is probably best to keep your toddler clean with all-over washes instead and to try the bath again after a gap. It is sensible to take things slowly, she may prefer to have a bath with you or a friend at first.

Teeth

Your toddler will learn to brush her teeth during this stage, but she will need your help for a few more years. Use a small baby-sized soft toothbrush.

● Keep to small amounts of child-strength toothpaste only because your child is bound to swallow some and she could end up getting too much fluoride from the toothpaste.

● Replace toothbrushes when they're flat or looking worn.

● Brush morning and night.

● Make a first appointment with the dentist some time around the age of two-and-a-half years old.

● Disclosing tablets are fun. A toddler can use them, supervised, from the age of two.

189

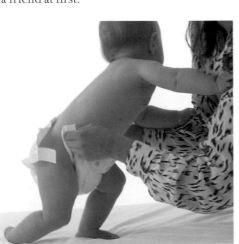

POTTY TRAINING

Most toddlers become used to the potty or the lavatory at some time before the age of three – and they usually do so without much teaching. They learn simply by watching other people and copying. Most parents speed the process up, however, by active intervention. Here's what to do to make it easier and more enjoyable.

Vocabulary
The words you use are up to you, of course, but many parents these days teach their children the words 'poo' and 'wee' – more acceptable than some other equivalents, and unlikely to embarrass anyone unduly.

EQUIPMENT
Potty
Choose a sturdy, plastic potty with a wide base. Consider getting more than one, for use in different rooms. A splash-guard is useful for a boy, as is a lid for carrying it when full.

Climb-up stool
This makes it easy for your toddler to reach the lavatory or the washbasin. You can buy a toddler's 'grow tall' step as shown here but any strong, lightweight box or short-legged household stool will do. Check it is secure, and that your child can move it and stand on it confidently.

Toddler toilet seat
This can be useful for small toddlers when they start to use the lavatory.

WHEN TO START
There's no point in starting to potty train your child before he's ready to learn. This is unlikely to be much before the age of twenty months – and it could be quite a lot later (even two and a half or older).

You may hear about babies who were 'trained' sooner. It's unlikely that they reached true toilet independence, though – that means going to the lavatory without being taken or reminded, managing their own clothing, and washing and wiping without help. Early trained toddlers tend to need a good deal of parental help, even if they can manage to perform on the potty when it's offered.

On the whole, it's easier for you to wait until your toddler can understand simple instructions, can go a couple of hours without urinating (you can watch for this on the beach or in the garden if he is without a nappy, or check his nappy every so often), and can pull his clothing up and down without too much assistance. It also helps if your toddler knows that wees and poos come from his body, and recognizes when he has a wet or dirty nappy. Some toddlers will make this obvious by pointing at their nappy while they are doing a wee or a poo.

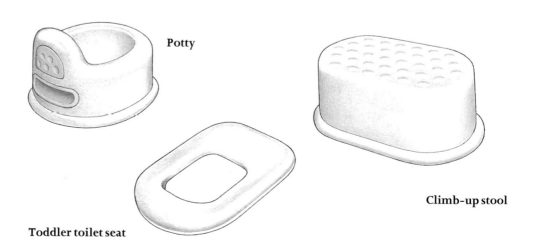

Potty

Toddler toilet seat

Climb-up stool

Your toddler may enjoy sitting on her potty so let her take her time.

Introducing the potty

Have the potty around in the bathroom for some weeks before you begin training so your toddler can sit on it when he has no clothing to bother about. He just might do something in it. But don't think you've cracked it. It could just be luck! But it helps him to make the link between the potty and the lavatory, which he'll have seen you use.

See if older children will oblige by using the potty for you. These practical lessons are far more effective than trying to tell your child what to do in words. Ask your child to sit on the potty at more frequent times in the day, and give praise whenever he does anything in it.

There may be times when he is happy to sit there for several minutes. But never force your child to sit on it, or get cross if he doesn't want to.

See Bathing and Everyday Care, page 221, for night-time dryness

If your toddler doesn't want to sit on the potty, don't force her. Leave it for a while and try again another time.

192

Managing accidents

Most children have 'accidents' from time to time during training. Make as little fuss about them as possible. This really is a learning process, and while it's human nature to feel a bit irritated and inconvenienced, be sure to show you understand. Your child probably forgot, or didn't realize he needed the potty until it was too late. 'Hanging on' is a skill that comes later. Encouraging your child by telling him that he'll remember next time is better than showing him how to make you really cross, which will only upset him.

Help your child to take responsibility by teaching him what to do with his wet or dirty clothes and where to find the clean ones, and giving him a cloth to help wipe up as well.

OUT AND ABOUT

At first, you'll probably still put your child in a nappy when you're out, or visiting, but you could think about using trainer pants instead. The paper throw-away ones look like pants, and pull up and down as easily (and tear off if a quick change is necessary). An absorbent core makes them cope with any accidents. Remember to take a spare pair with you, just in case.

If you prefer to use ordinary pants, you'll again need to take an extra pair with you,

plus a change of clothes. Try to encourage your child to use the potty or lavatory before going out – but remember younger toddlers can't do anything to order for a while yet. They have to feel the sensations of needing to 'go'.

DRY AT NIGHT

Most toddlers need a night nappy for longer than a daytime one, although a few achieve night-time dryness at about the same time. Once you notice the night-time nappy is occasionally dry in the morning, try leaving it off, telling your child why.

Even if the nappy is always wet, leave it off and see if not having a nappy helps your child to wake if he needs the lavatory. It sometimes seems that wearing a nappy holds a child back from developing night-time dryness.

LEAVING IT TILL LATER

If you wait until your child is about two-and-a-half before thinking about training, you may find the process surprisingly quick and easy. Children of this age may be mature enough to hang on to a full bladder for a time, and they may even be able to use the lavatory without much help – bypassing the potty altogether. This could be helpful if you've already got your hands full with a new baby or a house move.

TIPS
● Let your child get used to the lavatory from the start.
● A piece of lavatory paper in the bottom of the potty before your child uses it makes for easy cleaning.
● Keep a pair of rolled-up pyjama trousers in a plastic bag in your bag at all times, in case of accidents (they look like jogging bottoms but take up less room).

YOUR QUESTIONS ANSWERED

My daughter's been dry for a few months now, but she always waits until she gets her night nappy on before doing a poo. She won't do it in the potty.
Many children develop a habit like this. Some hang on, and become very constipated, which makes the problem worse, as they then have an accident when they can't keep it in any longer. It's best to accept your daughter's resistance, as she's likely to grow out of it. You could try putting a nappy in the potty, so she does it 'in the nappy' – some children have been won over in this way.

We've tried lots of times to train our son, but he still has as many accidents as successes. He's twenty-six months, and I feel he knows what to do, but doesn't care.
You may be right. Potty training is nearly always more important to the parents than the child! The fact that your son is having some success shows he is on the way to being trained, so don't give up hope. If you're getting sick of the situation, put him back in nappies for a few weeks and then try again. Alternatively, you could try involving him in his accidents (see page 192).

My son is two, and he is reasonably reliable about the potty – but he seems to need me to remind him, or he'd just forget. I check every half hour or so by asking him if he needs a wee. How can I encourage him to be more independent? I get the impression that he finds my constant reminders rather irritating!
Most children need some reminders at the start of potty training, but you don't need to check as often as this. He'll be helped if you start to trust him for longer, though he may continue to forget at first. Aim to leave it up to him to decide when and if he wants to use the lavatory or potty.

I've heard it's possible to train children early, so they're out of nappies by eighteen months. Is this true?
A few children really are clean and dry by this age, though they are still not totally independent, as they need quite a lot of adult help with clothing, and sitting comfortably, and they probably can't use the lavatory very well. Some children do seem to train themselves as early as this, but it's more likely that they've reached this stage after a lot of intensive 'training'. This means hard work on the part of the adults looking after them, producing the potty after every meal for months for example, and at intervals between meals, too. As long as it's done kindly and without any punishment for a lack of result, then this method probably does no harm – apart from being rather boring and time-consuming. If you wait until later, however, you'll probably find potty training much easier.

My daughter was dry for a couple of months but now she's suddenly started wetting again. Why is this happening and what can I do about it?
It could be that your daughter has a urine infection, and you should see your family doctor to have this checked out. Or it could be that she has been frightened in the lavatory, and has become worried about it as a result. Some children respond to stress and change in their lives by regressing to more babyish behaviour – and that includes wetting. Thinking about whether this is the case with your daughter, and giving her plenty of love and support and reassurance should help her to cope and she should regain her potty skills soon.

Why does my four-year-old son still insist on using the potty, and not the lavatory, for a poo? I am particularly concerned because he's starting school soon and will need to use the lavatory.
This is another fairly common situation. He may have been frightened and uncomfortable on the lavatory in the past, and simply be refusing to repeat the experience. You may be able to encourage him by rewarding him for sitting on the lavatory, fully clothed, for a short time. Get him to use the potty in the bathroom, so it's at least near the lavatory, and let him empty it afterwards. Make sure the lavatory is comfortable for him (try a child's seat and a box for his feet to rest on, see equipment, page 190) – and give him lots of praise when he tries again.

SLEEP AND BEDTIME

● **Keep bedtime rituals simple, and don't let your child make them never-ending. Yes, kiss teddy goodnight, and maybe rabbit, too – but don't get into the pattern of kissing every soft toy in the room.**
● **If you say this is the last story, mean it and don't change your mind.**

Sleeping – or not sleeping – is one of the prime concerns expressed by parents with toddler-aged children. To a certain extent, we expect babies to wake up in the night. Even when a baby is a little older, we have a whole bundle of explanations for why a baby might wake – hunger, colic, wind, teething, fear, loneliness . . . But a child who's walking and, if not actually talking much, certainly understanding a lot of what's said to her – why does she wake? And why doesn't she want to stay in bed when she's told she must?

If you are the parent of a wakeful toddler, then you may find you have to cope with other people's criticism, or your own self-criticism and maybe a lack of confidence in yourself. You may ask yourself, 'What am I doing wrong?'

NIGHT WAKING AND DIFFICULTIES IN SETTLING

You can't make a toddler sleep, but you can make it easier for her to settle, and to go through the night without needing attention. There are different ways of making bedtimes easier, if your toddler often objects to going to bed:

● Adopt a regular bedtime routine (see page 157) and make sure bedtime is always quiet and non-stimulating.
● Put her in her cot when she's almost asleep.
● Stay with your toddler in the bedroom until she drops off.
● If your toddler takes ages to get to sleep, distance yourself gradually by going from the bed to a chair, then move the chair nearer the door, then stand at the door.
● Leave her, saying you're just going for a cup of coffee, but you'll be back. Do go back (your child has to trust you). You may find that after a few nights the child falls asleep in the meantime.
● Try the 'checking' method of leaving your child and returning every few minutes to offer reassurance without taking her out of bed.
● Try just a brief 'check' when your child wakes in the night.

● Bring your child into bed with you when she wakes, though this may become a habit that's hard to break.

It's not helpful to:
● Constantly chop and change your method of settling.
● Talk about what an awful sleeper/settler your child is in front of her.
● Try one method (such as checking) for a few nights only. It may take a fortnight to work properly.
● Sometimes let your child in your bed and sometimes not (unless she is old enough to understand why – for example, when she's poorly you may say 'yes').
● Let your child come downstairs to watch TV with you or have a drink.

AVOIDING THAT LATE NAP

Most toddlers still need some sleep in the day. But if your toddler has a late afternoon or early evening nap, her bedtime could be severely delayed, as she'll be full of beans until 10pm.

Sometimes you can't avoid this happening. Tired toddlers may flop wherever they are because sleep just overwhelms them. But here are some ideas to try:
● Adjust the timing of any other daytime nap to avoid late-afternoon exhaustion (you may need to make the nap after lunch, rather than before).
● If you're out with her in the buggy, let her walk some of the way.
● Immediately rush home at the first sign of drooping eyelids.
● Talk to her, play with her and get her involved in what you're doing.

HOLIDAYS AND VISITS

Your toddler's routine is bound to be disrupted occasionally with visits and holidays, or simply an outing that ends late. This needn't disrupt your everyday life. Stick to the usual order of activities (for example, tea, bathtime, story or play, then bed) when you can and, once you're back to normal, go back to your regular timing.

194

OPPOSITE *When your bedtime is near, your play and wash in the bath are over and your tummy is full, it's lovely to be cuddled as you look at the pictures in your book and listen to the story.*

See Sleep and Bedtime, page 157, for bedtime routine

COT TO BED

At some time between the age of eighteen months and two-and-a-half, your child may become too big for her cot or you may be expecting another baby. Whatever the reason, you can make the transition to bed easy if you tell her in advance what you're going to do. Try not to make the change just as the new baby needs the cot – leave a few weeks' gap.

EARLY MORNINGS

Lots of families enjoy a morning cuddle in bed with their early waking toddler. This is often easier to manage than trying to convince your child to stay in her own room until you decide she can get up.

You may be able to get an extra half hour or so of sleep by leaving a drink your toddler can reach when she wakes, and by making sure some safe toys are in or near her cot or bed. Thick blinds or curtains in the room will help prevent bright morning light disturbing your child.

NIGHTMARES AND FEARS

Toddlerhood can be a time when fears and anxieties develop. They can show up more acutely at night – and as everyone knows the occasional bad dream can happen to anyone. Few toddlers have adequate language to express their fears in words, and it can be hard to offer the right reassurance if you don't know precisely why your child is upset and afraid.

If your toddler is going through a stage when you feel she is upset or frightened at night, she may need to see you at night and be aware of your comforting presence. A nightlight, a landing light shining through an open door or even the glow of a streetlight, can be comforting to a child who's afraid of the dark.

MUSICAL BEDS

Few families manage to get through the early years of parenthood without having at least a few nights when one or more of the family members wakes up in a different bed

Would you ever have imagined – before you had an early waking toddler – that you could enjoy playing a game of fitting shapes into spaces at the crack of dawn?

196

See What Your Child May Need, page 224

A young child who's feeling poorly nearly always likes someone close at hand all the time. Cuddles, attention and time are some of the simple ingredients you can put in the recipe for a speedy recovery.

from the one they fell asleep in the night before. For some it goes on for a long time, usually because a child needs company or comfort to get to sleep again. One parent gets out of bed to share a single bed with a child, and the other parent shares the double bed with another child.

There's nothing wrong with this; it can be the best way for everyone to get more sleep. If it bothers you, however, and you want to stop, you have to be consistent. Take your child back to her bed, again and again if necessary if she wakes and wanders, after a quick cuddle. This will work eventually, although you must be firm otherwise you will confuse your child.

FAMILY BED
An alternative is the family bed, or co-sleeping – the usual way for families to sleep until we all had bedrooms. Some people feel this is the natural way to sleep, as babies and toddlers are close to the warmth and comfort of the parent, and the mother's breast – but you can only do it in comfort if you have a huge bed or mattress. Also there is a suggestion that it may be safer for a baby under twelve months

of age to sleep in her own cot because of the risk of cot death from overheating (see page 118). Parents who adopt co-sleeping find that as children get older, they gradually change to using their own room more and more as their independence and confidence grow.

WHEN YOUR CHILD IS ILL
Any period of illness is bound to affect your child's sleep. She may be extra sleepy in the day and, as she recovers (and children can do so very quickly), resist her usual bedtime. Parents sometimes find this sets up a new pattern, but if you put your old routine back into action and are consistent, you'll probably find things get back to normal soon.

'My fifteen-month-old has never been a good sleeper. I find that I can normally settle him back down to sleep the first time he wakes, but the only way to settle him the second time is to take him into bed with us. Although I don't sleep as deeply with him beside me, I actually like the togetherness of sharing a bed.'

WHAT YOUR TODDLER MAY NEED

Your very own 'grown-up' bed makes an excellent venue for entertaining. And you can also get out and go to the lavatory on your own at night, which you can't if you're in a cot.

All the safety precautions you've taken so far still apply but more so. Your child will soon be able to climb on to chairs or tables, so just moving things out of reach may not be enough. And it won't be long before he's ready to move into a bed, so it's time to think about rearranging his room.

A PROPER BEDROOM

Your child will be acquiring an ever-growing number of books, toys and clothes. It's great if you can plan his room so he can have all his things in there while allowing as much floor space as possible. It will then, eventually, become his playroom as well as his bedroom.

Plan of action

1. Remove the feeding chair, baby bath (if it was in there) and other unnecessary baby equipment. (You may still need the changing mat – but some mums find they have to change their child standing up as he won't lie down and keep still any more.)
2. Buy a bookcase or set of open shelves to fix to a wall (don't have free-standing stacking shelves as they can be pulled over too easily).
3. Buy a wardrobe.
4. Provide plenty of places to keep his toys.

STORAGE SECRETS

Encourage your child to be tidy from an early age by providing a place for everything. Tidying up can become fun if he can see a reason for it.

● Make cardboard-box beds for favourite toys, a box garage for the cars and find a small tray for the tea-set.
● Invest in a set of plastic stacking toy boxes. They're colourful and inexpensive.
● Cover ice-cream tubs or similar containers with sticky-backed plastic and label them for small items like farm animals, cars or the doll's tea-set.
● Label shelves or boxes with what goes on or in them – teddies, bricks, cars and so on. It will help your child begin to recognize words.
● Coat hooks on the back of the door are useful for his dressing-gown and any bags or holdalls.
● A shoe-tidy with several compartments hung on the wall (or behind the door) can be useful for small toys as well as shoes.

Secondhand bargains

Bookshelves, chests of drawers, wardrobes and tables can all be picked up for just a few pounds in junk shops, car boot sales and even jumble sales.

FROM COT TO BED

When your child is about two, you will probably be thinking about moving him into a 'proper' bed. Not just because he's too big for the cot, but if he's being toilet trained, he'll need to be able to get out of bed quickly to go on his potty at night. Remember to cover the mattress with a plastic sheet to prevent staining just in case he has an accident.

COT BED

If you have a cot bed, all you'll need to do is remove the sides and fit the lower foot-end panel if yours has one. But as it isn't a full-size bed you'll need to buy a larger one in a few years' time.

DIVAN

If you buy a good-quality one it will last for years – probably until your child is grown up. A divan has a box-sprung base with an interior-sprung mattress on top.
+ Suitable as an adult bed too.
– No space to store anything underneath.

BED WITH DRAWERS

Extra storage space under the bed can be an advantage. The drawers are accessible to your child which makes them good for toys.

+ Makes use of otherwise wasted space.
– Your toddler may constantly empty out the contents.

CABIN BED

Similar to the above but with the bed raised, giving both cupboard and drawer space underneath. This type of bed is good for a small room although it is not suitable for the under sixes.

CAPTAIN'S BED

A high version of the cabin bed, with a built-in wardrobe and shelves. It is not recommended for very young children because of its height off the ground, but worth considering for after a cot bed.

BUNK BEDS

If you are planning to have more than one child and want them to share a room, bunk beds are a good choice. There should be a safety rail on each side of the top bunk, although if there is a rail on one side only the beds should be pushed up against a wall.
+ Gives more floor space in a room where two beds are essential, and some convert to single beds later.
– The top bunk is not suitable for a child under six years of age.

BED SAFETY
● When transferring from cot to bed, have the bed against a wall and fit a bed-guard to prevent your child falling out.
● Children under the age of six should not sleep at an elevated height.
● Don't encourage bouncing on the bed – it is easy for a child to bounce off and crack his head on a radiator or sharp-cornered table.

199

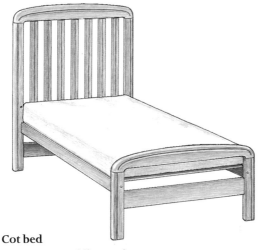

Cot bed
+ Gets your toddler used to a bed before moving on to a full-sized one.
– Only really suitable if you're not planning to have any more children within, say, five years.

Cabin bed
+ Both the cabin and the captain's bed are great space savers in small rooms.
– Not suitable for children under the age of six because of the height off the ground.

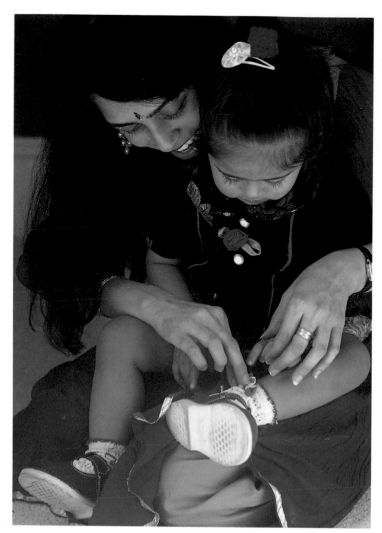

200

Small feet sometimes grow faster than you realize, so be sure to check regularly that your child's shoes fit correctly and aren't cramping the style of tiny toes.

BEST FOOT FORWARD

Don't put your child in shoes until he is walking unaided, then follow these guidelines:

● Get his feet measured every four months by a reputable retailer.
● Choose leather uppers for his 'proper' shoes as they let the feet breathe.
● Choose a buckled, laced or velcro-fastening style, not slip-ons.
● For playwear choose canvas as it also allows the feet to breathe and will 'give' and not restrict your child's toes. Plastic 'jelly' shoes are fine for the beach but shouldn't be worn every day.
● Don't buy wellingtons so big that they slop on and off, and don't let him wear them without socks as they can rub.
● Socks and tights must also fit properly. If they are too small they will restrict the growth of his toes; if they are too big the extra will bunch over his heel, or toes, and rub, causing soreness.

WALKING OUT

Your toddler will not want to be in his buggy all the time now and holding hands is not always enough for his safety. A pair of reins is useful equipment – especially in crowded places. Most safety harnesses come complete with detachable reins. A wrist extension – one end clips around your wrist and the other to your child's with a coiled lead in between – is an alternative if he won't wear reins.

COMFY CLOTHES

Toddlers are very active little people so they need clothes that are comfortable, still look good after loads of washing and also that don't need ironing!

The most practical, and also the most popular outfits for both boys and girls are jogging suits because they're soft, easy to wear and durable. Other favourites are dungarees or pinafore dresses with T-shirts, blouses or jumpers underneath. Dungarees aren't so good when you're toilet training your child, however, because they take too long to undo and pull on and off. It is a good idea to avoid tights for girls if you're at that stage too. Buy trousers a size bigger if your child still wears a nappy.

DINING CHAIRS

There comes a point when your child no longer wants to sit in his highchair. First take off the highchair tray so he can sit at the table. You could then try a table-mounted seat which clips on to any suitable stable surface and is useful when travelling as it can be packed easily. Or a sit-at-table seat, as below, can be turned over to give two heights. A strap secures it to the base of most dining chairs and the raised sides prevent your child from falling off.

Sit-at-table seat
+ Much safer than a pile of cushions or a dining chair.
– Some children want to be the same as everyone else from an early age and won't sit on it.

Dressed for all weathers

For outdoor wear in winter a machine-washable, zip-up snowsuit is fine, although an anorak with matching salopettes or quilted dungarees is even better. Avoid winter coats that need dry-cleaning. When it's really cold your child will also need a hat and mittens.

In summer keep your child's shoulders covered if the weather is very hot and make sure he wears a sunhat.

Underwear

Four of each of the basics – vests, pants, socks or tights – is the minimum. If your child is just out of nappies, choose vests, not pop-under bodysuits. You'll need at least six pairs of pants to allow for accidents. (Boys may need extra pairs of trousers at this stage for the same reason.)

And so to bed

Nighties and pyjamas take over from stretchsuits now. If your child tends to kick off his bedclothes, put him in a fleecy sleepsuit (you'll need two) over his pyjamas in cold weather. This will also double as a dressing-gown (which he'll need for evenings and mornings when it's cold if he doesn't have a sleepsuit).

Good, sturdy but supple, waterproof shoes are suitable for walking outside come rain or shine. And dressed in a warm, comfortable, colourful outfit you feel ready for anything.

COMMON CONCERNS

How do I cope with tantrums? My toddler is so wilful and I just don't know how to deal with it. She is nearly two.
It's a shock to every mother when her baby suddenly asserts herself and won't do what you want her to. She may hit you, break things, lie on the floor and scream, throw her food or drink away, or even break her favourite toy.

Tantrums are mainly caused by frustration. Your toddler may desperately want something that she can't have or may not be able to explain to you what she does want; or she may want to perform some task which is beyond her ability. Because a child can't have everything she wants, she has a tantrum. The best thing to do is not to let your child's tantrum anger you. If you can, ignore it, but don't leave her alone. When she is feeling better, then you can comfort her, explain that you understand why she is upset, and welcome her return to good humour. Find her something else that is interesting to do, and don't make the mistake of allowing her to have what she wanted once the confrontation is over. Often tantrums occur when your child is tired; a sleep or a period of quiet play may be the answer.

My toddler is very aggressive. At playgroup she hits the other children and is always snatching or throwing things. What should I do?
Aggression in a young child is very common, especially if she has a younger brother and sister. She may take out her jealousy on other children or adults. It helps not to reward bad behaviour; remove toys that she throws or uses as a weapon, take her firmly away from any child she is bullying, and perhaps leave the playgroup or situation altogether if she persists. Often aggressive behaviour is a way of getting attention, so try to provide this when she is playing well rather than when she acts badly.

Remember not to hit your child or punish her physically for being aggressive, as this will give your child the message that aggression pays and that hitting is an acceptable form of behaviour.

I'm expecting a second baby in a month; how can I prepare my toddler so that she won't be jealous of the new arrival?
Most children feel some jealousy of a new baby brother or sister, and they also feel affection for them. However, there are ways in which you can help make things easier for your child.

It helps not to describe the baby as someone to play with; she won't be that for a very long time. Explain that babies can be boring in some ways but that they become more interesting with time. Make sure you still play with your toddler and that the new baby doesn't get all the attention from visitors. If you can, arrange for your toddler to see her own friends and go on some outings to keep her busy. Stressing all the things that your toddler can do which the baby can't can help her feel more grown-up and important.

My toddler is getting out of hand – my whole day is a battle. I don't want to smack her, but I really don't know how else to get her to do what I want.
Toddlers need firm handling. She is too young to understand properly if you try

When a new baby demands your mother's time, you can always look after your doll. Most young children have mixed feelings about a new arrival in the family – they may love the baby but don't always like her.

202

See Dealing with Feelings, page 250

to reason with her and if you smack her she won't understand why. It helps to try to be firm and consistent. Don't let her do one thing one day and the next day forbid it, perhaps because you're tired and in a hurry. Always take things away when they are abused. Provide lots of distractions to avoid conflicts and try to avoid situations which always lead to tears. Most important, give her attention when she's being 'good'.

It may help not to provide too much choice. If you offer her a choice of orange or apple juice she won't know which to choose and may change her mind several times and end up crying because she can't have both. Don't make an issue out of things that aren't important but be firm over things that really matter which might affect her safety.

Make your house toddler-proof so that she can play and explore without you having to say 'no' all the time. Provide alternatives to things she can't do – find an old radio with knobs that she can twiddle instead of the knobs on the oven or the video, or a toy with buttons she can press instead of the phone.

Should I keep my toddler on reins? She seems to hate them and cries to have them off.
Reins can be a very practical way of keeping your toddler safe while you are shopping, making journeys on buses and trains, or in crowded places, especially if you also have a young baby to look after. If you use reins every time you go out as soon as your child can walk, she will get used to them and won't protest. If you start later, perhaps because of some near-accident, be firm and perhaps offer some reward. Don't pull on the reins all the time or use them to drag her along; have them there as a back-up in case you need them, but still hold her hand if she wants you to. If she also resists holding your hand, it can help to offer her a choice of the right or left hand. But in some cases, such as crossing roads or walking along crowded pavements, you can't afford to argue about it, her safety depends on it. Don't embark on journeys that are too long or tiring for her and perhaps take the pushchair with you so that you can use this as a last resort.

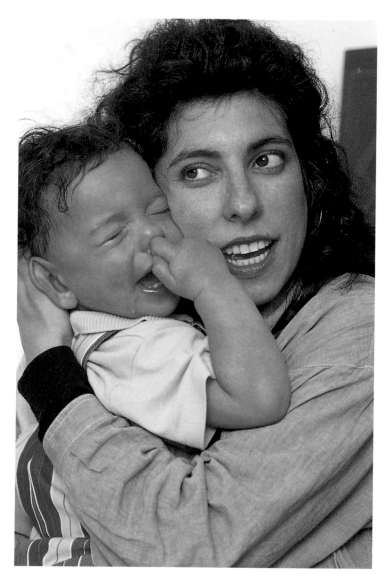

My toddler has started scribbling on the walls and has also damaged the wallpaper. I've told her off but she keeps on doing it. How can I discourage her?
Some children love drawing and there is something irresistible about a large blank space. You can try pasting up an area of lining paper, perhaps in the child's room, where you can allow her to scribble but make it clear that she mustn't do this anywhere else. Keep an eye on her if she tends to wander off with a pen in other people's houses. While she goes through this phase, create plenty of opportunities for her to draw and paint where you can supervise her, on the kitchen table or in her room.

If you are decorating, try to have smooth washable surfaces in areas where there will be a lot of wear and tear such as the hallway, stairs and kitchen, so you can wipe away scribbles and sticky fingermarks.

Toddlerhood can be a confusing time for your child and he'll need your love and support at all times.

203

See Growing and Learning, page 233, for learning rules; Positive Parenting, page 266, for further information on discipline

GROWING AND LEARNING

Is it really a year since your baby was born? He has grown and learned so much during that time. Perhaps now you should pat yourself on the back, because much of this learning has come from you – without you, he'd never have got so far. Now, however, he's about to make that leap between babyhood and childhood. He'll learn to walk (perhaps he's doing so already) and to talk. You'll probably find that his mind is running ahead of his body – he'll want to do things which he can't physically achieve yet. And it's frustrating both for him and for you (when you have to cope with the angry tears). He's doing things that he shouldn't – like opening forbidden cupboard doors – and he's testing you to see how far you'll let him get away with it. It's one of the toughest stages for you as you have to be constantly on the alert but it's one of the most exciting times for him. You *can* help each other – and here's how.

GETTING MOBILE

Your child will probably already be heaving himself up on the furniture (see Growing and Learning, page 171). And, even if he's not walking, he might be standing if only for a few seconds before he realizes he's doing it – and tumbles down. At the same time, you can watch him squat down to pick up a toy and then rise to his full height again. He'll want to climb up stairs and you'll have to teach him how to come down backwards on his tummy or on his bottom. Before all this you can help him take that first step by:
● Standing a short distance in front of him and holding out your arms.
● Supplying a push-along toy.

Increase those faltering few steps by:
● Holding his hand and walking with him from the kitchen to the sitting room and back again, if he can manage it.

YOUR CHILD'S PHYSICAL DEVELOPMENT

Learning to stand fairly and squarely on your own two feet requires plenty of concentration and practice ... as the saying goes, 'If at first you don't succeed, try, try, try again.'

● Pointing out other 'juvenile walkers'. Toddlers love to copy.

● Not pushing him if he doesn't want to do these things. It will come when he's ready and it may be that he's happy crawling for the time being.

USING HIS HANDS

Now's the time to plug into your child's enthusiasm and help him play more complicated games. Sit him down on the carpet (or at a small chair and table) and help him push plastic rings over stacking poles. Show him how to turn on his toy radio. And help him 'draw' by placing a wax crayon in his hand and guiding it over a piece of paper. At first, his movements will seem very clumsy and the drawing will be no more than widely sweeping lines, but by the time he's two, he could be making more controlled lines (perhaps even a circle) and holding the crayon with his thumb and first two fingers. But don't worry if he is still making scribbles only, so long as he is enjoying it.

Let your own artistic talent run free too! Anyone can draw a large circle with a small one on top and two triangular ears sticking out. Add some whiskers to the top circle and a tail to the bottom and you have a recognizable cat. Now your toddler can colour it in.

If it's summer, you can help him develop his manual dexterity in the sandpit. Teach him to fill the bucket with sand and turn it upside down. Bathtime is another playground for hands. Tipping water out of plastic cups provides endless fun and you'll have trouble getting him out. Don't worry if your child prefers the destructive side of building to the constructive. It still takes some dexterity to knock down a sandcastle or a tall tower of bricks.

MAKING CONNECTIONS

This is a marvellous 'matching and linking' stage when you can see the growing and learning process really coming together. Watch how your child's mind is beginning to work. By pushing that railway piece into

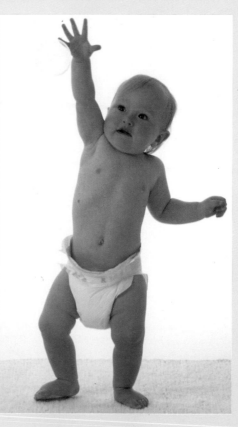

This is exciting . . . Whoops! Glad there's a soft carpet . . . A little bit more upright this time . . . There, I've done it. Now is definitely the time to 'toddler–proof' your home.

A shape sorter provides a wonderful opportunity for experimentation and practice at matching shapes together and is almost always a very popular toy.

to life. Plasticine, an old favourite, can be used for teaching colours too. Don't forget that he'll have his own preferences. Not every child likes jigsaws, just as many adults find them tedious, but others may enjoy turning round the pieces in their hands until they finally fit.

LISTENING AND TALKING

You'd be amazed at how much your child can understand even if he can't talk much. Encourage this by issuing instructions in your daily routine ('Get your coat on, please'). When you praise him for putting on his coat, he'll want to do it again. He'll also remember the key word (coat).

Some mothers become quite competitive about how many words their child can say. A two-year-old should probably have about thirty words at his command, but don't worry if his vocabulary is less extensive; provided he can say a little more than simply 'Mum' or 'Dad', there is no cause for concern. Some letters are easier to say than others – p, d and g sounds trip off the tongue better than sh or ch. You'll find your child attempts to make these sounds but that the word comes out with chunks missing. As long as he's trying to make the right sound, it doesn't matter. So 'car' may sound like 'aar' and 'shoe' like 'oo'. Gradually it becomes clearer, and 'naar' for 'no' becomes a 'no' to rhyme with 'know'.

During the second year, your child will join two or more words to make phrases like 'Dad's oo' for 'Daddy's shoe'. There will always be some prodigy who can say a lot more, but try not to worry or compare. Speech usually comes with time. If it doesn't – and you really feel your child is lagging behind – ask your doctor to refer you to the audiologist in case your child can't hear properly. It's also worth remembering that third (and subsequent) children often speak later than the first or second ones as they have older siblings to translate for them. What is the point of speaking if you can simply grunt and a brother or sister will carry the required toy to you? Some children take in more than you realize, and when they finally talk (rather late), come out with complete phrases without any of the usual babytalk.

another, he can make a circular track. That doll on the bedroom floor looks like the one in the picture book – and your child will tell you so with excited cries of 'doll'. He'll even be able to link people with their photographs and tangible objects with their names. 'Where's my hairbrush?' you might say to yourself. He will go racing out of the room, to return triumphantly clutching the lost object in his hand.

He won't always hit the nail on the head, however. It's very common for toddlers to generalize. All food is 'fish fingers' or all four-legged animals are called 'Tizzy', after the cat. But it will come, and by the age of three he'll understand the difference between next door's cat and his own.

Creative play is invaluable in linking shapes and concepts. Simply browse through the art section of the toyshop for ideas that you can adapt at home without having to spend any money. (See Make your own car, page 210). Bricks which are easy to join will bring all sorts of fantasies

HELPING HIM TALK

You can help your child learn to talk:

● Pick a quiet time (no radio, television or other children) and sit your child on your knee – close contact helps him relax. Look through a picture book and repeat easy words, such as boat and ball, clearly. Avoid words he won't identify easily; zebra crossings have little meaning if you live out of town. Say the word clearly and encourage your child when he repeats it. Don't correct him, simply say the word again clearly.

● Place a selection of toys behind your back and bring out one at a time. Name it clearly, for example, cup, doll, car, and make sure he is watching you.

● Encourage telephone playing (hello, goodbye). Let your toddler talk to his father or someone else he knows well if they ring.

● Sing nursery rhymes, or listen to nursery rhyme tapes which have clear pronunciation. Children love hearing the same phrases repeated over and over again.

● Speak in simple, uncomplicated sentences. 'Get your coat on' rather than 'Hurry up. Get your coat on. Now, where on earth did I put it? Do you know?'

● Point out words during your daily tasks, for example 'Look, there's a *car*'. Count as you go up and down steps. 'One, two, three, etc'. Soon your child will say the numbers with you.

● Look at your child when speaking to him, so he can watch your lips.

● Don't speak too fast.

Stammering

Some children stammer slightly when learning to talk. Often this is a perfectly natural phase of development. Sometimes it's because they're trying to get out too many words too fast, or perhaps they're so keen to get the right sound out that it's making them nervous. Help your child relax. Don't be quick to criticize when he says the wrong word or stammers. Often young stammerers grow out of the habit after a few months, but if it persists, mention it to your health visitor. There might be a developmental problem such as difficulty in getting his tongue around the words, or perhaps your child is emotionally upset about something such as family problems or a new baby. See also A-Z of Healthcare, page 301.

Mummy's elbow . . . my elbow. Mummy's toe . . . my toe. Mummy's nose . . . my nose. A simple game like this helps your toddler to recognize different parts of the body as well as giving her great pleasure.

207

Sharing toys is a social skill that takes time to develop. Encourage your child by taking an interest and commenting warmly when he is sharing, rather than by telling him off when he isn't.

BECOMING A PERSON

Your toddler is such a strong personality now that it's easy to forget he's still a baby. He wants to do so many things for himself that you may be excused for expecting him to act like an adult in other ways too. 'Sit still while I brush your hair', you may demand, forgetting that he's still very young.

Try to make allowances when everything goes wrong for him. He may find it very hard to bear when the jigsaw piece won't go in, or he wants another drink when you think he's had enough, and this is when the dreaded temper tantrums may occur (see Common Concerns, page 202, for advice on how to deal with them).

LOOKING AFTER HIMSELF

Your toddler can do so much now on his own that it's not surprising he wants to be independent. It can be very frustrating for you, however. Something as trivial as wanting to put his leg into his trousers himself, or deciding that, no thank you, he'd rather not wear a vest today, can cause ructions. Those newly acquired verbal skills can seem quite annoying when your child loudly and persistently demands yet another 'dink' (drink).

WHAT YOUR CHILD WILL DO

By the time he reaches two-and-a-half years old, your toddler will probably:

• **Know his name and even recognize the shape of the first letter in it. You can encourage this with magnetic play letters on the fridge.**

• **Recognize certain colours (red and blue are easy ones to start with).**

• **Try to press the doorbell to hear the sound it makes, and pick up the phone when it rings (although you may not want your toddler to do this).**

• **Differentiate between shapes, especially if he has a shape sorting box.**

• **Understand the difference between him and babies. ('What a big boy you are now!')**

• **Try to put a key in the door (and lose it around the house if you're not careful).**

• **Jump, skip and turn somersaults.**

At other times you're filled with pride when he announces his need for a wee or learns to sit on the lavatory. He might now be happy to play on his own for a while or run off with friends at mother and toddler group instead of clinging to your legs.

Such independence varies among children – girls are often more competent at an earlier stage than boys, for example, at holding their training cup and so on. But whatever your toddler's level of independence, let him go at his own pace and never push him.

Help him become independent

• Allow extra time before going out so he can put on his own coat without making you late.

• Read a magazine at the table to distract yourself if your toddler insists on messily feeding himself without any help from you. After all, it can't be pleasant to have someone hanging over you and shoving in every mouthful even if you do spill a bit when you do it yourself. It does get better – really – even though some toddlers take longer than others at aiming each mouthful accurately. They all get there in the end.

• Make allowances for your child when he's ill or under the weather. He may be less independent and need your attention more for a while.

SOCIAL SKILLS

His social skills with other children may vary from day to day (and mood to mood). One day he might play beautifully with a friend, but the next he'll be turning over chairs and even kicking his chum to get your attention. If this happens try to distract him or take him away from the situation for a short while. It may be better to arrange to meet the friend on common ground such as at a park where they can share the amusements instead of squabbling over their own favourite toys back home.

Household chores can help him learn social skills too. Let him hand you the pegs when you're hanging out the washing, or show him how to put his pyjamas under the pillow or give him a cloth and let him help with the dusting.

PLAY AND TOYS

MAKE YOUR OWN CAR
● Find a cardboard box big enough for your toddler to sit in. Stick two paper plates on either side at the base level for wheels.
● Using a paper fastener, secure apaper plate to the inside front of thebox, so it turns, for a steering wheel.
● Attach a kitchen towel tube at the side with another paper fastener for a 'brake' or 'gear stick'.
● Let your toddler help paint it.

You no longer have a baby to look after, but an active little person with abounding energy and enthusiasm. It's an exciting time for her. Every day will be a rollercoaster of adventure which can be very tiring for you. As she plays she will be discovering and developing all the time, and whenever she masters a new skill she will become more confident. She will also become increasingly frustrated if she fails, which is when tantrums can occur. So toys must be pitched at the right level for her – to stretch her development, not thwart it.

Now too is the time that your toddler will begin to enjoy the company of other people, particularly children.

These toys also help her develop in other ways. On a sit 'n' ride car, she'll make pretend engine-noises, perhaps imagining she's driving to work, or taking her family on an outing. A doll in a buggy, of course, opens up a whole world of role playing. It's her chance to take control. Most of these toys need space to be enjoyed. If you value your paintwork, you may prefer to keep them for outdoor play in your garden, if you're lucky enough to have one, or in your local park.

Long-handled brooms, carpet sweepers and wheelbarrows come into their own now too. All huge fun and very good for learning through role play.

210

Free from your local shop or supermarket and needing only a little imagination, a large cardboard box readily doubles as a police station, hideout, lorry, ship or train.

SHE'S OFF!

A sturdy toddle truck with bricks is the ideal push-along toy for when your toddler is learning to walk. As she progresses and can walk confidently by herself, she'll enjoy a whole range of mobile toys including sit 'n' rides, rocking horses and other push-along toys. All of these will help to strengthen her legs and enable her to develop her balance.

OUTDOOR PLAY

If you have a garden, you may be tempted to buy a whole range of equipment. Some children love slides, swings and so on, while others aren't so keen. Alternatively, take a trip to your local park and let your toddler play on the swings and slides there.

It's also worth remembering that most garden toys are more fun when there are siblings or friends to play with.

Finger-painting can be just as creative as painting with a brush. You can use your fingers, palms and the sides of your hands to paint with and you can make your own hand — or even foot — prints.

MESSY PLAY

Your toddler will enjoy playing with substances like sand, mud, water, playdough and paints. Through such activities, she'll learn about textures, colour and shape, how to manipulate different media, and how to express herself, but best of all, she'll have a lot of fun in the process.

Sand

Sand is more versatile than you may think. Dry, it can be used rather like water – to pour from beaker to beaker, to swish about, to pour through a sieve. When damp, it becomes a modelling medium for making sandcastles, or for building hills, roads and tunnels. When very wet, it becomes deliciously sloppy for stirring, mixing and spooning.

The ideal is to keep it in a sandpit in the garden, but it can be played with in a washing-up bowl or the baby bath indoors on a large sheet to contain the mess. Buy 'washed' play sand as builder's sand is coarser and stains everything.

If you have a garden, you don't have to invest in a sandpit – as long as you don't mind your toddler getting dirty. Set aside a small patch of ground and give your child a bucket, spade and some water in a little watering can. She'll discover what the earth is really like . . . so remember to put her in old clothes!

Playdough

To start with, your child will like trying to roll out and cut the dough with plastic pastry shapes. Later she can use it to make models or pretend food. Buy tubs of playdough or make your own (the salt in the home-made variety makes it much less likely to be eaten):

1 cup plain flour
$^{1}/_{2}$ cup salt
1 tbsp oil
2 tsp cream of tartar
225 ml (8 fl oz) water
few drops of food colouring
Blend all the ingredients in a saucepan until smooth. Bring to the boil, stirring, until the mixture goes all lumpy then leaves the sides of the pan clean.

Turn it out on to a board, cool slightly, then knead until smooth and allow it to cool. Store in an airtight container for up to six months.

Tip: If you make double the quantity, don't add the food colouring at the start but cook it, then divide it into four and colour each piece a different shade by kneading in some colouring.

Painting and drawing

Painting doesn't have to be confined to the kitchen table. It's an ideal outdoor activity. Use bulldog clips to hold paper in place on a table or easel. Don't try to guess what your

PLAY SAFE
● **Don't let your child throw sand –
it can scratch
or irritate eyes.**
● **Cover a sandpit
when not in use.
Cats and dogs find it
an irresistible toilet.**
● **Never leave her
alone in a paddling
pool or near any
water. A child can
drown in just a few
centimetres/inches –
even in a little water
in a bucket.**
● **Check all garden
equipment regularly
for wear and tear.**

child's picture is meant to be, it's fun
for her if you let her tell you.

Buy washable non-toxic paints or try
making your own:

● Blend 1 tablespoon of plain flour or
cornflour with 300ml (10 fl oz) water.
Bring to the boil, stirring until thickened
and smooth.

● Divide into small portions, colour with
food colouring and leave to cool with a
circle of wet greaseproof paper over each
portion to prevent a skin forming.

Scribbling is most toddlers' first step
towards writing and drawing. Choose thick
wax crayons and soft-leaded pencils which
are easy for tiny hands to hold and make
marks with. Help your toddler by guiding
her hand across the paper.

or cooking the meals. This should all be
encouraged either with suitable bought
or home-made toys or by providing 'real'
items for her to play with.

Play house

A wooden, plastic or material-covered Play
house or a play tent is always popular. Your
child will want you to play in it with her –
and, of course, friends or siblings.
Mummies and daddies, hospitals and shops,
are all games which help her learn to live
in the world around her.

**FITTING, SORTING AND
CONSTRUCTION**

Your toddler will find it hugely satisfying
when she can fit shapes into the right holes

*The joy of a play tent
improvised from chairs
and blankets is that you
can make a different one
each time, it doesn't need
storing and it's free.*

ROLE PLAY

If you listen to your toddler chatting to her
toys, you'll most likely hear her praising
them, just as you praise her. She'll pick up
other mannerisms of yours, too, such as the
way you toss your head or clear your throat.
She'll love dressing up in your clothes and
shoes and having tea parties, doing the
housework, pretending to go to the office

or lift and discover what's under pieces in
a play tray. Jigsaws with just a few big pieces
are also good at this stage.

Now is the time to choose simple
construction toys with pieces that fit
together. A basic set of bricks is a good
start. Choose a brand that offers a wide
range of toys in the series, so the set can
be added to as she grows.

BOOKS

Big colourful picture books about real things are the most popular at this stage. Look at them together and make up stories about the pictures.

Your child may be familiar with certain TV or video characters. If so, books with big pictures and very simple storylines will also be greatly enjoyed.

Looking at books together will help your toddler learn to talk.

MAKING FRIENDS

If she's got older brothers or sisters she will already be used to playing with other children, but at this stage it can be helpful if she sees playmates of her own age. She will learn a good deal of her social behaviour from playing with her peers. And also creative play becomes more fun if you've got someone else to copy, just as pretend play is much more fun when you've got someone your own age to pretend with.

MUMS AND TOTS

Make the effort to go to a parent and toddler group with your child. It's good for you as well as her to get out and meet people. She will learn so much from her peers and you will get support, feedback and friendship from the other mums. It will also help your child get used to being in a group, ready for the time when she may go to playgroup or nursery before starting school.

TOYS FOR YOUR TODDLER

WHEN your child: can walk unaided.	WHEN your child: stops putting everything in her mouth.	WHEN your child: can hold small objects and transfer them from one hand to the other.	WHEN your child: starts to copy you.
WHAT she will enjoy: sit 'n' rides, push- and pull-along toys, rocking toys, hobby horses.	WHAT she will enjoy: sand, earth, water, playdough, finger paints and colouring.	WHAT she will enjoy: simple puzzles, posting toys, shape sorters, big building or fit-together bricks.	WHAT she will enjoy: dressing up clothes, real and pretend household equipment, dolls and cuddly toys, toy cars, a Wendy house, etc.
WHY she needs them: to strengthen her legs. To improve her balance. To discover the sensations of speed and movement.	WHY she needs them: to discover, recognize and enjoy texture, colour and shape. To help her express herself.	WHY she needs them: to encourage her to think for herself and solve problems. To help her recognize colour, and shape. To help hand and eye co-ordination.	WHY she needs them: to develop her imagination and social skills. To help her adjust to and grow up in everyday life through discovery and pretend play.

213

THE
OLDER CHILD
2¹/₂-5 years

Your child is ready to spread his wings and learn more about the world around him. With his increasing command of words he understands a great deal and expresses his thoughts and feelings too. He becomes a fascinating, if sometimes exhausting, companion as he talks and questions with enormous enthusiasm and perseverance.

Nowadays he likes playing with friends, learning to give and take and share. Sometimes you'll notice him mimicking things you've said and done as he plays imaginative games – you are his main teacher and he'll watch and copy you whenever he can. These are the days when mastering everyday activities boosts your child's ability and creativity and brings confidence and delight.

YOU AND YOUR OLDER CHILD

The days are full of chatter and questions as your child becomes increasingly fluent with speech. You'll hear 'Why?' over and over again as he strives to learn and understand, fuelled by never-ending curiosity. And, at the most unexpected times, you'll find yourself trying to answer such queries as 'Why doesn't the sun fall out of the sky?' or 'Why has Auntie Lin got a big tummy?' To your child you are a living encyclopedia who knows the answer to everything.

At the same time as his vocabulary and ability to string words together are growing, your child is also learning to think in more abstract ways. He'll link memories about what has happened in the past to what is going on now, and he'll also be able to talk about the family's plans for the future. He is good company and able to have lengthy conversations. Your views and attitudes are just as important as your explanations because now is the best time for developing a sense of fairness, good and bad, and right and wrong.

The years before going to school are a time when your child loves to be with you; helping, talking and investigating, from dawn to dusk. He identifies with you and may find it hard if you want to go out without him. The good thing is that you can begin to reason with him and he can understand that although you may spend time elsewhere, you love him and will come back to him. Hugging a favourite cuddly toy or a familiar blanket helps many a young child of two, three or four bridge the gap and feel more secure.

These are also the years when he will become more interested in playing with other children, rather than simply alongside them. This is a good time to have friends with young children round to your home so they can play together under your eye. You may decide to take him to a playgroup or put him in a nursery school so he can have the opportunity to interact with other adults, play with different children and enjoy new toys and play equipment. As you listen to your child

Your older child may benefit from the wide range of activities which are available at a playgroup or nursery school as well as from the enjoyment of playing with other children.

216

playing, you'll hear him saying things to his toys and friends that he's heard you say to him. 'Careful, you've spilt it – let's wipe it up together' or 'You're tired out – what you need is a lovely long sleep,' roll off his tongue just as they have rolled off yours so many times before. He is learning your style of parenting ready to practise on his own children one day.

Constant activity and increasing agility and confidence are hallmarks of this age, and running, jumping, hopping, skipping, climbing and taking things from one place to another take up a lot of time. A promise to visit the playground with its slide, swings, climbing frame and see-saw gives a whole new meaning to going shopping. Young children love to watch older children on the apparatus and then have a go themselves, though you need to stay close to lend a helping hand if they get into any trouble, like going too fast down the slide or getting stuck on the climbing frame.

Quieter activities also come into their own, with looking at books, drawing and painting, playing with sand and water, dressing-up, and sticking, cutting and making things being very popular. Be ready to collect everything you need to re-create models shown on children's television. Most young children can't wait to get started and thoroughly enjoy the actual making but aren't so keen on the putting away, which can take much longer.

Many young children are becoming more aware of how others are feeling and you may find your child making down-to-earth comments like 'Mummy's tired – Mummy go to bed now,' or 'You don't like that bad man, do you Daddy?' They are also very in touch with their own likes and dislikes and have no hesitation in stating them, wherever they are.

By now you have a much clearer idea of your child's characteristics and personality. You know him better than anyone else does and he knows you love him. That's an excellent base from which he can enter the next stage – going to school.

Dr Penny Stanway

OUR CHILDREN

Penny Stanway: 'My mother gave me the books she'd kept from when I was a child but my three were never very interested in them – I think they liked the colours and presentation of modern books better. They liked to look at their favourite books over and over again.'

Daphne Metland: 'I thought things would get easier after toddlerhood, but Sam and his best friend Ben used to get into awful scrapes; at four they discovered that easystrip wallpaper comes off in whole sheets, and managed to strip a complete wall before I found them!'

Gillian Fletcher: 'I remember when Robert was four and had watched the David Attenborough *Life on Earth* TV series. Andrew, his older brother, asked his Dad, "Who was the first man on earth?" With no hesitation, Robert replied, "David Attenborough, of course." I think it's important to remember those moments when your children say something funny, as it's so easy to forget them.'

Heather Welford: 'I can understand why parents get frustrated when children develop likes and dislikes. There's no logic to some of them! A friend of mine had a daughter who refused pasta when it wasn't "squiggly enough".'

Carolyn Humphries: 'James has always been tractor-mad, and his pedal one with a trailer was the best buy ever. He still careers round the garden on it (he's now seven) and even helped me move some ballast when we were having some building work done recently.'

Maggie Jones: 'Starting school was the big anxiety at this stage with my first child and he clung to me for weeks when he first started, while four years later the third gave a cheery wave and rushed in without a backward glance. For the first child, school was an alien environment, while the third had been in and out of schools since he was a week old and knew that mothers didn't stay.'

Jane Bidder: 'When my eldest child, William, went to nursery at the age of two and a quarter, he was only just learning to put two words together. After the first morning his vocabulary improved dramatically. 'What did you do at nursery?' I asked, not expecting to get a very illuminating reply. "Mrs Saunders say 'No jumping on table'," came the reply. I didn't know whether to applaud him for such a long sentence or hide from Mrs Saunders the following morning.'

FEEDING YOUR CHILD

PARTY TREATS
● Don't over-estimate children's appetites for sweet foods at parties. They love tiny savouries served on cocktail sticks or as mini-sandwiches.
● Try soft sliced bread spread with cream cheese and then rolled up and sliced to make pinwheel sandwiches.
● Spear grapes and cubes of cheese on sticks.
● Serve natural fromage frais and yogurt as dips with vegetable sticks.

Food and drinks often taste so much better outside in the fresh air, especially when you have your very own picnic box and flask and a friend to share the sunshine with.

Between the ages of three and five your child is likely to spend an increasing amount of time eating away from home – possibly at nursery school or playgroup and then at school – and as a guest in other children's houses. You may find that any fussiness and food fads – still quite common in this age group – become far less apparent once she moves outside the family. They then start to disappear at home, too – though don't expect your child to like everything.

HELPING OUT
Your over-three may now be a genuine help in the kitchen. She can be relied on to help fetch items from the fridge or cupboard for you. You can also encourage her to clear away the table after a meal, and to help put dirty cups and plates by the sink or in the dishwasher.

With careful supervision, she can even chop some foods with a knife, although she'll probably find it easier to use scissors for some things, such as mushrooms.

PACKED LUNCHES
A healthy packed lunch is no less nutritious than a cooked one. If you make it the night before it's needed, keep it in the fridge to maintain the freshness.

Make sure it contains some carbohydrate such as bread, in the form of a sandwich or bun; some protein (such as cheese or chicken, possibly in the sandwich as a filling); some fruit or vegetables (a small salad or a piece of fruit); and a milk product such as a yogurt, a milk-based dessert, or a fromage frais.

Here's an idea of what this might mean:
● Buttered wholemeal sandwich, with cheese/tuna or ham filling, with salad.
● Apple and yogurt.
● Orange juice.
or:
● Cold pasta salad with pasta shapes, peas, sweetcorn and chopped ham.
● Banana and fromage frais.
● Blackcurrant juice.

What about crisps and biscuits?
Biscuits and crisps are high in fat. However, they are short on several nutrients, so they shouldn't form the main part of any meal, whether it be packed or otherwise. As an extra, they have a part to play, if your child enjoys them. However, it's actually better for your child's teeth to eat a biscuit as part of a meal rather than to have it as an in-between snack.

GRAZING
Most children enjoy snacks and there is no harm in them so long as they usually include healthy items such as fruit or vegetable sticks. If, however, your child is constantly filling up on sweets, biscuits and crisps and not eating her main meals then you should encourage her to change her eating habits. Don't buy any biscuits or crisps. Explain that there aren't any of her normal snacks in the house and offer her healthier alternatives. Serve up her meals as usual.

If you're consistent, she will change – and that will make you both happier. In time, you can offer her a biscuit or packet of crisps as an occasional treat. The best time may be after she has finished her meal.

MILK
Current guidelines are as follows:
● Breast milk or formula milk for the first six months at least and ideally for the first year. Whole pasteurized cow's milk in small quantities for cooking after six months. You can continue with breast milk for as long as you and your child like.
● Whole pasteurized cow's milk for drinks until two years old.
● Semi-skimmed (not skimmed) or whole milk until five. Whole milk if the child isn't taking a good range of other foods.

A few children are intolerant of cow's milk (always get this diagnosis checked by a specialist). Speak to a dietitian about substitutes such as goat's milk or soya milk.

WHAT ABOUT A LOW-FAT DIET?
A low-fat diet isn't recommended for healthy growing children.

BATHING AND EVERYDAY CARE

It's now a good idea to start helping your child to learn about using the lavatory and the washbasin as independently as possible, so that when he's at playgroup, nursery or school he doesn't need to rely on the staff. Explain the basics of hygiene to your child – at this age, he can understand the concept of germs and bugs, and why we need to stay clean.

SETBACKS IN TRAINING

Ask your health visitor for support and advice if you feel you're making little progress with toilet training. It may be that a star chart will help. This rewards him with a star (leading to a present or a treat

when he's dry). Never punish him when he's wet. Check that your child is not constipated, or suffering from an anal fissure (see A-Z of Healthcare, page 288) which makes him reluctant to go. Hanging on . . . and on . . . will make him even more constipated and makes accidental soiling more likely.

Prolonged or unaccustomed daytime wetting can be associated with a urine infection, so it's a good idea to ask your doctor to check for this. Sometimes a child who has been reliably clean and dry reacts to stress or change by going backwards – and that means he may start to wet and soil. Getting angry with a child who does this, or who has yet to be trained, doesn't help but can make things worse. If it's difficult for you not to be angry, think about putting your child back into nappies for a short time to take the heat out of the situation.

USING THE LAVATORY

Your child will probably be able to use the lavatory by now, though he may need your help to get on it if he's small. He will also need help with wiping his bottom at first – aim to teach him by the time he gets to school and teach girls to do it front to back.

A stool or box to climb on, especially one that's high enough up to rest his feet on when he's sitting on it, will keep him stable. It will also help him to go – perched with feet dangling is not actually a very comfortable way to do it although some children don't mind at all. Little boys can stand up to wee. Teach them how to aim, and to shake off the last couple of drops.

Your child will probably be able to sit on the lavatory now, although if he is small a special step to climb on will help him.

'When Owen was two years and eight months old I started "potty" training him. He was quite happy sitting on the lavatory so we bypassed the potty stage and he was out of nappies almost immediately. I didn't think he would be dry at night as easily so I put him in a nappy at bedtime but after a fortnight of dry nappies, I didn't bother any more.'

See Potty Training, page 190; A-Z of Healthcare, page 284, for bed wetting

220

KEEPING CLEAN

Your child can now wash his own hands after using the lavatory and before meals and will only need your supervision and maybe a bit of help in getting washed in the mornings. Bathing still needs your help to ensure safety and to make sure it's properly done, as does hair washing (especially rinsing). Carry on helping with teeth brushing, too. Teach your child to spit out the toothpaste instead of swallowing it (though this may take time).

NIGHT-TIME DRYNESS

If your child isn't already dry by now, the chances are he will soon get there. However, a sizeable minority of children are still wet at night until the age of five or six, and most children's doctors don't suggest intervening

You may avoid the odd wet bed by 'lifting' your child to use the lavatory late at night. Always wake him when you do this; otherwise you're teaching him to wee in his sleep – which prolongs the problem. Don't restrict drinks in the evening. No evidence has been found that this stops bedwetting. Obviously, it is a good idea to encourage your child to use the lavatory just before he goes to bed, whether or not he wets at night. A potty by the bed may help if your child is scared of going to the bathroom alone.

Always remember that your child can't help wetting at night. He does it in his sleep. You may be able to encourage him to wake with the sensations of a full bladder with a star chart, however, from the age of about three or four (see left). However, if your star chart doesn't look like working, don't persevere –

When he can reach the basin and knows how to work the taps, encourage him to wash his hands after using the lavatory and before meals.

with any special programme until the age of seven. As so many children simply grow out of the tendency to wet at night, it seems that it is part of the maturing process. Any setbacks do not automatically signal underlying emotional disorder – though children who have been dry and then start wetting again may be expressing some distress or anxiety, or reacting to major changes in their lives.

abandon it.

Large-size nappies are available for older children, but there'll come a point when you feel your child is really too old for them – even if he is still wetting, or your child may refuse to wear them. Nappies are for babies, after all. Protect the bed with a waterproof cover. You can buy special covers for duvets, too, to avoid having to wash them again and again.

SLEEP AND BEDTIME

ABOVE When your child is tired but none too keen on going to bed, it helps if he knows that someone understands his fears and concerns even though you expect him to be in bed.

222

OPPOSITE 'Hello, Mummy and Daddy, I've come to join you.' Coming into your bed in the middle of the night makes everything feel better but some parents would rather it didn't become a habit.

Here's a suggested bedtime routine for your three-to-five-year-old:
- **Tea or supper at about 5.30pm.**
- **Bath about 6pm.**
- **Snack and drink, followed by teeth brushing, at about 6.30pm.**
- **Story, quiet time, from about 7pm until about 7.30pm.**

Most children over the age of about three have stopped having a regular daytime nap – though an active day, or a series of later-than-normal nights might still mean your child drops off in the car or the pushchair, or even sitting on the sofa. Most have a long, uninterrupted sleep of twelve hours or so every night. Nevertheless, wakefulness and problems with settling aren't uncommon in this age group.

NIGHT WANDERINGS

You'll probably want to keep up a bedtime routine. Parents often find the hours between tea and bedtime a special, close time, and now your child can talk, you can discuss the goings on of the day and enjoy being together. This time can be especially important if you have been at work all day.

Your child needs to know that once she's in bed she should stay there unless she needs to go to the lavatory or wants a drink of water. It's not a good idea to make it difficult or impossible for your child to open the door of her room, or to put a stair gate in the entrance. Making her room a prison won't help her to like it, and in an emergency she may need to get out quickly. (Although, as a safety precaution, it's probably wise to leave a stair gate shut at the top of the stairs,

especially if you have gone to bed.) Instead, keep taking her back to her room if she wanders. You may want to compromise; coming into your bed is all right if you're actually there, for example. If you want to try to stop her from sharing your bed, however, a star chart may help. Every night she stays in her own bed she is awarded a star and after she has earned so many, she gets a special treat.

Many children of this age still need some form of comfort to help them get to sleep, such as a special blanket, a soft toy, thumb-sucking, a dummy or some comfort sucking at the breast. This is normal, and your child will grow out of it in time.

DISTURBED NIGHTS

Bad dreams are part of life, and they're bound to happen occasionally, but if your child regularly becomes distressed after a bad dream, or finds it difficult to settle, try to find out what might be worrying her. Perhaps she needs reassurance about family problems, or the chance to talk simply about her feelings. This is also an age of powerful imaginings, and she may tell you she's worried about monsters, or dragons, or dinosaurs. At this age, she's still confused about the differences between thoughts and reality – and while she can accept that there aren't any dragons under the bed when you look for them, she may be genuinely afraid they'll come back when you're not there.

It may help to acknowledge your child's fear by saying, 'We'll chase that nasty dragon away for ever.' Or, you can make friends with the dragon and discover, together, that it's a kind, protective dragon after all. Night terrors are frightening episodes where the child screams and fights in distress and can't be calmed down. She has her eyes open, but seems unable to relate to you, or even see you. Usually, the terrors disappear in time. They're not thought to indicate a serious disturbance, though sometimes they are related to stress. They can be upsetting, however, so if you're worried, ask your doctor for advice.

WHAT YOUR CHILD MAY NEED

Your child may already have started at playgroup or nursery school or, if not, he probably soon will. He will be getting used to mixing with others and having friends round to play. You may feel you've got more independence too when he and his little friend go off to his room to play while you and the friend's mother are left to have coffee and a chat downstairs.

A ROOM TO PLAY IN

This is where his room comes into its own and although safety is still of paramount importance, he is old enough to have simple safety rules explained to him – like not jumping off the bed or climbing on the

A proper easel is a luxury but an ordinary table will do just as well for your budding young artist to practise drawing, using colours, chalks, crayons and paper to make his mark.

224

table. As your child's confidence grows, he will spend more time playing out of your sight. Make his room as pleasant as possible in the following ways:

- Make sure his toys are easily accessible.
- If there is space, provide a desk, work-surface or table and chair so he can draw or do puzzles on a firm surface.
- Give him a large jar or desk-tidy for crayons and pencils, and save any junk mail that has writing on one side only – the plain side is great for scribbling on.
- Encourage tidiness by having drawers that are easy to open and label them for clothes and toys.
- Hang a mirror at the right height for him so he can brush his own hair.
- Make sure bookshelves are big enough for large picture books or buy a pair of bookends to stand on a chest of drawers.
- A blackboard and easel will give your child hours of fun.
- Fix a pinboard to the wall to display his drawings and paintings.
- If there's room, a beanbag makes a pleasant place to flop and look at a book, rather than lying on the bed.

A ROOM FOR TWO

If you're redesigning your child's room because his little brother or sister is about to move in, there are several things to bear in mind. Your child may not be too thrilled at the thought of having to share his room. Involve him in the planning and re-designing, so he feels it's partly his idea, but don't automatically think you're compromising him – children often like the company of a little brother or sister until they're a bit older.

- Your older child will need some privacy, so make a large part of the room very definitely his.
- Put the baby's cot along one wall, with a changing area nearby and, perhaps, have a piece of furniture coming out from a wall to make a divider.
- Buy an anglepoise light which can be directed away from the baby, lighting up the older child's part of the room

if he wants to look at a book in bed before he goes to sleep.

● If the sleeping arrangements are going to be long-term, it may be a good idea to invest in bunk beds (see From cot to bed, page 199). Remember that the top bunk is not suitable for a child under the age of six years. Your older child could sleep in the bottom bunk at first, then progress to the more exciting top one when his little brother or sister is ready to move into a bed and can go into the lower bunk.

CAR SAFETY

At around four years, your child will grow out of his car seat. He still won't be big enough to see out of the window and an adult belt won't fit in the correct position on its own, so he'll need a booster seat.

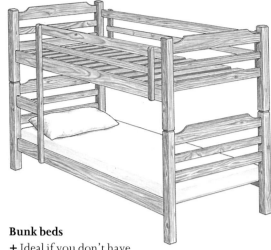

Bunk beds
+ Ideal if you don't have much space and want your children to share a room.
– A child under the age of six cannot sleep on the top bunk.

WHAT YOUR CHILD MAY NEED

225

Some children enjoy their own company much more than others, but most value a little bit of privacy from time to time, not to mention a place which is all their own.

Some lightweight car seats (see What Your Baby May Need, page 164) convert into a booster seat. If you don't have rear seatbelts, it can be used with a junior harness which has to be anchored to the car following the manufacturer's instructions. Remove the seat when not in use – in an accident it could fly through the air and injure the driver or other passengers.

NEVER use an ordinary cushion for your child to sit on with an adult belt. In an accident, the cushion could slide out and he could be injured by the belt.

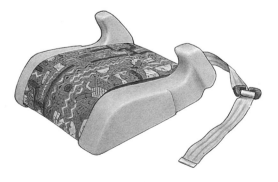

Booster seat
(from around four years or from 25kg/55lb).

See What Your Toddler May Need, page 199, for more information on choosing beds

COMMON CONCERNS

TV sometimes has an unfairly bad press. Ration the time spent watching and turn off anything you don't like but take advantage of some of the worthwhile and well-made programmes.

My child is very shy and unsociable – how can I encourage her to make friends?

At this stage your child will probably be attending some kind of playgroup or nursery school. Some children adapt very easily to this sort of social group, learning to share, take turns, and negotiate; others find these skills more difficult and need help to learn what is acceptable to other children.

If your child is shy, it can help to invite other children to your house for short visits. You may need to play with both children at first to break the ice and get them happily engaged in something. In the same way, staying with your child for a short while when she first starts at playgroup can help too.

My child watches far too much television, and when I turn the television off she has tantrums and complains that she is bored. How much television should I let her watch and how can I ration it? And does television violence really affect her?

Surveys have shown that the average pre-school child watches as many as thirty-five hours of television a week, or five hours a day, a lot of time to spend in a purely passive activity. Most children under five cannot concentrate on television for long periods; after watching for between half an hour and an hour you will notice the child may well appear bored, or be rocking or sucking her thumb, drumming her feet, or wriggling in her chair. Eventually she may not be watching at all, even though she complains when it is switched off.

It's best to ration television to several short sessions a day rather than one long one. There are some excellent educational programmes aimed at young children; often these show how to paint, draw or make something and you can encourage your child to switch off and try it. If you have the television on as a constant background noise, your child is less likely to be able to choose what she wants to watch and turn off when it is finished. If your child acts aggressively after programmes with some violence, try to avoid them.

Don't let your child watch programmes intended for a much older age group, especially if there is a lot of violence. This can sometimes be difficult if older brothers and sisters are watching a particular programme. Some children act aggressively even after violent cartoons.

The best way to prevent your child watching television is to provide other interesting activities. Invite friends round, take your child to the park or swimming to get physical exercise, read books or play board games.

Keep videos out of sight and out of reach and reserve them for a special treat. If you are firm, your child will respect this and soon find other things to do.

My child is so disobedient. I ask her to do things and she just says 'No'. She never helps me and is always pointing out what I've done wrong. How can I make her less difficult?

As your child gets older she has a larger vocabulary and is is able to express her feelings much more clearly. The wordless tantrums of the toddler are replaced by arguments and wilful disobedience. Often life is hard for an elder child because it may well be that too much is being expected of her, especially if you are busy with a baby. Remember she is still very young herself and allow her to be a baby sometimes.

It can be hard for parents when children start to talk and answer back, or offer their own view of the situation. It helps to keep good-humoured. Offer rewards and praise and encourage your child when she does help. Try to pay attention to good behaviour and not to end up constantly nagging. Sometimes it is a good idea to compromise and go halfway by aiding her in carrying out some task, such as clearing up her toys.

How can I warn my child about the risks of strangers without frightening her unduly?

It is a fact that more abuse of children is carried out by relatives or acquaintances whom they know than by complete strangers. However, as your child begins to spend more time away from you, at playgroup, nursery school, school or at the homes of friends, you will inevitably worry about whether she is safe.

It is important to give your child the self-confidence to say 'No' in situations she doesn't like. Make sure that you always know where she is; double-check arrangements for your child to be collected from school; always tell the teachers if you will not be there to meet her yourself; and always ask other parents to let you know what is happening if there is any change of plan. Tell your child that you must *always* know where she is and that you'll be very worried if you don't know where she is, just as she gets very frightened if she doesn't know how to find you. Teach your child her address and telephone number so that she can be brought home to you in an emergency.

My child has started taking things from other children's houses and lies about it when I confront her. What can I do?

Children of this age are not really deliberately lying because they may not know the difference between fact and fantasy. Similarly, they may not understand the principle behind stealing. Make it a rule that if your child does bring something back with her, it is always returned. Don't get angry with the child; just be casual and matter-of-fact, and point out that she wouldn't like it if someone took one of her toys home with them.

Sometimes persistent lying may be hiding anxieties, it can mean that the child is unhappy or afraid. Help your child be truthful by not punishing her if she admits to something she's done wrong; and of course it follows that you should always be truthful yourself.

A bamboo pole has plenty of possibilities on a summer's day. Reinforce the idea of playing safely by making positive, encouraging comments when he is being careful rather than just pointing out the dangers.

See Positive Parenting, page 266, for more information on behaviour

GROWING AND LEARNING

It probably seems as though your child has been with you for ever, even though he's only two and a half. Sometimes it helps to remember what a short timespan this is. Your child has grown and learned so much since babyhood that it's natural to expect him to behave like a five- or six-year-old – especially if you have older children who are already sitting still at the table and who no longer indulge in difficult or anti-social behaviour.

The problem is that at times your two-and-a-half-year old will be very grown-up. This can be great fun – particularly when he chats to you and comes out with some wonderful phrases which you'll chuckle over for years to come. Often, he's *too* independent for his own good (and yours). He'll thrash like mad when you're trying to put on his car seatbelt, and insist on feeding himself even when half of his lunch ends up on his clean jumper. At other times, he'll revert to babyhood – especially if, by now, there's another baby in the house. He might whinge like a one-year-old or insist on a breastfeed or his old bottle instead of his trainer mug or cup.

This can be hard to deal with, but you can make yourself feel better by trying to understand how your child's growing mind is working. If you suddenly discovered you could clear a high jump or play at Wimbledon (your child's equivalent to running across the lawn or straddling the cat), would you really appreciate someone saying 'Don't do that'? Your child has been given the key of the door marked 'growing up' and he's not going to let you take it away. And why should you – unless it spells danger for him or anyone else?

YOUR CHILD'S PHYSICAL DEVELOPMENT

Like an athlete in training, your child will get an enormous amount of pleasure from learning and polishing the skills she needs to be more and more agile and always on the move.

228

LIVING WITH AN ACTIVE CHILD

As you may have already suspected, some mothers find this the toughest stage of all. So take heart – once you've got through this, life will get easier. Try to remember that you're not the only mother whose child runs off in the supermarket or who wanders off in the house and hides behind a chair while you're frantically calling for him. It's all part of using his increasing powers of mobility.

Just watch him skip and jump with delight. His movements are much more controlled now. Play a game: take a little jump yourself and tell him to jump, too. Repeat. He'll love it and you won't feel so silly after a while. He's beginning to master the art of balancing – you can see it for yourself, when you watch him on the climbing frame. And you and he can play catch with a ball now. He might even be able to throw it reasonably accurately. Some children have more natural sporting ability than others, just like adults. Your child may enjoy turning somersaults or hopping on one leg; others are not so co-ordinated.

Learn to enjoy this mobility (even though it's often exhausting for *you*) by:

● Setting the base rules as soon as possible. Reins will be worn when you walk anywhere – even if it's just a quick trot to the corner shop. Safety has to come before exploration. If he buckles his legs in protest, stay firm. Wait next to him until he'll walk properly, but don't remove the reins or he'll know he's won.

● Helping him burn up all that energy, just as if you had a boisterous puppy. Take him for walks (lots of fresh air) and do something physical which won't destroy the home, such as garden or park ball games or tricycle rides.

● Enrolling him at a toddler gym or visiting the playground regularly.

● Taking him swimming.

Whether jumping up and down or hopping around on one foot, your older child has masses of energy and may easily keep going from dawn to dusk before giving in and going to sleep exhausted.

229

STAGES IN DRAWING A PERSON
● Roundish circle which may not be closed up.
● Circle containing smaller circles/dots inside for eyes, nose and mouth.
● Stick-like arms and legs without width.
● Clothes added on to stick limbs (like a triangular skirt).

Learning about letters is a really good game when you're matching shapes – like you've done with your posting box – and having plenty of feedback, encouragement and praise.

230

CREATIVE PLAY

This is a lovely phase. Even if you have never considered yourself creative, you will be in your child's eyes. A simple yogurt pot filled with dried haricot beans and sealed with a lid makes a marvellous shaker to beat time with during nursery rhymes. Like magic, a plasticine ball rolled into a sausage can then be coiled into a snail shape.

By now, your child will enjoy using his hands and his imagination to make all kinds of interesting bits and pieces. Encourage independent play by keeping a box of odds and ends such as material scraps, cotton reels and so on which he can fiddle with on wet days. His hands will be working well now. At first, those drawings seem no more than scribbles. Then, as the months go by, you can make out figures or pictures of houses. You'll also be able to tell whether your child is left- or right-handed. It might well still be a bit of both. Some children as old as nine still wield a bat with their left hand but do everything else with their right. It's still early days and many children continue writing certain letters of the alphabet back to front until they are five or older.

I WANT TO DO IT MYSELF

Independence is really the name of the game here. One day your growing child decides that no thank you, he's not going to sit in that highchair any more. Maybe he's right. Perhaps it does feel too restricting, so compromise – instead he could sit on a tall chair (with a cushion). If he keeps hopping up and down, put him back in the highchair. He'll learn eventually to sit still.

Maybe he'll also want to sit on the adult lavatory instead of his potty. He sees you doing it, so why can't he? It's all progress, so buy a trainer seat or simply hold him in place. Now he wants to wash his own hands, and no, he doesn't want you to roll up his sleeves first. Frustrating, isn't it? Nevertheless, it's part of growing and learning. He'll soon learn to keep his sleeves dry.

He may also want to dress himself. When you're in a hurry (especially if there are other children to get to school), this can be pretty frustrating, so remove temptations such as other clothes which he'd rather wear and you don't want him to. Put out the outfit of the day but provide

some leeway – perhaps he could choose his socks. This will also help him learn colours (red or blue today?) Your child will also be growing out of his cot. He's now big enough and strong enough to climb over the side – which can be dangerous. Perhaps he's ready for a bed.

Choices

Learning to make choices is part of growing to be independent. As your child gets older, he'll start to choose his own food. You may not appreciate this – carrots are *good* for you, but maybe he dislikes them as much as you dislike rice pudding. You may have to just accept it. On the other hand, he also has to listen to you. It's no good letting him put on his own shoes if he insists on wearing the left shoe on his right foot. Compromise by steering one foot into the correct shoe, but in such a way that he thinks he's doing it himself.

GETTING READY TO READ

● Buy magnetic alphabet letters for the fridge door. At first, he'll play with them without realizing what they are. Then help him find the letter with which his name begins, then the second, and so on. You can also buy magnetic numbers. Don't assume your child is too young for this – some children recognize letters and numbers before their second birthday so by two-and-a-half he should be ready.

● Look at picture books together at least once a day. Pick a quiet time (after lunch or his bath) and point out letters which you've already spotted on the fridge door. Don't worry if you find you are reading the same favourite story again and again – recognition is comfortingly familiar for a child.

● Buy picture games where you match the picture with the right word.

● Trace around familiar letters with his finger so he gets to know the shape.

● Point out signs on shop windows and other notices. Pick out a letter he might be able to recognize.

● As your child gets older, label familiar household objects with a clearly written word (e.g. pin or stick a label saying 'curtain' on a curtain).

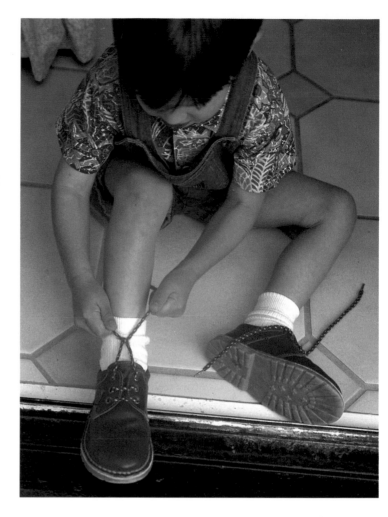

231

WHAT YOUR THREE-YEAR-OLD MAY DO

● **Dress and feed himself.**

● **Hold intelligible conversations.**

● **Think logically ('I'm too hot to wear this jumper').**

● **Match shapes (as with jigsaws) and identify what is the 'same' and what is 'different' (a picture of a ball on the newspaper's sports page is like his own football).**

● **Begin to count and perhaps recognize certain letters (see Getting Ready to Read, left).**

● **Understand location terminology such as on, under, behind.**

● **Know the difference between night and day. 'Yesterday' and 'tomorrow' might not mean much until he's about three and a half or four.**

● **Understand the difference between short and long.**

Your child is becoming increasingly independent and will want to do things for himself such as learn to tie his shoe-laces which takes time, much practice and concentration.

WHY IS THE GRASS GREEN?

'Look at that, Mummy – what *is* it?' This type of question can come at the most inconvenient time, such as when you're driving and concentrating on the road. Nevertheless, try to see it as a challenge. It shows your child's mind is growing – he needs to know. Try to stop yourself from being angry that your concentration has been disturbed, and answer with something like 'I'm driving at the moment so I can't see. Tell me what it looked like. What colour was it?' Even when you're not driving, childish questions can be very complex and difficult to answer, such as 'Why is the grass green?' (why indeed?) or 'Where does rain come from?' Try to explain life simply ('rain comes from the clouds in the sky').

Some subjects are easier than others. Many parents find death a hard topic to discuss with a child who wants to know where Granny has gone. Make the answer as simple as you can, according to your faith. Try comparing it with a situation you've already come across: 'Granny has gone to heaven like the rabbit did, last year. She can still see you even though we can't see her'. Death, in fact, can be a far more distressing subject for the explainer than for the childish questioner, who will often be very matter of fact, once he's received a satisfactory reply. Details which seem very trivial to us can be of the utmost importance to a child. 'But what does Granny eat for breakfast in heaven?' you may be asked. Keep your response as calm and down to earth as the question. For instance: 'Cornflakes, I expect.' Other children, however, may not wish to discuss the death of a loved adult and their silence on the subject should be respected.

DOING AND THINKING

Your child will now be able to do a wide variety of practical things. He can turn keys (and lose them). He can turn on the bathtaps if you're not looking, and he will sort out his own socks if you leave him to it. By the age of five he may be better at using the video than you are. He can also remember much more than you may give him credit for. 'I've seen that house before – we came here last year,' your four-year old might say, on visiting friends.

In the early days, your child's understanding doesn't quite match his wordpower. Two-and-a-half-year-olds often say no even when they mean yes and vice versa. Or they might nod their heads when saying no and shake them when saying yes. This is quite natural – rather like playing a piano when your left hand has to co-ordinate with the right; it's difficult at first but it comes with time.

FEELINGS AND BEHAVIOUR

Never underestimate a child's feelings. An unhappy incident, such as a death in the family or witnessing an accident, can remain in his mind for life. So can a smell which is associated with a particular event. Listen to your child about whatever is upsetting him, regardless of how young he is. As has been said before, he can understand more than you might think. Sometimes, in fact, your child can shock you with his adult-like emotions. Anger

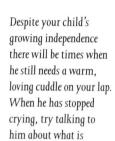

Despite your child's growing independence there will be times when he still needs a warm, loving cuddle on your lap. When he has stopped crying, try talking to him about what is upsetting him.

232

See Dealing with Feelings, page 250, for more information on your child's feelings

is a good example. Look how he clenches his hands and stamps his feet when another child hijacks his trike at the mother and toddler group. Now's the time to talk. You could say, 'I understand why you're angry that James has taken your bike, but it's friendly to share things, isn't it?' Your child will probably still feel angry, but at least you've talked about it rather than trying to repress his feelings. The message about sharing will go in, eventually.

Serious discussions work better during quiet, relaxed times (cuddling up on the sofa with an after-lunch book, perhaps). Hold your child close to you – there's nothing more comforting than body warmth. Look him in the eye with a kindly smile. Looks say everything – and he's more likely to open up if he feels he has a sympathetic listener. Perhaps your child is feeling bad (and behaving badly) because of developmental problems. These could be serious – is your child being teased because he has a large birthmark on his leg? The problem might seem relatively minor to you, yet huge to him. Talk to your doctor or health visitor – if that birthmark is really troubling your child, you could explore the

medical options; laser treatments are now very effective, for example. If the developmental blockage isn't medical, talk to your child about it. Don't just dismiss his feelings as 'silly'.

If your child still won't talk, it might help to draw a picture of your situation. You could draw Susie kicking her Mummy and say something like 'Poor Mummy – look at that purple bruise on her leg. Maybe that will help Susie to realize that kicking people hurts . . .' Books can draw out feelings as well. If jealousy is the problem find a picture of a little boy with a new baby sister. Is he looking rather cross? That's your cue for explaining simply that you understand why he's angry because you have a new baby to look after too. Try making him feel big: 'You're so grown up now that you can help me change the baby's nappies.'

Tell your child stories about what it was like when you were young and how you felt when you lost your favourite teddy or you cut your knee on a pair of scissors. Children love to hear of your own childhood, just as you did at that age. It means a lot to know that Mummy also did naughty things . . .

As children grow older they spend longer amusing themselves with constructive and imaginative games and activities. It's even better if there's a co-operative friend, brother or sister around.

233

LEARNING RULES
● **Safety must come first. Establish the fact that he can't walk along the pavement unless he's wearing reins or holding your hand or that he mustn't touch the fire or cooker because it is hot and will hurt him.**
● **Establish table rules. If he gets down from the table, he's obviously finished. He will miss pudding.**
● **Be consistent. Don't give in one day and be strict the next.**

PLAY AND TOYS

Your walking, talking little person will now have acquired many skills. She is capable of performing simple tasks like helping to cook something, laying the table or dressing herself. Don't expect too much though and always be there to help, encourage and praise her achievements however small they may seem.

LET'S PRETEND

Your child will probably spend more and more time playing pretend games, especially with her friends or siblings. She'll love dressing up and creating 'situations', so be sure to save empty packets and jars so she can play shops. Toy money doesn't cost much and will help your child get used to giving money in exchange for goods and receiving change. When you're out, let her hand over the money for the loaf of bread, for example. Toy food is expensive – but great fun. Alternatively, you could help your child make some with playdough for playing shops or cafés.

If she likes 'writing' and being more businesslike you could help her make an 'office'. A toy telephone, a typewriter (either toy or an old manual one), a desk and chair, paper and pens and, perhaps, a rubber stamp are all you need. A post office is another popular idea.

A dolls' house, farmyard or castle would all make good toys now, and if you are choosing a train or road set, buy one with a wooden or plastic interlocking track. The setting up of all these things is often the best part of the game!

TOY WEAPONS

Some people think that if you let children play with toy guns, they'll develop a taste for violence, but to most children, playing cowboys and Indians, knights in shining armour or Robin Hood and his Merrie Men is just innocent role play. If you ban toy weapons, boys in particular tend to use sticks, pieces of construction kit or even rulers as guns or swords, so don't make a big issue of it!

Save interesting old clothes, shoes, hats, belts, bags and jewellery for dressing-up and sort through secondhand things at car boot and jumble sales to add to the collection.

TV AND VIDEO

TV and videos can play a valuable part in your child's development but shouldn't be used as an excuse to ignore her. Don't regularly plonk her down in front of the screen just to keep her quiet (though this can be a saving grace if you are at the end of your tether and need some 'space'). She's much better off playing with you or other friends for the most part, although watching a TV programme or a video can be a good 'wind down' after a busy day at playgroup or some other activity. Use videos as a treat, not an everyday pastime and limit TV viewing to 'her' programmes. Don't let her automatically switch the television on and watch whatever appears, as it may not be suitable.

COMPUTER BRAIN

Don't rush out and buy all the latest computer toys on the market because you think you should 'cram' your child for school. You will be able to tell when she's ready to learn by her questions. For instance, if she starts asking what time lunch is, or what time a particular programme comes on television, it would be a good idea to get a simple toy clock to teach her the basics of time-telling.

Pair and matching games are particularly good for developing her recognition and memory, but they don't have to be advanced-technology models. Simple snap cards and picture dominoes are fine. The only advantages of computerized versions are that most children are fascinated by flashing lights and push-buttons; they give the games an added dimension and can help them become computer-literate from an early age. The disadvantage is that they cost a lot more. Some computerized toys are extremely good, although others can be a huge disappointment. Always try a computerized toy before you buy and make sure that it can grow with your child. If she can master all it has to offer in the first week, then it'll be a wash out. If you have a real computer, you could buy a pre-school game package for it instead.

236

ACTION PLUS

Most children between the ages of three and four can master pedals. First trikes or other vehicles tend to have the pedals attached to the front wheels, but these are often more difficult to master than one with a chain. Let her try it out before you buy and make sure there is somewhere flat for her to ride it.

Catch

Simple throwing and catching games are good for hand-eye co-ordination. A small home-made beanbag is easier to grasp than a ball. Indoors, just keeping a balloon off the

ART AND CRAFT

Most children will spend hours painting, colouring and drawing. Ready-mixed bottles of poster paint in large plastic bottles are one of the best buys. Choose the primary colours – red, blue and yellow, plus black and white. Your child can then mix any colour she needs (with your help at first).

Give her thick stubby brushes to start with. One for each colour is better than trying to get her to rinse her brush – she'll forget and all the colours will get mixed up. If she has difficulty holding her crayons, buy a little grip which fits on to the pencil with

Having your very own three-wheeler is an enormous help when you have to take your Aerobie a long way in the garden! Giving your child wheels opens up a whole new dimension.

ground will give hours of fun and won't cause any damage.

Other physical activities she'll learn now are climbing, hopping, skipping, jumping and running. You could buy a climbing frame, trampoline or rope ladder, if you have somewhere suitable to put them, or devise a simple assault course: a plank supported on two bricks, a ladder on the ground to step across, a hula-hoop to jump in and out of and an old mattress or piece of foam to do somersaults or to fall and jump on. Indoors, a large beanbag makes a comfy seat and is great for tumbling on.

the finger positions moulded in it. It will also help when she comes to learning to write. Don't spend a fortune on paper – computer printouts, old wallpaper and large envelopes are ideal.

THE LITTLE HELPER

Your child will enjoy helping you with the following chores inside and out:
● Washing up: Let her stand on a chair beside you with an apron on.
● Washing clothes: Give her some doll's clothes or her own socks and pants and let her wash them in lots of lovely suds.

● Cooking: Give her her own piece of pastry or bread dough to shape and roll.

● Cleaning: A toy vacuum cleaner, broom or carpet sweeper is a good idea. Provide her with her own duster and let her help polish the table and chairs.

● Sewing: She'll be fascinated watching you sew. Teach her by skewering some holes in a piece of card. Give her a blunt bodkin threaded with wool and let her sew in and out of the holes.

● Shopping: When you go to the supermarket, let her help.

● Gardening: Give her a child-size wheelbarrow. She'll love collecting fallen leaves or grass cuttings.

● Car wash: Give her a large sponge or soft cloth and let her help.

STARTING PLAYGROUP

Children need to mix with other children. They learn from each other to share, interact and relate to other people. They also learn socially acceptable behaviour, how to communicate, and how to become independent. All of these skills are achieved through playing together. Your child will need to build up her confidence ready for school. Joining a playgroup will help her enormously.

START YOUR OWN GROUP
If there isn't a suitable group locally, you could consider starting one yourself. Contact the Pre-school Playgroups Association (see Useful Addresses, page 314) for further information.

TOYS FOR YOUR OLDER CHILD

WHEN your child: shows pleasure in role play.	WHEN your child: can master a sit 'n' ride toy easily and has developed strong leg muscles.	WHEN your child: can recognize shapes and colours and can hold a brush or crayon.	WHEN your child: can recognize tunes and sing along.
WHAT she will enjoy: a doll's house, train or road set, castle, farmyard or zoo animals, etc.	WHAT she will enjoy: pedal trike or other vehicle.	WHAT she will enjoy: matching and memory games, picture and story books, painting, drawing, cutting and pasting.	WHAT she will enjoy: musical instruments like a whistle, keyboard, xylophone or cassette player.
WHY she needs them: to develop her imagination and ability to concentrate and to help her construction and organizational skills. To help her to learn to cherish her possessions by encouraging her to collect items for her set over a period of time, for example, different animals for a farmyard.	WHY she needs it: to develop her balance and co-ordination. To learn to manoeuvre, which means developing her ability to think and do. To enjoy the sensation of speed.	WHY she needs them: to encourage creativity, imagination and concentration. To develop her memory and thought processes. To relax.	WHY she needs them: to develop her sense of rhythm and an awareness of and pleasure in different sounds, music and songs. (Some children enjoy playing with these even earlier than three.)

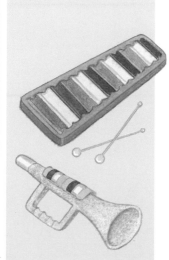

237

PRE-SCHOOL PLAY AND LEARNING

● Most pre-school education is privately run and costs vary from area to area.
● There are a few state-run nursery schools (contact your local Social Services department for information).
● Most playgroups and nursery schools limit the time your child can attend to about three mornings a week.

Play is already an important part of your child's life – and has been ever since he first learned to shake his rattle or make faces with you in the mirror. After the age of two, you'll notice your child needs to do a little more – perhaps some colouring or making playdough animals. Don't worry if he puts down the crayon after a few minutes or gets bored with the playdough. A young child's concentration is very limited at first. Try to increase it by sitting down and playing with him for a set amount of time per day (perhaps ten minutes).

Of course, this won't be easy, especially when there's all that washing to be done or you simply want five minutes to close your eyes . . . which is why a pre-school playgroup can be so important. It gives your child a chance to play with other adults and children, and it helps you both to have some time away from each other. It will also help him to acquire important social skills such as learning to share and play with other children.

IS YOUR CHILD READY?

Playgroups and nursery schools generally take children from the age of three, although some areas take them from two-and-a-half. A playgroup or nursery school should not be confused with a day nursery which accepts little ones from birth. Needless to say, one three-year-old can be very different from another. Your own little chap might be a happy socializer who'll run into playgroup without as much as a backward glance, while your friend's son might cling to her knees at the door. So how can you tell if your child is ready for this first parting? Generally speaking, most three-year-olds need some sort of stimulus – preferably outside the home – as part of their social development. Imagine if you spent all your time with just one person. You'd eventually get bored, wouldn't you? Even an extremely clingy three-year-old might be fine once Mummy has finally gone and isn't hovering by the door, wearing a worried expression and making him feel confused.

A good playgroup or nursery school will provide plenty of activities for your child.

Being on top and singing 'I'm the queen of the castle', is much more fun when there are other children around to play with than when you're on your own.

239

PREPARING YOUR CHILD

Play-acting is a natural way to explain many new situations to children. Just as a game of 'doctors and nurses' can introduce the idea of hospital, playing 'schools' is a fun preparation for playgroup or nursery school. Make sure it's positive play – you want to make your child *want* to go to playgroup, not dread it. 'Let's practise drawing red circles,' you might say. If he picks up the blue crayon, you can gently guide his hand towards the right colour with the words '*Here*'s the red crayon.'

However, don't become competitive and beware of comparing your child's academic abilities with those of your friends' children. Some children pick up pre-school skills earlier than others but when they start school most children are on a similar level. Remember he's still only young and social preparation for pre-school education is just as important as academic ability.

Ask the playgroup or nursery school leader for the names of two or three local children who might be starting at the same time. Invite them (plus mothers) round to play. If you do this regularly before your child goes to playgroup or nursery school, he will recognize some familiar faces when he starts at the group.

Many pre-school groups have familiarization days before the start of a new term. If yours doesn't, ask if your child can spend an hour or two there before he begins properly. Some playgroups aren't insured to take under-threes (even for trial mornings) so you may need to stay with him.

Check too (with the playgroup/nursery school leader) whether a child has to be toilet trained before starting. This can cause tremendous anxiety among parents in case they can't train their children in time. If you still haven't succeeded before the beginning of term, explain the situation to the head. Most are sympathetic enough to know that potty training doesn't always succeed by the age of three.

240

PLAYGROUPS AND NURSERY SCHOOLS

The basic difference between playgroups and nursery schools is that playgroups aim to teach children through play rather than formal lessons. A typical playgroup might have several 'activity tables' with helpers guiding children who are sticking shapes on to paper, making playdough figures, and so on. There is not so much formal teaching at playgroups although many have 'rising five' sections to teach letters.

Playgroup leaders do not have to be trained teachers. Many are mothers who have taken a Pre-school Playgroup Association (PPA) training course – although they do not have to. In fact, anyone can start a playgroup (see What to look for, below). The leader usually has at least one paid helper, but parents generally take it in turns to help out.

Nursery schools tend to emphasize more formal teaching at an earlier age, but they do so in a non-demanding way, like joining dots to form the outline of a letter. A three-year-old might also start to learn numbers through games and colouring in. Most nursery schools are run by trained teachers and many are attached to schools, which can be helpful to your child if it means he will already be familiar with the place when it's time for full-time schooling.

'I DON'T WANT HIM TO GO'

It is obvious that playgroups and nursery schools have a lot to offer a child, but maybe your child doesn't like going. If so perhaps you should postpone sending him and try again the following term. Formal playgroup or nursery school education is not compulsory – unlike school, you don't *have* to send your child. You can do a lot to stimulate your three- to five-year-old at home, providing you can make the commitment; and if he plays with similarly aged friends regularly, he'll be equipped with the social skills needed for school. Do beware, however, of keeping your child at home for your own sake.

STARTING SCHOOL

When will he be going to school? That depends very much on the area you live in as well as on individual schools and their own age-guidelines. Some state schools take rising fives in the term before their fifth birthday. If your child is five in September, you might find that his prospective school considers him too young to start in the previous summer term.

Private schools often take children earlier – some from the age of four. This might be too young for your child. On the other hand, you may feel your child needs that extra input. The decision is yours. Only you know what is best for him.

WHAT TO LOOK FOR

Don't be afraid to ask staff a few questions as you look round. If they don't like it, maybe it's not a suitable environment. You have a right to make the following checks:

● Staff attitudes. Are they welcoming when you visit? Do they talk to your child as well as you? After all he is the important one.

● Staff qualifications. A natural affinity with children is worth more than a piece of paper, but there should be at least one member present who is trained in basic first aid. A good playgroup should have staff who've been on a PPA training course.

● Ratio. The PPA recommends a minimum of one adult per five children aged three to five years and one adult per four children aged two to three.

● Safety. Is there a safety chain on the door to prevent would-be truants? Is a register taken when children arrive? If not, how will staff know if a child never arrived that day or if he did and he's missing? Are parents asked to tell staff if someone else will be picking up their child that day? Is the outside play area safely cordoned off from the road?

● Discipline. Ask how the staff handle bad behaviour. Some have a 'naughty' corner (chair turned to the wall) which you might not approve of (or thoroughly agree with!).

● Hygiene. Pop into the children's lavatory while you're there. Is there adequate soap and are the towels clean?

OPPOSITE By the time your child starts school she'll be ready to respond to fresh challenges, make the most of a variety of opportunities and enjoy new friends and freedom.

FAMILY MATTERS

0-5 years

A child learns her first lessons about life in the heart of her family, for it's there that she can first feel what it's like to be loved and to love, to be sad and happy, angry and excited, afraid and full of hope. And it's within the family that she learns how to react to the world and to other people.

Families – and mothers and fathers in particular – are hugely important but never perfect. Problems arise for all of us, as well as normal, everyday joys, encouragements and rewards. Yet each of us can go on finding out how best to handle these very human experiences and, in so doing, we can give our children one of their most useful lessons – how to keep learning, growing and hoping.

BECOMING A PARENT

When you and your partner have your first baby, you start a brand-new extended family. The child links your fathers and mothers, grandmothers and grandfathers, and brothers and sisters, and the new arrival kindles hope for the future.

Giving birth also brings change, however. Both of you have to adjust to the baby's constant presence and your new responsibilities. Most new parents find that the reality of being a mother or father is very different from what they imagined.

Thankfully the thrills and pleasures of parenthood usually more than compensate for the tiredness and loss of your freedom as a couple, and these rewards can make the years spent caring for a child into a time of golden opportunity.

You'll find that life with a baby is very different from your pre-baby days. Some people say it's better. Others say it's difficult or even a shock.

Many new mothers give up paid employment outside the home when they have a baby. Many find that being based at home for the first time in their adult life – without contact with colleagues, the stimulation and pay of their former work, and the routine of travelling – is one of the biggest changes in their new lifestyle. A baby turns a couple into a threesome, which inevitably affects how you and your partner get on together. And if you have other children they too will need reassuring that they're still important.

THE REALITIES OF BEING A PARENT

You may find yourself wanting to change decisions you made before you had the baby. Perhaps you decided to bottlefeed, but found the idea of breastfeeding much more attractive the moment you held your warm and fascinating baby with his wonderful smell. On the other hand, you may wonder why no one told you that breastfeeding isn't always plain sailing. The same goes for work. Whatever your antenatal plans, you may want to change your mind when you see what being a parent is like.

Perhaps the biggest surprise is when it sinks in that you'll be a parent for the rest of your life. And just as your parents have an important influence on you – and you on them – so it is with you and your child.

TIREDNESS

There's no getting away from the fact that looking after a baby or young child is hard work, however rewarding it may be. You'll probably find you're very much more tired at home with your baby than you were when you went out to work. The main reason is broken sleep. But you're also using up energy adapting to your new lifestyle and focusing attention on your little one. And childbirth, however wonderful, is intrinsically stressful, not only for you but also for your partner. Looking after yourselves as parents is never more important than it is now. It's an absolute necessity when you're so tired.

Taking your baby with you has never been easier – thanks to ingeniously designed, state of the art equipment such as this strong portable babychair which is a joy to use.

244

See Your Day Together, page 82

'THE EMOTIONAL ROLLERCOASTER'

Some women readily adapt to motherhood. Others find it difficult and become flat and depressed, or swing between feeling low and on top form. Men, too, can run the gamut of emotions: joy over the beauty of the baby; anxiety that life will never be the same again; excitement on becoming a father; resentment of the responsibility; deeper feelings of warmth and intimacy with their partner; jealousy of the time the woman gives the baby; and frustration at not having sex for some time.

Some feelings which may crop up, such as pride, pleasure, excitement and fulfilment, are readily acceptable and pleasurable. Others, such as boredom, irritation and feeling inadequate and lonely, are unexpected and uncomfortable but can be managed and dealt with (see page 250).

SUPPORTS

Parents of young children arguably have the most important of all jobs. However, there are times when they need help to do this job well. Don't be afraid to ask for help but make sure it's constructive help which meets your actual needs.

Tip: Make it easier for people to help you by telling them exactly what you'd most like them to do.
- If you're exhausted, ask them to take the baby out for a ride in the pushchair so you can have an uninterrupted rest.
- If you've too much to do, ask them to go to the shops, do some of the housework, or prepare the supper.
- If some exercise would buck you up, ask them to come with you to the swimming pool or an exercise class so they can look after the baby.

Family size makes a big difference to the support others can give you. For instance, a couple may have twice the time and energy of a single parent, and available grand-parents add an extra dimension. Whatever your family size, you can weave a network of people who might help when you need them by making friends and joining in local activities.

The support and advice of your family doctor and health visitor are there for the taking, and local groups of the National Childbirth Trust and La Leche League provide a source of information, support and potential friends.

Rewards

Take time to recognize and enjoy the things that give you pleasure: it may be
- Your baby's smile.
- Or the delight of a cuddle or the thrill of the first steps.
- Or feeling closer to your partner.
- Or maybe you simply love your baby and are delighted by being a parent.

'Looking after Debbie keeps me going all day and a lot of the night too, and she's only two months old. My trouble is that I use the times when she sleeps in the day to get on with other things. It might be better if I caught up on some lost sleep instead, or used the time for myself rather than on the house.'

Your baby needs you for comfort and love, food and company, and every basic care, so never be too proud to ask for as much practical back-up and emotional support as you need for your important role.

245

BEING A FATHER

One of the most important and far-reaching things that can happen to a man is becoming a father. From the moment you know your partner is pregnant, you see life from a different perspective. When the baby is born your life changes even more, and gradually you realize life will never be the same again.

A GOOD TIME TO BE A DAD

The world of today is a particularly good place to be a father. This is partly because we now know so much about the importance of fathering that the average good dad can be satisfied with what he does.

One reason why fathering is so important is that your child's first close relationship with a man is with you. Psychologists say the father-child relationship colours all future relationships with men. You are your son's main male role-model as he travels on the long journey towards manhood. As for your daughter, you are the one from whom she learns what to expect from other close male relationships she will have in her life. At some level she will always compare her male friends and significant others with you.

This may sound as if you have to be a perfect father but this is not necessary, and in any case it is doubtful whether such a thing exists. Psychologists believe a man

need be only a 'good enough' father, not a perfect one, for his children to feel loved and loveable – two things that are invaluable for their well-being.

Another reason why it's a good time to be a father is that a growing number of men have more opportunities to be involved with their children. No longer do we have to keep within the rigid boundaries that once defined what men did.

MEN'S WORK AND WOMEN'S WORK

The definitions of 'women's work' and 'men's work' are evolving year by year. This allows many a man to see more of his children and home than previous generations did. Society once expected a father to be the sole breadwinner, but nowadays many men don't have to shoulder this burden single-handed. The majority of young women expect to share financial responsibility. Although most take a meaningful amount of time off paid work to care for their young children, nearly all return some months or years later, albeit mostly part-time until the children are older.

However, surveys show that women still do the lion's share of childcare and household tasks – though this is usually because the couple chooses this division of work, rather

BELOW This child is having an exciting new experience and learning important lessons about the boundaries of fear and safety at the same time.

BELOW RIGHT Having your child a helping hand could have unexpected spin-offs for you as you shed the burdens of your working day and focus on the importance and thrill of those early steps.

than automatically assuming it will happen. Occasionally a couple decide he will stay home with the children and she will be the main breadwinner. And sometimes both do paid work outside the home.

MANAGING THIS STAGE OF LIFE

Most men take a delight and pride in their new baby. At the same time, however, that baby can come as something of a shock. And for some men this stage of life precipitates an identity crisis.

The Chinese pictogram for 'crisis' incorporates two symbols, one for danger and one for opportunity. New fatherhood, like any time of change, can feel dangerous in that it alters your familiar lifestyle. But it also lays before you a pathway paved with life-enhancing possibilities. The secret of coping with these two very different aspects is to be aware of your mixed feelings, and not imagine you ought to be delighted by everything and coping brilliantly. It's perfectly normal to feel ambivalent – even about something as wonderful and important as your own child. It's far healthier to allow any difficult feelings to come to the surface than to pretend they don't exist.

Sometimes it's difficult to see the rewards you will gain from being a father, especially if you're tired from having broken nights and then getting up early in the morning to go to work. Add to this your partner being tired and disrupted too, and it's easy to see why some new fathers feel upset.

One way of managing this is to see the situation in perspective. In becoming a father you take on an important and demanding new role. If this sometimes seems overly stressful and overwhelming, concentrate on finding effective ways of meeting your needs. This is especially important if you become depressed – as psychologists believe happens to about seven in a hundred new fathers.

MEETING YOUR NEEDS

Most men, like most women, want simple things: rewarding and productive work, enjoyable free time, a loving friendship and good sex life with their partner and to be able to love and care for their children. Finding ways of meeting your needs is important not only for your own sake, so you can enjoy this time, but also so you have plenty of energy and motivation to protect your partner and child and enjoy being with them and providing for them. Here are some suggestions:

- Eat a healthy diet.
- Experiment with more effective stress-management techniques when necessary.
- Spend time with your friends.
- Meet your needs for sex by cuddling your partner and by masturbating until she is fit, well and ready for full intercourse again.
- Take moderate-to-high-intensity aerobic exercise, preferably daily or as often as possible.

On the subject of exercise, quite a lot of fathers know they could do more. One way of fitting this into a busy schedule is by combining exercise with childcare. Some of the newest strollers, for example, have over-sized wheels that enable the pusher to jog rather than walk. (The wheels of a regular stroller are so small that the baby wouldn't get a comfy ride.) If you were to go stroller-jogging with a friend, you could enjoy socializing as well as keeping fit. Another idea is for you and your partner to take the baby to a swimming pool and take it in turns to look after the baby or have a swim yourself.

WHEN THINGS GO WRONG

Many couples who are parents find a successful way of living together as friends, lovers, parents and workers. But when things go wrong in a relationship then there is often hurt on both sides and you may need to seek help and advice (see page 258).

There are two particular groups of fathers who feel excluded and unhappy. Some separated or divorced men are unhappy because they have only limited access to their children. And some men who have fathered a child out of wedlock discover too late that the mother wants to be independent, remain single, and exclude them from their child's life.

Yet men who are fathers have just as many rights to care for their children as women who are mothers. So if this happens to you, ask a lawyer to point you to someone who can help you to resolve the situation.

ABOVE No-one adds a thrill to a weekend walk like a Dad – remember how your dad used to do just the same to you?

247

WHAT CHILDREN NEED

That sleeping baby looks so lovely that you just want to give his hand a big kiss, then you and Mummy can quietly creep away to spend some time together playing without him.

Children need people to love them. Being loved makes them feel lovable, special and important at a deep level. It gives them a sense of security and a feeling that everything will work out all right, and helps to establish confidence and self-esteem. Moreover, being loved and feeling lovable enables children to love others.

Children need to know that their parents will always root for them. That they can always go to their mother or father for a cuddle, reassurance, encouragement or help, and that even if their parents sometimes disapprove of what they do, they will always love them.

BEING WITH YOU
One form of showing your love is to give your child time on a one-to-one basis. Children naturally try to get attention, as any parent knows, and not always when it's most convenient. You, or whoever is with your child, need to take the time single-mindedly to enjoy playing or listening carefully to them, giving them what is known as quality time.

It's no good 'saving up' or rationing quality time, children need to refresh themselves by constantly 'plugging in' to it at intervals throughout the day.

LEARNING ABOUT RELATIONSHIPS AND BEHAVIOUR FROM YOU
Your child learns about relationships as your apprentice. Children soak up what it means to be listened to and to listen, to love and hate, to be angry, happy, sad, excited, afraid, worried or joyful, at their parents' knees.

Your baby will scrutinize you and your reactions, including the expression on your face, your body language and your tone of voice. You'll be rewarded with a smile, a delighted wriggle, a roar of laughter, or a gurgle or coo. And all the time you're engaged in this you're teaching communication skills better than any qualified teacher. An older child practises relating with a doll, teddy, brother or sister. Years later that grown-up child may behave with a partner just as you now behave with yours, and imitate your parenting with your grandchild.

LIVING FOR THE PRESENT
Many religions and philosophies teach the importance of living moment by moment – of savouring the flavour of the present, but some of us spend too much time worrying, reminiscing about the past or longing for the future. Sometimes you'll look forward to your child's bedtime, or the time when she will be mobile, or off to playgroup. That's only natural, but it's a shame if it stops you making as much as you can of the here and now.

Obviously when times are tough you may wish you were a million miles away but, otherwise, try to live in the present and appreciate the good things you and your child have going between you.

CUDDLES, HUGS AND MASSAGE

Your cuddles convey your love. Babies and adults nearly all enjoy being held and babies in particular need hugs and physical contact to thrive. Massaging your baby is a lovely way to show you care and many people say that giving a massage is almost as relaxing as receiving one. Try it even if you've never done one before. There are many good books on the subject that may help with practical advice.

LAUGHTER

When you have nothing to laugh about, think of something funny or láugh just for the sake of it. You'll probably feel much better. Sometimes it's easy for people to be over-serious when they become parents. Making time to enjoy yourselves and have a good laugh is most important. And children love to laugh with their parents. A good laugh is a highly effective way of unwinding and putting life in perspective.

Handling and cuddling your baby is second nature to you, so try massaging his chest, tummy, back, head, face, feet or limbs with gentle, slow, rhythmical movements. You'll probably both love it.

Warm the room and collect towels, sheets, massage oil and a blanket in case the person being massaged becomes cold. Massage babies on the floor because oil makes them more slippery than usual. The floor gives a lovely firm base when massaging an adult too. Spread a sheet on the carpet first, then a large soft towel for the person to lie on.

Use a 'relaxing' massage oil from a shop or, for an adult, mix a tablespoon of carrier oil (such as soya or grapeseed) with two or three drops of your favourite relaxing essential oils. Essential oils are plant extracts containing the 'essence' and fragrance of the flowers, leaves, seeds, stems or roots they come from. Lavender oil is useful for any age, as are rose and neroli oils. Make up a smaller amount of massage oil for a baby – one drop of essential oil to a dessertspoonful of carrier oil will do.

ENCOURAGEMENT, AFFIRMATION AND PRAISE

You can change someone's behaviour, confidence level and happiness by encouraging, affirming and praising instead of only pointing out what's wrong or putting them down. Try the following for a few days:

1 Focus on what you like about your child's – or partner's – behaviour or attitude. (The smallest thing will do.)
2 Then describe it to them, say why you like it and tell them how it makes you feel.

Encouragement makes loved ones feel warm and heartened; affirmation (highlighting the positive things about them) firms up their belief that you approve of and love them (and helps them love themselves); and praise helps them believe in themselves. Experiment with anyone, not only your child and partner.

DEALING WITH FEELINGS

OPPOSITE *A lovely warm feeling fills the air when the two of you have time to listen and talk, time to understand and be understood, and time simply to enjoy each other's company.*

Dealing with feelings is very important to parents and children because family problems, like problems between any human beings, can be rooted in poor communication.

Sometimes the most difficult things to communicate are your feelings, but how is someone to know how you feel if you don't tell them? 'If they loved me, they'd know how I feel,' you might say, but some people are naturally better at sensing emotions and it isn't helpful to blame those who aren't so good.

WHEN PARENTS KEEP FEELINGS TO THEMSELVES

You may have become quite an expert at keeping yourself to yourself, and you may bury difficult feelings so well that even you don't know they're there.

The snag with buried feelings is that it takes a lot of energy to keep them from bothering you, so you may end up feeling tired or low. Habits such as drinking or eating too much, working unnecessarily hard, or channelling emotional problems into bodily illness can be ways of protecting ourselves from coming face to face with problem feelings. Unfortunately, these habits can harm you and, possibly, those you love. There comes a time when it's easier to bring them out into the open and learn to deal with them differently. You may be able to do this on your own but it's more likely that you'll need someone else to listen to you and help you.

YOUR PARTNER AND CHILD'S FEELINGS

Perhaps you're an ace at recognizing how your partner or child feels. But do they know you know? If you tell them about the feelings you think you're picking up, they may feel better. You may not always be right, but they know you care enough to try to understand.

Feeling understood is wonderful, and sharing your understanding of your partner or child might help them understand themselves and their situation better too.

LISTENING TO YOUR PARTNER, CHILD AND SELF

However good a listener you are, you can learn how to deal with feelings better by trying to empathize with the person you are talking to, whether this is your partner or child. This means trying to imagine what it must feel like to be that person, not what you would feel like in their circumstances.

How to listen to your partner or child

● Choose a time when you're both alone and unlikely to be interrupted.
● Lay aside what's on your mind. Many things can interfere with listening, for example, noise, physical discomfort, or important issues on your mind.
● Try to identify their main feelings. You may detect emotions in the words used, the sound and rhythm of the speech, their body language, or somehow through your intuition or sixth sense. Sense the feelings as accurately as you can, and try to spot the deeper ones as well as those which are easy to recognize.
● Reflect back the feeling you think you have identified by saying something like 'It seems to me you're feeling...' This is the part of good listening that is so helpful but which many, even very sensitive, people neglect. (If you identify their feelings wrongly, they'll soon put you right.)

But remember, if you want to be good at listening, you must practise listening to yourself as a priority. When you regularly listen to yourself and try to work out your own feelings, you'll automatically listen more helpfully to others.

'Marina, who's three, kept pinching Nathan's wrist when he was lying in his cot. She said she wanted to be my baby and wished we didn't have Nathan. I told her I understood that she sometimes hated Nathan. She perked up and later said that although Nathan was sometimes a nuisance, she loved him.'

LISTENING TO YOURSELF

● Choose a convenient, quiet time when you're unlikely to be interrupted. (The time isn't always right to listen to yourself – or anyone else, for that matter.)

● Be relaxed and still. If your mind is racing, try to calm yourself, perhaps by lying down and doing some deep-breathing relaxation exercises.

● Name the emotions you're experiencing They may flit through your mind or they may be overwhelmingly powerful. Be as accurate as you can and don't try to feel what you think you should.

What then?

Simply recognizing your feelings may help. You may also find you can release difficult feelings constructively through such activities as work, sport, reading, cooking or listening to music. Or perhaps you'd feel better if you talked about them with someone you trust, such as your partner, parent or friend.

Listening better

It's easy as a listener to develop bad habits which put people off telling you how they feel and spoil your ability to recognize feelings. It's possible to curb these habits if you know what they are, so use this chart to find out. Tick if, when you're listening, you frequently find yourself:

❑ Interrupting.
❑ Criticizing.
❑ Judging.
❑ Explaining.
❑ Finishing their sentences.
❑ Switching off because you've heard it all before.
❑ Switching off because you think you know what they're going to say.
❑ Being distracted because your own feelings are stirred up.
❑ Advising.
❑ Feeling impatient.
❑ Asking questions for your own curiosity.
❑ Rescuing by reassuring.
❑ Competing for attention by talking about your own experiences.

COPING WITH DISAGREEMENTS

Disagreements are normal, but people cope with them in different ways, some better than others. Good communication combined with sensitive listening helps sparring partners feel understood. It's useful with children too, as long as you don't expect your child to listen in the same way

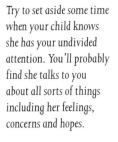

Try to set aside some time when your child knows she has your undivided attention. You'll probably find she talks to you about all sorts of things including her feelings, concerns and hopes.

to you. If your feelings are simmering, express them, if appropriate, but don't expect your child to be able to help – ask an adult to do that later. Having said this, children learn how to cope with conflict by watching their parents. Listening to your child's feelings can pay off as your child learns to copy you.

Who first? When you disagree or have a row or argument, both parties may have strong feelings. Each needs these feelings recognized as soon as possible.

Whose problem is it? Whose problem began the disagreement or row? That person may need to be heard first. Because you listen first it doesn't mean that you are without feelings or needs.

When you don't want to listen. Sensitive listening is hard or even impossible when you're angry and upset. This is because it's difficult to put your own mood aside so you can tune in to the other person's feelings. When your feelings are running high and you can't listen properly, tell the other person you'll listen when you've calmed down. First, you need to let them know how you feel.

When you're angry. When you're upset, frustrated, cross, furious or plain angry, you may feel better if someone recognizes how you're feeling. It isn't easy to listen to yourself when your feelings are very strong. However independent you usually are, it's surprising how much it can help when someone tries to understand you.

'You' and 'I' Language. Use 'I' language when talking about your feelings. For example, say 'I feel so angry,' rather than 'You make me feel so angry when . . . .' 'You' language can be unnecessarily inflammatory, whereas 'I' language reminds you both that you're a separate person entitled to your own feelings.

When your partner or child irritates you. Try saying 'I hate finding all the dirty pans in the sink,' rather than 'I hate you when you leave the dirty pans in the sink.' Let the other person know it's their action you dislike, not them. You may love them but loathe what they do. Let them know you accept that they are feeling as they do. They'll feel better and it doesn't mean you've given in or lost the argument.

253

NEGOTIATION

You may find 'The Three Cs' useful tools when it comes to settling conflicts: these are Capitulation (one of you – not always the same one – gives in to the other), Compromise (both make concessions), and Coexistence (you agree to do things differently). Don't feel as if you have failed if you resolve a conflict using one set of terms and then find that in a similar situation later you have to use a different approach. Do remember that any relationship is constantly changing and a certain amount of renegotiation is probable and could be essential. Capitulation might leave one partner feeling somewhat resentful. However, if you take it in turns to 'give in' and try to see capitulation as an adult way of choosing to deal with the problem, it has a rightful place alongside compromise and coexistence or choosing to do things differently.

Trying to listen to your friend on the phone with your baby in your arm and your young child at your knee is a skilful business and it may be easier and less stressful to phone back when things are quieter.

BEING ASSERTIVE

Being assertive means knowing your feelings and what you want, and letting others know when appropriate in a simple, straightforward way, without belittling or hurting them. It's an important skill for women who are mothers. Some mothers become so used to looking after their family that they forget their own needs.

Caring for others can be wonderful, but not if you are trampled on and uncared for yourself. Remember, being a doormat is no fun, and no example to set your children or partner.

When explaining your position, be clear and concise, so that the other person understands. They may try to change your mind. Stay firm by acknowledging what they say then repeating your statement. Don't spoil things by rambling, explaining or apologizing.

Help yourself to become more assertive:
● Make time to listen to yourself.
● Decide how you feel and what you want.
● Say so using 'I' language (see page 253).
● Say it again if necessary.
● Listen to the other person and learn to negotiate together.

POSTNATAL DEPRESSION
Feeling low soon after your baby is born is very common, but as many as one in ten women become much more depressed. A few are very ill indeed.

There are many triggers for postnatal depression. Becoming a mother brings enormous changes. You gain a lot but you lose a great deal too. It's perfectly normal to like some things you've gained and dislike others, just as it is to regret some things you've lost and be pleased about others.

'I used to be exhausted at the end of the day because so many people popped in. Now I've learnt to say calmly at the doorstep, "I won't ask you in because I haven't time now but I'd love to see you – how about . . ." (and I'd suggest a day and time).'

However, it's a problem if the bad bits seem to outweigh the good. Sadness and resentment are difficult to cope with if you're tired and motherhood seems strange. If you feel guilty at admitting to such feelings, it's even worse. Depression is your unconscious mind's way of coping, but it isn't easy to live with.

When you're depressed you may feel flat, gloomy, tearful, helpless and hopeless. Nothing seems exciting or pleasurable, you may not be eating or sleeping properly and you may find it hard to concentrate or make decisions. It may also affect your relationship with your partner. However, there are positive steps you can take to overcome your depression:
● Talk to someone about how you feel – your partner, a friend or relative, a neighbour, the midwife, or the health visitor or doctor. Don't waste precious time alone in your depression. You need someone with the time and experience to listen sensitively. If you've people to talk to but you're feeling no better, tell your health visitor or doctor. Some doctors prescribe anti-depressant drugs, but that shouldn't be instead of looking at your feelings.
● Find out about any local groups where women in your situation can talk in the presence of a skilled leader, or arrange to see a counsellor.
● Go to a parent and baby group to meet other mothers.
● Be assertive by asking for practical help – say what you'd like done.
● Eat a healthy diet with plenty of vegetables, fruit and foods rich in vitamins B and C, calcium, iron, magnesium and zinc, especially if breastfeeding.
● Exercise every day to boost your circulation, make you feel warm and increase the levels of chemicals called endorphins in your blood. These natural opiates (morphine-like chemicals) will make you feel more relaxed and help you cope better with stressful situations.
● Have at least an hour outside each day, preferably at mid-day in winter. Daylight may help your depression.

254

See Healthy Eating, page 40, Exercise During Pregnancy, pages 47-51, and Postnatal Exercises, pages 84-9

Eating a healthy diet with plenty of fresh fruit and vegetables will keep you fit and well and better able to manage your demanding new role.

VITAMINS AND MINERALS
- **Vitamin B: dairy foods, eggs, fish, meat, whole grains, green leafy vegetables, mushrooms, brown rice, nuts and seeds.**
- **Vitamin C: fresh fruits and vegetables.**
- **Calcium: dairy foods, shellfish, beans and peas, green leafy vegetables, carrots, parsnips, nuts and seeds.**
- **Iron: meat, shellfish, fish, whole grains, brown rice, beans, peas, green leafy vegetables, dates, figs, nuts and seeds.**
- **Magnesium: meat, fish, whole grains, beans, peas, green leafy vegetables, mushrooms and nuts.**
- **Zinc: dairy foods, eggs, fish, meat, whole grains, beans, peas, root vegetables, nuts and seeds.**

255

COPING WITH TIREDNESS

It can be tough caring for a baby alone if your partner is out all day. If you're a single parent the whole responsibility falls on your shoulders. And if you're working as well as coping with shopping and housework, it would be surprising if you weren't tired out.

Two things will help you to avoid becoming exhausted. Firstly, ask for help with practical domestic matters from your partner, family, friends or neighbours. Secondly, look after yourself (see page 256). Not only are you a very important person in your own right, but you have a very important baby to care for too.

KEEPING HEALTHY

Looking after yourself, coping with tiredness, meeting your needs and managing stress will go a long way to keeping you healthy. Your doctor and health visitor are there when you need them for

Looking after yourself isn't a luxury — it's a necessity, so remember that even if you have only a little time to yourself, you can do things like exercise with your baby there too.

you or your children, and you may like to explore other forms of healthcare in combination with conventional medical care. Homeopathy, aromatherapy, osteopathy, herbal medicine and acupuncture are just some of the many alternative or complementary therapies available. Check first that the practitioner or therapist is well qualified (see Useful Addresses, page 314).

LOOKING AFTER YOURSELF

It may help to look at this section with a paper and pencil to hand.

Diet: List everything you've eaten in the last two days, including when you had it, how long your meal took, and what else you were doing at the same time. Try to assess whether you're eating healthily. For example, do you eat several pieces of fresh fruit and several helpings of salad and vegetables each day? Also look at whether mealtimes are relaxed or stressful. *How* you eat can be just as important as *what* you eat.

Rest and relaxation: Look at how much you rest. If you're not sleeping well, can you catch up during the day? List the things

you find relaxing. Sometimes quite ordinary, mundane activities are profoundly relaxing.

Exercise: This is so important for parents of young children but is often squeezed out of busy schedules. Make time for it for your own sake.

Relationships: There's no time like the present to improve your relationships and thus the quality of your life. Talking and listening to your partner in a sensitive way is an excellent place to begin.

The inner self: Many parents find this is a time when they become especially sensitive to the beauty of the world around them. There can be a sense of awe at having a baby. Sometimes there's a greater awareness of the spiritual side of life. Allow yourself to use and enjoy these feelings and experiences to the full.

MEETING YOUR NEEDS

Do you look after yourself and try to meet your own needs? Use this exercise to look at how often you do the things which give you pleasure.

- Write a list of the things you most like doing.
- Choose the three you like best that you could do every day.
- Put these in order.
- Work out and write down how often you actually do them.
- Repeat, choosing three things you could do each week.
- Think about whether you can and will do more of the things you like.

The point is to see whether you can realistically adjust your current lifestyle to make it more pleasurable. You can use the same exercise to look at how often you relax, see friends, take exercise, and so on.

SUPERWOMAN AND SUPERMAN

There's no such thing as a perfect parent, just as there are no prizes for being a superwoman or superman. Pushing yourself on all fronts means something has to give. That could be your health, so watch for the warning signs.

You may be trying too hard to be a 'superparent' if you:

- Always rush everywhere.
- Put on or lose weight without wishing to.
- Wake up worrying.
- Have no free time in your day.
- Are frequently ill.
- Never let off steam.
- Feel depressed and anxious.
- Feel exhausted.
- Never say 'no'.
- Never ask for help.

STRESS MANAGEMENT

Stress is an inevitable part of life, but too much stress handled in the wrong way can make us ill. Handling the stressful parts of life well can make all the difference to the effects they have on us. Simply identifying the stresses is a good start. Getting a perspective is important too, for example – how long will this go on, whose problem is it, do I have any control over it, or can I alter my reaction to it?

Coping by taking too much responsibility on your shoulders, becoming ever more busy, doing everything yourself, keeping a stiff upper lip, pretending to yourself and others that everything is fine, smoking, eating or drinking too much or eating too little, are just some of the many destructive ways of coping with stress.

We all need to work out ways of handling stressful situations that don't hurt us. And it's helpful to have learned some relaxation techniques for when times are tough. Breathing exercises, lying down with your eyes closed and tensing and relaxing all your muscles one by one, having a long bath, exercising (see pages 84–9), enjoying a delicious meal, a football match, film or TV programme, or making time to read, are all ways of relaxing.

It makes good sense to identify the sources of your stress, work out whether they can be altered, learn to say 'no' to unnecessary demands, delegate, ask for help, put the things you need to do in order of priority, and spend some thoughtful time planning. If your life seems stressful, why not think things over by yourself or talk through what is worrying you with a friend?

There's a wonderful world out there for free, with hidden insects to admire together, exquisite little wild flowers to find, and the whole of nature to delight the soul and soothe stress away.

257

WHEN THINGS GO WRONG

Children sense their parents' every mood and notice every facet of behaviour, so if you are both upset try to talk things through so hidden messages don't upset your child more.

Things may sometimes go wrong with your relationship, which is quite normal. But there may come a time when the disadvantages of the relationship outweigh its advantages. You then have three options. You can let things deteriorate; you can separate or divorce; or you can learn the skills you need to make things better.

RELATIONSHIP SKILLS

Studies show that communication problems are a major cause of misunderstandings in relationships. Individuals may have trouble understanding and being understood, but it's quite possible to improve your communication skills by giving encouragement and praise (see page 249), learning how to listen (see page 250), managing disagreements (see page 252) and being assertive (see page 254).

Looking after yourself (see page 256) is, ironically, a relationship skill too. Doing it helps you to feel good about yourself, and it reinforces the message most of us receive as babies – that we are valuable and loved. If you feel like this, it's easier to care for and love another person, whereas if you put yourself down, neglect your needs, and don't value, honour or respect yourself, you'll find it very hard or even impossible to do the same for your partner.

TOLERANCE AND PATIENCE

The nature of things is that one of you will progress faster than the other with relationship skills or one may have a head start. This imbalance can cause problems between you. If you feel miles ahead of your partner, for instance if your partner seems hopeless with feelings and doesn't seem to understand you, consider accepting the difference between you and patiently waiting for your partner to catch up. Use your understanding of the situation and of your different abilities to let go of your anxiety and feel tolerant and at peace. You may need to wait a long time for your partner's relationship skills to improve, but it will be worth it. And one day he – or she – may do the same for you. We all make progress in life at different speeds and at different times. It is perfectly natural for two people in a partnership to be sometimes out of sync.

COUNSELLING

This may or may not save your relationship, but even if you do break up it generally has other spin-offs, such as helping you to understand the part you played in what went wrong. A counsellor can also help you to communicate better with each other by teaching you more effective ways of listening and coping with disagreements. Finally, you may have a chance to begin working out what's best for the children.

Individual counselling

Sometimes only one partner will go for counselling. Don't be put off by going alone – it may be the best thing you've ever done, and you never know – your partner may eventually join you.

SEPARATION AND DIVORCE

Some couples are quite certain about splitting up. Others waver for a long time, while a few keep returning to try again. Deciding whether or not to stay living together is a major task. It may seem easy for those who always decide things quickly, but an impetuous decision could be wrong and can hurt the other person so much in its suddenness that it reduces the chances of getting back together.

A solicitor experienced in marital matters will help to clarify what you want to do. For example, he or she may point out that seeking legal advice can be a way of communicating to your partner just how desperate you're feeling.

LEGAL HELP

If your relationship has broken down irretrievably, a solicitor can help with the conciliation work that will make the split less damaging to you, your partner and your children. You'll need to make acceptable arrangements about the custody, access to, financial support and education of the children, and decide what will happen to your home and other assets.

the burden of painful feelings going unheard. Besides giving your child a chance to talk about feelings, give simple updates and explanations about what is happening. Saying 'Daddy and I have decided to live in different places for a while because we've been arguing so much' is honest and straightforward, as long as you don't make promises about being together again which you can't keep. If your child asks you when you'll get back together, say you don't know, if that is the case. And as for awkward questions like 'Is Bob going to live here with us instead of my Daddy?', be as direct as you can. Children often sum up situations and people better than adults.

Some children who live with one parent after a separation or divorce continue to see the other parent, but a lot don't. That's a shame because it's generally preferable

259

A good friend with a sensitive listening ear is an enormous help when your life is difficult. She'll be ready to hear you puzzling over the same things again and again as you work out what's best to do.

HELPING YOUR CHILD THROUGH SEPARATION AND DIVORCE

Managing this long process well depends on parents listening to each other, trying to understand one another's feelings, and not taking their own feelings out on the children. It's essential for someone to recognize a child's feelings and feed back their awareness of them so that the child feels understood.

Sometimes someone else can convey this understanding better than parents, but it must be done if a child is to avoid

for a child to maintain links with both parents and both sides of the family. Unresolved custody and access problems can be a way in which one or both parents try to continue their relationship. One may be trying to hang on to the other. Some, on the other hand, consciously or unconsciously exclude their partner from their child's life as a punishment. However tempting it may be to criticize your partner in front of your child, try to resist it because it will be unhelpful and may be destructive to their relationship.

ONE PERSON, MANY ROLES

We prepare for parenthood by observing our own parents for years, but it isn't until we become parents ourselves that we really understand the responsibilities and emotions involved. At that point some people begin to think of themselves as parents first and people second. They find that being a parent overshadows all their other roles in life.

Juggling roles isn't easy. The duties and demands of being a mother or father, wife, husband or partner, daughter or son, sister or brother, and friend are one thing, but life goes on and these very same people also have to be breadwinner, shopper, cleaner, tidy-upper, gardener, chauffeur, handyman or woman, domestic secretary, cook and bottle-washer. Couples have to sort out who does what, and for some the decision about whether or not the woman will care for the child or go outside the home to work is the most complex.

BELOW Moments of shared interest and delight give parenthood — and childhood — their sparkle. And they help to forge happy memories of the pleasure of being together.

OPPOSITE Feeding other people is a skill learnt early — who knows what other skills this child will need as she in turn grows up and chooses what roles to take on board?

A few couples decide that the man will stay at home while the woman works. Many say the decision is thrust upon them by a combination of factors.

THE STAYING AT HOME/WORKING DILEMMA

In some societies most women work, while in others the reverse is true. People usually take the word 'work' to mean paid work. However, many other sorts of work, including voluntary and domestic work, can separate mothers from their children. A woman has to make up her own mind whether she is going to look after her children or arrange for someone else to do so. However, it's a sad fact that many are swayed by what they perceive other people doing, or by money. Ideally, every woman should be free to stay with her young child if that is what she wants and if her heart tells her that it is best.

Women's thoughts about working or not working don't only centre around money (though this is often given as the main reason). They also involve image, social contact and stimulation, career, relationships with partner and children, and whether a woman wants to be with her child all the time. Many women find the whole subject confusing and fraught with anxiety. If only we could be a little more honest with ourselves about our feelings, things might be clearer. The fact is that many women find it hard to be with their baby or young child all the time, but admitting this to yourself or anyone else may be much less acceptable than saying you want to work. Being as honest as you can gives you more choice. Instead of seeing work as the only acceptable way of getting away from your child, you might opt for arranging some regular periods of alternative childcare to give you some time to yourself.

The issues for the child are simpler, though extremely important. They concern whether or not his needs for mothering are met by the mother or another carer. Those needs include not only the basics of being

ONE PERSON, MANY ROLES

protected, kept warm, fed and played with, but also the vital need for sensitive, responsive, one-to-one attention from someone who is loving, on their side and readily available.

If you're deciding whether or not to go out to work, try to be clear about your situation, aims and objectives, bearing in mind that no decision is everlasting or irrevocable. For example, many women ultimately choose to stay with their babies and young children even though before becoming a mother they had planned to continue working. Others delay going back to work, cut down to working part-time, or arrange to work at home.

Although women have struggled for years for equality of opportunity, that doesn't mean that the exact structure and detail of their working lives has to be like that of most men in our society.

Use the chart (see right) to help you create lists of advantages (pros) and disadvantages (cons) of staying with your child or being separated. Remember these pros and cons may change as your child grows older or if you have another child.

TO WORK OR NOT TO WORK?

	Pros for you	Cons for you
Full-time mothering		
Part-time work at home		
Part-time work outside the home		
Full-time work at home		
Full-time work outside the home		

	Pros for child	Cons for child
Full-time mothering		
Part-time work at home		
Part-time work outside the home		
Full-time work at home		
Full-time work outside the home		

261

Excitement and pleasure at greeting the childminder may be tinged with initial wariness and reserve, but young children adapt well to being looked after by someone else.

262

CHILDCARE CHOICES

In the UK two out of three families with children under five use some kind of regular childcare, with family, friends and nursery schools being the most common. Working mothers use childcare most, but one in two non-working mothers uses some sort of childcare too.

Choosing childcare is hugely important for the simple reason that some carers are good and some bad. Some parents care well and others badly too, of course, but there's rarely any choice in such circumstances other than for the parents to learn better parenting skills.

A formal training in childcare isn't essential for 'mothering' a child well, but it can turn an inexperienced or mediocre carer into a good one, so always ask about it. Basically, these are your choices:

● Childminding at home by your partner, the child's granny, grandpa, or a nanny, mother's help or au pair.
● Childminding outside the home by your child's granny, grandpa, other relative, neighbour or friend, a registered childminder, day nursery, playgroup, or nursery school.

'I always take our two-year-old out on Saturday mornings so Sarah, my wife, can have a few hours free. I look forward to having Robert on his own and I know Sarah can always use the time to herself.'

When making your decision, consider whether you would prefer your child to be cared for in your own home, which has the advantage of being familiar and may make an anxious child feel better about your leaving. It also has the huge benefit of you not having to take or pick up the child from a minder or nursery.

MANAGING CHILDCARE

Good managers know what they want or, if they don't, they find out through consultation and discussion. They let others know what they have decided. They also check that their wishes are met by direct supervision and meetings. They express their feelings about work done. They encourage and affirm others, and are attentive to feelings, attitudes and ideas.

These management skills are simply communication skills. Use them with the person caring for your child and you'll find they help a great deal.

The advantages of a place with a childminder or in a playgroup or nursery are that there are usually other children to provide ready-made company, and that you can't be let down by your sitter not turning up at your home for some reason, though of course a minder, like anyone else, can be ill. A workplace nursery means your child has to travel to and from work with you, but you are close at hand to visit (if you need to) in the day.

If you need reliability so you can work, it's better perhaps not to rely on friends. Hours are important too – a playgroup, for example, provides only very limited hours and then only during school term-times.

When you're choosing someone to care for your child, look for a person with common sense, emotional warmth and the wish to play, spend unlimited time with the child and make life interesting. Also they should be someone you like and who is prepared to look after your child as you wish. Most important, get references for anyone you don't know.

If you're considering an au pair, remember that her (or his) working hours are limited. Also most stay only for six months, which means that you will have a rapid staff turnover.

Clarify with your child's carer such things as: what your child will eat and when, and who is providing the food; payment; holidays; what happens about payment if your child is ill and stays with you; what happens if the carer is ill and can't have the child; starting and finishing times; likely sleep times and whether your child likes a story, cuddle, light, special toy, drink, and so on; use of the phone; whether visitors are allowed; whether you expect any jobs done in your home; how to lock up your home; who you are happy for your child to visit; which other children you would like invited round; and how much television is acceptable to you.

fully understand that you're leaving them with someone safe and reliable, who will meet their needs. All they know is that you are going and this makes them feel abandoned, afraid and lonely. Yet after you've gone, your child will probably settle down with the other carer and though perhaps unsettled at first, will soon be content enough again. When you return, there may be another noisy display of feelings – anger that you ever left, bottled-up fear of being without you, or perhaps sheer delight at your return.

Tell a child who's old enough how long you'll be away and stick to it. And try not to leave him while he is asleep because it

Almost everyone benefits from a change and the opportunity for a child to spend some time with a loving grandmother or grandfather can be enormously beneficial for all concerned.

A CHILD'S HIERARCHY OF AFFECTION

Children have favourites. Babies over five months usually make their favourite clear, especially when upset. Young children are often, but not always, less choosy except in times of trouble.

Help your child get to know a future babysitter by the two of you spending time with her. Then, when you leave him, you'll know he's familiar with her.

It can be hard for a parent leaving the home if a baby or toddler protests vociferously, as if their hearts were breaking. This reaction is a primitive attempt to alert their favourite person to the danger they sense on being left. They don't

can be frightening to wake up with someone unexpected. Leaving at a time of day when your child is bright and alert gives him a better chance of settling with the minder.

Mothers who decide to work while their children are young often feel guilty. However, few things in life are perfect and choices must be made. You're free to change your mind, but it isn't sensible to indulge in guilt as this saps strength and energy and increases stress. Feeling guilty is a way of avoiding the feelings of loss at leaving your child, besides perhaps being a potent way of punishing yourself for what at some level you may believe is wrong – or think others believe is wrong.

Planning your day

No plans you make last long with a baby. At home, unexpected things can happen such as your baby sleeping longer than usual, or a friend dropping in. If you're working, trains home can be delayed or your childminder may be ill. The best way of coping is to be prepared for anything!

Working mothers have to be well organized. Some women find their day fills up with all sorts of things, but they still have no free time to unwind and refresh themselves. Time management can help both working and non-working parents. Decide what you want to do and what must be done. Put the items in order of importance, then allot enough time to each of the things you have to do. Use the remaining time to do things you want to do or things which crop up out of the blue. And don't forget how important it is to make time to do nothing sometimes.

BEING A SINGLE PARENT

Most single parents – mothers or, much less commonly, fathers – bringing up a child on their own, find it hard work. A single mother's relationship with the child's father may be a help or a hindrance. Some ex-partners manage to maintain a mutually supportive relationship, others have no contact or a destructive relationship. Worst of all is if either mother or father takes out their dissatisfaction with the other on the child, or uses him as a sounding board for their anger or woe.

As a single parent you need practical and emotional back-up and support just as much – if not more – as parents who have partners, if you are to enjoy caring for your child. So swallow your pride and ask for help when you need it. Make looking after yourself a priority so you're fit and well both for your own sake and your child's.

When you're introducing your enthusiastic young apprentice to gardening you may not get all the weeding done, but you will spend plenty of time studying stones, worms and flowers.

Being with her father or other special man who is gentle, friendly and willing to listen and play helps a young girl take her first step towards learning to relate to the opposite sex.

ONE PERSON, MANY ROLES

265

FINDING IDENTITY

Children learn about themselves and who they are primarily through their relationships with their mother, father or other close or important people. They learn many things, but most important are whether or not they feel loved and therefore lovable and valuable, and whether they learn to think of themselves as good or bad.

GENDER IDENTITY

Boys and girls grow up knowing very early whether they are male or female. They learn about what being a man or woman means, and about the various roles associated with gender, from society in general (for example, via TV) and from the local community, friends, family and parents in particular. Children identify to some extent with both parents, but before going to school they tend to imitate and identify more and more with their same-sex parent.

Today's parents have rather less gender-stereotyped roles than did their grandparents. Fathers may be more likely to help with childcare and running the home, and mothers may have paid employment in or outside the home. Traditional roles for men and women are valuable in many ways, for instance in that children grow up knowing what society and family expect of them, but too great an emphasis on them can stifle individual development and potential in the modern world.

The people around us have great influence on gender identity, but genes and hormones make men and women biologically different, too. However, what matters even more than maleness or femaleness is that children should grow up able to communicate, to listen and to understand other people, regardless of their gender, and with their individuality recognized and their unique gifts and abilities treasured. This is what they, in turn, will pass on to their children.

But we don't just learn about gender identity from our same-sex parent. Many pre-schoolers go through a stage of being 'in love' with their opposite-sex parent – with boys sometimes talking about marrying their mother and girls their father. This first 'love affair' sows the seeds for all future relationships with the opposite sex.

POSITIVE PARENTING

OPPOSITE *Try making some time at the end of the day when you and your child think of all the enjoyable and interesting events that have happened, and you remind him of the new things he's learned.*

It's often said that today's children don't know the difference between right and wrong. Certainly there's a lot of juvenile crime in certain groups. If children grow up in a family which teaches the difference between acceptable and unacceptable behaviour in a loving way, they'll develop their own values and moral code.

Teaching children about right and wrong isn't something you can put off until they're older. They have to learn it gradually so it becomes almost instinctive. When your parents have constantly guided you in your behaviour, you don't have to ask anyone how to behave – you know.

Parents have different styles of disciplining their children – or guiding them as to how to behave. What's important is to be quite clear about what you find acceptable.

The issue of smacking or hitting children is a controversial and vexed one. Physical punishment may teach a child that this form of punishment is acceptable as a way of releasing anger or revenge or teaching others how to behave, and you may find your child hitting other children. If it's done in the heat of the moment, the adult may not necessarily have full control and may hurt the child badly. Physical punishment which is delayed until later seems a bad idea; either the child has to suffer the agony of waiting for it to happen, or the child may develop a very hard shell of 'not caring'.

ENCOURAGEMENT AND ATTENTION FOR 'GOOD' BEHAVIOUR

Children need attention and if they aren't getting it, they'll probably make a fuss until you notice and give it to them. (A few, though, withdraw into a shell.) It's better to be a positive parent, by giving attention and demonstrating your pleasure in 'good' behaviour, rather than interacting with the child only over 'bad' or unacceptable behaviour. Positive parenting of this type is very powerful and means you're not always having to be cross with your child.

Even if you're doing something else while your child is playing, you may be able to find time to take a frequent interest. You'll notice that your child loves the extra attention and you may hear him repeating some of what you've said as he plays.

BEREAVEMENT

When someone important or dear to us dies, we have a lot of grieving to do and you may wish to protect your child from such sadness. However, your child needs to come to terms with the loss too and should be involved. Young children are usually affected by bereavement only if their lives are disrupted or if they were particularly close to the person. They are likely to take their cue as to how to handle bereavement from you.

Helping a child with bereavement
- Tell your child why the person died.
- Don't deny your own feelings.
- Listen to your child's comments and feelings.
- Consider including your child in the funeral arrangements.
- Talk about the dead person.
- Answer your child's questions about death and dying.
- Respect your child if she does not wish to talk about the person who died, no matter how unfeeling this may seem to you.

CHILD ABUSE

Sadly, child abuse continues, though greater awareness may one day encourage abusers, family members or older abused children to seek help, and others connected with an abused child to raise the alarm.

Child abuse can be verbal, physical, sexual or purely emotional. It's a terrible thing because it can have such catastrophic long-term effects on a child's emotional development, and also because an abused child can become an abused or an abusing wife, husband, partner, or parent.

If you think your child is being abused then seek skilled help. You won't regret it in the end.

See Growing and Learning, page 232, for more information on your child's feelings

CELEBRATIONS

Your little girl may put just as much concentration and effort into blowing out the candles as you have put into collecting the ingredients and making and decorating her birthday cake.

Birthdays and birth-days, weddings, christenings, Christmas, Boxing Day, pancake day, Valentine's day, Mothering Sunday, Easter, Father's Day, harvest festival and Guy Fawkes' night are just a few of the many festive occasions your family may celebrate. Then there are the fourth of July celebrations on American Independence day, bar-mitzvahs and all manner of other special days according to your nationality, culture and religion.

Taking time and making the effort to mark special days is worthwhile. It gives a sense of the cycle of the year and it marks important stages in life.

Most importantly, celebrating special occasions together strengthens family bonds, provides a sense of anticipation and excitement, and creates a bank of memories from which your child may one day draw when bringing up her children. You should find much to celebrate if you simply think about the ordinary everyday happenings in your lives.

Tips:

● Make your own celebrations to colour your family's life. You could celebrate your baby's first tooth, mark the anniversary of your kitten coming, or have a TGIF (Thank Goodness It's Friday) party.

● Organizing celebrations can be exhausting, but everyone would rather you enjoyed yourself than be tired out and irritable. There are no prizes for the best decorations or food, so relax!

● Half the fun of a celebration can lie in the preparation, so let your child join in with planning, preparing food and choosing and wrapping presents.

PETS

Many of us have a great affection for domestic animals as pets and they can benefit children in many ways. Depending on the animal, a pet can be a playmate, friend, and listening ear. Pets can offer a window on the 'facts of life' and they can also provide an opportunity to learn about taking responsibility by helping with feeding, exercising, grooming and cleaning out. Never expect a young child to take full responsibility for a pet. An animal's life and wellbeing are your responsibility, not the child's. Not until the child is much older can you hand over a pet's care.

What could they be celebrating? Perhaps it's the white rabbit's first excursion to the park … or the first day of autumn? Or maybe they're simply taking a delight in being together with time to play.

● Home-made cards can be cheap, easy and enjoyable to make. There must be few people who would rather have a shop-bought card than one illustrated by a young child. Stick a fresh piece of paper on to cardboard from an empty cereal packet, cut it to size, fold it in half and your card is ready for customizing.

● At the end of the day take the time to chat with your child about all the good things that have happened, then together look forward to the next day.

Dog: choose a reliable dog but never let a child tease it, don't leave them alone together, and worm the dog regularly.

Cat: never leave with a sleeping baby as cats sometimes sleep on warm faces, don't let a child tease it, and worm it regularly.

Fish: fun to watch occasionally, but *you* must clean their tank.

Rabbit, guinea pig or mouse: enjoyable to stroke and watch, especially in the summer, but rabbits can scratch when cuddled, and you will have to look after all of these.

PLANNING ANOTHER BABY

Women have always attempted to space their babies. Breastfeeding in such a way as to prevent ovulation for at least a year and maybe more is the most usual method worldwide. It's a good enough method, though not always reliable, and tends to space babies with about two or three years between them, *provided* breastfeeding is *unrestricted* day and night, the baby and mother sleep in the same room together, there are no long gaps between feeds, the baby doesn't use a dummy or suck fingers or thumb for long periods, a younger baby doesn't have any drinks other than breast milk, and an older baby still takes most of his fluid from the breast. But few women in developed countries choose to use it nowadays or understand how to make it as reliable as it can be. Most choose between the pill, condom, diaphragm, coil, withdrawal, or abstinence as forms of contraception. Others use natural family planning with the sympto-thermal technique (using awareness of the timing

You can't necessarily plan when – or if – your next baby will come along but when you do become pregnant, make time to imagine what being an older brother or sister will mean to your child.

and signs of the stages of the menstrual cycle to predict the fertile days).

Whatever the gap between your children, you can be sure that having more than one child will make a big difference to your family's lifestyle, although it will probably not be as big as that which accompanied the first child.

AGE GAPS
You may be interested in the effect of different age gaps on children as they grow and develop. These effects on behaviour and personality can shape adult life too. Psychologists find that there tend to be strong similarities between children of the same pecking order in different families, though these effects are usually cancelled out if the age gap between children is larger than five years. They are most pronounced among children of the same sex. And, of course, nature and nurture – the inbuilt blueprint and the type of upbringing – both have a large influence.

Like any other child, one with Down's syndrome needs to be loved and accepted by the family as a person with likes, dislikes, abilities and individual personality traits all of her own.

271

Eldest children
- Are used to looking after others and being in charge, so are good managers but sometimes bossy too.
- Are responsible and protective.
- Want things done well, if not perfectly, which can be very stressful as they demand high standards of themselves and others.
- Assume they can (and have to) do things better than others.
- Are hard-working, high-achieving, competitive, serious and successful.

Younger children
- Are used to more freedom.
- Are accustomed to being managed/bossed/looked after.
- Don't expect to be first or top.
- Get on well with others.
- Are easy-going, optimistic and charming.
- Expect to be liked.
- Get others to do things for them.
- Are familiar with taking risks .

Middle children
- Are sensitive to others.
- Get on well with others.
- Are independent, sociable and flexible.
- Are good negotiators and peacemakers.

Only children
- Are responsible.
- Get on well with adults and, later, people in authority.
- Are used to pleasing adults.
- Feel special.

CHILDREN WITH SPECIAL NEEDS

All expectant parents hope for a normal baby, but many harbour the secret fear that something will go wrong. For some it does. It can be a harsh blow to any parent to realize that your child won't ever be as you hoped. Mercifully, some parents have a time of respite to get used to the idea before the full extent of the problem is revealed.

Problems vary from genetic defects such as Down's syndrome to long-term handicaps such as cerebral palsy. Other children start off well then develop an illness such as cystic fibrosis, severe asthma, or muscular dystrophy.

Whatever your child's condition, you may need help from the health and helping agencies, and perhaps from family, friends and neighbours too. After all, bringing up a child who has learning difficulties or is 'differently abled' in some other way requires much time and attention.

You may decide to join a self-help information and support group relevant to your child's condition, as sharing your experiences and learning from others can make a great difference to your quality of life.

Caring for a child with special needs can strain your emotional and practical resources. However some parents find the experience brings totally unexpected blessings and rewards.

MOTHERING MULTIPLES

RIGHT *Sometimes you'll want to feed both babies together. At other times, perhaps when one is still sleeping, it's more convenient separately. And that baby can then enjoy some valuable one-to-one attention.*

Imagine the scenario. You go to the antenatal clinic. The doctor says you're big for your dates. Then the scan reveals you are carrying not one baby, but two, three or even more! Women who've had this experience report one or more of a wide range of feelings in the rest of their pregnancy. They might feel excited, delighted and even overawed. Or they might also feel shocked, anxious and even desperate. Whatever your emotions, realize it's acceptable to have them. Most women in this situation have mixed feelings, as do their partners.

The next few months before your babies are born is an excellent time to get in touch with your emotions and those of each other. Aim to recognize, name, accept and, if necessary, discuss them. You can then incorporate your enhanced emotional sensitivity into your daily management of the challenges of being parents of 'multiples'. This 'emotional intelligence' will be particularly helpful once you are both busy with feeding and other babycare.

FEEDING

However you feed your babies, feeding will occupy a lot of the day. One of your first decisions is how to feed them. The advantages of breastfeeding are just as important for your babies as for a singleton, and most women can provide all the milk twins need. Some mothers of triplets supply a large proportion of their daily milk requirement. And many women with quads or more give as much milk as they can, knowing that even a little is very beneficial.

Get off to a good start with breastfeeding by arranging for someone else to be there during feeds to look after other children, to give you drinks or anything else you need, and to help position the babies. You'll soon find you can feed two babies at the same time by positioning each of them, for example, in the football hold (see left).

If you encounter discomforts such as sore nipples, get expert information and advice rapidly, as well as any extra practical support you need. Your midwife, doctor and health visitor will provide professional back-up, and breastfeeding self-help organisations such as La Leche League and the National Childbirth Trust will put you in touch with a voluntary breastfeeding helper.

If you do some breastfeeding and some formula-feeding, or if you give only formula milk, you will also need effective and practical support and advice available from either your doctor or one of the organizations mentioned on page 314–5.

SLEEPING

It's inevitable that with more than one baby you'll be woken more often at night. Some parents adapt to broken nights by catnapping during the day. It's worth learning to snooze whenever all the babies are asleep at home during the day. Another idea is to have someone else take the babies out in a pram after they've been fed. You can then silence the phone and put a note on the front door to say you're sleeping. This way you can be assured of at least an hour or so of restorative, unbroken sleep.

BATHTIME

Arrange, if possible, for someone to help you with the babies at bathtime, at least in the early weeks. Alternatively, get into the habit right from the beginning of bathing one baby at a time. Bathing the babies after they have been fed and are contented means that both you and they are likely to enjoy bathtime more.

TIME FOR YOURSELVES

Having twins or more can mean double, triple or more of the enjoyment. At the same time caring for several babies entails more work, and this will sometimes be challenging and very exhausting. What's more, looking after multiples who don't all sleep at the same time can be more demanding than two full-time jobs, one by day, one by night! So it isn't surprising that parents of multiples are often relatively deprived of time to themselves.

One practical way of carving out some time is to encourage the babies to sleep at the same time. Another way is for a couple to take it in turns to care for the children and to give each other some time off.

A good idea is to arrange for a regular babysitter to give both of you some time off which you can enjoy together. Maintaining and nurturing your relationship with each other may seem like an impossible dream early on. This is why you – even more than parents of singletons – must make time together an absolute priority.

SIBLINGS

An older child may have very mixed feelings about the new arrivals. Excitement, curiosity and pride may mingle with anxiety, jealousy and even loneliness. Help by talking to your child and trying to gauge how they are feeling. Then name and, perhaps, explain these emotions, so the child feels understood.

Aim to give the child some one-to-one time each day and, when possible, arrange outings just for the two of you together. Explain to your child how the babies will develop and grow, and how long it will take before they become good company. Many an elder brother or sister is disappointed to find that the younger ones can't walk or talk for what seems to them an eternity.

Older children are often keen to help with caring for their younger siblings. Don't forget, though, that they should always be supervised, however busy you are and however mature the child is.

THE SAME OR DIFFERENT?

Other people are always fascinated by the differences between one twin (or other multiple) and the other, as well as by their similarities, especially so if they are identical. So it's all the more important for you to focus on each child as an individual, and to encourage others to do so too.

Emphasize the uniqueness of each one's personality by not dressing them the same, or expecting them to like the same things. A little time each day spent focusing on one as a special person in their own right will pay great dividends to that child's development, and confidence and self-esteem. It also gives you the chance to get to know each child better and to have more time for the vital mother-baby intercommunication that sets the scene for language development.

ASKING FOR HELP

- Buying the clothes and equipment you need for more than one child can be very expensive. However, there are ways of getting cheaper things for your children. The Twins and Multiple Births Association (TAMBA) can supply details of your nearest twins club. The parents there should be a valuable source of second-hand items. Don't forget to check out second-hand equipment thoroughly for safety.

- Accept all offers of help from friends and neighbours. Alternatively, jot their name and number on a list and ask if you can come back to them when you need help.

- Aim to delegate to your helpers the tasks that will free you for what you really want to do. Many mothers of twins or more particularly enjoy being able to give one child some one-to-one attention.

- The changes in lifestyle associated with caring for multiples, combined with all the hard work, means postnatal depression is more common than in mothers of a single baby. Don't ever delay seeking help because you think you should be able to manage everything. See your doctor sooner rather than later, because postnatal depression is a treatable condition.

A-Z OF HEALTHCARE

0-5 years

When your baby or young child is ill it helps if you have some idea of what's going on, what's likely to happen and what you can do to help. Most childhood problems are simple and short-lived, from nappy rashes to coughs and colds, and there's a great deal of ordinary, common-sense care that you can give in your own home, using simple home remedies, nursing care and first aid if necessary. Yet there may be times when you feel confused or worried by your child's appearance or symptoms yet unsure whether you should speak to the doctor. You know your child better than anyone else does so, if you are anxious and don't know what to do, then it's wise to trust your instincts and to ask for help.

YOU AND YOUR SICK CHILD

When a young child is sick it's natural for parents to be worried. A baby or toddler can't tell you what's wrong in words, so you have to recognize illness in other ways. Sometimes the first signs of sickness are crying and being fidgety and irritable. But some young children become quiet, withdrawn and sleepy. Other indicators include a fever, not wanting to feed, eat or drink, a cough, runny nose, or vomiting.

Parents are usually expert in what's normal and what isn't in their child, and with experience they come to learn the particular way their child looks and behaves when unwell. A parent can often spot early signs of illness even when others notice nothing wrong. Be guided by instinct and intuition or 'sixth sense' as well as by rational judgment because you are your child's all-important safety net.

When you are feeling ill or out of sorts, there's nothing like having your mother sit by you, with her arm round you, reading you a familiar story.

SEEING THE DOCTOR

When you are concerned about your child but don't know what to do, visit your doctor or ask for a home visit if your child is too ill to go out. Phone the surgery and describe what is wrong if you are uncertain what to do. The receptionist will ask the doctor if in doubt. Act sooner rather than later with a young baby and consult your doctor about any illness or worrying or unexplained change in behaviour.

Your doctor will examine the child and may be able to spot things you hadn't noticed. Sometimes the cause of a child's problem isn't clear and either some further investigation or test may help or it may be best to wait and see what happens. Discuss with your doctor how to treat any troublesome symptoms in the meantime. She may want to see the child again or ask you to bring your child back if you feel it's necessary. Always err on the safe side and don't be put off visiting the surgery for fear of being thought a fussy parent.

Before you leave, check that you know how to give any medicine prescribed. Some medicines need to be stored in the fridge while others can go in the cupboard. Some must be given with food and others on an empty stomach. And some need to be continued until all the medicine is used up, while you can stop others when your baby or child is better.

TREATING ILLNESS

Many minor illnesses get better on their own with no treatment other than 'tlc' (tender loving care). Some conditions cause unpleasant symptoms which you can treat with medicines or remedies you have bought over the counter, and with traditional home nursing techniques. Always check with the pharmacist (or with the label on the container) that bought medicines are suitable for your child's age.

The commonest cause of childhood illness is an infection, usually caused by viruses but sometimes by bacteria or other micro-organisms. Doctors give antibiotic medicines only if they believe the infection is – or might be – bacterial. The vast majority of feverish colds and sore throats are viral, which means that antibiotics will not be any help at all. Antibiotics can give a child diarrhoea and should be used only if necessary.

Tell your doctor if your child develops any new symptoms such as a rash or tummy-ache because these might be caused by the medicine you're giving.

If your child has an infectious illness but is well enough to go out, keep away from crowded places where she might cough and sneeze over other people and spread germs. And always warn friends who have young children or who might be pregnant so they can keep away if they wish.

ALWAYS CONSULT THE DOCTOR IF YOU NOTICE ANY OF THESE SIGNS

Headache	(if continuous, recurrent, or accompanied by repeated vomiting, fever, a stiff neck or severe pain elsewhere)	Vomiting	(if frequent, violent, or accompanied by a headache, fever or neck stiffness; or it lasts more than one hour in a baby or 4-5 hours in an older child)
Rash	(unless you're sure it's nothing to worry about)	Diarrhoea	(if it lasts for more than a day)
Thirst	(if excessive, especially if the child is also losing weight, though remember a feverish child needs lots of drinks)	Urine	(if little or none is being passed)
Fever	(if over 39.4°C (103°F), you're worried, or there are other signs of illness)		
Appetite loss	(if accompanied by other signs of illness)		
Breathing	(if shallow, unusual, noisy, difficult, or apparently painful)		

CONSULT THE DOCTOR URGENTLY IF YOUR CHILD DEVELOPS ANY OF THE FOLLOWING:

Loss of consciousness
Convulsions
Breathing difficulties
Severe or prolonged pain
Persistent vomiting or diarrhoea
A rash that looks like bleeding beneath the skin
Blue lips or face

Nursing your sick child

A child who is very unwell will want to lie down and you'll have to decide where is best. Ill children usually want company wherever they are. Some want a great deal of attention but others simply feel better if they know someone is there. The advantage of the child being in bed in a bedroom is that it'll probably be quiet. But the advantage of being in the living room is that you can get on with household tasks, and talk to and watch your child at the same time. Also your child may enjoy having a special bed made for her on the sofa.

A child who is recovering and feeling a little more active may like you to read a book out loud, help do a jigsaw puzzle on a tray, do some drawing, play games, listen to a tape or watch TV.

Children who feel poorly often go off their food and there's no need to worry unless the illness continues a long time. Milky drinks, fruit juices and soups may be more attractive than food.

YOUR CHILD'S TEMPERATURE

Many parents like to take their child's temperature to check if there is a fever, though this isn't necessary. You can tell when a child is hot by feeling the forehead, seeing flushed skin and asking.

To measure the temperature accurately, use a fast-reading plastic digital thermometer in the mouth (in a very young child – under three years of age – put it under the armpit) or put a fever strip on her forehead for a few seconds.

You can measure your child's temperature with a fast-reading digital thermometer by placing it under your child's armpit (right). You'll know it's ready to be read when you hear a bleeping noise. Alternatively, place a fever strip on your child's forehead for 15-20 seconds (far right) and read the highest box that remains coloured for a guide to your child's temperature. Anything over 37.5°C (99.5°F) is a fever.

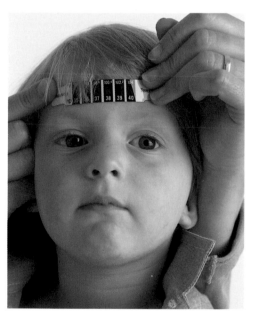

EATING AND DRINKING

Give your sick child plenty to drink, especially if there's a fever, vomiting or diarrhoea. It's possible to become dehydrated with this extra water loss and babies are most at risk. Check that your baby's nappies are as wet as usual and if not, encourage him to drink more. A breastfed baby may want to stay at the breast as much for the comfort of sucking as for the extra milk. Make up bottlefeeds accurately because too much milk powder is dangerous when a bottlefed baby is sick.

You can make a feverish child more comfortable by removing bedclothes and blankets or duvets, leaving only a sheet as a cover. Sponging with lukewarm water probably isn't a good idea, though it used to be recommended. It lowers the temperature only very temporarily and may make the child more uncomfortable as feverish skin is sensitive and prickly. Paracetamol elixir in the correct dose stated on the bottle lowers the body temperature and acts as a painkiller so may help relieve your child's symptoms.

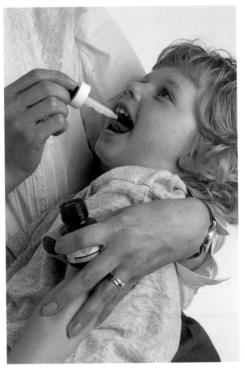

Your child may not like having medicine, so the quicker it's over, the better. You can use a spoon (far left) or you may find a dropper useful, especially for a younger child. Place the dropper in the corner of the child's mouth and gently squeeze the teat (left).

279

GIVING MEDICINE

- Children's medicine can be given by spoon or dropper.
- Always read the instructions on the bottle carefully and take care to measure the doses accurately.
- Remember to keep the medicine out of your child's reach.
- Discard old medicine safely down the lavatory or return it to your local chemist who will dispose of it.

GOING INTO HOSPITAL

Hospital can be an exciting or a frightening place, depending on your child's previous experience and current condition. Babies and young children benefit from having their mother (or father) with them. This is because anxiety caused by being separated can interfere with a baby's recovery. Most hospitals, therefore, make provision for a parent to stay. They also know that children need a special recognizable nurse who will take the mother's place when she has to go away.

Let your child know what is going to happen and how long the stay will be and try to recognize how your child feels. Children imagine all sorts of things and simply talking about what is going on can be greatly reassuring.

HOLIDAY HEALTH

You can take many simple precautions to prevent or cope with holiday illness.

- Organize all necessary immunizations for the country you are visiting several months ahead of your departure date. This will enable your doctor to work out how to fit them in without disrupting your child's existing routine immunization schedule.
- Put together a first-aid kit of plasters, medicated wipes, antiseptic cream, dressings, bandages, blister or burn dressings, cotton-wool, insect repellent, sting-relief, a high factor sun cream (at least factor 15) and calamine lotion.
- Arrange medical insurance if you are going abroad.
- Pack any medicines your child is taking and also any that he may need from time to time, such as an asthma inhaler.
- Make sure you have enough of your child's medicine to last you for the whole time you are away.
- Reduce the risk of foreign holiday tummy by avoiding raw unpeeled fruit or vegetables; using bottled water both for your child to drink and to clean her teeth (as young children often swallow tooth-cleaning water), and avoiding ice unless the tap water is safe, and not drying clean hands on a dirty towel.

See Common Concerns, page 202, for tantrums

COMPLEMENTARY REMEDIES

ABOVE Prepare a fragrant blend of oils ahead of time, then sit on the floor in a warm room with your baby on your lap, ready for a five to ten minute session of gentle massage.

When your child feels poorly, the first thing to do is assess what the problem is and how serious it is. Most ailments are common conditions (such as colds, coughs, bites and stings, tummy aches and headaches) that you can readily treat at home. About four out of five of such ailments will get better on their own whatever you do.

Most parents treat their children with a combination of 'tlc' (tender loving care) and one or more trusted home remedies and therapies. Some are called 'complementary' remedies and therapies, because they can safely be used alongside any 'orthodox' treatments that may be recommended by doctors or bought over-the-counter from the pharmacy. Finding the best balance of orthodox and complementary treatments helps your child to feel better and get well.

The following complementary remedies and therapies for domestic use are among the most popular:

- Massage
- Acupressure
- Heat and cold therapy
- Dietary changes and food supplements
- Aromatherapy
- Herbal and flower remedies
- Homeopathy

MASSAGE

Parents often use massage instinctively when their child is unwell by, for example, rubbing a sore place better, or giving a back rub to a child who feels tired and out of sorts. There are no rules when it comes to giving a massage. You simply do what you think is best, then you either stop if the child doesn't like it or continue for a while if he or she finds that it's beneficial. Be guided by what feels good to them. You can massage your child either through clothing or on bare skin. A little sweet almond oil to lubricate the skin helps your fingers to glide more easily.

One way in which massage can help is by encouraging the relaxation of tense muscles. A second is by providing a stimulus that may effectively block the passage of pain signals. And a third is by boosting the level of natural 'feel-good' chemicals called endorphins in the child's body. But probably the most important of all is the fact that they know that you care.

ACUPRESSURE

You may sometimes give yourself acupressure without realising – for example, when you have a headache and automatically want to press your fingertips into your temples. Acupressure involves pressing on points on the body known as acupoints. Pressing appropriate points in certain ways is said to relieve symptoms either by releasing blocked energy, or by strengthening or decreasing the energy flow. The benefits may be near the acupoint chosen or at a distance.

HEAT AND COLD THERAPY

It's sensible to warm a child who feels cold (unless this is due to feverish shivering), and to cool a feverish child (but not too much, or the body's temperature-balancing mechanism may react by raising the temperature even higher).

You can also use local heat or cold for certain conditions. A sprain, for example, may respond to something cold, whereas aching muscles might prefer some heat. Apply local heat or cold with:

- An ice pack – use a packet of frozen peas or a polythene bag full of ice cubes or crushed ice; wrap the pack in a towel to avoid 'freezer burn' to the skin.
- A compress – dip a flannel or folded tea towel in hot or cold water, wring out and lay it over the area to be treated. Cover a hot compress with a thick towel to retain the heat.
- A hot water bottle or heated pad.

DIETARY CHANGES AND FOOD SUPPLEMENTS

An ill child may not feel like eating, in which case it's probably better simply to give them whatever they fancy. A child with any infection needs plenty of immunity-boosting nutrients, so offer foods rich in beta-carotene, vitamin C, flavonoids and zinc. You could also give vitamin C and flavonoids as a supplement, using the dosage recommendations on the packet. Both infections and other forms of inflammation may respond to anti-oxidants in the form of foods rich in beta-carotene, vitamins C and E, flavonoids and selenium. And if your child's doctor diagnoses a food allergy or intolerance, you'll obviously need to exclude the culprits in question from your child's diet – though some children with a mild sensitivity can tolerate small amounts of these foods.

AROMATHERAPY

Using essential oils extracted from plants is a delightful way of treating several common ailments in children. Choose good quality undiluted oils and keep them in a cool dark place where your child can't get at them. You also need to buy a 'carrier' oil, such as sweet almond or macadamia oil, with which to dilute the essential oil. Only lavender oil and tea tree oil should ever be used undiluted on the skin.

One way of using essential oils is by incorporating them into a massage oil. The child benefits from the active substances in the oils mainly by inhaling their vapour. This comes from the oil evaporating from the warm skin.
● Make an all-purpose massage oil by putting a tablespoon of sweet almond oil into a small bowl and adding a drop of lavender oil. You can then add a drop or so of any other oil that is appropriate to the child's symptoms. Ideally it's best to warm the oil before you massage your child. Do this by standing the bowl in a little hot water in a basin for a minute or two.

Another popular use of essential oils is in an inhalation mixture; the child then breathes in the scented steam. Inhaling eucalyptus oil is particularly beneficial for children with colds or respiratory problems.
● Make an inhalation mixture by pouring just-boiled water into a basin, adding a drop of eucalyptus oil, and stirring. Put the bowl on the table and seat the child so he or she can lean safely over the bowl and breathe the vapour. Drape a towel over both the child's head and the bowl to help prevent the scented steam from escaping. Caution: this needs careful supervision and is unsuitable for a young child who might upset the bowl.

HERBAL AND FLOWER REMEDIES

Remedies made from leaves, stems, flowers, fruits, seeds and roots have been used in home remedies for thousands of years. Herbal remedies are available in many forms, such as tablets, capsules, tinctures, creams, ointments, infused oils and teabags. You can also use herbs directly on the skin, perhaps inside a compress, poultice or plaster.
To make tea directly from herb leaves:
● Put two ounces (50g) of fresh, or one ounce (25g) of dried, herbs into a cup.
● Add boiling water.
● Let stand for 10 minutes.
● Strain and sweeten if necessary.
To make tea from roots, seeds or bark:
● Crush or pound the plant matter.
● Boil it in water for 10–15 minutes.
● Strain and sweeten if necessary.

HOMEOPATHY

Homeopathic remedies can come as liquids, creams, ointments, granules or little round pellets called 'pillules' that you place under the child's tongue. They contain an immeasurably tiny amount of the substance it's made from. The 'vibrations' from this remedy are said to trigger healing – whereas if the substance itself were taken, it would actually cause the same symptoms. To determine the best remedy for your child to try, you choose one made from a substance that is capable of causing similar symptoms. In practice, most parents either consult a trained homeopath (who may also be a doctor), find an appropriate remedy from a homeopathy book, or ask a pharmacist.

LEFT *Sipping a glass of camomile flower tea – hot in winter, cold in summer – is an excellent way of unwinding. Some say this herb has a delicate pineapple scent – see if you agree.*

A-Z OF HEALTHCARE

The entries on these pages cover the most common upsets and illnesses of the first five years of life. Many of them are not serious and most young children, however healthy, will have their share of coughs, colds and rashes. You should always contact your doctor if you are worried about your child's health, well-being or behaviour; most parents know instinctively when something is wrong.

A

Abdominal pain
(*See* **Tummyache**)

Abscess
An abscess is a pocket of pus which can occur anywhere in the body as a result of infection. The formation of an abscess is one of the body's defence mechanisms. By separating infected pus from surrounding healthy tissue, the spread of infection is prevented. A child with an abscess may feel unwell and feverish, but other symptoms depend on where the infection is. For example, with a cervical abscess (in a lymph node in the neck) the child has a tender red lump on the side of his neck, whereas an abscess in the lung, which cannot be seen, may cause the child to breathe faster than normal and to cough. An abscess deep in the body, such as a lung abscess, is more serious than one on or near the skin's surface.

Sometimes an abscess 'points' to an area where it can burst. If this occurs internally it results in further spread of the infection, but when it bursts on the surface of the skin the pus escapes and the condition spontaneously improves. To speed up the healing of an abscess, a doctor may open up the infected area and allow the pus to drain out. In a few cases he may prescribe antibiotics to prevent the abscess from getting worse.

Adenoids
The adenoids are pieces of tissue lying either side of the air passages behind the nose and throat. Their main function is to prevent infection of the upper airways and in most children they do this effectively. However, they can become enlarged and this can have two effects.

Firstly, they may block the nose so that the child constantly has to breathe through the mouth. Secondly, they may obstruct the Eustachian tubes' which connect the nasal passages to the middle ears. If this occurs, fluid from the middle ear each side cannot drain into the throat and this results in poor hearing and frequent ear infection. In such cases, the doctor may recommend an operation to remove the adenoids so that hearing and breathing are improved. This minor operation is known as an adenoidectomy and is sometimes performed at the same time as surgical removal of the tonsils.

(*See also* **Deafness, Glue ear**)

The Adenoids

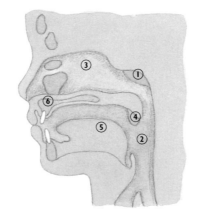

1. Adenoid	**2.** Throat
3. Nasal cavity	**4.** Tonsil
5. Tongue	**6.** Hard palate

*The **adenoids**, which are small at birth, begin to grow when the child is about three years old. Enlarged adenoids can block the nose or the Eustachian tubes (see diagram, page 290).*

Allergic rhinitis
Allergic rhinitis is an allergic reaction of the lining of the nasal passages which causes a blocked or runny nose and, sometimes, watery eyes and sneezing. It's better known as hay fever when it results from air-borne pollens, but it can occur throughout the year as a reaction to other substances, such as house dust mites, fur and certain foods.

It helps to minimise contact with the pollen or other allergen. For example, when the pollen count is high, you can help a pollen-sensitive child in various ways. Keep him indoors with windows closed when possible; close car windows; remove and wash his clothing and wash his face when he comes in; wash his hair before bed-time; avoid grassy and weedy places; and give him wraparound sunglasses to lessen the amount of pollen landing on his eyes. These precautions are particularly helpful in the early evening and before, during and after a thunderstorm, when the pollen count rises.

Eating a daily teaspoon of local honey for two or three months before a child's expected hay-fever season may also help prevent hay fever. This is because the tiny amounts of pollens in the honey have an immunising effect.

If necessary, your doctor can arrange have skin-prick tests to help to determine the allergen that's responsible. There are various remedies from the pharmacist such as nose-drops, sprays and anti-histamine tablets which can relieve nasal congestion. Other treatments include bathing sore eyes and nostrils with 600ml (1 pint) of water to which you've added two teaspoons of witch hazel or a pinch of salt. Adding garlic to food is said to relieve a stuffy nose, as may a twice-daily cup of elder-flower or nettle tea. You can make this by pouring a cup of boiling water over a teaspoon of dried elderflowers or nettle leaves, steeping for five minutes, then straining and sweetening with honey if desired.

Allergy

An excessive reaction of the body to substances with which it comes into contact is known as allergy. The body can react in many different ways – a rash, bowel disturbance, runny nose and sneezing, or breathing difficulties. When an allergen enters the body, the immune system calls up part of its defence force called immunoglobulin E (IgE) antibodies. These trigger the release of chemical messengers, including a powerful hormone called histamine that widens blood vessels. The nasal cavities and sinuses may become blocked, and muscles in the airways may go into spasm, constricting the breathing passages and making breathing difficult. There may be sneezing and a runny nose and eyes. The purpose of this reaction is to counteract damage by the allergen, but the side-effects of the antibody-allergen battle – in other words, the allergic symptoms – can be unpleasant or even dangerous.

Many things can cause allergy in susceptible children, including certain foods, pollens, dust, animal fur, feathers and insect bites. The tendency to develop allergy often runs in families.

Drugs such as antihistamines and corticosteroids may dampen an allergic reaction. It's also worth giving foods or supplements that are rich in natural antihistamines such as vitamin C and flavonoids.

(See also Allergic rhinitis, Asthma, Coeliac disease, Eczema, Food sensitivity, Urticaria)

Anaemia

The colour of blood is red because of the presence of red pigment (haemoglobin) in the blood cells. Anaemia occurs when the haemoglobin concentration falls below its normal level. This may be because the haemoglobin content of the red blood cells is low or because the number of red cells is significantly reduced. Whatever the cause of anaemia, the child looks pale, is tired and may become breathless after exertion. If you think your child may be anaemic, take him to a doctor. The most common cause of anaemia is insufficient iron in the diet. Iron is needed to produce haemoglobin and it is present in meat, fish, eggs, peas, beans, nuts and green vegetables. Eating foods containing vitamin C along with iron-rich foods boosts the absorption of iron from the digestive tract. In contrast, caffeine reduces iron absorption so it is best not to drink tea, coffee or other drinks containing caffeine with meals or just after them.

Anaemia may also result from blood loss (for example because of bowel damage caused by sensitivity to cow's milk) and from certain rare diseases.

(See also Sickle cell disease, Thalassaemia)

Appendicitis

Appendicitis is inflammation of the appendix, a small sac which is attached to the bowel and whose function is unknown. If the appendix becomes inflamed it causes tummyache, which usually starts in the centre of the tummy and moves to the lower right-hand side. The child may have a temperature, vomit and lose his appetite. The pain tends to get worse the longer it goes on. If your child has these symptoms, call the doctor immediately. Treatment is an operation to remove the appendix.

Very occasionally the inflamed appendix bursts, causing the infection to spread throughout the abdomen. This is called peritonitis and, if it occurs, the child becomes very unwell and the pain worsens. In such circumstances, call a doctor urgently or take the child to hospital.

The Appendix

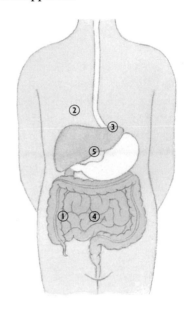

1. Appendix   4. Rectum
2. Liver   5. Intestine (bowel)
3. Stomach

*The **appendix** lies at the junction of the large and small intestine. With appendicitis the pain spreads throughout the abdomen, sometimes intensifying over the appendix.*

Asthma

Asthma, or repeated episodes of wheezing, is quite common in childhood. It is caused by the narrowing of the lungs' small breathing tubes (bronchioles) which transport air in and out of the body. This narrowing may occur as part of an allergic reaction or can be triggered by a viral lung infection, stress, exercise, cigarette smoke, fumes and extremes of temperature. Wheezing and asthma often run in families and you frequently find that another member of the family suffers from asthma, eczema or hay fever.

283

See Why is My Baby Crying, page 133, for colic

The child who has an asthmatic attack wheezes, breathes faster than normal and may struggle to get air. He may also cough and even vomit. There are a number of drugs which may be used during an asthmatic attack. Some of these are referred to as bronchodilators and they relieve the narrowing or spasm in the airways and so make breathing easier. They can be given as tablets or inhaled from a spinhaler or aerosol. A child who is wheezing often has little interest in eating or drinking. It does not matter if he does not eat for a few days, but you should make sure he takes fluids frequently and in small amounts, as he may vomit if given a large drink. A child who wheezes frequently may benefit from drugs which prevent the allergic reaction from occurring in the first place. These drugs have to be taken regularly, even when the child is well.

It may be worth trying to identify which substances trigger off an attack. The house-dust mite (which, as the name suggests, lives in house dust), pollen, some foods and animal feathers or fur can produce wheezing in susceptible children. If house-dust mites are responsible, keep a child's bedroom as dust-free as possible, wash bedding at as high a temperature as possible and consider replacing fitted carpets with hard flooring and washable rugs, so the mites can't easily multiply. You can destroy house-dust mites in soft toys by putting them in the freezer overnight or, if washable, by laundering.

One exciting but unproven therapy, is Buteyko breathing. This involves a child doing breathing exercises that help prevent her hyperventilating (breathing rapidly and deeply). People with asthma tend to hyperventilate between attacks. Early studies suggest that some people can reduce the frequency of their asthma attacks by learning to recognize and control

hyperventilation. This may be because hyperventilation makes a person breathe out too much carbon dioxide. A low carbon-dioxide level reduces the amount of oxygen available to the body's cells which, in turn, makes the child breathe even faster.

A healthy diet may discourage asthma that's related to allergy or infection; try giving your child oily fish (like salmon or herrings) three times a week, as well as plenty of foods rich in magnesium, and vitamins C and E. Adding garlic to meals may also be helpful.

Wheezing may start in the first year of life. At this stage it is impossible to say whether or not the child is going to develop asthma. The majority of children with asthma grow out of it during childhood and are left with normal lungs.
(See diagram opposite)

Athlete's foot
(See Ringworm)

B

Bed wetting
Some children become dry at night later than others. Twenty per cent of otherwise healthy five-year-olds still wet the bed whilst asleep but become dry at night within the next few years. After the age of five, bed wetting (enuresis), is slightly more common in boys than girls and the tendency may run in families.

As a child wets the bed without knowing, it is a mistake to blame her for doing it. She is more likely to grow out of it if she is treated kindly and praised when she does have a dry night. It may be helpful to take her to empty her bladder when you go to bed. In some cases children who have previously been dry at night

suddenly begin wetting again, perhaps due to some upset in their life. Bed wetting can also be caused by a urinary infection or a medical condition such as diabetes.

If the wetting is due to an infection, the child experiences discomfort when she urinates or may pass small amounts frequently. A child with diabetes passes a lot of urine during the day as well as at night and drinks more than usual. If your child has any of these symptoms, consult your doctor.
(See also Diabetes, Urinary tract infections)

Bee sting
(See First aid, page 313)

Birthmarks
There are several kinds of birthmark, most of which disappear during childhood without treatment. These include the stork mark – a pink patch on the neck, forehead or eyelids – and the Mongolian blue spot – a bluish mark across the back which is common in black and Asian babies.

A less common form of birthmark is the strawberry mark. This red mark is raised and feels a little uneven, but is not painful. Strawberry marks can occur anywhere on the body. They are not usually present at birth but more commonly appear during the first two months of life and gradually fade over a period of months. Most strawberry marks have disappeared by the time the child is five years old.

Port-wine stains, unlike strawberry marks, are permanent and present from birth, though some can be helped by laser treatment.

Bites and stings
(See First aid, page 313)

Bleeding
(See Emergencies, page 308)

Blisters
(See First aid, page 312)

Blood in urine or bowel motions

If you notice blood in your child's urine or bowel motions, you should consult your doctor. The cause is probably a minor one, but it could indicate a more serious condition. **(See also Constipation, Urinary tract infections)**

Blueness of the skin
(See Breath-holding, Bronchiolitis, Cyanosis)

Boils

A boil is a small abscess (collection of pus) in the skin, caused by a bacterial infection. The boil may throb, but the child is not generally unwell. Try to keep the child's skin, hands and nails clean to prevent the spread of infection. The doctor may treat the boil with antibiotics.

Bow legs

Bow legs are common in toddlers and can be considered as normal in this age group. Provided the bowing is symmetrical (that is, the same amount on each side) it is highly likely to resolve itself by the time the child is three or four. If the leg bowing is severe, asymmetrical or persistent, consult your doctor.
(See also Rickets)

Breath holding

Breath holding is usually caused by frustration and is similar to a temper tantrum in this respect. Attacks sometimes start towards the end of the first year but they are more common in the second or third year. They rarely occur in children over five. During an attack the child cries, breathes in and fails to take another breath for some time.

The symptoms which develop depend on the interval between breaths. Initially the child goes blue and stiffens, and she may become momentarily unconscious. Normal breathing usually starts again spontaneously – the child takes another breath and her colour gradually returns. If it does not, call a doctor at once.

Breath-holding attacks are frightening for parents, particularly as there is little that can be done once an attack has started. However, some parents find that giving the child a shake or a light slap makes her take another breath more quickly. Try to prevent an attack by avoiding situations which are likely to be frustrating for your child and distract her when she looks as if she is about to start screaming, although this is not always easy. It is also important for the child to learn that these attacks do not mean that she gets what she wants, or this will encourage her to behave in this way. Children always grow out of breath-holding attacks.

Broken bones
(See Fractures, page 311)

The Lungs

Bronchiolitis

Bronchiolitis is a viral infection of the bronchioles (the small breathing tubes in the lungs). It usually occurs in children under two and is most common in the first year of life.

At the beginning of the illness the child may have symptoms of a cold (a runny nose and sneezing), but as the infection moves down to the lungs she develops other symptoms such as coughing, wheezing and rapid breathing. She may also have difficulty getting her breath (particularly when feeding) and her lips may turn blue when she coughs.

Unfortunately, there is no treatment for bronchiolitis, although sometimes antibiotics can prevent secondary infection. Bronchiolitis gets better by itself in a week or so. Babies with bronchiolitis can develop feeding problems and quite severe breathing difficulties. If you notice these symptoms it is essential to

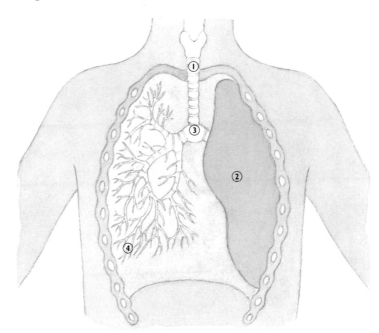

1. Windpipe (trachea) **3.** Bronchus
2. Left lung   **4.** Bronchioles

Each lung contains large breathing tubes which are called bronchi. These branch out into smaller breathing tubes (bronchioles). At the tip of each bronchiole are tiny air sacs (alveoli) where the exchange of oxygen and carbon dioxide takes place.
(See Asthma, Bronchiolitis, Bronchitis)

consult the doctor; he may suggest that the baby goes into hospital for observation and treatment.
(*See* **diagram, page 285**)

Bronchitis

Bronchitis is an infection of the bronchi (the large breathing tubes in the lungs) which is usually caused by viruses. The child with bronchitis has a cough and fever. She may also be breathing faster than usual and wheezing. If your child shows these symptoms, consult the doctor at once.

Antibiotics are sometimes used to prevent the development of secondary bacterial infection in bronchitis. Some children find cough mixtures soothing and occasionally an anti-wheeze drug from the doctor may help. A child with bronchitis may lose her appetite, but it is important to see that she has plenty to drink. Bronchitis usually gets better over a few days and does not cause permanent lung problems.
(*See* **diagram, page 285**)

Bruises

Bruises occur where blood has leaked into the tissue under the skin. They are usually caused by a knock or fall and will gradually disappear without treatment. If you notice your child develops excessive bruising, consult your doctor as it may mean that there is something wrong with the clotting mechanism of the blood.

Burns and scalds
(*See* **Emergencies, page 310**)

C

Car sickness
(*See* **Travel sickness**)

Catarrh

Catarrh is the excessive production of mucus by the lining of the respiratory passages in response to irritation. The most common form of irritation is infection from a cold. Allergic rhinitis also encourages catarrh. Catarrh may last for several days but usually clears up by itself. If it persists, however, you should consult your doctor.

Chest infections
(*See* **Bronchiolitis, Bronchitis**)

Chickenpox

Chickenpox is an infectious disease caused by a virus. It is characterized by little blisters which appear in crops on the body first, then the face and scalp and finally the limbs. The spots are itchy and easily broken, forming crusts or scabs. When the rash begins, the child often has a fever which may last for three to four days. The doctor may suggest giving paracetamol elixir to reduce the temperature. There is no specific treatment; just keep the child as comfortable as possible and try to stop him from scratching the spots because this can lead to secondary infection and scarring. The itching can be reduced by dabbing the rash with calamine lotion. Any scars which are left after the illness may take a while to disappear, although a few may remain.
(*See* **Quarantine chart, page 299**)

Chilblains

Chilblains are small red itchy areas on the tips of the fingers, toes or tops of the ears. Severe cold causes the blood vessels in the exposed parts to constrict so that for a while their blood flow is reduced and they appear white or bluish. Chilblains appear later and are usually at their most painful or itchy when the child is warm. Once they have developed there is no treatment but, if they are severe, the doctor may be able to give the child something to relieve the pain. Chilblains usually disappear over two to three weeks. To prevent chilblains, keep your child well wrapped up when out in the cold. If he is frequently troubled with them despite being protected against the cold, consult your doctor.

Choking
(*See* **Emergencies, page 308**)

Circumcision

Circumcision is the surgical removal of part of the foreskin of the penis. It is usually performed for religious and social reasons, rather than medical ones. In a baby the foreskin is fused to the tip of the penis and cannot be pulled back. As the penis grows during infancy, the foreskin gradually separates from the glans so that it can be drawn back in many boys by early childhood. If the child has a very tight foreskin or suffers repeated infections underneath the foreskin, such as balanitis, your doctor may recommend circumcision, but usually these conditions resolve in time without an operation.

Cleft palate

A cleft palate, either alone or in association with a cleft (hare lip), is an abnormality which is present at birth. The palate makes up the roof of the mouth and separates the mouth from the nasal passages. When it is cleft there is a central gap in the part of the palate that lies at the back of the mouth. An untreated cleft palate causes feeding difficulties and speech problems. It is usually repaired by surgery in the first year.
(*See also* **Hare lip**)

Clicking hip
(*See* **Congenital dislocated hip**)

Coeliac disease

This is a type of food sensitivity that results from damage to the lining of the small intestine. It results from eating foods containing gluten, a protein found in wheat, rye, barley and oats. When the child eats these foods, he produces antibodies to protect his intestine from gluten. These gluten antibodies circulate in the blood and may damage the bowel, flattening its normal finger-like projections and so preventing food from being absorbed properly. Children with coeliac disease fail to thrive, develop diarrhoea and may suffer from anaemia and vitamin and mineral deficiencies. The condition only develops after the child has been exposed to foods containing gluten. If a child with coeliac disease avoids all foods which contain gluten, the symptoms disappear and the damaged bowel returns to normal, but the special gluten-free diet must be followed throughout life.

Gluten sensitivity can also be associated with many other disorders, including blisters, mouth ulcers, pitted and discoloured tooth enamel, diabetes, convulsions, fatigue, depression and, in adults, fertility problems. Raised levels of gluten antibodies are more common in people with insulin-dependent diabetes, thyroid gland inflammation, and Down's syndrome. Some children suffer from one or more gluten sensitivity disorders but have no signs of bowel damage. For a reliable diagnosis of gluten sensitivity, a child needs a blood test for endomysial antibodies, followed, if positive, with a biopsy of the small intestine taken through a tube passed through the mouth.

Cold

This is a viral infection of the nose and throat. The child has a runny or blocked nose, may cough, complain of a sore throat and become feverish. Young children with colds often go off their food for a few days.

Antibiotics don't help, but vitamin C and elderberry extract, (given according to the packet instructions) may speed recovery. Paracetamol elixir can reduce a high temperature and ease a sore throat. In young babies a blocked nose can make feeding difficult, so your doctor may prescribe nose drops. Another idea for easing a blocked nose is to add a drop of eucalyptus oil to a teaspoon of sweet almond oil, and to smear some of this around the entrance to your child's nostrils. A little petroleum jelly gently rubbed in the same place helps prevent soreness from a runny nose.
(*See also* **Influenza**)

Cold sore

A cold sore typically starts as a blister on the lips or near the mouth. The blister, which may be painful, bursts, crusts over and heals without treatment within ten days and without a scar. Cold sores are caused by the herpes simplex virus and can recur when a child has a cold (hence the name) or chest infection, after exposure to strong sunlight or as a result of stress.

Colic

Colic is a type of tummy-ache which occurs in spasms. Infantile colic makes a baby draw up his knees and cry. It may occur a number of times a day, but in between the baby appears well. This type of colic, which occurs in both bottle- and breastfed babies, can be quite troublesome for the first three months of life or longer, especially in the evening. It may help to give the baby plenty of time at the breast and in your arms when he finishes feeding. Breastfeeding mothers may notice an improvement if they eat little and often throughout the day. Talk to your doctor if your baby has bad colic.

Colour blindness

Colour blindness is not uncommon in boys but is quite rare in girls. A colour-blind child has difficulty distinguishing reds and greens. This is often only discovered when a child is tested with special colour charts. It may run in families and there is no treatment to counteract it.

Coma

A coma is a state of unconsciousness from which it is impossible to be roused. It is very serious and may be caused by a head injury, poisoning, infections of the brain (meningitis or encephalitis), a low sugar level in the blood, diabetes or epilepsy. If your child becomes comatose, lie him on his side, so that if he vomits he will not inhale the vomit, and call an ambulance immediately.
(*See also* **Head injuries, page 311**)

Concussion
(*See* **Head injuries, page 311**)

Congenital defects

These are abnormalities with which a child is born. They range from relatively minor blemishes such as birthmarks to more serious abnormalities involving the heart, lungs or bowel.
(*See also* **Cleft palate, Congenital dislocated hip, Hare lip, Heart murmur**)

Congenital dislocated hip

The hip joint works like a ball and socket, the top of the leg bone being the ball and part of the pelvis (hip bone) being the socket. In some babies the socket is rather shallow and allows the leg bone to slip in and out. Although this is not noticeable at birth, a doctor can feel whether the hip joint easily dislocates when he examines the baby. It is more common for the doctor to feel a click as he moves the hip (a 'clicking' hip), without it actually slipping out of the socket. In this case all that is usually required is for the baby to be checked again several times to make sure the joint becomes completely stable over the first few months of life. Some doctors suggest using two terry towelling nappy squares during these early weeks to stabilize the leg bone in the socket. It is unusual for a simple clicking hip to need more treatment than this.

287

If the baby's hip does dislocate, the doctor will recommend an early visit to an orthopaedic surgeon (bone specialist) so that the hip can be placed in the best position for normal development. This may involve the baby wearing special splints and, very occasionally, a plaster or an operation may be necessary. If congenital dislocated hips are untreated they can lead to a limp and arthritis later on.

Conjunctivitis

Conjunctivitis, or pink eye, is inflammation of the conjunctiva – the outer surface of the front eyeball and the inner lining of the eyelids. It makes the white part of the eye appear red. Sometimes there is a yellowish discharge and the eye feels itchy. The causes include infection, allergy to pollen, or a foreign body in the eye. It is usual for both eyes to become inflamed with infection or allergy, but when conjunctivitis is caused by a foreign body only one eye is affected.

After consulting the doctor, the first thing to do is wipe away any discharge with some cotton wool moistened in clean water and carefully and, with expert help if necessary, remove any grit from the eye. If it has caused an abrasion the doctor may prescribe antibiotic eye drops (see below) or cream. He may also prescribe these if he suspects a bacterial infection.

Antibiotic creams should be applied, with clean hands, by pulling down the lower lid and placing a little cream on the eye. When the child blinks, the cream will be spread over the affected area. For allergic conjunctivitis the doctor may suggest some anti-allergic eye drops. If a child is suffering from infectious conjunctivitis, be careful to keep his towel and face flannel separate from those of the rest of the family. And keep the eye clean by washing it regularly with warm water.

Giving Eye Drops

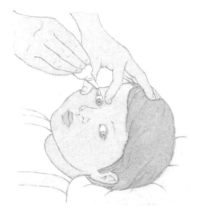

*To administer **eye drops**, tilt the child's head back slightly and put the drops in the outer edge of the open eye. When the child blinks the drops will flow over the eye.*

A mild form of conjunctivitis, called sticky eye, is common in babies. This is frequently made worse because a baby's tear ducts are too small to drain the eye properly. The baby's eyes should be bathed regularly with clean water and cotton-wool (using a separate piece of cotton-wool for each eye). Your doctor may also prescribe antibiotic drops.
(See also Allergic rhinitis)

Constipation

The number of times a day or week that a healthy child opens his bowels varies greatly. Constipation is when bowel motions are hard and difficult to expel. If your child passes motions of soft or firm consistency infrequently and without straining unduly, he is not constipated. If, on the other hand, the motions are hard, passed with difficulty and occasionally blood-streaked, he is likely to be constipated. Blood-streaking comes from anal fissures (little tears) caused by the passage of hard motions through the anus. In the vast majority of children constipation is a temporary problem which can be resolved by changes in the diet. A young child can be given more water or a little prune juice on a spoon. An older child's diet should

contain more fruit, vegetables and wholegrain cereals to increase the fibre content.

Some children become constipated because they put off going to the lavatory. This can happen when a child is away from home (perhaps on holiday) and feels anxious or takes a dislike to a strange lavatory. It might help to encourage the child to go at set times every day.
(See also Tummyache)

Convulsions

Abnormal bursts of electrical activity in the brain can cause convulsions. A convulsing child may have jerking limbs, become pale, be unresponsive or unconscious, and wet and soil himself. The vast majority of convulsions stop spontaneously after some minutes, but they can be frightening. There are many causes, but by far the most common are convulsions brought on by a high fever. These are known as febrile convulsions and occur in one in twenty normal healthy children between the ages of six months and five years. It is the raised temperature, often up to 40°C (104°F), which sets off the abnormal activity in the brain, so that the convulsion may occur at the beginning of an illness before the parents realize that the child is unwell. Infections of the ear, nose and throat are often responsible.

If a child has a convulsion consult your doctor at once. He may have to go into hospital, although the doctor may agree to look after him at home, particularly if he has had convulsions before. If the seizure is prolonged the doctor will give him an injection to stop it.

Once your child has had one febrile convulsion he is likely to have another, so you need to be aware of his temperature when he is unwell. If he becomes feverish keep him cool, give him paracetamol elixir to reduce the temperature and call your doctor.

See Sleep and Bedtime, page 118, for preventing cot death

The doctor may advise regular anti-convulsant drugs for children who have repeated febrile convulsions, but medical opinion is divided about this. Simple febrile convulsions do not cause brain damage and children grow out of them by the time they are four or five years old.

Much less common are convulsions caused by a brain infection, a low sugar or calcium level in the blood, or certain rare inherited diseases. If the doctor is uncertain about the cause of a convulsion he may recommend that the child is examined in hospital.

Other triggers include brain damage before, during or after birth; exposure to flashing lights (such as strobing lights in a cinema); and food sensitivity. Convulsions can sometimes occur in otherwise healthy children for no apparent reason. This is referred to as idiopathic epilepsy. In such cases the doctor may recommend that the child has regular anti-convulsant medication.
(*See also* **Meningitis, and First aid, page 312**)

Cot death

The sudden, unexpected death of a baby, usually while sleeping, is called the sudden infant death syndrome, or cot death, and it is something that every parent dreads.Many babies who die in this way are between two and six months of age and the majority appear perfectly healthy when put down to sleep. At present, research has not uncovered the cause, but a number of theories exist, including abnormal control of breathing, allergy, infection, sleeping on the tummy, breathing smoky air in a home where someone smokes and being too hot.
(*See* **Sleep and Bedtime, page 118, for prevention**)

Cough

Coughing is a mechanism that allows the body to cope with inflammation or irritation in the throat or breathing tubes in the lungs. The action forces air out of the lungs at high pressure and so expels any mucus, secretions or inhaled foreign body from the breathing tubes.

Coughs often occur with colds as part of a viral infection of the upper airways and throat. In this situation no special treatment is needed, although your doctor may prescribe medicine to soothe the cough.

A cough is sometimes the result of an infection in the lungs, such as bronchiolitis, bronchitis or pneumonia. It may also occur with asthma or following accidental inhalation of dust or a foreign body, such as a peanut.
(*See also* **Croup, and Choking, page 310**)

Cradle cap

Cradle cap is greasy yellow scales and crusting on a baby's scalp. Sometimes there are also patches of dry red itchy skin over the face, body and nappy area. This is a form of eczema known as seborrhoeic dermatitis. The scales on the scalp can be removed by daily shampooing, after they have been moistened overnight with an oily preparation such as olive oil. If the patches on the face or body are troublesome, you may need to get a special cream or lotion from the doctor, although often they will clear up spontaneously.

Croup

Croup is usually caused by an infection in the larynx (voice box). Other causes include an inhaled foreign body, allergy and even excitement or upset. More usual in winter, it is most common in toddlers. A croupy child has an unusual barking cough and noisy breathing which is often worse when he breathes in. He may also have a raised temperature. These symptoms can develop quite suddenly and can be frightening for the child and parents. Moistened air may help the condition and this can be provided in the home by taking the child into a steamy bathroom or by boiling a kettle (but make sure that the child cannot pull the kettle over). However, it is essential that any child who develops croup is seen by a doctor. He may suggest that the child goes into hospital for observation and treatment.

Cuts and grazes
(*See* **First aid, page 312**)

Cyanosis

Cyanosis refers to a blue appearance of the lips, fingers and toes. The blueness is caused by reduced amounts of oxygen in the blood and tissues and occurs with some diseases of the heart and lungs. If cyanosis develops, call your doctor urgently or take the child straight to a hospital accident and emergency department.

Sometimes a child's hands and feet go blue when they get too cold, but this is not serious and normal colour returns with warming. A child may go blue with a breath-holding attack, but normal colour returns when he takes another breath.

Cystic fibrosis

Cystic fibrosis is one of the most common inherited diseases. It causes repeated lung infections and difficulties with absorbing nutrients from food. Although both the parents of a child with cystic fibrosis are physically healthy, they each carry the abnormal cystic fibrosis gene and have a one in four chance of producing an affected child in each pregnancy. Researchers can now identify people who carry the cystic fibrosis gene and they can also use chorionic villus sampling to identify affected babies.
The condition is usually diagnosed when a child fails to thrive or has recurrent chest infections. Regular medical treatment, physiotherapy and attention to diet can help.

Cystitis
(*See* **Urinary tract infections**)

D

Deafness

To understand the different types of deafness it is necessary to have a little knowledge of the ear and how we hear. Sounds are vibrations of the air which enter the outer ear and strike the eardrum. On the other side of the drum, in the middle ear, are three tiny bones (the ossicles) through which the vibrations pass to reach the inner ear. This contains the organ of hearing – the cochlea – and within this are nerve endings which detect the sounds and relay them to the nerve fibres which carry them to the brain. The Eustachian tube connects the middle ear to the back of the throat, thereby maintaining the air pressure in the middle ear.

Deafness can be caused by a blockage somewhere along the passage from the external ear canal to the cochlea (conductive deafness), or by a disorder which affects the cochlea or nerve (nerve deafness). These two types can involve one ear or both, and the degree of hearing loss may be variable. The most common cause of poor hearing in children is temporary conductive deafness due to a blockage in the Eustachian tube. As a result, fluid collects in the middle ear and prevents the normal conduction of sounds through to the inner ear. This can occur with a common cold.

Conductive deafness can also be caused by glue ear, perforation of the eardrum, inflammation of the middle ear (otitis media) or damage to the ear bones. Deafness caused by maldevelopment or damage to the cochlea or its nerve is much less common but can result in partial or total deafness.

290

The Ear

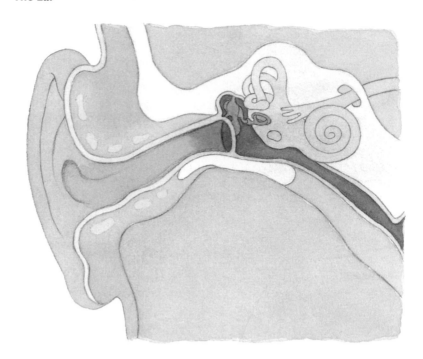

The human ear is divided into three different parts – the outer, middle and inner ear. Sound travels along the ear canal to the eardrum and then passes through the middle ear via three small bones (ossicles) to the cochlea in the inner ear.

1. Outer ear	**7.** Cochlea
2. Ear canal	**8.** Balancing
3. Eardrum	apparatus
4. Ossicles	**9.** Auditory nerve
5. Middle ear	**10.** Eustachian
6. Inner ear	tube

In childhood, hearing is essential for language development so any loss of hearing, however slight, is best diagnosed as soon as possible. Routine examination of a baby's hearing is carried out at child health clinics and if any abnormality is detected the baby is assessed in a special hearing clinic. However, if you think there is something wrong with your child's hearing you can have her checked at the clinic or consult the doctor. Treatment for children born deaf may involve inserting a cochlear implant – an electrode that receives sound signals in the inner ear.
(*See also* **Ear infections, Glue ear**)

Dehydration
(*See* **Diarrhoea, Fever**)

Dental decay
After eating, a sticky layer called

plaque coats the teeth. Bacteria break down sugar in plaque and produces acid which eats into enamel and encourages decay. Some children are less prone to decay, perhaps because they form less plaque, have different bacteria, more resistant enamel, a better diet or take in more fluoride. Once decay reaches the tooth's nerve, the child has toothache.

Help to prevent dental decay by reducing the amount of added sugar in your child's diet and by brushing the teeth with a fluoride toothpaste. Never let your baby go to sleep while drinking a bottle of milk or juice because the resulting pool of liquid round a sleeping baby's front teeth does not get washed away by saliva as it does when she is awake.

Dermatitis
(*See* **Eczema, Nappy rash**)

Diabetes

Childhood diabetes results from a deficiency of insulin, a hormone that controls the sugar level in the blood and tissues. This is because the pancreas – a gland in the upper abdomen, behind the stomach – fails to produce sufficient insulin This results in a high blood-sugar level, which makes the child feel thirsty, drink excessively and pass a lot of urine. She may also lose weight and feel unwell. Treatment with insulin injections daily enables the blood sugar level to return to normal, while a special diet and regular monitoring of the amount of sugar in the urine or blood can help to control the condition.

Diarrhoea

Diarrhoea is the frequent passing of loose watery motions. In childhood it usually occurs with gastroenteritis, an infection of the bowel.

It is very important for a child with diarrhoea not to become dehydrated. This will happen if she is losing more fluid in the diarrhoea than she is taking by mouth. You should therefore give plenty of fluids, especially to young babies, who become dehydrated very easily. It's best to give small amounts of fluid frequently. If you are breastfeeding, continue but give more feeds than usual and drink plenty yourself. A bottle-fed baby can have extra fluids as boiled water. Suggestions for older children, including babies on a mixed diet, include water, diluted fruit juice, weak tea, or thin vegetable soup.

Your doctor may recommend oral rehydration salts that you make up with water. Alternatively, prepare a home-made oral rehydration mixture by adding one level teaspoon of salt and eight level teaspoons of sugar to one litre (1 3/4 pints) of water. Both shop-bought and home-made oral rehydration mixtures provide energy in the form of sugar, as well as replacing minerals lost in the diarrhoea, and correcting the acidity balance in the child's body.

Less acute forms of diarrhoea may result from sensitivity to certain foods, respiratory infection, anxiety and other problems of the bowel. In such cases the child does not usually become ill suddenly, but may fail to gain weight in the normal way. Contact your doctor without delay if your child can't keep fluids down; has diarrhoea severely for twelve hours, or mildly for twenty-four hours; or has repeated vomiting, or blood in the faeces. One hygienic precaution to prevent any infection from spreading is extra careful hand-washing by your child after using the lavatory – and by you after helping him, or after touching soiled nappies, clothing or bed linen. Another is to wash crockery and cutlery in hotter water than usual. Easily digested foods for a child recovering include stewed apples, ripe bananas and brown rice. A little live yogurt each day helps restore a normal population of helpful bowel bacteria. (*See also* **Coeliac disease, Gastroenteritis**)

Diphtheria

Diphtheria is a serious and highly infectious bacterial disease which causes inflammation of the nose and throat. This inflammation may become so severe that it interferes with the child's breathing. Every child should be protected against diphtheria by immunization, which is part of the triple vaccine (tetanus, whooping cough and diptheria) given in the first few months of life. (*See also* **Immunization chart, page 131**)

Dyslexia

Dyslexia is difficulty in reading or learning to read. It is sometimes accompanied by writing and spelling problems. Affected children do not show backwardness in other school subjects and many of them are of average or above average intelligence. Dyslexic children usually benefit from extra specialized help with reading and spelling. Research indicates that some children with dyslexia can see words more clearly if they have glasses with tinted lenses. The precise tint needed varies from one child to another.

E

Earache

Earache can be caused by infection in the outer ear (otitis externa), inflammation of the middle ear (otitis media). It can also be caused by a sore throat and dental decay. (*See also* **Ear infections**)

Ear infections

Otitis externa is inflammation of the external ear canal. It is caused by a bacterial, viral or fungal infection. The inflammation causes pain or itchiness in the ear canal and sometimes a discharge. After examining the ear canal the doctor will probably prescribe ear drops. It is important that the ear canal is kept dry until the infection clears, so take care when washing the child's hair and do not allow him to swim.

Otitis media – inflammation of the middle ear – is common in young children. The illness can be caused by a bacterial infection and may be accompanied by a cold or tonsillitis. The child is usually unwell and feverish and may complain of earache or headache; he may also be slightly deaf. As the inflammation progresses the middle ear fills with fluid and this causes the pain and deafness to worsen. Sometimes the only indication of infection in a young child is that he repeatedly pulls or rubs his ear. If your child has any of these symptoms, consult your doctor. Treatment may include giving paracetamol elixir to relieve pain and fever, nasal decongestants to assist drainage of the middle ear, and antibiotics to clear the infection. Sometimes the eardrum ruptures with the pressure of fluid. This relieves the pain and produces a discharge from the ear. Consult your doctor if this happens.

If a child has repeated attacks of otitis media the doctor may recommend that he is seen by an ear, nose and throat (ENT) specialist. Treatment may include the insertion of grommets (tiny plastic tubes) in the eardrums to help drain the infected material from the ear, and removal of the adenoids. **(See also Deafness, Glue ear, and diagram, page 290)**

Eczema

Eczema is a form of dermatitis that is characterized by a red itchy rash. The most common type is atopic eczema. Often there is a family history of asthma, eczema or hay fever.

Eczema often starts in the first four months of life and at this stage affects the body and face. As the child gets older it tends to involve the crook of the elbow, the back of the knee and the wrists and ankles.

Eczema can be a very uncomfortable condition. Sufferers should avoid wearing tight-fitting, rough-fibred garments – loose, cotton clothing is best. Consult your doctor about special emollients, moisturizing creams and bath oils which can help to ease it. Eczema is sometimes worsened by a food sensitivity, so your doctor may recommend 'a carefully supervised triple-elimination-and-challenge diet (see the section on Food sensitivity for more details on this).

House-dust mite droppings are another possible trigger. (For suggestions about reducing the population of mites in your home, see the section on Asthma).

Contact (allergic or irritant) eczema is also common and is often provoked by prolonged or repeated contact with various substances, including bubble bath, saliva (leading to a rash caused by excessive dribbling), orange juice, detergent, sap, nickel (some jewellery), and a wet or dirty nappy; by plants such as chrysanthemums and primroses; by ointments or sprays containing neomycin, antihistamines or local anaesthetics; and by skin infections such as ringworm and impetigo.

Another type of eczema is seborrhoeic dermatitis which occurs with cradle cap in some babies and is treated similarly. **(See also Asthma, Cradle cap, Food sensitivity)**

Electric shock
(See Emergencies, page 310)

Enuresis
(See Bed wetting)

Epilepsy
(See Convulsions)

Eye infections
(See Conjunctivitis, Styes)

Eye injuries
(See First aid, page 312)

F

Febrile convulsions
(See Convulsions)

Fever
Fever occurs when the body temperature rises above normal (37°C/98.6°F) and usually represents a reaction to infection. The temperature often has an obvious cause, such as a cold, but it may be advisable to have a feverish child examined by a doctor.

A high temperature is not usually harmful, though in some young children it causes febrile convulsions. A feverish child is more comfortable if she is cooled down. This can be done by giving her paracetamol elixir in the correct dose. A feverish child will not feel like eating, but encourage her to drink as much as she can. Her appetite will return as the fever subsides.

Fifth disease (slapped cheek disease or erythema infectiosum)
So-called because it was once placed fifth in a list of common infectious diseases of childhood which have a similar rash, fifth disease is caused by parvovirus B19 infection. The average incubation period for this is sixteen days and the rash lasts on average for eleven days.

The cheeks look as if they have been slapped, and there may also be a blotchy rash on the forearms, lower legs and slightly on the trunk. The rash may itch and it feels worse when the skin is hot. Other symptoms can include a cold, sore throat, headache and diarrhoea. No specific treatment exists although calamine lotion may soothe the itching and paracetamol elixir can relieve a headache.

Fits
(See Convulsions)

Flat feet
The feet of infants and young children are fatter, wider and flatter than those of older children and adults. In young children fatty pads create a fullness on the undersurface of the foot so that

the arch is not visible. This is quite normal. As the child grows older this fatty pad will disappear and the arch is revealed. Consult your doctor if your child's feet hurt during exercise.

Food sensitivity

Food sensitivity is four times as common in young children as it is in adults. Several things encourage it, including a family history of any allergy, bottle-feeding, a missing digestive enzyme, gastro-enteritis, repeated antibiotics, and a poor diet. Food sensitivity can lead to a wide variety of symptoms, including flushing, tummyache, diarrhoea, vomiting, wind, joint pain, rash, headache, fatigue, weakness, palpitations, cough, runny nose, convulsions, depression, nerve disorder, blisters, mouth ulcers, and pitted and discoloured teeth. However, each of these conditions has many other possible causes, so it's best to track down the real underlying problem with your doctor rather than rush to blame food sensitivity.

There are four main types. The first is a non-allergic immune reaction, which often result from a common food such as wheat, milk and yeast, and many other foods can act as triggers. This may alter the level of an antibody called immunoglobulin G (IgG) and, perhaps immunoglobulin E (IgE) too, but it isn't actually allergic (even though it's sometimes called 'delayed-onset food allergy'). One example is gluten sensitivity (see Coeliac disease). Non-allergic immune reactions begin within seventy-two hours of eating the food. The symptoms tend to be vague, which makes pinpointing the cause difficult. One explanation for this reaction is the 'leaky gut' phenomenon, in which some sort of damage to the intestinal lining allows poorly digested food particles to pass into the bloodstream and trigger an immune reaction.

The second type of food sensitivity involves a reaction to a toxin (for example, from food-poisoning bacteria), an irritant (such as some spices), an additive (such as tartrazine, the flavour-enhancer monosodium glutamate, or MSG, the sweetener aspartame), or a pharmacologically-active substance (such as caffeine).

The third type results from a missing digestive enzyme such as lactase, the enzyme that digests milk sugar (lactose).

'The fourth is a 'true' food allergy, and is associated with a raised level of IgE antibodies. It begins within two hours (sometimes sooner) of eating a tiny amount of a food such as eggs, fish, shellfish, wheat, milk, nuts, nut oils, seeds and strawberries. Usually only one or at the most two foods act as triggers. Food allergy may cause urticaria, asthma, allergic rhinitis, migraine, vomiting, diarrhoea, swollen lips, tongue and throat, wheezing, chest pain, fainting and severe shock. A severe reaction (anaphylaxis) requires urgent treatment with an injection of adrenaline.

The best treatment for most food sensitivities is to use a food-diary to discover the culprit, then to arrange for your child to avoid it, eat smaller amounts, or eat it less frequently. Some children can eat a problem food if they have only a little of it no more often than every three or four days. However, if the initial reaction was serious, consult your doctor first and give the food under medical supervision.

The best way of identifying food sensitivity is with a triple-elimination-and-challenge diet. However, because this often involves eliminating a basic food, it's advisable to have a doctor's or dietitian's help so you can still provide your child with essential nutrients. The diet involves eliminating the suspect food for three weeks. If the symptoms settle, challenge your suspicion by offering the food again. If the symptoms then reappear, eliminate the food for a week, then do a second challenge; if they return, only to disappear when you next eliminate the food and come back with the third challenge, you can be reasonably sure you have correctly identified the culprit.

If your doctor suspects a food allergy, he will recommend skin-prick and blood tests. Such tests are unhelpful for non-allergic immune reactions. Tests are best done by an allergist. Some children need to be tested for lactose intolerance or gluten sensitivity. There are also other methods available such as kinesiology (muscle-strength testing while holding samples of food), dowsing (swinging a pendulum over the child or over foods) or hair testing, but there is no scientific proof that any of these are effective. (*See also* **Eczema, Urticaria**)

G

Gastroenteritis

This is infectious diarrhoea which is usually accompanied by vomiting. Most attacks are caused by a bacterial or viral infection of the bowel and they are not usually helped by antibiotics or medicine that slows down the frequency of bowel motions. The child may be generally unwell with a tummyache and fever, so consult your doctor about treatment. It is most important to give him plenty to drink to prevent him from becoming dehydrated.

Gastroenteritis usually clears up

after a few days, but very occasionally a child who is suffering from a severe attack has to be admitted to hospital for treatment for dehydration.

Gastroenteritis occurs less often in breastfed babies as breast milk contains antibodies that help protect against infection.
(*See also* **Tummyache, Diarrhoea**)

German measles
(*See* **Rubella**)

Glue ear
Glue ear is a condition in which the middle ear becomes filled with a fluid which is thick and sticky like glue, and which prevents sound vibrations passing through to the inner ear. There is no pain or fever, but the child's hearing is impaired. Glue ear affects one or both ears and usually follows an infection of the middle ear (otitis media) in association with a blocked Eustachian tube. This blockage is often caused by enlarged adenoids.

Treatment includes antibiotics and nasal decongestants, but if these fail an operation may be necessary. The adenoids are removed and the 'glue' is sucked out through a slit made in the eardrum. A tiny plastic tube called a grommet is inserted into the slit to allow air to pass into the middle ear and the fluid to drain out. While a child has grommets in he should keep his ears dry and avoid swimming. Grommets usually fall out after some months and the eardrums will heal without any further problem.
(*See also* **Deafness and diagram, page 290**)

Growing pains
Children sometimes complain of pain in their legs and occasionally in their arms. These pains keep the child awake at night, although he is otherwise quite well. The cause is unknown but may relate to swelling of the muscles after strenuous

exercise. Whatever the cause, growing pains are not serious and disappear in time. Massaging the limbs and putting a warm hot water bottle on or near them may ease the pain. If the pain persists or is associated with other problems, or should you feel uneasy, then you should consult your doctor.

Gum boils
(*See* **Mouth infections**)

H

Hare or cleft lip
A hare or cleft lip is a congenital abnormality of the lip which may occur with a cleft palate. It can vary from a small notch in the upper lip to a complete cleft that extends into the nostril. Treatment involves surgery, usually within three months of birth.
(*See also* **Cleft palate**)

Hay fever
(*See* **Allergic rhinitis**)

Headache
A headache is a common childhood complaint with many possible causes including a fever, toothache and earache. Treatment for the complaint itself normally relieves the headache. Recurrent headaches, when the child is well in between, may have an emotional basis or may be migraines, and you should consult your doctor.

A headache in conjunction with a temperature, vomiting, drowsiness and reluctance to look at the light may indicate more serious disease, such as meningitis. If your child has these symptoms, consult your doctor immediately.
(*See also* **Meningitis**)

Head banging
Many children make repetitive

movements at some stage of development – head banging, rolling and rocking are examples of these.

Head rolling and rocking may be seen in the second six months of life. The baby rolls her head from side to side and may rock when she is put down in her cot. Some children find these movements comforting and generally stop after a while or rock themselves to sleep.

A child between the ages of one and two may bang her head on the side of the cot, wall or floor. This can be due to a temper tantrum or to seek attention. Kind and firm handling may help prevent these episodes, but if they do occur the child should be protected from damaging itself, though it is rare for children to do themselves any actual injury.

Frequent and persistent head banging is a cause for concern. Your doctor may be able to offer advice or refer you for more specific help.

Head injuries
(*See* **Emergencies, page 308**)

Head lice
It is not uncommon for pre-school children to have head lice. They are transferred from child to child and their presence does not indicate any lack of hygiene. The eggs of the louse, called nits, are laid on the hairs and appear as small grey-white specks which do not brush off. If you look carefully you may see a louse moving on the scalp. The lice cause the child to scratch her scalp and this can lead to skin infection if left untreated. A safe, effective treatment is to wash hair, load it with conditioner, comb it with a wide-toothed comb, then remove the lice with a fine-toothed comb. Dunk the comb into a bowl of water after each combing to drown the lice. This removes only the adult lice, not the nits, which remain stuck to the hairs. Some of these nits contain immature

See **Nappy Changing, page 110**, for nappy rash

lice. However, if you repeat the treatment twice a week for two weeks, you'll catch the newly hatched lice from these nits too before they can lay more eggs. This treatment is just as simple as using a pesticide-containing lotion or shampoo, and avoids any potential danger from pesticide being absorbed through the warm scalp into the bloodstream.

Other members of the family should be closely examined for nits, and if there is any sign that they are infected they should be treated too.

Heart murmur

Murmurs are noises heard when listening to the heart with a stethoscope. They result from a disturbance in the flow of blood as it passes through the heart. The disturbance can be caused by a structural abnormality of the heart, as in congenital heart disease, or may just relate to the actual flow of blood itself. Some healthy children with perfectly normal hearts have a murmur caused by the blood flow. These are referred to as innocent murmurs; they are harmless and disappear as the child gets older.

Herbal medicine

Most of the medicines now used in orthodox medicine originated from plants, though many today are synthetic copies and those few which still come from plants are highly purified. Some people believe that herbal remedies in which plant material is gathered at particular times and processed as little as possible have greater healing powers than the material which has been extracted, purified and altered.

You can obtain herbal remedies from a medical herbalist or some pharmacies. Follow the instructions carefully because these remedies can have side effects just as orthodox medicines can, and remember to tell your doctor or pharmacist before giving your child combinations of herbal remedies and other medicines.

Hernia

A hernia is a protrusion of tissue through the wall of the cavity which contains it. Hernias in the groin (inguinal hernias) are not uncommon in young children. They produce a swelling in the groin which may be visible only when the child cries or coughs. Any child who has such a swelling should be seen by a doctor as the minor operation needed to repair the hernia should not be delayed.

Umbilical hernias are swellings through the belly button. They do not cause problems and do not need any treatment because they get smaller and disappear as the child gets older.

Herpes simplex
(See Cold sore)

Hives
(See Urticaria)

Homeopathy

Homeopathy is based on the idea that ill health responds to remedies containing infinitesimally small amounts of substances (often plant extracts or minerals) which, in larger doses, would cause the same symptoms as the illness. Diluting a substance thousands of times is believed to increase its healing power. There is relatively little scientific proof of the value of homeopathy, but it provides treatments which are gentle and have no side effects and some people prefer it to orthodox medicine or use homeopathy and orthodox medicine in parallel.

Homeopaths are highly trained and may be medically qualified as well. They prefer to base their treatment on a thorough knowledge of a person's individual characteristics. The time and courtesy they give to those who consult them may be important factors contributing to healing. Homeopathic remedies bought direct from pharmacies can be useful for minor ailments.

Hyperactivity

Many toddlers are extremely active and appear never to tire. These children are normal. Hyperactivity refers to those children who combine frenetic activity with an inability to settle. Their behaviour often appears impulsive and restless, they have poor concentration and are easily distracted. A hyperactive child may be unable to concentrate at school, resulting in serious setbacks to learning. A small proportion of hyperactive children are mentally retarded, but the majority of them are otherwise well.

The cause of hyperactive behaviour remains uncertain, but sensitivity to certain foods and food additives may play a part in some cases. If your child shows signs of being hyperactive, consult your doctor.

Whatever the cause, hyperactive children benefit from consistent, firm and kind handling within an orderly environment without too many distractions. The condition usually improves with age.

I

Impetigo

Impetigo is a skin infection caused by bacteria. It can occur anywhere on the body, but it usually begins on the face with red spots which rapidly become little blisters and then pustules. These spots weep and form yellow crusts. The infection can spread to other parts of the body if the child scratches the spots, and it can also be passed on to other children very easily.

The doctor will suggest localized treatment, such as dabbing the crusts with an antiseptic solution three or four times a day. Washing with medicated soap may also help, but the infection clears more rapidly if treated with antibiotics.

Influenza

Influenza, or flu, is an infection caused by influenza viruses. It usually lasts for about seven to ten days. Typical symptoms are fever, aches and pains, a headache and a cold. A child who has influenza goes off his food and may vomit.

Antibiotics have no effect, but studies show that vitamin C supplements and elderberry extract, taken according to the packet instructions, can speed recovery. If the child is feverish, paracetamol elixir helps bring down the temperature and ease aches and pains.

Contact a doctor if your child becomes very unwell or if she has very cold hands and feet, feels sick or unusually thirsty or has a rash. This is because very occasionally these are early signs of septicaemia (blood poisoning) from unrecognized bacterial meningitis. Another reason is that if the child already has long-term heart, lung or kidney disease, diabetes or poor immunity, she has a higher than average risk of complications.

A new drug, Zanamivir, can reduce the risk of complications. An annual shot of flu vaccine is a wise precaution for a child with one of these conditions too.'

J

Jaundice

Jaundice is a yellow discoloration of the skin which is also visible in the whites of the eyes. It is the result of too much yellow pigment, called

bilirubin, in the blood. Jaundice is common in newborn babies. It usually develops on the second or third day of life and disappears without treatment after about a week. Be sure to tell your doctor if your baby's jaundice persists, as if it is left untreated the condition could cause brain damage. The treatment involves putting the baby under ultra-violet light for several hours each day.

Jaundice in older children is uncommon and never normal. It can be an indication of infectious hepatitis and the jaundiced child should be seen by a doctor.

K

Knock knees

This is when a child cannot put his ankles together while his knees are touching. Some toddlers have mild knock knees which improve on their own by the time they are six or seven years old. If the condition is marked, does not disappear with age, or appears to be getting worse, consult your doctor. If necessary, the doctor will refer the child to an orthopaedic surgeon (bone specialist) for advice on future treatment.

L

Laryngitis

Laryngitis is inflammation of the larynx (voicebox). In adults and older children it usually produces hoarseness and sometimes loss of voice; in young children who have a smaller voicebox, the inflammation may lead to an attack of croup and they should be seen by a doctor.
(See also Croup)

Lice
(See Head lice)

M

Measles

Measles is an infectious disease caused by viruses. Because it is such an unpleasant and often serious illness, children should be immunized against it as soon as possible. This usually happens in their second year. If you are unsure whether your child has been immunized or not you should check with your health visitor or doctor.

The first symptoms of measles are snuffles, fever, conjunctivitis and a cough. These symptoms are followed four to five days later by a red blotchy rash which begins on the face and then spreads to the body and limbs. As the rash spreads, the fever often continues, but it usually settles a day or so after the rash appears on the legs. After this the rash also begins to fade.

Before and during the time that the rash is appearing, the child can feel miserable and develop a chest or ear infection. There is no specific treatment for the rash, but you should consult your doctor about treatment to relieve other symptoms. He may treat secondary infections with antibiotics and suggest paracetamol elixir to reduce the temperature. The child may not feel like eating much, but should have plenty to drink.
(See also Quarantine, and Immunization chart, page 131)

Meningitis

This is an uncommon but serious bacterial or viral infection in which the tissue covering the brain and spinal cord become inflamed. The child may complain of a headache, may vomit and be feverish.

Light may hurt his eyes, it may be painful for him to bend his neck, and he may be drowsy. He may have very cold hands and feet, and be unusually thirsty. He may also have convulsions and a rash. A baby with meningitis cannot complain of a headache, but he will have a temperature, may vomit, and be irritable and disinterested in his feeds. The soft spot (fontanelle) on his head may be fuller than usual, and he may have a convulsion.

A rash that doesn't fade when you press the base of a drinking glass against the skin suggests bacterial meningitis. However, a meningitis rash does sometimes blanch this way, especially early on. A child with these symptoms should see a doctor urgently. If there is any suspicion of meningitis, the doctor will admit the child to hospital. And if there is any suspicion of bacterial meningitis, antibiotics are begun at once. However, it's only by examining the fluid around the brain and spinal cord that a definite diagnosis can be made.

Sometimes a type of blood poisoning (septicaemia) from bacterial meningitis begins before there are any signs of meningitis. Indeed, you may think your child simply has flu. So get urgent medical help if a child with 'flu' has very cold hands and feet, or a rash, or feels sick or unusually thirsty, or if your sixth sense tells you something more serious is going on. **(See also Mumps)**

Mouth infections

The most common mouth infection in babies is thrush. It is caused by a yeast infection which produces white patches on the tongue and the inside of the cheeks. It can also occur on the baby's bottom and cause nappy rash.

Thrush is not serious but it can cause discomfort when sucking or feeding. The infection may have been passed on by the mother at the time of birth, or have come from thrush on her nipples if she is breastfeeding, or can develop after taking a course of antibiotics. It can also arise if bottles have not been sterilized properly. Your doctor will prescribe antifungal drops to clear the mouth infection.

Children occasionally develop mouth ulcers, which usually appear on the gums or the insides of the cheeks. They are caused by a viral infection and should disappear within a few days.

Less commonly, herpes simplex viruses, which also cause cold sores, may be responsible for a severe mouth ulcer. The child becomes unwell and feverish, with small blisters on the tongue, gums, palate and insides of the cheeks which burst to leave painful ulcers. Eating causes discomfort, but the child should be encouraged to drink plenty as this helps to keep the mouth clean and prevents dehydration. The doctor may prescribe a soothing cream, but occasionally sufferers need to be nursed in hospital because they require extra fluids. The condition usually clears up after about ten days.

Mouth ulcers
(See Mouth infections)

Mumps

Mumps is an infectious disease that is caused by a viral infection. The illness begins with pain and swelling in one or both of the parotid glands, the saliva-producing glands on either side of the face, in front of and below the ear. The swelling usually reaches its peak two or three days later and subsides over the next few days. Swelling of one gland may precede that of the other by one or two days. The child may be feverish and feel lethargic.

There is no specific treatment, but the child should be kept as comfortable as possible and can be given paracetamol elixir if he has a fever or the swelling is painful.

He will be infectious for about two weeks after the onset of the swelling.

Rare complications include mild meningitis and inflammation of the testes (orchitis). Orchitis may occur in boys about eight days after the parotid swelling. The testes become swollen and sore for about four days, but the inflammation settles down without treatment. No damage to the testes results, but if mumps is contracted by an adult male it can occasionally cause a degree of infertility.
(See also Quarantine)

N

Nappy rash

This red blotchy rash in the nappy area is common in babies. It can be caused by a fungal infection, such as thrush, or by a reaction of the skin to wet and soiled nappies. To prevent or clear the rash, keep the baby's bottom as clean and dry as possible. This is best done by changing the nappy frequently and leaving it off whenever possible to expose the skin to the air. At each nappy change clean the baby's bottom and apply a barrier cream such as zinc and castor oil ointment. Avoid waterproof pants as they keep the skin moist which exacerbates the problem. If you use terry towelling nappies, avoid washing them with biological soap powder or strong detergent and rinse them thoroughly. If thrush is suspected your doctor will prescribe an antifungal cream which should clear the rash up within a few days.

Nettle rash
(See Urticaria)

Nosebleeds

Nosebleeds are rare in young babies, but are not uncommon in older

297

children. The bleeding usually results from an infection of the lining of the nose or because of persistent nose picking; it may be alarming but is rarely severe. Bleeding is best controlled by pinching the soft part of the nose to close the nostrils. Apply pressure for at least five minutes to allow a clot to form. The child should sit up and lean forwards so that no blood drips down the throat.

Try to stop the child touching or blowing her nose as this can lead to more bleeding. A child with frequent nosebleeds should see a doctor.

Obesity

Many babies who are overweight in the first months of life lose their extra weight in the second year when they become more mobile. Remember also that most toddlers have little pot bellies and this does not mean that they are overweight. However, fat or obese children are more likely than those who are average weight to become fat adults – a condition which increases the risks of heart disease, high blood pressure and diabetes.

You should avoid giving children too many stodgy, high-calorie foods such as ice cream, sweets, cakes, crisps and fizzy drinks. If obesity is a real problem, your doctor may advise you on an appropriate diet.

Otitis externa and Otitis media
(See Ear infections)

P

Phobias

A phobia is an irrational and intense fear of something. For example, a child may have a fear of tigers, ghosts or robbers in her bedroom at night or may be afraid of the dark. These fears are usually a passing phase but may represent hidden anxiety – perhaps she is worried about a problem in the family or at school – so they are best handled with sympathy and reassurance.

If a phobia persists, mention it to your doctor because she may be able to give advice on how to handle the problem.

Pica

Normal infants and toddlers put all sorts of unsuitable things into their mouths; they may even eat them. Such behaviour is part of a natural exploration of the world, but should be discouraged as the child may inadvertently eat something harmful.

If dirt-eating becomes a habit, it is referred to as pica, and should lead to concern about the child's general wellbeing. If you suspect that your child has pica, consult your doctor or health visitor.

Pigeon toes

This condition describes the position of the feet when they are turned inwards. As a result of pigeon toes a child may trip over her feet when she runs. Many toddlers are pigeon-toed, but this tends to correct itself as the child grows and usually disappears completely by the age of six or seven years. In most cases no treatment is required, but if the condition does not improve, or gets worse, you should consult your doctor. She may refer the child to an orthopaedic surgeon (bone specialist) for advice.

Pink eye
(See Conjunctivitis)

Poisoning
(See Emergencies, page 311)

Prickly heat

Prickly heat is an itchy rash caused by blockage of the sweat glands in the skin. In a hot humid atmosphere a baby or child may develop tiny pin-point blisters of sweat, particularly on the face, neck and nappy area. No treatment is necessary as the rash disappears by itself after a few days, but you can prevent prickly heat by keeping your child cool in hot weather – dressing him in cotton clothes will help.

Pyloric stenosis

Pyloric stenosis is a narrowing of the outlet of the stomach into the intestine. The narrowing is due to excessive muscular development which constricts the outlet and prevents milk and food from leaving the stomach normally. As the quantity of milk filling the stomach increases, the baby automatically vomits. In some cases vomiting is projectile (spurts out forcefully), which can be alarming for parents. The result of repeated vomiting is that the baby receives insufficient nourishment from her food and loses weight. Despite this, she usually feeds well. Pyloric stenosis typically occurs in the first three months of life and is more common in boys than girls; the cause is unknown. A minor operation may be necessary to relieve the obstruction.

Quarantine

Medical opinion is divided about the value or necessity of keeping children in quarantine. The quarantine period of an illness is the time during which the infected child can pass the disease on to someone else, but as the most infectious stage is often before there are any outward signs it can be

QUARANTINE CHART

Disease	Incubation*	Infectious period
Chickenpox	2-3 weeks	2 days before the rash shows until all the spots have crusted. If the child is in contact with a pregnant woman during this period, advise the woman to consult a doctor.
Measles	1-2 weeks	A week before the rash appears until 5 days afterwards.
Mumps	2-3 weeks	A week before the onset of the parotid swelling until 2 weeks afterwards.
Rubella (German measles)	2-3 weeks	A few days before the onset of the rash until 1 day after the symptoms go. If the child is in contact with a pregnant woman during this period, advise the woman to consult a doctor.
Whooping cough (pertussis)	1-3 weeks	4 days before until 21 days after the onset of the cough (unless on erythromycin, in which case isolate for 7 days from starting the antibiotic).

*The incubation period of a disease is the time from exposure to the disease until the first symptoms show.

difficult to know when to isolate a child. However, in some cases it is necessary for other members of the family or friends to be protected from an infectious disease. Your doctor can advise you about how best to do this. The chart above gives quarantine periods for the most common infectious diseases in childhood.

R

Rash
(See **Eczema, Nappy rash, Prickly heat, Urticaria**)

Rickets
A lack of sunlight on the skin is the most common cause of rickets. Sunlight enables the skin to make vitamin D, which is also obtained from fatty foods such as milk, fish, liver and cod liver oil, and what helps to control the amount of calcium in the body. Calcium helps build strong bones and teeth and, as a result of calcium deficiency, children with rickets have soft bones which may become deformed (for example, leg bowing). There may be some swelling at the wrists and ankles.

A few hours spent outside every day in the summer will help to build up body stores of vitamin D for the winter. Rickets is unusual in the developed world today because of improved nutrition, but a vitamin D supplement may be advisable for children who don't have enough sun or whose diet is very poor.

Ringworm
This condition is caused by a fungal infection. It results in red scaly circles on the skin which may be very itchy. The scalp, body, groin, nails and feet may all be affected. When it affects the feet it is known as athlete's foot. Ringworm on the body is sometimes contracted from an infected pet. You can clear ringworm with anti-fungal ointment or tablets from the doctor. Alternatively, smooth on two drops of lemongrass oil mixed with a teaspoon of calendula cream, or one drop of eucalyptus oil mixed with a teaspoon of jojoba oil.

Other ways to help remedy the situation include vacuuming carpets and upholstery more often if you have pets; washing clothes, bed-linen and towels more frequently; and not sharing towels and flannels. Take a pet that is scratching a lot to the vet.

Rubella
Rubella (German measles), is an infectious viral disease. It produces a red blotchy rash, a mild fever and enlargement of the lymph nodes (glands) at the back of the neck. It is not a serious disease when it is caught by children and generally lasts for only a few days. However, if the disease is contracted during pregnancy (particularly in the first three months), it can damage the baby in the womb. Because of this very serious complication it is now recommended that all children should be immunized against rubella in their second year. Rubella immunization is usually combined with measles and mumps in the one-shot MMR vaccine (measles, mumps and rubella).

Any child with rubella is highly infectious to other people who have not had the disease from a few days before the rash appears to one day after the symptoms go. If the child comes into contact with a pregnant woman during this time, you should advise her to consult a doctor immediately.

(See also Quarantine)

S

Scalds
(*See* **Emergencies, page 310**)

Scoliosis
Scoliosis is an abnormal curvature of the spine. It is an uncommon condition which may be caused by an abnormality of the bones, nerves or muscles of the back, although in some cases no underlying cause is found. A child with scoliosis will probably be referred by the doctor to an orthopaedic surgeon (bone specialist) who will give advice on how to manage the condition.

Sickle cell disease
Sickle cell disease is an inherited blood condition which affects some people of African, Indian and Mediterranean origin. It results in anaemia and episodes of pain in various parts of the body due to blockages of the blood vessels. These episodes of pain are known as 'sickle cell crises' and are often provoked by infections. A child with sickle cell disease has two abnormal sickle cell genes in each body cell. If a child has a single abnormal sickle cell gene in each cell (sickle cell trait) he will only suffer from mild anaemia and is unlikely to have problems.

There is no cure for sickle cell disease, but blood transfusions can correct anaemia and prompt medical treatment helps to relieve the painful crises. A child with sickle cell disease has inherited an abnormal gene from each of his parents and the parents have a one-in-four chance of having a similarly affected child in each subsequent pregnancy. Screening tests of newborn babies identify those who are affected so that they can be given daily penicillin and folic acid (a B vitamin) to reduce ill health.

Sleep walking
Sleep walking is more likely to occur in children of school age than younger children. The cause is unknown, but it may be associated with periods of stress, such as starting school, so try to find out if your child is worried about anything. A child found sleep walking should be gently directed back to bed.

Children who walk in their sleep rarely harm themselves, but this can happen. If a child has a tendency to sleep walk, make sure that there are no immediate dangers (for example, an open window).

Sore throat
Four out of five sore throats are caused by viral infection and the rest by bacteria. The tonsils usually become inflamed and so does the back of the throat. Acute inflammation is known as tonsillitis. A sore throat can occur by itself or with a cold or infection of the ears (otitis media) or sinuses. Apart from soreness of the throat, there may be tummyache and earache, a fever, irritability, loss of appetite, a cough, a runny nose and swollen lymph nodes (glands) in the neck. Mild sore throats usually last for only a few days and need no treatment.

Keep your child at home while he feels ill, cool him down if he has a fever, and let him eat and drink as he wants. A twice-daily cup of echinacea tea sweetened with a little honey is thought to boost immunity. Alternatively, you can offer a twice-daily glass of hot lemon and honey, made by pouring 600ml (1 pint) of very hot water over the juice and rind of two lemons and adding honey to taste. You may help your child feel better and speed recovery by giving foods rich in vitamin C and flavonoids, or a supplement of these nutrients. Your child may feel more comfortable with a scarf around his neck, but take care that a young child doesn't become over-heated, especially if he has a fever.

If very carefully supervised, an older child may find that an inhalation of scented steam soothes his throat; the steam may also help kill off a viral infection. Fill a bowl with very hot water, and add a teaspoon of menthol and eucalyptus inhalation mixture (from the phamacy), or two drops each of eucalyptus and tea tree oils. Sit the child with his head over the bowl. Put a towel over his head and the bowl and let him breathe in the vapour for five minutes.

Don't let anyone smoke at home, as smoke irritates an inflamed throat. Because some sore throats are due to bacterial infection, and because one sort of streptococcal bacterial infection can occasionally lead to kidney inflammation (nephritis) or rheumatic fever, some doctors like to give antibiotics every time, while others prefer to send a throat swab off for tests and only give antibiotics if these tests suggest they are necessary. Any complication of a sore throat, such as an ear infection, sinusitis, or laryngitis, may need further medical treatment.

Get medical help if the child finds it difficult to breathe, or starts to breathe noisily.

Speech disorder
(*See* **Stuttering**)

Splinters
(*See* **First aid, page 313**)

Sprains
(*See* **First aid, page 313**)

Squint
A squint is when the eyes do not look in exactly the same direction. It may result from short-sightedness in one eye or an imbalance in the control of the eye movements. Newborn babies sometimes have a temporary squint

The Eye

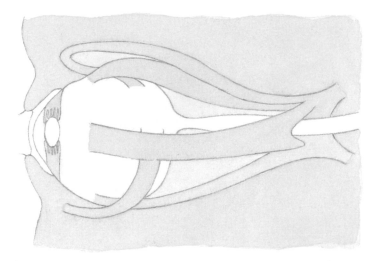

1. Eyeball	**3.** Eyelid
2. Muscles	**4.** Optic nerve

*A **squint** results when the muscles controlling each eye fail to co-ordinate the eye movements.*

which they quickly lose as control of the eyes develops. However, a persistent squint may prevent proper development of vision, so any child or baby who appears to have one should be seen by a doctor, who may refer him to an ophthalmologist (eye specialist). The treatment which the specialist recommends depends on the underlying cause, but may involve patching the good eye to encourage the squinting one to work harder. Occasionally the problem requires surgical correction.

Stammering
(See Stuttering)

Sticky eye
(See Conjunctivitis)

Stings
(See First aid, page 313)

Stomach upsets
(See Gastroenteritis)

Stuttering
Children between the ages of three and four often stumble or stutter over words when they are excited or trying to describe something that has just

happened. This is a normal phase of language development which generally disappears by the time the child goes to school. Faltering speech is not helped by an authoritarian attitude, so it is better not to tell the child to slow down and repeat what he is saying because this may frustrate and inhibit him. If he does stutter, listen to him patiently and try not to draw attention to it.

Should the problem persist, consult your doctor who will probably refer you to a speech therapist who can provide further advice.

Styes
A stye is a pimple, or tiny boil, at the base of an eyelash. The doctor will prescribe an antibiotic ointment to treat this, but cotton-wool soaked in warm water and applied to the stye may help to alleviate discomfort in the first place. Styes usually heal in a few days.

Sudden infant death syndrome
(See Cot death)

Sunburn
Babies and young children have very delicate skin and can become

sunburnt easily, so it is important not to expose them to too much direct sunlight. If the child is out in the sun for any length of time, make sure that they are protected with a sun hat and sun cream. A pram or pushchair canopy can provide protection from the sun for a baby.

If sunburn does occur it is often not be noticeable straight away, but appear some hours later in the form of reddened tender skin and possibly blisters. Soothe slightly sunburnt skin by applying cool water, calamine lotion or aloe vera gel. Other remedies include calendula cream or a compress soaked in cold chamomile tea. Make this tea with a teabag, or by adding a cup of boiling water to a teaspoon of dried chamomile flowers (or two teaspoons of fresh ones). Steep for five minutes, and then strain them. Cool the tea before applying the compress to the skin. Some after-sun lotions are also very soothing: choose ones containing vitamins.

A supplement of beta-carotene and vitamins C and E may also help the skin to heal. However, if the sunburn is severe, give the child plenty of fluids and speak to a doctor to get further advice immediately.

Swallowed objects
(See First aid, page 313)

Swollen lymph nodes (glands)
The lymph nodes are situated throughout the body, but can sometimes be felt in the groin, armpits and neck when they become swollen in response to infection. For example, with a sore throat the neck nodes become enlarged as a defence mechanism and can be felt as small rubbery lumps under the skin. As the infection settles they gradually return to their normal size. If your child has persistently enlarged nodes he should see a doctor in case something else is wrong.

The Lymph Nodes

1. Cervical lymph nodes ('glands')
2. Axillary lymph nodes ('glands')
3. Inguinal lymph nodes ('glands')

The lymph nodes ('glands') are part of the body's defence system. Sometimes they swell while they are fighting an infection. The main groups of nodes are in the neck, the armpits and the groin.

302

T

Temperature
(See Fever)

Testes
The testes are the male sexual glands which develop in the abdomen prior to birth. While the baby is still in the womb, the testes move down from the abdomen into the scrotum. Occasionally this descent is incomplete at the time of birth so that one or both of the testes are undescended and cannot be felt in the scrotum.

Most undescended testes come down into the scrotum during the first year, but when this does not happen, a small operation can fix the testes in the scrotum where they can develop normally.

A retractile testis is one that intermittently escapes from the scrotum into the groin. It differs from an undescended testis in that it can be coaxed down into the scrotum and requires no treatment as it will remain permanently in place in time.

Torsion of a testis occurs when it twists on its stalk. This causes sudden pain in the testis, the child may feel sick and vomit and the testis may be swollen and tender. If a child has these symptoms, consult your doctor at once. The condition will have to be treated surgically.

The Testes

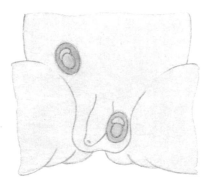

1. Undescended testis
2. Scrotum
3. Testis in correct position

Tetanus
Tetanus is a serious illness caused by a type of bacteria that lives in soil, dust and water. The bacteria gain access to the body through open wounds and produce a toxic substance which puts the muscles of the body into spasm. The condition can be prevented by a tetanus immunization, which all children should have during the first year of life. A tetanus booster is given at the age of five, or to any child who sustains a dirty injury and has not had a booster for the past five years.
(See also Immunization chart, page 131)

Thalassaemia
Thalassaemia is an inherited blood condition which affects the blood cells and results in anaemia. The thalassaemia gene is found quite frequently in people of Mediterranean, African or Asian extraction. A single abnormal thalassaemia gene in each body cell (thalassaemia minor) does not cause significant anaemia, but if a child has two abnormal genes in each cell (thalassaemia major) she will develop anaemia and require regular blood transfusions and therapy. A child with thalassaemia major has inherited one abnormal gene from each parent and the parents will have a one-in-four chance of producing another affected child in each subsequent pregnancy.

Threadworms
A number of worms can live as parasites in the bowels. The most common are threadworms, which live in the lower bowel and lay their eggs around the anus. These tiny worms do not usually cause any symptoms, but they may make the child's bottom itchy. The eggs are too small to be seen with the naked eye, but occasionally worms may be seen around the anus or on the bedding; they are about 1cm ($\frac{1}{2}$in) long and look like slender white threads. The infection is passed on by scratching the bottom, getting the eggs on to hands and then putting the fingers into the mouth.

The doctor may ask you to put some sticky tape over part of the child's bottom at night so that she can examine the tape under the microscope the next day and see if there are any worms or eggs. Threadworms are common in schoolchildren and can easily be eradicated with a special medicine which your doctor will prescribe.

Thrush
(See Mouth infections, Nappy rash)

Tongue tie

Sometimes the tissue that joins the tongue to the floor of the mouth extends to the tip of the tongue and stops it from protruding normally. In the vast majority of cases this presents no problem to the child and improves as she gets older, but very rarely a tongue tie may be tight enough to prevent a child from making certain sounds properly. In this situation a simple operation is needed to release the tongue.

The Tonsils

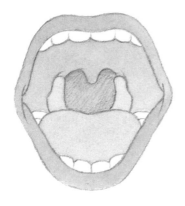

1. Palate   3. Inflamed tonsils
2. Tongue

The tonsils are two pieces of lymphoid tissue which may become swollen and inflamed due to infection, causing a sore throat.

Tonsillitis

The tonsils are patches of lymph tissue on either side of the back of the throat. Tonsillitis occurs when the tonsils become inflamed due to a bacterial or viral infection. The child with tonsillitis has a sore throat and fever, and may feel generally unwell and be off her food. The lymph nodes under the chin and neck, which drain the tonsils, also become enlarged. If bacterial tonsillitis is suspected the doctor will prescribe antibiotics; otherwise treatment includes paracetamol elixir and plenty to drink. You can also use the home remedies suggested for a sore throat.

Tonsillitis usually gets better after three to four days. Removal of the tonsils used to be carried out very often, but it is now usually considered to be unnecessary.

Toothache

Toothache can be caused by decay of a tooth (caries), inflammation of the root of a tooth (a tooth abscess) or a gum infection. Sometimes pain caused by inflammation of the ear or jaw-bone can feel like toothache. A child with toothache should be seen by a dentist first, but if the dentist can find nothing wrong with the child's teeth, consult your doctor.

Travel sickness

Travel or motion sickness is a tendency to feel sick and vomit while travelling. It is the movement which causes the sickness, so it can occur in a plane, boat, car or even on a merry-go-round. If your child readily vomits in such situations, encourage her to sit still during journeys, preferably by an open window and looking in the direction in which she is travelling.

Antihistamines may be helpful in preventing travel sickness, but they should be taken at least half an hour before the start of the journey.

One useful tip for preventing travel sickness is to give your child some form of ginger. One idea is ginger tea, made from a ginger teabag, or by pouring 600ml (1 pint) of boiling water over 50g (2oz) of grated fresh ginger root, boiling for ten minutes, straining and sweetening as desired. You can take this with you in a vacuum flask. Another idea is for your child can suck a piece of crystallized ginger.

Acupressure may help travel sickness. Press on the point two little-finger-widths up your child's arm from the centre of the crease on the inside of the wrist. Continue until the child feels better, or until you can see that it clearly isn't working. Most

children grow out of motion sickness in time.

Tuberculosis

Tuberculosis (TB) is a bacterial disease which primarily causes inflammation of the lungs. However, it can affect other parts of the body, such as the brain, neck lymph nodes ('glands'), bones and kidneys. Treatment for the disease is with antibiotics and therapy has to be continued for some months. During the early part of this century it was a relatively common disease in the UK. Now it occurs only rarely, though it is becoming a little more common among some immigrant groups and drug users. It is acquired either through close contact with someone who has TB of the lung or by drinking milk from infected cattle. Since 1960, TB has been virtually eliminated from cattle in the UK. Immunization with the vaccine BCG can be used to protect young children with an increased risk of catching tuberculosis. Occasionally, where there is felt to be a particular risk of contracting the disease, BCG vaccination is given to babies soon after birth.

Tummy-ache

Tummyache or abdominal pain is a common childhood complaint with many causes, most of which are not serious. Children can have tummy-ache with something as simple as a sore throat or cold. This is because the lymph nodes ('glands') in the abdomen become enlarged as part of the body's reaction to the infection, causing irritation to the bowel and thus pain. This type of pain settles without treatment, but make sure your child takes plenty of fluids.

Sometimes children complain of tummyaches when they are anxious. These pains are similar to the tension headaches which some adults develop when stressed. In between the bouts of pain the child is well and no treatment is required, but it may be helpful to find out what is upsetting them. This occurs more frequently in schoolchildren than toddlers.

Tummyache may also occur with other symptoms. When accompanied by frequent vomiting or a change in the bowel motions (diarrhoea or constipation) it could be caused by an infection of the bowel, such as gastroenteritis, by appendicitis or by an obstruction in the bowel. A tummyache combined with blood in the bowel motions may be caused by a bowel infection or obstruction. If the child is urinating very frequently, the pain may be due to a urinary infection. A child who has any one of these complaints appears unwell, loses her appetite and energy and may be feverish. The pain probably comes and goes, but even when it is not acute the child is not her usual self.

Other causes of tummyache include food sensitivity, asthma, sickle cell anaemia, cystic fibrosis, diabetes, lead poisoning and indigestion. A child who experiences severe or prolonged abdominal pain, particularly if associated with any of the above symptoms, should be seen by a doctor.
(See also Appendicitis, Colic, Gastroenteritis, Urinary tract infections)

Typhoid
(See Holiday health, page 279)

U

Ulcers
(See Mouth infections)

Upper respiratory tract infection
Infections of the upper respiratory tract encompass coughs, colds, tonsillitis and otitis media. These

are often caused by viruses and are generally less serious than those infections of the lower respiratory tract, such as bronchitis, bronchiolitis and pneumonia.

Urinary tract infections
The urinary tract includes the kidneys, ureters, bladder and urethra. Urinary tract infection can involve all or part of this system. When the kidneys are primarily involved the condition is called pyelonephritis; when the infection is mainly in the bladder it is popularly called cystitis.

Urinary infections are caused by bacteria. The symptoms may include fever, pain on passing urine, needing to pass urine more frequently than usual, passing blood in the urine, abdominal pain, vomiting, irritability, unwillingness to feed and loose motions. A urine sample can be tested to discover what sort of infection (if any) is present. If the child is very young, the doctor will provide a special bag for collecting the urine sample.

If urine infection is confirmed, the child should be given plenty of fluid and the doctor will prescribe the appropriate antibiotics.

Cranberries can help a child with a urine infection. This is because pigments (flavonoids called proanthocyandins) from the berries enter the urine and make it hard for bacteria to stick to the inside of the bladder. Your child can drink cranberry juice, take cranberry extract tablets or eat cranberry sauce twice a day.

Other helpful foods include asparagus, beetroot and raw garlic. Ease symptoms with home-made lemon barley water, made by boiling barley in water for forty-five minutes, straining and flavouring with lemon juice and honey. Alternatively, make the urine less acid by adding half a level teaspoon of sodium bicarbonate to every third glass of fluid the child drinks, or giving potassium citrate

or flavoured 'cystitis salts' (from the pharmacy) in the right dose for your child's age.

When the course of antibiotics is finished, a urine sample should again be checked to make sure that the infection has been eliminated. Some children need further investigation to rule out an underlying urinary tract abnormality.

Urinary System

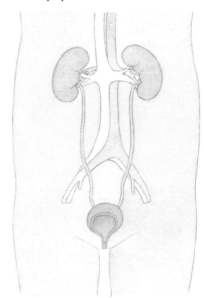

| **1.** Kidney | **3.** Bladder |
| **2.** Ureter | **4.** Urethra |

Urine is filtered by the kidneys and passed to the bladder, from where it is expelled from the body via the urethra. Urine infection can be caused by bacteria spreading from the urethra to the bladder, and can pass up to the kidneys.

Urticaria
Urticaria (also known as nettle rash or hives) is an allergic skin reaction which results in itchy weals and blotches. The rash usually clears up after a few days, but calamine lotion may be soothing and antihistamines can reduce itchiness.

Urticaria can be caused by allergy to certain foods, by stinging nettles, pollens, drugs, flea bites, infections and physical factors, such as water or cold weather.

V

Vaginal infection

A vaginal discharge of thick white mucus is normal in newborn girls; occasionally it is accompanied by a small amount of blood staining. Both symptoms result from the effect of the mother's hormones on the glands of the baby's cervix, but they usually disappear in the first two weeks.

In young girls the skin of the vulva and vagina is very delicate so that irritation or infection can easily cause inflammation and a discharge. Tight trousers and rough-textured tights should be avoided as they rub against the skin. Some types of bubble bath also cause irritation. Occasionally the bottom scratching associated with threadworms can damage the vulval skin and cause a slight infection. If a child has a sore vulva, with or without a discharge, it may be helpful to use mild soap for washing, avoid bubble bath and see that she wears cotton pants. Your doctor may prescribe a hormone cream to increase the skin's resistance to irritation. If the discharge is due to a bacterial infection, antibiotics will be prescribed to treat it.

Occasionally little girls push small objects into their vagina. This can result in a persistent infection and discharge, which will only clear when the object is removed.

Verruca
(See Warts)

Vomiting

Vomiting is the expulsion of the stomach contents due to infection, or because of an obstruction to the passage of food in the bowel. Sometimes it is not significant and may relate to a minor infection such as a cold or tonsillitis, but if the vomiting is persistent and occurs with a tummyache, headache, diarrhoea or feeding difficulties, or if your child seems generally unwell, consult your doctor.

Vomiting should not be confused with possetting, which is when babies regurgitate a small amount of excess milk after a feed.

W

Warts

These are small skin growths caused by viruses. They are common in childhood and not serious, although they may be uncomfortable and unsightly. Warts are usually found on the fingers, hands and elbows, and there may be one or more. Consult your doctor about treatment. Chemical paints or freezing with carbon dioxide snow may get rid of the warts, but sometimes they recur after treatment. If left alone they disappear by themselves.

A verruca is a wart on the sole of the foot. Because of its position in the thick skin under the foot it produces a small hard lump. A verruca is painless, except when a child is standing or walking, when it presses into the foot and may feel like a pebble in the shoe. Verrucas can be treated in the same way as other warts, but the doctor may also pare down the lump of hard skin so that it does not press into the foot. None of the numerous home remedies for warts are guaranteed, but you might still want to try. They include painting with clear nail varnish; putting on a plaster soaked in cider vinegar, or containing a sliver of raw garlic, and changing it daily; and dabbing with tea tree oil.

Wax in ears

It is natural for yellow wax to be formed in the ear canals. Its function is to cleanse the ear of dust particles and protect the ear lining. When cleaning your child's ears it is only necessary to wipe wax from outside. Do not poke deep into the ear with the edge of a towel or a cotton wool bud as you could damage the eardrum.

Wheezing
(See Asthma, Bronchitis)

Whooping cough

Whooping cough, or pertussis, is a respiratory infection caused by bacteria. It generally begins with a cold, followed a few days later by a cough characterized by a whooping sound as the child catches his breath. The cough comes in spasms and usually makes the child red in the face. He may also vomit after an episode of coughing. The number of coughing bouts per day varies and the condition may continue for several weeks, with the child remaining infectious for up to three weeks after the cough begins.

Whooping cough is most dangerous in small babies because the coughing spasms interfere with normal breathing and feeding. If you notice any of these symptoms consult your doctor at once. Once whooping cough is established, antibiotics will not alter its course, but they may make the child less infectious.

Whooping cough can be prevented by immunization. Whooping cough immunization is usually administered with diphtheria and tetanus vaccine, but it may not be recommended if your baby suffers from fits or has brain damage, or if a close relative of the child (parents, brothers or sisters) has a history of fits or epilepsy. If you have any doubts about whether your child should be immunized against whooping cough, consult your doctor. **(See also Immunization chart, page 131)**

Worms
(See Threadworms)

SAFETY AROUND THE HOUSE

Accidents are now the major cause of death for young children, and accidents in the home are second only to road accidents. You need to think ahead and plan how to organize your home before your child reaches the next stage of her development – you may not know that she can crawl until the day she crosses the room and reaches out for the electric fire.

Scalds and burns are among the most common and most serious injuries in the home. Always make sure that fires are properly guarded, saucepan handles are turned inwards out of reach, pans of hot fat and boiling water are not left unattended with children in the room, and pots and cups of hot coffee and tea are not left in reach of little hands. All poisonous substances, such as medicines, bleaches, household cleaners and garden pesticides, should be kept locked away out of reach. Falls are a common risk with small children; make stairs safe by using stairgates, put stops or safety catches on windows, and keep your active baby safely harnessed in her pram, pushchair and highchair.

Make sure that all toys are of a reputable make and put away any sharp or breakable objects which could cut. Avoid loose flexes so your child can't pull heavy objects down on top of her and see that all electrical appliances are safely switched off and put away. Most electric sockets are safe nowadays but remember that a child can get an electric shock if she half-pulls out a plug that is attached to a working appliance and then touches the pins of the plug.

Always make sure that equipment for your child has been checked for safety. Many products are covered by British Standards or other approval or certification schemes. Keep all equipment like pushchairs and swings in good condition by regular maintenance checks.

General safety points
● Keep all open, gas or electric fires guarded, preferably with a fixed guard which attaches to the wall. Never dry clothes over a fireguard.

GARDEN
● Always lock up sheds and garages where you keep garden chemicals and dangerous tools. Don't leave gardening tools lying about.
● Make sure you don't have any poisonous plants.
● Teach your child not to eat any plants or berries from the garden.
● Cover garden pools and rainwater butts securely or get rid of them. Never leave buckets of water around.
● Supervise water play all the time.
● Fit a child-proof catch to the garden gate.
● Make sure that children don't play with cats' and dogs' excrement. Keep sandpits covered.
● Make sure that climbing frames, swings and all outdoor play equipment are in good order.
● Always use a pram net to protect your baby from insects.

BATHROOM
● Keep all medicines, cosmetics, household cleaners and razor blades well out of reach, preferably in a cupboard with a childproof lock.
● Run the bath before the child gets in and check that the water is not too hot. Never leave your child unattended in the bath as she could drown in even a few centimetres of water.
● Never use a portable electric fire in the bathroom.
● Adjust the thermostat so the water is never dangerously hot.
● Keep the lavatory seat down.

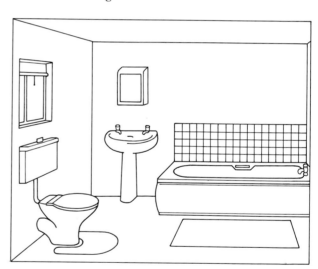

LIVING ROOM
● Keep all breakable objects out of reach.
● Use cable clips to secure trailing flexes.
● Disconnect your television when not in use.
● Don't put hot drinks on a low table and keep alcoholic drinks out of a child's reach.
● Never hold or pass hot drinks over your baby.
● Make sure that rugs cannot slip under your feet. Use non-slip floor polish.
● Make sure shelves and bookcases are secure and can't be pulled over.

● Put safety film over glass-panel doors and table-tops or fit safety glass.

● Fit safety covers to electric sockets not in use.

● Use safety plugs and plugs with lights which show when they're switched on.

● Keep cigarettes, cigars, lighters and matches out of a child's reach.

● Never leave plastic bags lying around or store them within a child's reach.

● Fit safety catches or window stops to all windows that are above ground level, and all cupboards and drawers.

● Put away keys to all doors so that your child can't lock herself into a room or outside the house where you can't get to her.

● Never lock a child into a room.

HALLWAYS AND STAIRS

● Keep hallways well lit. Never leave toys lying around where you could trip over them.

● Hold on to the banister while carrying a child downstairs.

● Check that banisters are secure and that a small child can't get between the rails.

● Always use a safety gate on the stairs and make sure the gate at the top is closed at night once a young child can get out of bed unaided.

● Don't let your child walk around carrying things like scissors or sharp pencils in case she falls on them.

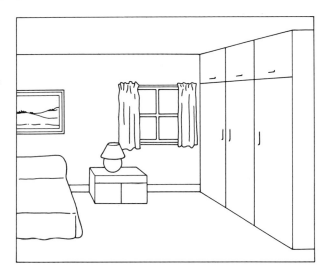

BEDROOMS

● Don't leave cosmetics, perfumes, breakables, nail scissors and so on within a child's reach.

● Make sure that wardrobe doors can be opened from the inside in case your child gets shut in. Make sure cupboards are not top-heavy and can't be pulled over.

● Don't leave an electric blanket on if the child is alone in the room.

● Disconnect and put away electrical equipment such as hairdriers when not in use.

CHILDREN'S ROOM

● Make sure that all equipment is stable and toys are safe.

● Store any toys for older children which contain tiny pieces out of reach of young ones.

● Never use a pillow for a baby under one year old.

● Never put your child to sleep with a bib on, or a garment with drawstrings round the neck, as they could catch on something and strangle her.

● Remove hot-water bottles before you put your baby or child to bed.

● Nightwear should not be made of inflammable fabric.

307

KITCHEN

● When possible, keep your child out of the kitchen.

● Keep all bleach, household cleaners and detergents well out of reach, preferably in a locked cupboard.

● Turn all saucepan handles inwards and fit a cooker or hob guard. Don't let your child play with the knobs.

● Never leave a chip pan unattended.

● Make sure your child is sitting at the table or harnessed in her highchair before you serve hot food.

● Make sure your child can't get at the rubbish bin.

● Always disconnect electrical appliances when not in use. Use curly flexes where possible.

● Avoid highly polished floors and loose mats or rugs. Always wipe up spills immediately.

● Don't use long tablecloths which a child can pull.

● Keep knives and other sharp tools out of reach or in drawers or cupboards with safety catches fitted.

● Keep a fibreglass cloth handy to smother any fires.

● Never leave an iron or kettle where a child can pull it down.

EMERGENCIES

EMERGENCY ACTION

If you are alone, urgent first aid is your priority. If someone is with you, one of you can get help.

● If it is a serious accident – dial 999 immediately and call an ambulance.
● For an emergency such as suspected poisoning, take the child to the nearest hospital accident and emergency department.
● In less urgent situations phone the doctor or hospital.
● Do not give the child anything to drink after an accident in case he needs an anaesthetic.

As a parent, there may be a time when quick and knowledgeable action on your part could save your child's life. Learning first aid skills from a book is not easy, especially with techniques such as mouth-to-mouth ventilation and heart massage for which you really need detailed instruction and practice. Find out who runs first aid courses locally and take the trouble to go along. The British Red Cross Society, St John Ambulance and the Royal Life Saving Society organize such courses (see Useful Addresses, page 314). The Royal Society for the Prevention of Accidents runs road safety classes

through Tufty Clubs, and you can find out where your nearest classes are from RoSPA. Many public swimming pools run special classes to teach young children to swim. These can be great fun, as well as giving your child a skill which could save his life.

A child should always be taken to hospital after an accident if he is unconscious, in pain, drowsy or vomiting, has bleeding or a discharge from the ears or nose or has lost a lot of blood. Find out where your nearest accident and emergency department is and plan how you would get there in an emergency.

MOUTH-TO-MOUTH VENTILATION

Learn how to do mouth-to-mouth ventilation (the 'kiss of life') from a trained instructor so you are ready for an emergency.

Check whether your child is breathing by listening with your ear close to her mouth, and watching for chest movements. If your child has stopped breathing, mouth-to-mouth ventilation should be given immediately. Do this even if you think it is too late – it may not be.

The air you breathe into your child's lungs contains enough oxygen to make it a potential life-saver. If there is a telephone nearby and you need to summon help, give ten breaths of mouth-to-mouth ventilation first, then quickly phone before you continue with the ventilation.

1 Lie the child on his back. Clear his mouth of any foreign bodies, blood or vomit.

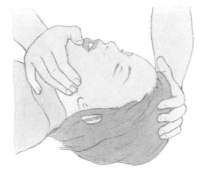

2 Tilt the head back slightly with one hand and lift the chin up and forward with the other so that his tongue is not blocking his throat.

3 Pinch the child's nostrils to close off the nasal airway and seal your mouth over his open mouth (for small children and babies, cover their mouth and nose). Blow into the child's mouth and check that the chest rises.

4 Remove your lips and allow the chest to fall.

5 Give one breath about every three seconds and keep on with this until the child starts to breathe, or professional help arrives.

6 When the child is breathing again, gently turn him over and place him in the recovery position (see right).

HEART MASSAGE (CHEST COMPRESSIONS)

If after the first attempts at mouth-to-mouth ventilation the child is very pale or a blue-grey colour and not breathing, the heart may have stopped.

Check the pulse in the child's neck (just below the jaw bone and in line with the earlobe) and, if absent, give heart massage as well as mouth-to-mouth ventilation.

Lie the child on his back and kneel beside him.

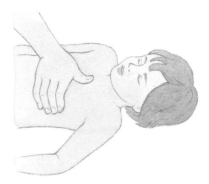

1 For a child of one year or more, press gently but firmly on the lower part of his breastbone with the heel of your hand. Press down to a depth of 3cm (1¼in) (at a rate of about 100 compressions per minute – that's faster than one a second).

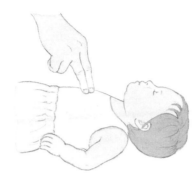

1 For a baby, use two fingers and press down to a depth of 2cm (¾in), about 100 compressions per minute.

2 After every five compressions give one mouth-to-mouth ventilation. If there is someone with you, one of you can do heart massage, stopping after five compressions for the other to breathe into the child's lungs. This means you'll do about twenty breaths a minute into the child's lungs. Check for a pulse at least every three minutes.

3 Once you can feel the child's pulse, stop heart massage. Carry on with mouth-to-mouth ventilation until breathing starts, or a doctor or ambulance crew arrives to take over.

THE RECOVERY POSITION

It is dangerous for someone who is unconscious to be lying on their back as the throat can be blocked by the tongue or by vomit. If the child is unconscious or drowsy but breathing place him in the recovery position, propping a baby if necessary.

1 Kneel beside the child, tilt his head back and lift his chin up, then straighten his legs. Put the nearest arm at right angles to the body, elbow bent and palm uppermost. Bring the furthest arm across the chest, holding the hand, palm outwards, against the child's cheek nearest you.

2 Using your other hand, pull the knee furthest from you up, with the foot flat on the ground. Pull that leg's thigh towards you to roll the child on to his side. The hip and knee of this upper leg should now be bent at right angles. Tilt the head back to keep the airway open.

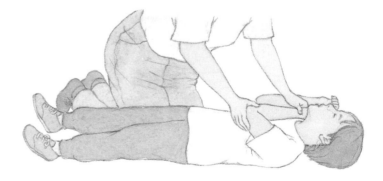

EMERGENCIES

BURNS AND SCALDS

A burn can be caused by fire, chemicals, electricity or contact with a very hot object. A scald is caused by steam or hot liquid.

A burn or scald is serious if it covers a large area, is very deep or is on the face or any other particularly sensitive part of the body. The danger with serious burns or scalds is that fluid (plasma) can be lost from the skin. This is particularly serious in young children, when it can rapidly lead to **shock** (see opposite).

1 Immerse the burnt or scalded area in cold water for at least ten minutes to take the heat out of the skin.

2 Take off tight clothes as the skin will swell up.

3 For a serious burn, call the doctor or take the child to hospital.

For minor burns or scalds, put a clean non-fluffy cloth or gauze (or even clingfilm) over the burn to stop it from becoming infected.

CLOTHES ON FIRE

If there is plenty of water to hand, douse the child's clothing with it. If not, get him on to the ground and smother the flames by covering him with a heavy rug, blanket, towel or coat. **Don't** use synthetic fabrics.

As a last resort, use your own body to smother the flames. However, make sure there is no gap between your bodies where air might get through and fan the flames. When the flames are smothered, immerse the burnt area in cold water. If clothes

are stuck to the skin, **don't** pull them off and **don't** burst any blisters. Give the child sips of water and take him to hospital immediately.

CHOKING

First look in mouth and remove any **obvious** object.

1 **For a child over one year**, lie him over your knee with his head down. Give him five sharp slaps between his shoulder blades to dislodge the object.

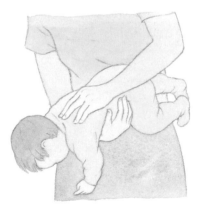

1 **For a baby**, hold him face down over your arm (or pick him up by his legs and hold him upside down) and give him five sharp slaps between the shoulder blades.

2 Check mouth again for easily removed object. Don't remove anything at the back of the throat as you may wedge it in further.

● If this doesn't work, **for a child**, give five chest thrusts similar to chest compressions but slower (about 20 per minute). Follow with five further back slaps. If necessary, follow this by lying the child face up and giving five short sharp thrusts to the upper

abdomen (between the navel and breastbone). Repeat the sequence of back thrusts, chest thrusts, back slaps, abdominal thrusts.

● **For a baby,** follow the five back slaps with five chest thrusts and repeat the sequence of back slaps with chest thrusts. Do not do abdominal thrusts on a baby.

● Give **mouth-to-mouth ventilation** if breathing stops.

DROWNING

Get your child out of the water, if possible. If it isn't, give emergency first aid in the water.

1 Empty the child's mouth and, if breathing has stopped, **give mouth-to-mouth ventilation.**

2 Send someone to call a doctor or ambulance and carry on with mouth-to-mouth ventilation until help arrives. **Be prepared to start heart massage**.

ELECTRIC SHOCK

Don't touch the child as the shock can be transmitted to you.

1 Switch off the source of electricity at the mains immediately or pull out the plug. If this is not possible, break the electrical contact with something which does not conduct electricity, such as a wooden broom, and push your child away from the wire or socket. If there is water around, do not stand in it as water conducts electricity.

2 Check your child's breathing and, if he is breathing but unconscious, place him in the **recovery position** (see previous page).

Your child may need to be treated for burns or for **shock** (see right) so take him to the nearest hospital with an accident and emergency department or call a doctor without delay.
● If the electric shock is minor, comfort him until he is feeling better.

FRACTURES AND DISLOCATIONS

A fall or injury may cause a bone to fracture or a joint to dislocate. A fracture is when a bone is broken or partly broken; a dislocation occurs when a bone is wrenched out of its socket at a joint (such as the knee, elbow or thumb). It may be difficult to distinguish between a fracture and a dislocation, so follow the same emergency procedure for both. **Don't** move the child unless you have to, especially if you think he might have injured his back or neck. Make him comfortable and get medical help.
● If you have to move the child, immobilize the affected limb.

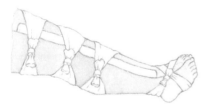

For a broken leg, place some padding between the legs and tie the injured leg gently but firmly to the other leg with bandages.

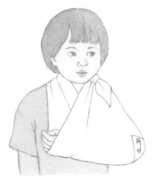

For a broken arm, use a triangular bandage to make a sling. Gently bend the injured arm across the chest and

slide one end of the bandage between the elbow and the chest and over the shoulder. Bring the other end over the arm and wrist, and tie the two ends at one shoulder. Pin the excess bandage carefully at the elbow.

HEAD INJURIES

Bangs on the head are common in childhood and usually cause no lasting harm. Consult your doctor if you think your child is ill or behaving strangely in any way after a blow to the head, even if it is hours after the accident.
● Take your child to hospital if he shows any of the following signs or symptoms: vomiting, drowsiness, dizziness, a severe headache, or a discharge from nose or ear.
● If the child's condition changes, and especially if he becomes unconscious, make sure he is seen by a doctor at once. The child may be concussed or have had a fit which caused the fall.

HEAVY BLEEDING

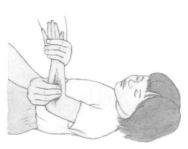

1 Take any piece of clean cloth (such as a laundered handkerchief) – or use your hand – and press firmly on the wound. At the same time, raise the affected area to help stop the bleeding. Keep the child still.

● If there's a bone protruding, or a piece of glass or sharp object in the wound, press around the edges of the wound, not directly on to it. **Don't** remove anything from a wound as it may be acting as a plug to stop the bleeding.

2 To prevent infection, cover the wound with a bandage. Make sure

your child is seen by a doctor as soon as possible as the wound may need stitching.

3 Comfort your child and watch for signs of **shock** (see below).

SHOCK

If a child is pale, sweating and unwell after an accident, he may be suffering from shock, which can be a serious condition. Other signs of shock are: faintness and nausea; rapid pulse and breathing, and delirium.

Make the child lie down with his head turned to one side. Loosen clothing and raise his legs. Keep him warm but not too hot (for example, lightly cover him with a blanket but don't give him a hot-water bottle). If the child becomes unconscious, place him in the recovery position and seek medical help immediately. If the child is conscious, but remains shaken by the experience, you should consult your doctor.

POISONING

If you suspect that your child may have swallowed something poisonous, take him to hospital immediately. If you know what your child has swallowed, take the container to the hospital, too, so that they know what kind of poison it is and how to treat it.
● If the child is vomiting, hold him with his body bent forward so that he can't choke.
Don't try to make the child sick by giving salty drinks, or by any other method – you could cause more harm, especially if what he's swallowed is corrosive.
● If the child has swallowed corrosive poison which has burnt his lips, and if he is still conscious, give him frequent sips of cold milk or water.

SMOTHERING/SUFFOCATION

1 Quickly remove whatever has smothered the child.

2 If he has stopped breathing, give him mouth-to-mouth ventilation (see page 308).

FIRST AID TREATMENT

The entries on these pages cover the less serious injuries and scrapes of childhood. It is a good idea to keep a first aid box (see below) in your home for such eventualities, so that you can act at once if your child is hurt. The box should be kept in a safe place, out of reach of children, but not locked away where you might not be able to get it easily when you're in a hurry.

Animal bites

If the bite is superficial, clean the wound with warm water and apply a sterile dressing if necessary. If it's a serious wound, or on your child's face, take him to a doctor at once. For both minor and more serious wounds, your child may need a tetanus booster, if he has not had one recently. See also Snake bite.

Blisters

Blisters usually occur as a result of friction or a burn. Never prick a blister as it forms a protective layer between the skin and damaged area which protects against infection. Cover the blister with a non-adherent dressing kept in place with sticking plaster. If the blister bursts, keep it clean and dry.

Convulsions

Never leave a child during a convulsion (fit) in case he vomits and chokes.

Put him in the **recovery position** (page 309) and loosen his clothing. *Don't* try to restrain him.

When the convulsion is over the child may be confused, or drift off to sleep. Always seek medical advice.

Crushed fingers

This is a fairly common accident with small children, who may inadvertently trap their fingers.

Comfort your child as the wound will be painful and run his hand under cold water, or apply a cold compress, to help ease the pain and swelling. Painkillers are not necessary, but you could cover the hand loosely with a clean handkerchief to protect it from further knocks.

If the pain doesn't subside after a few hours, or if there is any damage to the fingers, consult your doctor.

Cuts and grazes

If a wound is deep or bleeding profusely, follow the advice for heavy bleeding (page 311).

Minor cuts and grazes can be treated at home. Clean the wound with warm water, wiping from the middle outwards. Use each swab once only to help prevent cross-infection. Pat the skin round the cut or graze, dry and cover with a dressing or sticking plaster.

Eye injuries

Small objects, such as grit or dirt, can usually be washed out of the eye by bathing with water. If you can see a foreign body in the eye, remove it gently with the tip of a clean handkerchief before bathing. *Don't* let your child rub the eye, especially if you think something sharp has got into it.

If your child's eye has been injured in any way, take him to the doctor or to the hospital accident and emergency department.

If the injury has been caused by a chemical, put the child's head on one side and flush the eye with cold water. Be sure to wash from the inside corner of the eye outwards. This ensures that chemicals are not washed across the face and possibly into the other eye. Apply an eye pad and take the child to hospital at once.

Foreign body in the ear

Don't try to remove the object yourself as you may wedge it in more firmly. Take the child to the doctor or local hospital – a nurse or doctor will probably syringe the ear to get the foreign body out.

If an insect has gone into the ear, lie the child on his side and gently pour warm water into it so that the insect floats to the surface. If this doesn't work, get medical help. *Don't* pour water into the ear if the child has grommets fitted (these are tiny tubes used to treat glue ear), or if there is a foreign body other than an insect, as it could cause the object to swell.

Foreign body in the nose

An unpleasant discharge from one nostril is often a sign that something has been pushed into the nose. Tell the child to blow through the affected nostril, while you cover the other one.

If this is not successful in dislodging the object, take the child to hospital or to the doctor's surgery.

FIRST AID BOX

- Box of assorted sticking plasters
- Packet of absorbent cotton wool
- Box of sterile gauze dressings
- Roll of 5 cm (2 in) gauze bandage
- Non-adhesive sterile dressings (for burns and blisters)
- 2 or 3 crêpe bandages for sprains
- Sterilized eye pad with bandages
- Large triangular bandage, or a piece of clean white linen, to use as a sling or dressing for burns and scalds
- Safety pins and surgical tape for securing bandages
- Scissors
- Blunt-ended tweezers
- Paracetamol elixir
- Calamine lotion for soothing sunburn and stings
- Thermometer or fever strip
- Tube of eye ointment
- Antiseptic wipes for cleaning around a wound

Heatstroke

Never let small children or babies become too hot – they can't control their body temperature very well and should not be in full sunlight for any length of time.

Heatstroke can be a serious condition, so watch out for signs of overheating. For example, if your child becomes restless, very hot or flushed, or unwell with a raised temperature, seek medical advice as soon as possible. In the meantime, keep the child cool and still, remove her clothes, and give her sips of cold water to drink.
(*See also* **Sunburn, page 301**)

Insect bites and stings

Insect bites (such as from a mosquito or flea) can be soothed with calamine lotion. It may help to cover the bites to prevent your child scratching, as this only makes the irritation worse.

A bee or wasp sting can be very painful and alarming. If you can see the sting, pull it out with a pair of tweezers, but if you can't – or it's too deep – don't try to squeeze it out or you'll cause more pain and inflammation. A piece of cotton wool soaked in a solution of bicarbonate of soda (diluted vinegar for a wasp sting) and held over the sting is a good household remedy. A cold compress helps reduce pain and swelling.

If the child has been stung in the mouth there may be a lot of swelling. Call your doctor immediately, and, while you are waiting for him, get the child to rinse his mouth out with a solution of bicarbonate of soda and give him a lump of ice or an ice lolly to suck.

Snake bite

If your child has been bitten by a snake, lie him down and keep him as still as possible to prevent the poison from spreading. *Don't* raise the affected limb. Wash the wound thoroughly with soap and water. Send for medical help, and reassure your child. Tell the doctor what the snake looked like, so that the right anti-venom can be given.

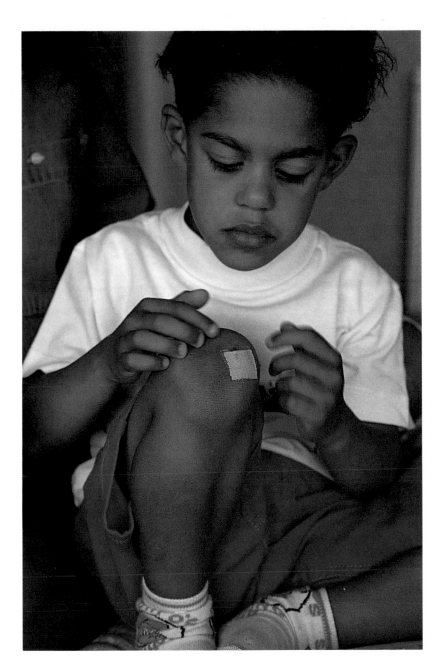

Splinters

Small splinters may work their way out of their own accord, but if there's a bit of the splinter sticking out, you can pull it out with a pair of tweezers. A splinter under the skin can be squeezed and taken out with a sterilized needle that has been passed through a flame and cooled. Calm and reassure your child as you remove the splinter as it is likely to be painful. *Don't* try to pull out a splinter of glass or metal yourself but leave this to the doctor. If the area of skin becomes infected, bathe it in warm water, apply antiseptic cream and take the child to the doctor.

Sprains

Get your child to take his weight off the sprained limb and rest it in a comfortable raised position. Apply a cold compress to ease the swelling.

Swallowed objects

Small children often put small objects into their mouths and may inadvertently swallow them. This is not an emergency unless the object was sharp or the child chokes (see Choking, page 310). Many objects simply pass through the digestive tract and come out at the other end. However, if you are worried, take your child to the doctor.

313

USEFUL ADDRESSES

When writing for information please enclose an SAE.
All addresses are correct at the time of going to press.

PRECONCEPTUAL AND ANTENATAL CARE AND BIRTH

Active Birth Centre
113a Chetwynd Road
London NW5 1DA
Tel: 0171 4825554
Fax: 0171 2679683
Website:
www.activebirthcentre.com
Postnatal courses also available - call for catalogue.

Family Planning Association
(FPA) Helpline
0171 8374044

Foresight Charity
for Preconceptual Care
28 The Paddock
Godalming
Surrey GU7 1XD
Tel:01483 427839

Life
Life House
Newbold Terrace
Leamington Spa CV32 4EA
Tel: 01926 311511
Fax: 01926 336497
website: http://www.lifeuk.org
Practical help and counselling for women with an unplanned pregnancy; post abortion counselling; accomodation for homeless pregnant women.

National Childbirth Trust (NCT)
Alexandra House
Oldham Terrace
London W3 6NH
Tel: 0181 9928637
Fax: 0181 9925929
Information and support during pregnancy, childbirth and early parenthood to help parents to make informed choices.

Pre-Eclampsia Society (PETS)
Eaton Lodge
8 Southend Road
Hockley
Essex
SS5 4QQ
Tel: 01702 205088

Stillbirth and Neonatal
Death Society
28 Portland Place
London
W1N 4DE
Tel: 0171 436 5881

POSTNATAL SUPPORT

Association of
Breastfeeding Mothers
26 Holmshaw Close
London SE26 4TH
Tel: 0171 8131481

The Association for
Postnatal Illness (APNI)
25 Jerdan Place
Fulham
London SW6 1BE
Tel: 0171 3860868
Fax: 0171 386 8885

BLISS
(Baby Life Support Systems)
7-21 Emerald Street
London WC1N 3QL
Tel: 0171 831 9393
Support and information for parents of premature and special care babies.

La Leche League
BM 3424
London WC1N 3XX
Tel: 0171 2421278
Helpline: 0500 618140
Breastfeeding information and counselling.

Meet-a-Mum Association
(MAMA)
58 Malden Avenue
London SE25 4HS
Helpline: 0181 7680123
Contacts for all mothers and support for postnatal depression.

Miscarriage Association
c/o Clayton Hospital
Northgate,Wakefield
West Yorkshire WF1 3JS
Tel: 01924 200799

Twins and Multiple Birth
Association (TAMBA)
Harnott House
309 Chester Road
Little Sutton
South Wirral
L66 1QQ
Tel: 0870 121 4000
 0151 3480020
Fax: 0870 1214001
 0151 3450765

SUPPORT AND
INFORMATION FOR PARENTS

Al-Anon Family Groups
(UK and Eire)
61 Great Dover Street
London SE1 4YF
Tel: 0171 4030888

Al-Anon Information Centre
(Scotland)
50 Warrington Street
Room 338
Glasgow G2
Helpline: 0141 2217356

British Association
for Counselling
1 Regent Place
Rugby
Warwickshire CV21 2PJ
Tel: 01788 578328
Lists of local counsellors.

Marriage Care
Clitherow House
1 Blythe Mews
Blythe Road
London W14 0NW
Tel: 0171 3711341
Fax: 0171 3714921
Website:
http://www.marriagecare.org.uk

Compassionate Friends
53 North Street
Bristol BS3 1EN
Tel: 0117 9665202
*(Administration phoneline and fax number) Helpline: 0117 9539639
Support over the death of a child.*

CRY-SIS Support Group
BM Cry-sis
London WC1N 3XX
Tel: 0171 4045011
Support for parents whose babies cry excessively.

Foundation for the
Study of Infant Deaths
14 Halkin Street
London SW1X 7DP
Tel: 0171 235 0965 (enquiries)
Helpline: 0171 235 1721
Fax: 0171 8231987
Website: http://fids.org.uk/fsid

Gingerbread
16-17 Clerkenwell Close
London EC1R 0AN
Tel: 0171 3358183
Advice line: 0171 3368184
Advice for lone parents and a network of self-help groups. (Freephone number will be available Autumn 1999)

Institute for Complementary
Medicine (ICM)
PO Box 194
London SE16 1QZ
Tel: 0171 2375165
Information about organisations and lists of trained therapists.

National Council for
One Parent Families
255 Kentish Town Road
London NW5 2LX
Tel: 0171 4285400
Helpline: 0800 0185026

Parentline
Endway House
Endway
Hadleigh
Essex, SS7 2AN
Helpline: 01702 559900
Tel: 01702 554782

The Parent Network
Room 2
Winchester House
11 Cranmer Road
London SW9 6EJ
Tel: 0171 7351214

Relate (National Marriage
Guidance)
Herbert Gray College
Little Church Street
Rugby CV21 3AP
Tel: 01788 573241
Fax: 01788 535707

The Samaritans
Head Office
10 The Grove
Slough SL11QOP
Tel: 01753 2165000
Consult your telephone directory for local offices.

National Stepfamily Association
18 Hatton Place
London EC1N 8RU
Tel: 0171 2092460
Helpline: 01702 559900
Support and information for stepfamilies and those who work with them.

SERVICES FOR ALL
CHILDREN IN NEED

Child Poverty Action Group
94 White Lion Street
London N1 9PF
Tel: 0171 8377979

The Children'S Society
Edward Rudolph House
69-85 Margery Street
London WC1X 0JL
Tel: 0171 8414400
Fax: 0171 8370211

Barnardo's
Tanner's Lane
Barkingside
Ilford
Essex, IG6 1QG
Tel: 0181 5508822

Women's Royal Voluntary
Service (WRVS)
Tel: 01235 442900
*(See telephone directory for your local branch.)
Runs mother and baby clubs, playgroups, etc. and offers practical help.*

CHILDCARE, PLAY
AND EDUCATION

Action for Sick Children
1st Floor
300 Kingston Road
Wimbledon Chase
London SW20 8LX
Tel: 0181 5424848
Fax: 0181 542 2424

314

National Childminding
Association
8 Masons Hill
Bromley
Kent BR2 9EY
Tel: 0181 4646164
Pre-School Learning Alliance
69 King's Cross Road
London WC1X 9LL
Tel: 0171 833 0991

CHILDREN WITH SPECIAL
EDUCATIONAL NEEDS

British Dyslexia Association
98 London Road
Reading
Berkshire RG1 5AU
Tel: 0118 9662677
Helpline: 0118 9668271
Fax: 0118 9351927
Email: info@dyslexiahelp-
bda.demon.co.uk
Website: http://www.bda-
dyslexia.org.uk
National Association for Gifted
Children
Elder House
Milton Keynes MK9 1LR
Tel: 01908 673677

CHILDREN WITH
PARTICULAR PROBLEMS

Association for All Speech
Impaired Children (AFASIC)
347 Central Markets
Smithfield
London EC1A 9NH
Tel: 0171 2363632
Association for Brain-Damaged
Children and Young Adults
Clifton House
3 St Paul's Road
Foleshill
Coventry CV6 5DE
Tel: 01203 665450
Association for Spina Bifida and
Hydrocephalus (ASBAH)
ASBAH HOUSE
42 Park Road
Peterborough PE1 2UQ
Tel: 01733 555988
Fax: 01733 555985
British Diabetic Association
10 Queen Anne Street
London W1M 0BD
Tel: 0171 3231531
British Epilepsy Association
New Anstey House
Gateway Drive
Yeadon
Leeds LS19 7XY
Tel: 0113 2439393
Helpline: 0800 309030

Cancer and Leukaemia in
Childhood Charity (CLIC)
12-13 King Square
Bristol BS2 8JH
Tel: 0117 9248844
Cleft Lip and Palate
Association (CLAPA)
235-237 Finchley Road
London NW3 6LF
Tel: 0171 4310033
Coeliac Society
PO Box 220
High Wycombe
Buckinghamshire
HP11 2HY
Tel: 01494 437278
Contact-a-Family
170 Tottenham Court Road
London W1P 0HA
Tel: 0171 3833555
Website: www.cafamily.org.uk
Email: info@family.org.uk
Cystic Fibrosis Trust
11 London Road
Bromley
Kent BR1 1BY
Tel: 0181 4647211
Disabled Living Foundation
380-384 Harrow Road
London W9 2HU
Tel: 0171 2896111
Helpline: 0870 6039177
Minicom: 0870 603 9176
Open 10-4 Monday-Friday.
*Provides practical information and
equipment.*
Down's Syndrome Association
155 Mitcham Road
London SW17 9PG
Tel: 0181 6824001
Haemophilia Society
3rd Floor
Chesterfield House
385 Euston Road
London NW1 3AU
Tel: 0171 3800600
Hyperactive Children's
Support Group
71 Whyke Lane
Chichester
West Sussex PO19 2LD
Tel: 01903 725182
(10-1 Monday-Friday)
Fax: 01903 734726
ICAN
4 Dyer's Buildings
Holborn
London EC1N 2QP
Tel: 0870 0104066
Fax: 0870 010 4067
*National educational charity for children
with speech and language difficulties.*

Lady Hoare Trust for
Physically Disabled Children
87 Worship Street
London EC2A 2BE
Tel: 0171 3777567
MENCAP (Royal Society
for Mentally Handicapped
Children and Adults)
Mencap National Centre
117-123 Golden Lane
London EC1Y 0RT
Tel: 0171 4540454
Muscular Dystrophy Group
7-11 Prescott Place
London SW4 6BS
Tel: 0171 7208055
The National Asthma Campaign
Providence House
Providence Place
London N1 0NT
Tel: 0171 2262260
Helpline: 0845 7010203
Fax: 0171 7040740
National Autistic Society
393 City Road
London EC1C 1NG
Tel: 0171 8332299
ring in half an hour
. National Deaf Children's Society
15 Dufferin Street
London EC1Y 8UR
Tel: 0171 4908656
Helpline: 0171 2500123
From 10-5 Monday-Friday
(10-7 on a Tuesday)
National Eczema Society
163 Eversholt Street
London NW1 1BU
Tel: 0171 3884097
Fax: 0171 3885882
Research Trust for Metabolic
Disease in Children
The Quadrangle
Crewe Hall
Weston Road
Crewe CW1 6UR
Tel: 01270 250221
Fax: 01270 250244
*Contacts, information and support for
families.*
Royal National Institute
for the Blind (RNIB)
224 Great Portland Street
London W1N 6AA
Tel: 0171 3881266
Royal National Institute
for the Deaf (RNID)
Tel: 0171 3878033

Sickle Cell Society
54 Station Road
London NW10 4UA
Tel: 0181 9617795
Website:
www.sicklecellsociety.org.uk
Email:
sicklecellsoc@btinternet.com
Scope
6 Market Road
London N7 9PW
Tel: 0171 6197100
Spinal Injuries Association
76 St James's Lane
London N10 3DF
Tel: 0181 4442121

GROUPS CAMPAIGNING ON
SPECIFIC ISSUES

Maternity Alliance
45 Beech Street
London EC2P 2LX
Tel: 0171 5888583
*Experts in maternity employment,
benefits and rights*

INFORMATION ON
SAFETY AND FIRST AID

British Red Cross Society
9 Grovesnor Crescent
London SW1X 7EJ
Tel: 0171 2355454
British Standards Institute
359 Chiswick High Road
London W4 4AL
Tel: 0171 6299000
Child Accident Prevention Trust
4th Floor
Clerks Court
18-20 Farringdon Lane
London EC1R 3HA
Tel: 0171 6083828
Health Education Authority
Trevelyan House
30 Great Peter Street
London SW1P 2HW
Royal Society for the Prevention
of Accidents (RoSPA)
Edgbaston Park
353 Bristol Road
Birmingham
B5 7FT
Tel: 0121 2482000
St John Ambulance
1 Grovesnor Crescent
London SW1X 7EF
Tel: 0171 2355231

INDEX

A

abbreviations, co-operation cards 26
abdominal exercises 51, 51, 86-8, 86-8
abscesses 282
accidents 306-9
activity centres 176, 179
additives, baby food 105
adenoids 282, 282
aerobics 47, 50
afterbirth see placenta
afterpains 72
age gaps between children 270-1
aggression 208, 226
alcohol 10, 38
allergic rhinitis 282-3
allergies 90, 100, 104, 146, 283, 293
alpha-fetoprotein test 28
alphabet 230, 231
amniocentesis 29, 33
amniotic fluid 16, 29, 33
anaemia 283, 300, 302
anal fissures 220, 288
anger 232-3, 253
animals 269, 312
antenatal care 22-7
antenatal classes 36-7
antenatal clinics 24-6
antibiotics 277
antibodies 90, 149
anxiety 169, 221
Apgar score 71, 74
appendicitis 283, 283
apples 104
arnica 72
assertiveness 254-5
Association of Breastfeeding Mothers 99
asthma 31, 90, 271, 283-4
athlete's foot 299
au pairs 262

B

babbling 79
baby bouncers 160, 160
baby foods, commercial 105, 152
baby gyms 122, 122, 138
baby oil 113
baby rockers 123, 123
baby walkers 160
baby wipes 110
back:
    backache 52, 58, 60
    massage 62, 62
    posture 47
backpacks 127, 127, 165, 165
baked-bean shepherd's pie 187
ball games 236
banana whip 187
barrier creams 110, 113
bath supports 128, 128
bathing:
    older babies 154, 154
    older children 221
    salt baths 72
    toddlers 188-9
    young babies 112-15, 112-15, 128, 138
bathrooms, safety 306
baths 112-3, 128, 128
BCG vaccinations 130, 303
beakers 106
bed wetting 221, 284
bedrooms:
    older children 218-19
    safety 307
    toddlers 198
    young babies 120
beds:
    bunk beds 199, 225
    cabin beds 199, 199
    captain's beds 199, 199
    family beds 196-7
    moving toddlers into 196, 199
    sleeping with young babies 116
bedtime routines 157-8, 194, 222
bereavement 266
bilirubin 75, 296
birth:
    birth pains 22, 24, 60
    birth plans 27
    birth certificates 81
    birth control 131, 270
    home birth 22-3, 55
    hospital birth 22, 58-9
    registering 81
    see also labour
birthmarks 233, 284
biscuits 218
bites and stings 312, 313
blankets 118, 121
bleeding:
    after delivery 70, 72
    emergencies 311
    in urine or motions 285
    miscarriages 30
    onset of labour 58
blisters 312
blood pressure 26, 30
blood tests 27, 27
boils 285
bonding 71
bones:
    fractures 311
    hips, congenital dislocated 130, 287-8

rickets 299
books:
    first books 179
    picture books 207, 231
booster seats 164, 225, 225
bottlefeeding 90-1, 100-3, 100-3, 132, 147, 184
bottom-shuffling 145, 171
bouncing cradles 122, 122
bow legs 285
bowel movements, babies' 111, 153
brain, development 170
bras 39, 39, 95
Braxton Hicks contractions 35
breakfast 147
breast pads 95
breastfeeding 71, 84
    comfort feeds 147
    contraception 131, 270
    cot death 118
    crying babies 132
    expressing milk 74, 94, 96, 96-7
    frequency 94
    special care babies 97
    toddlers 184
breasts, during pregnancy 39
breath, holding 285
breathing, during contractions 61, 62-3
breathlessness 52
bronchiolitis 285-6
bronchitis 286
bruises 72-3, 286
buggies see pushchairs
bunk beds 199, 225
burns 306, 310

C

cabin beds 199, 199
caesarean sections 22, 24, 30, 69, 84
calcium 43, 150, 255
caps, contraceptive 131
captain's beds 199, 199
carbohydrates 148
carpal tunnel syndrome 52
carrots 104
carrycots 116, 121, 124, 126
cars:
    car seats 126, 164, 225
    making your own toy cars 210
casein-dominant milks 100
cat nets 125
catarrh 286
cats 125, 269
celebrations 268-9
cerebral palsy 75, 271
cervix:
    dilatation 59, 60
    incompetent 30
    show 58

smear tests 131
chairs:
    highchairs 166-7, 166-7, 200, 230
    multi-purpose 123, 123
changing mats 128
cheese 148, 149, 150, 151, 153
chest compressions 309, 309
chickenpox 10, 286, 299
chilblains 286
child abuse 266
child health clinics 130, 130, 186
choking 310
chorion biopsy 29
chromosomal abnormalities 29
circumcision 286
clapping games 174
classes, antenatal 36-7
cleft palate 286
clingy babies and children 169, 238
clinics:
    antenatal 24-6
    child health 130, 130, 186
clothes:
    breastfeeding 95
    dressing babies 115, 115
    during pregnancy 44-5
    older babies 161, 161
    older children 230-1
    on fire 310
    toddlers 200-1
    young babies 56-7, 129
club foot 75
co-operation cards 26, 37
co-sleeping 196-7
coeliac disease 146, 286-7
coils, contraceptive 131
cold sores 287
colds 126, 287
colic 133, 133, 287
colostrum 93, 94
colour blindness 287
coma 287
comfort feeds 147
comforters see dummies
commercial baby foods 105, 152
complications, pregnancy 30-1
computer toys 234
conception: 14
    planning for 10
    signs of 12-13
condoms 131
conflicts 252-3
congenital defects 287
conjunctivitis 288
constipation 41, 42, 52-3, 153, 193, 220, 288
construction toys 212
consultant care 24
contact lenses 45
contraception 131, 270
contraceptive pill 10, 131

316

ACKNOWLEDGMENTS

The publisher thanks the following photographers and organizations for their kind permission to reproduce the photographs in this book:

14 above Science Photo Library; 14 below Kohlmeier/Picture Press/SOA; 42 John Kelly/Tony Stone Images; 43 left Lucy Tizard /Bubbles; 43 centre left Lucy Tizard/Bubbles; 43 centre right Lucy Tizard/Bubbles; 43 right Claire Paxton/Bubbles; 49 Anthea Sieveking/Collections; 240 left Sandra Lousada/ Collections; 240 right Laurence Dutton/Tony Stone Images; 241 Roger Ellis /Tony Stone Images; 262 Durichen/Picture Press/SOA; 270 Phillip Reeson/Retna; 271 Loisjoy Thurston/Bubbles

The publisher thanks all the parents and children and other people that took part in the photography: Jennifer, John and Ellie Alexander, Helen Angell, Louise and Katherine Arnot, Charlotte Atkins, Katherine Austin, Lucy and Imogen Bailey, Adrian and Yvonne Bazar, Katia Bazar Rosen, Giles Bidder, Karen Biggins, Francesca Birkbeck, Amelia Bowyer, Maurice and Harriet Cheng, Bridget and Jack Clarence-Smith, Charlotte and Sam Cliffe, Michela Cliffe, Hannah Copestick, Raymond and Margaret Copus, Eleanor Cross, Luke Courtier, Rachel Davies, Suann, Emmy and Marcus Daywill, Debbie, Christopher and Olivia D'Lima, Josh and Amy Dudack, Michelle Dudack-Green, Isobel and Thomas Duncan, Hannah Elmer, Maggie and Pippa Elms, Rakum Fagan, Hannah Felt, Keith Fernandez, Hannah Fickling, Martha and Blanca Garbo, Carol, Daryl and Troy Goldie, Andrea and William Grace, Julia Green, Malcom and Ilana Green, Chris and Florence Griffiths, Hattie Grylls, Annalise and Lauren Hanson, Jane and Toby Harris, Wendy, Dan and

Joseph Harris, Jo Harrison, Sophie and Lily Hartman, Gabbi and Sam Hertzberg-Slade, Kate Hopkins, Diane and Charlie Howard, Kathy and Alice Howes, Onita Hunte, Susanne and Nicole Hunte, Christine and Eleanor Jennings, Paris, Vanessa, Brogen and Amber Johnston, Christopher Julienne, Dharwinder Kang, Jamie and Pippa Kang, Jackie and Demi Kaye, Josh Kennet, Rosie Lakin, Nicola, Lauren and Adam Leach, Moussanda and Henrietta Lee, Colette, Lior and Shir Leshem, Helen Lewis, Natassia Lewis, Miriam and Jessica Lipman, Jane Maitland, Max Massiah, Benjamin James Muir, Tom Norris, Corinne, Tony and Tate Oulton, Harish, Keyuri and Karishma Patel, Lela Pattison, Dr Neomie Penna, Polly Powell, Many and Olivia Reed, Gillian Reynolds, Cindy, Jo and Ben Richards, Mark, Hunter and Rileigh Ruthven, Bridget Rose, Lisa, Xavier and Joshua Roupie, Sally Sadler, Helen Shamroth, Patzi and Mark Shepperson, Trudy Stonach, Vandana Talwar, Shiz and Felix Tao, Cassie and Eden Tarn, Louise and Francesca Taylor, Kelly Tilly, Karen and Daniel Tuhrim, Serena van der Hyde, Peggy Vance, Alexander and Archie Walters, Jessica Walton, Simon Webb, Zack Wellin, Debra West, Francesca Wickers, Lily Whitfield, Simon Willis, Natasha Wolfson-West, Anita Zehavi.

The publisher thanks the following people and organizations for their help in this book: Café Rouge, Julia Green and Crouch End Health Centre, Dance Bizarre, The Down Syndrome Association, Fleet Primary School, Fleet Road, Sabi Khan, Lingfield Health Club, Helen Shamroth, John Simons Hairdressers, Hampstead, St John Ambulance and St Thomas' Hospital. The publisher would like to give special thanks to the Tommy's Campaign, the charity helping parents to have healthy babies.